Politics & Society in Contemporary Europe

A Concise Introduction

Stephen Wright

LYNNE
RIENNER
PUBLISHERS

BOULDER
LONDON

Published in the United States of America in 2023 by
Lynne Rienner Publishers, Inc.
1800 30th Street, Suite 314, Boulder, Colorado 80301
www.rienner.com

and in the United Kingdom by
Lynne Rienner Publishers, Inc.
Gray's Inn House, 127 Clerkenwell Road, London EC1 5DB
www.eurospanbookstore.com/rienner

Library of Congress Cataloging-in-Publication Data
Names: Wright, Stephen, 1954– author.
Title: Politics and society in contemporary Europe : a concise introduction
   / Stephen Wright.
Description: Boulder, Colorado : Lynne Rienner Publishers, Inc., 2023. |
   Includes bibliographical references and index. | Summary: "A thorough,
   accessible, thematic discussion of politics and society in contemporary
   Europe, from the United Kingdom to the Russian Federation"— Provided by
   publisher.
Identifiers: LCCN 2022011952 (print) | LCCN 2022011953 (ebook) | ISBN
   9781955055512 (hardcover) | ISBN 9781955055529 (paperback) | ISBN
   9781955055727 (ebook)
Subjects: LCSH: Europe—Politics and government—21st century. |
   Europe—Social conditions—21st century. | European Union. | Policy
   sciences—Europe.
Classification: LCC JN13 .W75 2023 (print) | LCC JN13 (ebook) | DDC
   323.44/83094—dc23/eng/20220726
LC record available at https://lccn.loc.gov/2022011952
LC ebook record available at https://lccn.loc.gov/2022011953

British Cataloguing in Publication Data
A Cataloguing in Publication record for this book
is available from the British Library.

Printed and bound in the United States of America

The paper used in this publication meets the requirements
of the American National Standard for Permanence of
Paper for Printed Library Materials Z39.48-1992.

5 4 3 2 1

Politics & Society
in Contemporary
Europe

Contents

Europe, 2022

1

The Evolution of
European Identities

THE POLITICAL LANDSCAPE OF EUROPE IS IN CONSTANT FLUX, UNDER-
going significant change in recent decades and facing ongoing challenges
today. There are many important topics to consider in explaining contemporary
European politics. What are the main political, social, and economic issues that
shape the countries of Europe, and how do these trends differ across the continent? How do Europeans govern themselves? To what extent are national interests and sovereignty subsumed by the European Union (EU) for those twenty-
seven states that are members?[1] Can we speak of a common European identity,
or the commonality of policy and issues across Europe? Is the EU itself
increasingly shaping the nature of national policies through the trend of "Europeanization"? How are European states managing the challenge of the rising
power of China and Russia, or the temperamental relationship with the United
States? Do some European countries continue to wield global political and economic influence as in previous centuries, or are they declining in their status?
Is the EU increasingly a global actor in its own right? This book sets out to
tackle these and other issues.

Outline of the Book

Several key features collectively help to make this book distinctive. First, it
focuses on the essential information needed to grasp the essence of European
politics. It provides succinct analysis and meaningful examples in the form of a
primer, and tries to avoid the pitfall of overwhelming detail. It is comparative in

scope analyzing broad continental trends, rather than being solely country specific or focusing on a handful of countries.

Second, the book focuses on the contemporary *political* framework (policies and institutions) of European states. It seeks to draw on other approaches,
however, notably social, cultural, historical, and economic perspectives to provide a greater understanding of the political arena. Such inclusion is vital to
offer a more complete overview and explanation of contemporary Europe. The
book also offers insights into the relationship between European countries and
the outside world.

Third, the geographical scope of the book is broad. Although I include discussion of the customary handful of larger West European countries, I go
beyond this focus to consider political issues and structures in a broad array of
countries. This includes discussion of small (and very small) states, as well as
inclusion of countries such as Turkey and Russia that we often consider as non-
European, even though they are physically on the European landmass.

Fourth, while the book's focus is on the political environment within states,
we are interested in the shifting partnerships between these states. Such shifts
are obvious when one thinks of Europe over the centuries (including the fluid
borders of many states), but relationships in recent decades are important to consider. For example, a differentiation of "Western" and "Eastern" Europe, accentuated by the Cold War over the four decades before 1990, is less evident today,
especially as many states from both camps are members in the EU together. Yet
economic and social indicators of Central and Eastern European (CEE) countries remain different in some areas from those of Western Europe, even though
membership in the EU attunes political and social objectives to some common
objectives, notably democratization and liberalization.

Fifth, the EU and the member states are both critical sets of actors in terms
of their interrelationship in Europe. I do not treat the EU in a separate or distinct
manner, but study and integrate it as just another actor in European politics,
heavily influenced and arguably controlled by the interests of the members. The
EU is unlikely to supersede the states to form a "United States of Europe," nor
are states likely to undermine or abolish the EU. Their relationship is complex,
symbiotic, and fluid.

The book contains ten chapters, with important statistical and explanatory
country information provided in a country profiles section at the end. This first
chapter continues with an overview of contemporary Europe, explaining key
features of policy, and the degree to which we can identify through recent history the development of a common European identity. Chapter 2 explains policies of today's Europe through the lens of the legacies of the twentieth century.
It focuses in particular on events after 1945, notably the Cold War era and its

aftermath, the establishment and development of the EU, and the impact of decolonization on select European states.

The following three chapters focus on core political processes and institutions. Chapter 3 addresses the constitutional foundations of political systems in Europe, looking at such things as the separation of powers, federalism, and parliamentary options. Chapter 4 focuses on the role of governmental institutions and leadership, such as executives and legislatures. Chapter 5 looks at aspects of political contests and participation in Europe, focusing on elections, political parties, and interest groups. Chapter 6 examines the fabric of European social issues and society, and it considers how these shape contemporary political life. I assess such factors as language, ethnicity, religion, gender, class, migration, and environmental concerns. Chapter 7 highlights important debates over public policies in European states and the EU such as with health care, labor, and gender equity.

Chapter 8 considers the political and economic relationships between European states, and assesses the external policies (limited to within Europe primarily) of a number of governments. I discuss the factors that shape national policies, including the increasing influence of the EU. Chapter 9 considers the relationship of European states and the EU with the outside world, discussing Europe's relative status and attempts to retain and contest for global influence. The final chapter pulls conclusions together regarding contemporary Europe, and highlights trends to watch for over the coming decade. There is every indication that European politics will remain dynamic and unpredictable.

What Constitutes Europe?

Endemic wars and the rise and fall of empires have shaped the map and our conception of Europe over the centuries.[2] The twentieth century was no exception, especially with the impact of two world wars, and changes to the European map continue with the fallout from the breakup of the Union of Soviet Socialist Republics (USSR) after 1991 and the continuing power of nationalism, notably but certainly not exclusively in the Balkans.[3] Fundamental questions arise. What are Europe's actual geographical boundaries? How do states demarcate their borders, and how do they deal with borders that change in location or role? Has the EU altered the general perception of, and attitude toward, national borders and state identity?

Theories of nationalism, social constructivism, and political culture are important in helping to provide initial answers to these questions, in a geographical sense as well as in political and social understanding. These approaches also help inform the discussions throughout this book. Nationalism is a sense of belonging, with people linked together by a common bond of history, language, or religion, often strengthened by an attachment to some territory. The desire of national groups for statehood has been a driving force of European politics in recent centuries, arguably since the French Revolution of 1789. Different theories emphasize different elements, with some focusing on biological factors as primary and others seeing identity as learned or competitive vis-à-vis other identities.[4]

To some extent, a goal of the EU is to dull the potentially violent ramifications of nationalism wrapped around territory and borders, but still support those aspirations linked to embracing cultural diversity. The EU is an attempt to convert the in-group to a broader pan-European identity—as part of a regionalist or globalization perspective—rather than one purely based on national or nativist characteristics. It is an important element of this book to recognize that national identity remains a strong political force (though not automatically violent) even after seventy years of the EU—or perhaps because of seventy years of the EU. The United Kingdom's departure from the EU in January 2020 is just one example of the populist opposition to globalization and regional integration, and the rise of right-wing ethnonationalist movements in general is indicative of a nativist attachment to the state rather than to the EU.[5] These movements reflect the sense of winners and losers from EU integration and globalization. We also witness trends of a more divisive ethnic nationalism across the continent rather than a more collaborative multicultural civic nationalism.

Social constructivism emphasizes social and interactive learning and the construction of one's own reality, rather than some neutral observable facts. People, or groups of people, construct their own facts, and such facts can change or face manipulation.[6] This approach warns us against too rationalistic an explanation of European events, such as exemplified by the liberal intergovernmental approach that states always know what their interests are and go about pursuing them. As one scholar wrote before social constructivism was a formal approach, "Logical or rational action plays a relatively minor part in political and social change. For the most part it is a delusion to believe that in social life men take deliberate steps to achieve consciously held goals. Non-logical action, spurred by environmental changes, instinct, impulse, interest, is the usual social rule."[7] Perhaps we should not lose sight of rationality, but understand that decisionmaking is complex.

Social constructivism helps to point us, for example, toward an explanation of France and Germany's nationalistic hostility toward each other before 1945, then shifting and framing to a cooperative stance with the growth of the Cold War and the EU. As another example, European general tolerance toward minority populations changed significantly in the past decade as populists across the continent altered people's attitudes to those outside the "nation." Social constructivism helps citizens explain their relationship to their country and to the

EU as events unfold, but their "truth" is fragile and changeable. It also plays a critical role in shaping or framing what we view Europe geographically to be, and which states we perceive to be inside or outside the continent, and which people to consider as having an identity as "European."[8]

Political culture helps to explain ideas that hold people together within a society, and offers an explanation as to whether we can foresee a single European culture emerging, or only a diverse set of national cultures. Founded on Gabriel A. Almond and Sidney Verba's work on civic culture in the 1960s, it is particularly interesting to view the development of the EU and the democratization of CEE in the 1990s through this lens. Almond and Verba defined *political culture* as "attitudes toward the political system and its various parts, and attitudes toward the role of the self in the system," and as "the particular distribution of patterns of orientation toward political objects among the members of the nation."[9] Through comparative studies, they saw that democracies did best where there was a mix of passive and active citizens, and where significant trust existed to allow political institutions to operate without excessive interference. Almond, in a later work, saw that one of the greatest challenges to democratization and political culture across Europe was in the post–Cold War environment where CEE states emerged in the 1990s and sought a path to democracy and political stability as well as entry into the EU.[10]

Recent research suggests other factors to be aware of in understanding aspects of European political culture, notably the increasingly negative attitudes toward government, along with the growing apathy toward political involvement. This research shows increased levels of disenchantment and negativity in the newer democracies of CEE, and points to the need to emphasize national difference rather than see an emerging Europe-wide consensus.[11] Overall, political culture helps to explain the features and characteristics of national populations as they look inward, but also provides a filter to help citizens view others on the outside of their culture.

The map of the European continent evolved over time and with different frames of reference. The Treaty of Westphalia in 1648 helped to define concepts of state sovereignty and secularism, and moved the continent away from the "normal" acceptance of religious interference in politics. The 1789 French Revolution and the subsequent Napoleonic wars stoked the flames of nationalism across the continent, and further helped to shape perceptions of how states organize. The Treaty of Vienna, signed after the Napoleonic wars in 1815, brought a relative peace to Europe through the construct of the promotion of conservative values, so undermining alternative perceptions and challenges raised by the French Revolution. Yet the strength of nationalism ushered in the unification of Italy in 1865, and the unification of Germany in 1871. Prior to unification, both countries comprised a number of principalities. Earlier in the nineteenth century, France and then Austria occupied much of Italy. By 1900, a handful of dominant empires consolidated power (Poland or the Polish-Lithuania Commonwealth, for example, had disappeared from the map, along with Bohemia), with little love lost between them, and even less representation to minority peoples within the continent.

World War I (1914–1918) triggered the collapse of four of these European empires—Austria-Hungary, Germany, Ottoman, and Russia—and led to a massive nationalistic (or "self-determination" in the words of US president Woodrow Wilson) restructuring of Europe, most notably with the modern creation of Bulgaria, Czechoslovakia, Hungary, Poland, and Yugoslavia. World War II (1939–1945) brought about another major transformation of the map of Europe, forcibly changing nationalistic perceptions. This included the expansion westward of the Soviet Union, and the pushing of Poland across the map to the Oder-Neisse Rivers, with yet another demarcation of Germany's eastern border (only finally given international recognition in 1990).

Another transformation of the European map occurred after 1991, with the collapse of the USSR and the independence of many republics that had been part of it, including the (re)emergence of the sovereign Baltic states of Estonia, Latvia, and Lithuania, as well as states such as Azerbaijan, Belarus, Georgia, and Ukraine. As an example, the city of Vilnius, the capital of Lithuania today, began the twentieth century as Russian, then became part of Poland in the interwar period, then part of the Soviet Union after World War II, and only in the 1990s the capital of Lithuania. The city changed hands multiple times during both world wars. The end of the Cold War also contributed to tensions and civil war within Yugoslavia, which broke into its constituent ethnic units, as well as within Czechoslovakia, which also divided into Czech and Slovak states in January 1993. Russia's invasion of Ukraine in February 2022, and its desire to control the Russian-speaking enclaves of Donetsk and Luhansk and perhaps the whole of Ukraine, signaled the ongoing contest over the map of Europe.

If the physical borders of Europe proved fluid over the centuries, then the political question of what constitutes Europe also needs consideration. Who defined Europe as a separate continent? A dispassionate observer could simply perceive it as geographically a small appendage of Western Asia. Physically, Europe is small as a continent, but its historical power and prowess allowed Europeans to frame their land a continent. The West European core of countries that "shaped" and colonized the world in previous centuries possesses a small landmass as a fraction of Europe. In terms of landmass today, according to the World Bank, the EU total of twenty-seven member countries (EU27) has a land mass of 3,999,622 square kilometers, which puts the whole bloc at just one-sixth the size of sub-Saharan Africa, less than one-quarter the size of Russia, and less than half the size of China or the United States.[12] As a point of reference within the United States, the state of Texas has a landmass equivalent to Austria, Belgium, the Czech Republic, Denmark, Germany, the Netherlands, Slovakia, and Switzerland combined. As another indication of the compact size of Europe, following the nuclear disaster at Chernobyl (then inside the USSR, though today in Ukraine) in April 1986, nuclear fallout was recorded within a week across virtually the whole of Europe, including Italy, Spain, and the UK. In terms of population size today, the whole of Europe (including Russia) stands at 743 million according to the United Nations, just less than 10 percent of the total world population.[13] The EU27 population stands at 448 million, about 6 percent of the global total.

Observers generally demarcate Europe's western, northern, and southern geographical borders by water, either the Atlantic Ocean or the Mediterranean Sea. The eastern border, however, is more problematic and more difficult to pull together a consensus. Directly east, the end of geographic Europe, for many, runs along the Ural Mountains of Russia, dissecting that country into European and Asian sectors. An age-old question has centered on how "European" a country is Russia, if at all. Is a country European when several million of its citizens live east of Beijing, or when its eastern border is only 5 kilometers from the United States?[14] Russia has played a critical role in European politics for centuries, and borders five EU member states (plus Norway). It is a matter of framing as to whether we perceive it as European, or even whether it could become a member of the EU. Many include only Russia west of the Urals as European, but this is problematic as it excludes much of Russia that includes Siberia, itself a landmass the size of Europe. For some, the issue of Russia's Europeanness ties to its political situation. If the country were a vibrant liberal democracy, with Russians eager to tie themselves closer to Europe, perhaps more would frame Russia as a European country. This designation appears less likely following the near universal European opposition to Russia's invasion of Ukraine in 2022.

A similar question regards the status of Turkey. For many, the Bosporus divides Turkey into European and Asian segments, with the vast majority of Turkey physically in Asia. Historically, though, Turkey has been an integral part of Europe, notably through the Ottoman Empire, and today many perceive Turkey as European. For example, it has been a member of the North Atlantic Treaty Organization (NATO) since 1952—and is involved in ongoing and seemingly endless membership negotiations with the EU. Turkey first applied for EU membership in 1959, but the EU only accepted it as an official candidate for entry in 1999, some forty years later. Part of the reason for the delay was instability inside Turkey, and a military coup d'état in 1980. Negotiations on membership formally opened in 2005, but they continue to lead nowhere, even though such negotiations at face value point to the acceptance of Turkey as "European."[15]

EU officials offer various reasons for the delay in membership, such as the lack of democracy in Turkey, various human rights violations, the relatively underdeveloped economy, significant cultural differences, and the fact that it is largely a non-Christian country. Understated fears are that it would become the largest member of the EU by population (just ahead of Germany), and transform dramatically the nature of the organization, including potentially shifting its center eastward. Some opponents state that Turkey is "not European" because it is not Christian, supposedly making the argument for EU membership a nonstarter. If Turkey were to join the EU, then why not its neighbors sharing common borders, such as Georgia, Armenia, Iran, Iraq, and Syria?

The United Nations Economic Commission for Europe (UNECE), established in 1947, has a more fluid and functional concept of what Europe is.[16] Besides all the "core" countries of Europe as included in the EU, the UNECE

Box 1.1   The Ottoman Empire

The Ottoman Empire, founded at the end of the thirteenth century, expanded via war over the following centuries to occupy much of southeastern Europe (Greece, Hungary, Romania, the Balkan states, and parts of Ukraine), defeating weakening Christian forces. It inflicted the final defeat on the Roman Empire in 1453, with the help of the new weapon of gunpowder, after the Romans had held on to a truncated empire for a thousand years following the fall of Rome (in 476) in its eastern capital of Constantinople (called the Byzantine Empire).[a] The Ottomans eventually occupied all the land around the Black Sea, as well as much of what we call today the Middle East (though not Iran). Ottoman control also ran across North Africa, including Egypt, Libya, and Algeria. The empire expanded the influence of Islam into Europe, where it still has considerable impact on the politics of the Balkans, notably in Turkey as well as Albania and Kosovo (following their victory over the Serbs at the Battle of Kosovo in 1389). Its defeat in World War I enabled Britain and France to supplant Ottoman influence across the Middle East. Britain took control of Iraq, Jordan, and Palestine (Israel) along with its ongoing control of Bahrain, Kuwait, and Qatar. France took control of Lebanon and Syria. Britain and France along with Greece, Italy, and the Soviet Union had plans to dismember Turkey and share it among themselves, but a Turkish national uprising thwarted those plans and led to the creation of an independent Turkish state under Kemal Atatürk in 1923.

Note: a. Edward Gibbon, *The Decline and Fall of the Roman Empire*, abridged by D. M. Low (London: Book Club Associates, 1960), chap. 65.

membership of fifty-six countries includes many to the east, such as Armenia, Azerbaijan, Georgia, Israel, Kazakhstan, and Uzbekistan. Are these states European? Part of this categorization is because there is no other obvious or palatable region in which to put these countries, such as is true of Israel. The United Nations itself categorizes forty-four countries in Europe.[17] This list includes Iceland, Russia, and Ukraine, but excludes Cyprus, Turkey, and states on Turkey's eastern border. Many of these states are members of the EU's European Neighborhood Policy (ENP), whose original intent was to help some of these states prepare for EU membership.[18]

Psychological and cultural factors, along with geopolitical power, also shape the concept of boundaries. The British at the height of their global influence centered the world's maps and time zones on London (at the Royal Observatory in Greenwich), something that happened in practice before an international treaty signed in 1884 formalized it. Similarly, the larger West European countries shaped an image of themselves and their powers, and defined outsiders in terms of *Near East, Middle East,* and *Far East,* terms that still resonate today to Europeans even if they are politically inappropriate. As mentioned earlier, we can debate where the eastward border of Europe actually is, and how much we can embrace countries such as Ukraine, Belarus, Georgia, and Turkey as European. Where there are common land borders, it is difficult to say where Europe should end. Water barriers are perhaps more helpful in providing boundaries.

The English Channel has had a marked impact on Britain's political and social development in contrast to continental Europe, even though the distance from Dover in the UK to Calais, France, is a mere 21 miles (34 kilometers).[19] Although the UK may be physically part of the European continent, for long periods of its history it acted politically and psychologically aloof. Politicians and citizens alike, who wanted to reinforce this distinction, drove the UK's departure from the EU in January 2020, preferring to liberate the country from the shackles and the shadows of the EU. In terms of the potential barrier of water, one can raise similar questions about Iceland. It is 928 miles (1,494 kilometers) from the nearest European capital, Dublin, but considers itself European and is a member of the European Economic Area (EEA). Greenland is even further from the European landmass but, as a dependency of Denmark, it also perceives itself as European. Cyprus lies less than 200 miles from Syria and Lebanon, and to the east of Istanbul and Ankara. Malta, another EU island member, is a similar case, where it lies closer to the African capitals of Tunis and Tripoli than the nearest European capitals of Athens and Rome.

Why should Morocco not consider membership in the EU as it is only 8 miles (13 kilometers) from Spain, or Lebanon, whose capital of Beirut is only 129 miles (208 kilometers) from Cyprus? In centuries past, after all, these countries were part of Europe through their membership in the French Empire, or the earlier Ottoman Empire, or the even earlier Roman Empire. More recently, most of North Africa was part of Adolf Hitler's German Empire in the early 1940s. Some EU policies today, notably the intergovernmental Union for the Mediterranean (UfM), recreate the idea of a "greater" zone of Europe embracing all countries around the Mediterranean.[20] Do culture, language, and religion, however, preclude such states from being European, or could a change in perception accommodate this? Likewise, how can the Black Sea divide European states from outsiders? Are countries on the western shores of the Black Sea naturally European (Bulgaria, Moldova, Romania, Ukraine), whereas those on the eastern and southern shores non-European (Georgia, Turkey)? Membership of all these states with Russia in the Istanbul-based Organization of the Black Sea Economic Cooperation (BSEC) complicates this issue. The answer is perhaps how politics defines geography and culture.

We can see, then, that an easy definition of Europe is elusive, even in a "simple" geographical sense. Other ideas of Europe suggest it is held together by a shared set of ideas or memory, or by a common European culture, or by its interdependence physically and economically, a feature strengthened by the EU.[21] I explore these ideas further in this chapter and throughout the book.

European Society

The above discussion points to the fact that defining what constitutes Europe is not so straightforward, where political, historical, and cultural/social considerations as much as geography help to shape the answer. For the purposes in this book, I am adopting—for convenience rather than outright principle—the framework of the Council of Europe, which comprises forty-seven member countries. The Council of Europe, formed in 1949, is one of Europe's oldest organizations, and predates the EU. The list of countries includes all EU members, Russia, Turkey, and Ukraine, but excludes Belarus and Israel (which has observer status). The Council excluded Russia from membership in March 2022 after its invasion of Ukraine, so bringing the Council's membership to forty-six states, at least temporarily, although I will continue to refer to membership as forty-seven countries.[22] It includes other former Soviet republics on the east of the Black Sea such as Armenia, Azerbaijan, and Georgia, and microstates such as Andorra, Liechtenstein, and Monaco. These forty-seven countries provide a challenging focus of study at just under one-quarter the membership of the United Nations.

Population totals of European countries vary considerably. According to the World Bank, Russia has the largest population at about 144 million, but only five others are above 60 million (Turkey, Germany, the UK, France, and Italy, in order of population size). Looking from another perspective, twenty-nine states have populations less than 10 million. Four of these states have populations less than 100,000: Andorra, Monaco, Liechtenstein, and San Marino.[23] The Holy See (Vatican) has observer status at the Council of Europe, with a population of just under 1,000. Population density in Europe varies considerably, from Monaco with the highest density of just over 19,000 per square kilometer to Iceland with the lowest density of 3 per square kilometer.[24]

Another basic feature of European society is that it is relatively wealthy, although there are significant differences across Europe. According to the World Bank for gross domestic product (GDP) per capita 2019 current values, the range within the EU runs from Luxembourg at $114,704 down to Bulgaria at $9,838. Denmark tops the Nordic countries at $60,170. Microstates generally possess strong economies, but poorer countries are present as one moves eastward and southward across Europe. Albania, for example, has a GDP per capita rate of $5,353, with Ukraine a very low $3,659.

A shorthand way to approach the social geography of Europe is to differentiate core and peripheral areas. One can perceive the core of Europe to be inside of a line drawn between London, Berlin, Milan, and Paris. Within this area reside a majority of European citizens, and the area holds much of the economic and political strength of Europe. As a general rule of thumb, the poorest and least populated areas of Europe lie on the outer edges of the continent: northern Scotland; the southern regions of Portugal, Spain, and Italy; Greece; the Arctic Circle; and states in the extreme east of Europe. The countries of the periphery that have EU membership required significant financial investment and assistance to join the EU and to remain viable and competitive in the European arena. Certainly, there are success stories in those poorer regions.

This simplification of Europe creates some problems of course. Spain and Portugal recorded impressive economic growth since their admission to the EU in the 1980s. Ireland has shaken off its image as a passive agricultural-based economy to be a dynamic leader in new technology with a GDP per capita almost twice that of France. The Nordic countries are also vibrant economies with a significant role and stature in Europe. Similarly, the expansion to the EU27 has brought in new players, notably Poland, to the main table of Europe. Despite all these caveats, there is some truth in understanding the relative strength of the core of Europe, and this extends to the political leadership and policy direction of the EU—at least in recent years (see the Country Profiles section at the end of the book for more details).

Despite the ability of people to move and work freely across the EU27, there is relatively little migration within the EU, and most countries possess only small minorities of noncitizens. Belgium, hosting the EU's core institutions, has the

---

Box 1.2   What Is Scandinavia?

The term *Scandinavia* perhaps owes its origin to Pliny during the Roman Empire as a region beyond its control. Scandinavians embraced the term during the 1830s as it spread into a political movement, solidified by a poem by Hans Christian Andersen in 1839, "I Am a Scandinavian." Within the region, Scandinavia normally refers only to Denmark, Norway, and Sweden. For many outside the region, Scandinavia is a broader concept also including Finland and Iceland. These five countries form the *Nordic group of states*, a term widely accepted. These five countries have a long history of trade, war, and empire, and have occupied each other for long periods. For example, Sweden controlled Norway during the nineteenth century as the price paid by the latter for its support of Napoleon Bonaparte. The contemporary map of the region only came about after the independence of Finland from Russia in December 1917 in the aftermath of the Russian Revolution. For convenience, I refer to Scandinavia loosely as the five Nordic countries.

---

highest population of foreign residents, but that figure is under 10 percent of the total population. This is primarily due to cultural and language factors, in that most Europeans do not wish to move from their own countries. Inward migration from outside the EU has been much more of a contentious issue on the political landscape, with significant numbers of non-Europeans, legal and illegal, joining the workforce of many West European economies. The workforce of Europe has moved primarily into service industries, with manufacturing shrinking to less than a third of the workforce, and agriculture down to about 2 percent. Agriculture and fisheries are contentious economic sectors within Europe that bring regular clashes with countries beyond the continent, notably China. In terms of their contribution to Europe's GDP and workforce, however, they provide small contributions.

European states are not always homogenous, and cultural and linguistic differences provide fault lines inside many countries. Nationalism and time have erased some of the interesting historical examples, such as Spain controlling the Netherlands, or France parts of Italy. In Central and Eastern Europe today, these pressures can be witnessed in the push for the "velvet divorce" in 1993 of Czechs and Slovaks within Czechoslovakia, as well as the more stressful breakup of the former Soviet Union and Yugoslavia. In Western Europe, the nationalism of Welsh and Scots inside of the UK and their occasional calls for independence highlight the impact of culture and history in social life. The continuing British possession of Gibraltar, despite pressure from Spain for its return, is another example of history at work (see Box 1.3). Similarly, we see pressures in the Basque and Catalan regions of Spain, and in Corsica within France, displaying openly significant social and political divisions.

Box 1.3   Gibraltar: Why British?

Gibraltar is an interesting anachronism of European history. Occupied by the Moors in the eighth century, Spanish forces took control in the fourteenth century. Gibraltar was ceded to Britain in 1713 following Britain's partnership with the Dutch and Austrians (Habsburgs) to take control of Spain, and the UK has held the land since then. Today, Gibraltar is a British Overseas Territory with about 34,000 citizens, and a total territory of 10 square kilometers. In past EU elections, citizens voted as part of South West England. Spain has repeatedly negotiated for its return, but without success. Gibraltar proved immensely important as a British naval base in the nineteenth century, especially in battles at Trafalgar with Napoleon (1805) and against Russia in Crimea (1854–1856). The base was also important during the two world wars in the twentieth century, but with Spain's membership in NATO after 1982, the need for British control of the port diminished. However, the UK refused to give up the port on the southern tip of Spain. During the Brexit referendum, 96 percent of citizens in Gibraltar voted to remain in the EU as their economic livelihood requires an open border with Spain. Negotiations with the EU allowed a special dispensation to keep this border open and have Gibraltar join the Schengen zone, even though it remains a British possession.[a]

Note: a. Raphael Minder, "Gibraltar Gets a Deal of Its Own on Borders," *New York Times*, January 1, 2021.

War and Peace: Europe in Constant Flux

It is a cliché to say that things never stay the same, or that change is constant, but some ignore this adage when contemplating Europe's geographical development. Their perception is of an old, long-established continent, where countries and their physical locations have been stable for many years. This perception, however, is factually incorrect. The political and social map of Europe has constantly changed over the past 2,000 years, and continues to shift. War is a constant defining feature of Europe. This is evident dating back to the classical writings of Thucydides about the Peloponnesian Wars between Athens and Sparta from 431 to 404 BCE, as well as all the associated wars in the region during that period.[25] We can see this also in the writings of Niccolò Machiavelli, who examined the machinations of power politics in Italy in 1516, and wrote these immortal words about European politics: "A prince, therefore, should have no other object, no other thought, nor should he adopt any other art as his profession, than war and its rules and discipline . . ."[26] As Martin Wight summed up regarding sovereign states in Europe since the sixteenth century, "War is inevitable, but particular wars can be avoided."[27]

In the fourteenth century, there were hundreds of identifiable principalities in Europe. Today, with our adoption of the Council of Europe's membership, Europe has forty-seven countries. This is actually an increase in numbers from prior to World War I, and shaped particularly in the past thirty years with the collapse of the Soviet Union and the breakup of Yugoslavia into its component national parts. The transition of the European map weaves into the impact of war over the centuries, and we can briefly mention key events to highlight this.

The Greek city-states are often symbols of the beginning of democracy, but the Romans superseded the Greeks with arguably the strongest and most influential of empires, the first great (European) empire of a modern age, well documented and well preserved. The Romans left a legacy of law, language, and technology from Spain to Britain (though not Ireland or Scotland), from Greece to Germany, and their "European" empire included today's Middle East and North Africa. This empire lasted for centuries, until it finally started to fall apart from its own excesses and from external pressures. The continuation of the empire from its outpost in Constantinople (Istanbul), even after Rome collapsed, provided a significant legacy to Eastern Europe, most particularly in the Coptic Church, a conservative form of Christianity still prevalent in Russia and Greece today.[28]

In northern Europe, the broad sweep of the Vikings between the eighth and eleventh centuries left a lasting impression beyond their Nordic homeland in places such as Iceland and Ireland. The impact of Islam across southern Europe provides evidence of another major empire, dating from its control of Iberia in 711. Islam's influence was prominent in shaping mathematics and astronomy in Europe, contributing to Europeans' ability to later navigate and conquer the world. Islam's impact is still felt today in the Balkans, as the Ottoman Empire maintained its grip on North Africa and southeastern Europe until the early twentieth century. Once Iberia broke free from Islamic control, with the liberation of Granada in 1492, the Spanish and Portuguese expanded their overseas growth. Portuguese traders populated areas of Africa and the Far East while searching for the spice routes, and looked to the "new" world (as perceived by Europeans) of the Americas. The Spanish also ventured outside of Europe, though they clashed with the British for naval supremacy during the sixteenth century and beyond.

Martin Luther's challenge to Catholicism reverberated around the continent for several centuries (and arguably down to the present). The Thirty Years' War from 1618 to 1648 killed almost one-quarter of the European population, and led to an important shift in power in the Treaty of Westphalia signed in 1648. Under this treaty, the Pope agreed to recluse himself from political matters across Europe, so limiting somewhat the role of the church and marking the establishment of sovereignty and the modern state system in Europe. The treaty also tried to establish some norms of behavior to limit conflict.

The French Revolution of 1789 dramatically ended monarchy in France (though it briefly resurfaced during the mid-1800s), and threatened monarchical rule across Europe. The birth of modern-day nationalism gave a radical edge to French politics, and Napoleon Bonaparte made efforts to export that across Europe. He was finally defeated at the Battle of Waterloo, just outside modern-day Brussels in 1815, another critical turning point in European history, with the

---

Box 1.4   Pandemics in Europe

As the saying goes, the two inevitable things in life are death and taxes. In Europe, we can add wars and pandemics. The Peloponnesian War, between Athens and Sparta, was partly defined by a pandemic that swept through Athens and killed at least two-thirds of its citizens, weakening it to help facilitate Sparta's victory. Pandemics have been significant across European history. The bubonic plague swept the continent between the sixth and eighth centuries, killing an estimated 50 million people in Europe, contributing to the continuing decline of the Roman Empire and the rise of religion. In the fourteenth century, another bubonic plague known as the Black Death swept Europe killing up to half of the European population. The Great Plague in London in 1665 killed 20 percent of its population, but its end was helped by the Great Fire of London the following year. The Spanish flu of 1918–1920 killed about 50 million worldwide, and killed more people in Europe than the previous four years of World War I. The Covid-19 pandemic of 2020–2022 caused incredible dislocation to Europe and its economies, though with a death toll much less than the pandemics previously mentioned. As of May 2022, the death toll from Covid-19 for European countries stood at 1.97 million. The UK topped the list in Western Europe with 176,412 deaths.[a] The virus tested and exposed the limits of cooperation among European governments, and its impact will reverberate throughout the continent for some time. As a final note here, I should mention that Europeans have been responsible for the exportation of pandemics and deadly diseases to other continents over the centuries, often through their colonial policies. Whether across Latin America, or with Native Americans in what would become the United States, or Aboriginal citizens in Australia, European disease wiped out millions. At times, this unwittingly occurred, but there is some evidence that on other occasions there was no attempt at mitigation.[b]

Notes: a. Conor Stewart, "Number of New Coronavirus (Covid-19) Deaths in Europe Since February 2020." *Statista*, May 8, 2022, https://www.statista.com/statistics/1102288/coronavirus-deaths-development-europe/.

b. Alfred W. Crosby, *The Columbian Exchange: Biological and Cultural Consequences of 1492* (Westport, CT: Greenwood Press, 1972).

armies of Prussia joining British and other forces to tip the scales against Napoleon. The Concert of Europe, established in Vienna later that year, provided a novel mechanism for European peacekeeping, stability, and conservatism, as well as an attempt at an ongoing European diplomatic dialogue. This "Concert" included the five major European powers at the time—Austria-Hungary, France, Prussia, Russia, and the UK—and this had modest success in maintaining some peace, and averting revolutionary pressures, inside Europe over the following century, though Europeans exported their conflicts in the race for colonies and the "Scramble for Africa" in the latter half of the nineteenth century.

The Concert did not eliminate all wars from Europe, and nationalism remained a potent force.[29] One notable event was the Crimean War between 1853 and 1856, exhibiting the tension between the UK and its allies with Russia over access to India and parts of the Ottoman Empire, which changed the nature of warfare through use of the railway and the telegraph. This war was also famous for the work of Florence Nightingale in the treatment of war casualties. It was actually the Battle of Solferino in 1859, part of the War of Italian Unification, which shocked Henry Dunant over the treatment of soldiers on the battlefield and led him to launch the International Committee of the Red Cross in Geneva in 1863.

German principalities, led by Prussia, pursued their quest for unification and continental dominance through wars against Austria and France (then the leading continental powers) in the 1860s and early 1870s. Germany's defeat of France in 1870, and the proclamation of a new unified German Empire in January 1871 (at Versailles, just outside Paris, to heighten French humiliation), was important in several respects.[30] It marked the rise of a united German state to European great-power status, soon to surpass the UK to become the continent's dominant economy. This set off a battle for supremacy over Europe that was going to engulf the continent (and many parts of the world) over the next century. It also heightened the bitterest of rivalries between France and Germany, a rivalry that only seemed to be satiated with their partnership in the EU after three major wars over seventy years. The map of Germany changed numerous times over the next century, culminating in its current configuration after the reunification of the country in 1990. But its economic preeminence remained almost constant.

Attempts to maintain a balance of power and arms control measures within Europe and globally were promoted during the Hague peace conferences at the turn of the twentieth century (1899 and 1907), but their limited success was exposed in the breakout of the Great War, or World War I (as it later became known), in 1914. The end to major wars in 1815, 1918, and 1945 provides turning points in the political map of Europe. Likewise, these wars provided the impetus to new forms of political cooperation in Europe. The defeat of Napoleon in 1815 led to the Concert of Europe. The end of World War I in 1918 led to the Geneva-based League of Nations, which became essentially a club for European states dominated by France and the UK, as well as the creation of a swathe of newly recognized countries across Central and Eastern Europe. The defeat of Hitler in 1945 eventually led to the Treaty of Rome in 1957 and the creation of the EU, as well as to the United Nations (in 1945).

The recent bout of boundary redrawing brought about by the collapse of Soviet influence at the end of the twentieth century is almost complete, with outstanding disputes in the Balkans (e.g., with Bosnia and Herzegovina, Kosovo, and Serbia) edging toward potential settlement. Serbian threats in 2022 to undermine the power-sharing consensus in Bosnia and potentially tear the country apart point to the ongoing fragility. Russia's recognition of two separatist enclaves, Donetsk and Luhansk, in eastern Ukraine and its invasion of Ukraine in 2022 indicate Russia's willingness to continue to redraw the map of Eastern Europe. The dispute between Greece and Macedonia—Greece opposed use of the name Macedonia because of its territory in northern Greece of the same name—was resolved in 2019 with the adoption of the name of the Republic of North Macedonia.

The contemporary challenge of geography and maps perhaps relates less to political and military differences, although Russia's incursion into Ukraine and its annexation of Crimea and Sevastopol in 2014 (and its physical invasion of Ukraine in 2022) may be a partial exception, as there are cultural factors at work here also. More significant are social and economic factors, especially as the EU attempts to build cohesion and unity of purpose in many diverse areas across much of the continent. Rising subnationalism could still have significant repercussions on the map of Europe. Will Belgium, Spain, and the UK survive as currently configured, for example? Will Greenland wrest independence from Denmark?

European "Exceptionalism" and Identity

So, what contributes to the identity of contemporary Europe? What differentiates Europeans from each other, and what aspects of culture do they share? As mentioned earlier, much of our understanding of identity hinges on the work of social constructivism. Our identity is less an undisputed or neutral "fact" than a result of how we "frame" and view events. Our perception of the world or our country becomes our reality, and shapes the way in which we make decisions. There is no objective, neutral, or all-encompassing view of Europe, but rather how we picture Europe is a result of our perceptions. People across Europe view their continent differently, and view the history of Europe differently. Similarly, there are differences in how citizens of a country perceive their own country, as well as other countries.

With these caveats in mind, we can attempt to trace trends and factors that help to shape our views of contemporary Europe and what Europeans may have in common. Are there common threads that we can link to explain what binds Europe together, besides simple geographical proximity? Much of this hinges on the idea of the exceptionalism or the superiority of Europeans, that they were able to influence not only developments within the continent but also in the outside world. This hubristic narrative promoted and nurtured by Europeans sees the world revolving around Europe, a narrative under siege today as we will see. Trends discussed here primarily emerge from Western Europe, reflecting the historical dominance of these countries in the continent. Wars shape our understanding of the continent as discussed above, but here we turn to a broader and admittedly more sweeping consideration of the impact of ideas and ideologies.[31]

Philosophy

Europe has a strong philosophical tradition valuing the importance of ideas dating back more than 2,000 years. Philosophers of Ancient Greece, such as Aristotle, Plato, and Socrates, accompanied by the writings of Thucydides, remain central to modern discourse. Aristotle's classification of government into rule by the one, the few, and the many remains a basic starting point for much of our study of comparative government. The Roman Empire, though not necessarily renowned for its pure philosophical reflections, provided an important model of government and rule that shaped many aspects of European life—transportation routes, language, legal frameworks—that remain of interest to us today. This is not to say that Europeans were the only citizens philosophizing in ancient times, as clearly other civilizations were vibrant around the world, and from which Europeans often borrowed ideas.

Major changes in thinking slowly transformed European life, including the Renaissance (fourteenth to sixteenth centuries), the Reformation (sixteenth century), and the Enlightenment (eighteenth century). Each of these forced adjustments in thinking at the time, and transformed the debate about political, social, and religious structures. Martin Luther led the challenge in the sixteenth century against the excessive power of the Pope and the Catholic Church, leading to the growth of the "protest-ant" church in many areas of northern Europe. The printing of the Bible into German from Latin had some role in the steady development of German nationalism. European classical philosophers such as Immanuel

Kant, Jean-Jacques Rousseau, John Locke, and John Stuart Mill promoted concepts of liberty, democracy, and individual rights, whereas others such as Thomas Hobbes and Niccolò Machiavelli highlighted limitations. The development of the modern European state stemmed from these important philosophical debates—as well as brute military force, and resulting treaties, such as the 1648 Treaty of Westphalia—and the evolution of sovereignty and the secular state developed from these previous eras. In more modern eras, one can draw on philosophers such as Karl Marx, Jean-Paul Sartre, Michel Foucault, and Jürgen Habermas to continue this European tradition.

The importance of these philosophical concepts, however, has limitations. They are all rather elitist, as most Europeans then or now would probably not know many of these philosophers or what they argued, and their ideas do not necessarily transcend the continent. The impact of these and other European ideas are not necessarily positive for the continent. The religious intolerance by Christians during the Crusades in the twelfth and thirteenth centuries severely affected peoples of the Holy Land. The cultural arrogance and quest to exploit the "New World" (to Europeans) during the Age of Discovery in the fifteenth and sixteenth centuries, and again in the nineteenth-century Scramble for Africa, all led to incredible hardship and suffering for those at the brunt end of European ideas and conceptions of moral leadership and superiority. Imperialism, both economic and cultural, is a major European philosophy justified for many harsh actions around the world to benefit Europeans. In the twentieth century within Europe, ideology brought similar hardship and misery, and the killing of millions of citizens at the hands of their own egalitarian communist governments apparently following Marxism.

The impact of these philosophical approaches is uneven across Europe. The Reformation clearly did not spread much beyond northern Europe, as today's concentration of Catholicism in southern Europe and Islam in southeastern Europe portray. Likewise, Eastern Europe barely felt the power of the Enlightenment and ideas of political justice. For example, serfdom existed in Russia until the Emancipation Reform of 1861, and lingered until the 1906 revolution. The relative absence of political reform in CEE and Russia contributed to the continuing prevalence of autocratic rule and significant inequality into the modern era. This also should not detract from the awareness of massive squalor and inequality in Western Europe during much of this period.

Religion

A significant portion of European identity centers on the interaction among, and divisions between, major religions. Struggles have revolved around Catholic,

Protestant, Orthodox Christian, Jewish, and Islamic elements, drawing in political, social, and economic issues. Over much of the past 2,000 years, the Catholic Church has had an enormous amount of influence over large areas of Europe, including in the secular arena of national and European politics. In medieval times, the Pope was as much a political leader as a spiritual one, and heavily involved in the political machinations of the time. The division of the Catholic Church in 1054 led to a more "liberal" western faith and a more "orthodox" or conservative eastern faith, based in Constantinople, now Istanbul. The Crusades began in 1095, justified by Pope Urban II as a way for Christianity to pin back Islam, and continued for several centuries. The gradual expansion of Islam continued across North Africa, southern Spain, and the Balkans, until a critical battle outside Vienna in 1683 halted its path. After that time, the Ottoman Empire began to recede in terms of size and strength, leaving important pockets of Islam in the Balkans and European Turkey, and across North Africa.

The Reformation led by Martin Luther and John Calvin, as mentioned above, had an equally important impact on European life. The earlier consolidation of the Church of England by King Henry VIII in the 1530s led to a schism in British and European politics. This left a trail of war and destruction to today—Spain's efforts to overthrow the English Crown through the Spanish Armada in 1588, and the troubles in Ireland (from the Battle of the Boyne in 1690 down to the present) being just two examples. The Netherlands fought the Eighty Years' War for independence from Catholic Spain in the sixteenth and seventeenth centuries. Some countries, such as Ireland, Poland, Italy, and Spain, have an identity partly fashioned by the widespread Catholic faith held by the vast majority. Although lingering religious animosities remain across Europe (the Balkans and Ireland as examples, as well as religious differences between Christians and Muslims in many states, accentuated by populist parties), it is possible to say that wars of religion are less likely today, though religion remains an important factor of identity.

Those of the Jewish faith have always been in a minority within Europe, and over time large communities gathered together in cities such as Berlin, Paris, and Kraków, partly for security. Persecution of Jewish minorities within Europe has been regular and matter-of-fact, on cultural and political grounds. In history, one of the more famous episodes is the Spanish Inquisition, dating from the 1480s (and this included forcing Muslims also to convert to Christianity), but there are many others of note. Persecution reached its nadir in the holocaust of the 1940s, when millions of Jews died in German concentration camps. Hitler's thoughts were clear: "The Jew is the great agitator for Germany's destruction. The trend of thought in Jewry is clear. It is to . . . rot away German national intelligence, and so crush the forces of German labour. . . . The National Socialist movement must see to it that in our own country at least the deadly enemy is realized."[32] The holocaust significantly altered the presence of Jews in Europe, as many survivors fled to the United States or Israel. Eighty years on, Jewish communities have revived across the continent, though still much smaller than in the 1930s, and anti-Semitism is growing, often linked to the growth in populism.

The State

The contemporary global state system owes a large part of its development to events in Europe. Efforts to minimize religious interference in territories, combined with the desire of local leaders to formalize their control over citizens (and tax them) led to the establishment of the respect for borders and temporal leaders and princes. This trend was formalized in 1648 at the Treaty of Westphalia, then under Prussian rule, at the end of Europe's Thirty Years' War, which was fought over religious differences in Central Europe. The principles underpinning the state included the concept of sovereignty, there being no higher authority than the ruler of the land. The principles also included the need for legal recognition by other sovereign states, inviolable territory and borders, and a population over which the leaders could exert full control.

The European state system evolved over centuries and was not a simple process.[33] Although these principles of statehood gained legal and conceptual acceptance, states willingly disregarded them whenever they wished to invade another country, but they remain the basis today for European relations. Breaches of these principles in Europe are now rare and, when they do happen, they are widely condemned, such as with Russia's invasions of Ukraine in 2014 and 2022.

Europeans did not recognize initially the existence of sovereignty outside of their continent, and so continued into the twentieth century their occupation and colonization of foreign lands and peoples. In time, these territories were consolidated into states by European occupiers and granted independence, and international organizations such as the League of Nations and the United Nations became the primary mechanisms of recognition of states. The development of the European Union is a novel attempt to alter the concept of sovereignty, though to date states remain central to our understanding of European politics.

Ideologies

Much of the language of politics that we use today—the "isms" of ideology—traces its intellectual origins to Europe. *Nationalism*, so prevalent in the contemporary world, traces to the actions of Napoleon in the late eighteenth century, and the igniting of opposition to French aspirations of domination across

Europe. The unification of Italy in 1865 and Germany in 1871 are important examples, and the hypernationalism of Europe in the first half of the twentieth century is testimony to the lethal force of such ideas. The devastation caused by such intense nationalism contributed to the search for ways after 1945 to minimize and mitigate such tensions, and this led to the concept of *supranationalism,* or the giving up of some national sovereignty to promote the cooperative venture of the European Union.

The language of *liberalism,* both economic and political, developed out of eighteenth- and nineteenth-century Europe, although its political roots go back much further. The signing of the Magna Carta of 1215 in Britain indicated a desire to rein in kings, their heavy taxation, and their military adventures, and this normally acts as a starting point for considerations about democracy. It was several hundred years later, however, before anything resembling a contemporary democracy would emerge. The prevalence of democracy across Europe today is one of the most important shared attributes of European states, and a sine qua non for entry into the EU as part of the Copenhagen criteria.[34] For many CEE states, their first true experience with democracy came only after the end of the Cold War in 1990, so there are significant differences across Europe. Russia and Turkey normally face exclusion from recognition as European because of their lack of democracy along with their geographical location.

Alternative conceptions toward management of the state and its political economy are evident in the competing ideologies of *conservatism, liberalism,* and *socialism*. These provide intellectual strength to the issues of European political development, but also contribute to significant turmoil. *Classical liberalism*'s growth through the work of Adam Smith and David Ricardo in the late eighteenth century offered an explanation and rationale for the expansion of British trade and global power through ideas of free trade and comparative advantage, and contributed to more economic reforms within the rest of Europe.

Conservatism, shaped by the writings of the English politician Edmund Burke, tended to be the overarching political force on continental Europe for much of the nineteenth and early twentieth centuries, as empires were reluctant to offer much in the way of democratic reform or change. This ideology also underpinned the Concert of Europe system of the nineteenth century in keeping stability and stifling reform. World War I swept away many of the empires, and created newly constituted countries in the center of Europe. Increasingly repressive conservatism quickly quashed widespread hopes of liberal development, culminating in the growth of *fascism* in Germany, Italy, and Spain. Extremism in the politics of the 1930s was another nadir for political development in Europe, and *totalitarianism* left an indelible mark on the conscience of the continent and the world.

At the other nominal end of the political spectrum stands *socialism* as initially propounded by Karl Marx, a German who spent much of his adult life in Britain. Socialism made little inroad into the vocabulary of Europe during the nineteenth century, despite the social upheaval and revolutionary activities of 1848. It was the devastating impact of World War I in Russia, along with the inept and callous rule of the Russian royal family, which provided the environment for the 1917 Russian Revolution, an event that catapulted socialist ideology into the mainstream European political arena. The schism in European politics widened during the 1920s and 1930s, as Joseph Stalin gained total control of the USSR. Hitler's rise in Germany in the 1920s was partly fueled by a common fear of the impact socialism would have there, along with the frailty of the fledgling Weimar Republic.

As the two totalitarian countries of Germany and the Soviet Union faced each other in the 1930s across the weak territories of Eastern Europe, there was (at least with hindsight) a certain inevitability of a clash between them. The nonaggression pact signed between them bought each time to prepare for war, and the German invasion of Russia in Operation Barbarossa in June 1941 started what was to be the most brutal conflict in European history. It would be wrong, though, to see this war as simply a clash of ideologies: rather, it was a battle for land, resources, and control of Central and Eastern Europe—and, to a considerable extent, the whole of the continent.

Today, *social democracy* is an ideology and a form of government that many in Europe embrace. Social democratic parties since 1945 have controlled the governments of Europe in equal measure to conservative parties, and many conservatives embrace the core tenets of social democracy, including universal health coverage, collective bargaining, and progressive taxation. At the extremes, the radical Marxist left fared reasonably well in parts of Europe (France, Italy) in the postwar era, but declined significantly after 1989. Conversely, the radical right had little traction in the postwar era (with major exceptions such as Portugal and Spain), but gradually gained in strength since the early 2000s, especially in countries such as Austria, Belgium, France, and, most recently, Germany. Here, these parties draw from a nationalist reaction to the perceived overarching presence of the EU, as well as to the increasing number of migrant workers. The pull of nationalism is still strong in influencing the political outlook of many Europeans.

Capitalism

Capitalism has transformed itself over the centuries within Europe, and intertwines itself with parallel developments in ideology and social progress (or perhaps in a Dickensian sense, the lack of it). Small-scale local employment gave way to guilds of artisans, but the arrival of capitalist production displaced them. The timing of this varied across Europe. A rough rule of thumb is that it developed in Britain—symbolized by the writings of the Scotsman Adam Smith with his 1776 publication of *The Wealth of Nations*—at the end of the eighteenth century and spread eastward, but this was uneven in time and impact, and capitalist activity was certainly present before 1776. Not all of Britain, for example, equally industrialized, as the scandal of the Irish potato famine of the 1820s exemplifies, where millions died from starvation in what was then the world's wealthiest country (as Ireland was a part of the UK then). Industrialization did not get to Russia and pockets of Eastern Europe until the twentieth century, and even then in limited form, though Czechoslovakia was one of the leading industrial powers in Europe in the 1930s.

In a similar vein, Europe's participation in, and creation of, a global capitalist system was uneven. European trade expansion in the sixteenth and seventeenth centuries—led in different periods by Venetian, Spanish, Portuguese, Dutch, and British forces—provided an early push toward the modern global capitalist system, but geared itself more to slavery and the simple exploitation of resources. The brutal slave trade helped to generate the wealth in Europe on which capitalism flourished. Over time, European colonialism more fully integrated territories into a capitalist marketplace, and further expansion into Asia and Africa in the nineteenth century consolidated this. The empires operating within Europe displayed a different emphasis of global capitalism to those outside the continent. The Austria-Hungarian and Ottoman Empires, for example, maintained elements of feudalistic rule within their European territories, and economic exploitation followed a historical pattern similar to previous centuries. European empires in Africa, on the other hand, exhibited blatant exploitation of raw materials, cash crops, and people to fuel the burgeoning European economies.

The social impact of capitalism was complex. On the one hand, it brought great wealth and prosperity to elites within Western Europe and, allied to wealth brutally extracted from overseas colonies, pushed countries to unprecedented heights of economic development, exemplified by the boom in the great cities of Berlin, London, and Paris. Extraction also occurred in artwork and artifacts plundered to benefit European galleries and museums. On the other hand, those countries in the east of Europe lagged badly in economic development and industrialization. Capitalist development also brought misery to countless millions of workers, drawn into cities and workplaces far from beneficial to their health. The gradual yet uneven expansion of workplace protection legislation helped, but did not dissipate the inhuman impact of the modern economy. Industrial development also led to pollution at chronic levels not seen in Europe before, and these high levels of pollution continued well into the beginning of the twenty-first century. During the Cold War, industrial production in the USSR and Soviet-dominated Eastern Europe—though not on traditionally capitalist grounds—also decimated local environments through intense levels of pollution.

Capitalist development transformed the transportation systems and technology of Europe, supplanting canals and water transport to bring the railway to the fore in the nineteenth century as the major mode of transportation.[35] The military implications of this were also immense, as World War I was to prove, with key decisions leading to war partly based on the rail transportation of troops. In Western Europe, transportation systems linked to the ports and the rapidly growing transatlantic trade routes. In the east, the relatively slow development of rail communications further hampered economic development, and reliance on waterways for transportation weakened trade as those routes tended to flow eastward and away from the vibrant markets of Western Europe.

The impact of capitalism in changing society and the workplace—the "factory"—contributed to the growth of trade unions and social unrest in many parts of Europe at the end of the 1800s and into the early 1900s. The writings of Marx, though not widely available at the time, provided an intellectual assault against the excesses of capitalism. The extent of a European workers' solidarity was limited, but there was some development of cross-national workers' movements at the turn of the twentieth century. This led to the belief that workers' solidarity would prevent them from fighting each other in a major European conflict. The jingoism and exhilaration with which European workers enlisted and marched to the battlefields dashed these illusions, and showed how shallow any pan-European identity was in 1914. The carnage of World War I was cruel punishment for European workers, but the economic nationalism of the 1920s and 1930s served to divide and subjugate further the national workforces of Europe.

Colonialism

The year 1492 remains an important date in European history with Christopher Columbus's "discovery" of the New World for Europeans. This event is symbolic of a growing expansion of European political and commercial power around the world, the development of a global economy centered on European power, and the growth of European empires that were to stretch around the globe. It also symbolizes Europe's arrogance of power and its complete, vicious disdain for the peoples that it occupied. There is a case to make that the past 500 years exemplify Europeans' perception of preeminence in the world, but that self-image came to an abrupt halt after World War II. The legacies of such influence are widespread, and continue to evolve. They include cultural influences, such as the use of European languages in far-flung areas around the world—English in the South Pacific, French in the Caribbean, Spanish in South America, and Portuguese in Southern Africa—to strong economic and political ties. Many of these former colonies remain dependent on Europe for development assistance, and a small minority continues a formal connection to the European metropole in a legal sense.

Not all European countries were global colonizers, as touched on earlier. Some, such as nineteenth-century Austria-Hungary, focused their colonizing efforts within Europe. The Scandinavians had jostled with each other for power and territory over the centuries, but remained with little outside of continental Europe, except Greenland and Iceland. The Dutch were early pioneers of colonization as Europe's leading global power and trader in the sixteenth and seventeenth centuries—helping shape their desire for the creation of international law to protect their trade interests—but were left in the twentieth century with scattered possessions in the Caribbean and East Asia (Indonesia). Germany was late into the colonial game, only unifying its own numerous principalities into a country in 1871. Its desire for a "place in the sun" burned brightly for several decades, but the League of Nations stripped Germany's colonial territories (e.g., Namibia and Togo) after the end of World War I.

Spain's colonial pursuits were largely concentrated in Latin America, where gold and religious converts were in abundance. Its control of territory through much of the continent, except for Brazil, lasted several centuries, but buckled in the early nineteenth century through a combination of internal revolt and competing interests from the UK and an emerging United States. Its last grip over parts of the continent was lost at the turn of the nineteenth century in Cuba and Puerto Rico at the hands of an aggressive and expansionist United States. Spain had few territorial interests in Africa outside of the extreme northwest (Western Sahara), although it retains possession of colonial enclaves today inside of Morocco. Portuguese exploits not only were in Latin America (Brazil), but were liberally scattered around the world, from Angola in Africa to Goa in India. Although Brazil prized its independence early in the nineteenth century, the Portuguese colonies in Africa were involved in major wars of independence, only breaking free in the 1970s, and then for some, such as Angola and Mozambique, plunging into decades-long and debilitating civil wars.

France and the UK were the other major imperial powers of Europe, with far-flung empires lasting for centuries. Each had parallel interests in the Caribbean, across Africa and the Middle East, and through parts of Asia and the Pacific. At times, the two powers cooperated in their colonial endeavors, whereas at other times they were mortal enemies. Such a history played out in their control of Canada and the United States, though these countries were relinquished much sooner than most of their other colonial territories. The final defeat of the British in the United States at New Orleans in January 1815 was significant in this regard, though the British eased their pain by extolling their important victory (with needed allies) over Napoleon at Waterloo in the same year. The toll of World War I weakened their control over their empires, but the devastation of World War II led to rapid decolonization of the British and French empires. I discuss these issues of decolonization in depth in the following chapter.

A European Identity?

Is there such a thing as an unambiguous European identity? Are the component national parts stronger than the European whole? What, if anything, binds Europeans together? Are there differences in attachment to Europe at a technocratic-legal level than to a cultural and spiritual level? Such questions are difficult to deal with, but begin to get at the problem of trying to judge what constitutes a European, how to perhaps differentiate between insiders and outsiders, and how effectively the EU is generating a European identity. These are themes that I continue to raise and address in subsequent chapters, but can introduce here.

If one works through a checklist of cultural factors, it is difficult to see from where a common European identity emerges. For example, language, religion, or ethnicity do not provide anything that Europeans share.[36] In poll after poll, the majority of European citizens outside of the Benelux core (Belgium, the Netherlands, and Luxembourg) do not fully align themselves with the EU or the broader concept of Europe. They do see themselves broadly, however, as citizens of Europe in addition to citizens of their own country, so with multiple identities. For example, a Eurobarometer survey in 2020 found about 70 percent of EU citizens polled felt comfortable perceiving themselves to be citizens of Europe, which is different from having an attachment to the EU. Not all Europeans normally approve of the major legislation of the EU, such as the introduction of the euro currency in 2002, or the European constitution in 2003. Despite some notable efforts at winning popular support, the EU administration in Brussels is aloof from everyday Europeans, and so has little ability to garner greater support for a European consciousness. Although the EU bureaucracy is often perceived to be all-powerful and menacing to Europeans, it accounts for only about 1 percent of European GDP, and operates on a small budget and with a small bureaucracy. With only twenty-seven members, the EU itself is not synonymous with all of Europe, especially in terms of the distinctiveness of Russia and Turkey, as well as the UK after 2020.

At a vaguer, more philosophical level, it is possible to suggest some factors that might tie Europeans together in a common consciousness beyond simple geographical proximity. The history of the Renaissance, the Reformation, the Enlightenment, and the two world wars in the twentieth century can possibly provide some sense of a shared experience. The impact of these events, however, was different in various parts of Europe, and so is difficult to judge in any concrete fashion. For the wars in particular, there were winners and losers, and so the experience (and memory) of these differed markedly. There are modern cultural events that bring Europeans together in competitions, such as the Champions League football/soccer season, the Tour de France cycling, and the Eurovision Song Contest. These are, however, insufficient to create a common identity and, if anything, pit countries (or competitors identified as representatives of their country) against each other. There are few examples where Europe fields a common team—the Ryder Cup in golf perhaps—but these have limited impact in building a European consciousness. When the European Commission entered its own song into the Eurovision Song Contest for the first time in 2021, there was significant opposition to this example of Europeanness. The resounding victory of the Ukrainian entry in the 2022 contest, however, displayed an emotive level of European solidarity and togetherness brought about by the depth of opposition to Russia's invasion of that country.

A country's perception of Europe and a shared identity links to its own historical and cultural experiences. So, for example, the UK's lukewarm support for Europe is understood in terms of the country's own history of perceived separation from continental Europe, geographically and figuratively, and a sense of superiority to the rest of Europe. Similarly, Russia's attachment to Europe appears to ebb and flow in history depending on numerous factors, not least the whims of the rulers at the time. The thrust for membership in the EU by a number of countries in CEE has perhaps less to do with a longing to share a European identity, and more to do with economic and security considerations.

Overall, then, the concept of a developing overarching European identity is problematic, and continuing national identity within Europe remains prevalent. As one survey bluntly put it, "People have no sense of a 'European character'—a set of characteristics that are common to Europeans. There is no equivalent to the set of myths or stories that make up national identities. There is no overarching narrative that makes sense of European history or the European project."[37] The EU seems unable and unlikely to dislodge states and national interest. Such issues receive further discussion in later chapters. There are arguments that Europe had more of a common identity during the nineteenth century than today. Then, it was possible to travel freely across Europe, trade within the region as a percentage of total trade was as high as it is in the twenty-first century, and some semblance of linguistic unity—at least for the elite—existed through the common use of French. The two world wars and the intense nationalism of the interwar period, combined with the Cold War division of Europe after 1945 and the renewed nationalism and subnationalism post-1989, have all arguably served to undermine a common European spirit—the best efforts of the EU notwithstanding.

The EU has succeeded in creating a mountain of common objectives and policies, codified in numerous treaties and the *acquis communautaire* (which roughly translates from French as the "acquired law of the community"), the body of laws that is at the heart of the EU, and to which all potential new members must agree prior to entry. Covering tens of thousands of pages, or thirty-five chapters now for negotiations with Turkey and other candidates, the *acquis* displays successful agreement on common policies.[38] All this does not come easily, however, and is normally the result of massive bargaining and dealmaking among the member states. In the earlier days of the EU, all members held a potential veto over all policies. Increasingly, as I show later, a system of qualified majority voting has been introduced, but even here policies are often boiled down to the lowest common denominator to gain approval—and can still be blocked by a national veto, especially by one of the larger members. An increasing trend in the EU has been for members to opt out of various aspects of legislation—such as defense, immigration, and the euro—so that there is a multispeed or differentiated EU, whereby member states are formally pursuing different objectives with different partners with different levels of enthusiasm.

At a more general level, however, one can make the case that the EU has helped to define a common policy agenda for Europe, and in many areas has successfully harmonized EU objectives and policies. At a specific level, we can talk about policies on competition between companies, and the liberalization across Europe of such economic sectors as transportation and telecommunications. The European Commission acts as the watchdog to make sure that EU members (and significantly those outside who trade with the EU) play to the same rules. At a broader level, it is possible to argue that the EU has helped to foster common political goals for the whole of Europe—democracy, capitalist economic development, social welfare, peace—and though vague, these are nevertheless worthy goals to pursue and achieve. How well the EU27 can maintain a focus on common objectives remains a question for later discussion, though clearly there are continuing policy divergences.

Another question to raise is the extent to which the EU is likely to become a United States of Europe, a federation of states resembling the federal United States. The term *the United States of Europe* has been around for a long time, perhaps first coined in the modern era by Winston Churchill soon after the end of World War II. Of course, in an involuntary way, many Europeans have been forced into a united Europe in the past, dating back to the Roman Empire. Churchill's view, like many others, was of a Europe loosely linked by economic and political commonalities, but not a federation in the sense of a single country or government or culture. That supranational view, however, is prominent among many of the political elite in Europe, dating back in the modern era to Jean Monnet, one of the founders of the EU. The voluntary relinquishing of sovereignty to create a United States of Europe gained ground as a specific policy objective, and has many concrete successes. These include the removal of national frontiers across much of Europe, the adoption of the euro currency by nineteen states, and the increasing governmental role played by the EU institutions in Brussels.

There are numerous limitations to this idea, however. Probably the single most important distinction is in the cultural area, where linguistic differences between Europeans make any true "United States" hard to imagine. Because of these differences, media coverage tends also to be language- and nation-based, hindering a more pan-European perspective. Although English may become the lingua franca of Europe (despite the UK's departure from the EU), national languages remain central.[39] It is highly unlikely that a federal European state will emerge whose system of government is similar to that of the US model. Whereas that might have seemed a distant possibility in the EU of six members, it is hard to imagine in the EU27 or beyond. Indeed, framed somewhat cynically or just realistically in a long-term historical perspective, the EU is perhaps just another transitory attempt to garner peace and unity in Europe after a war, with limited chance of permanence.

Conclusion

This chapter introduces some common themes and questions to form a basis for later chapters in the book. Besides offering a quick overview of the continent, it explored ideas of European culture and identity, bringing in a longer-term historical perspective. Agreeing on the exact boundaries of Europe is difficult, but a working definition was chosen to utilize the membership of the Council of Europe, including Russia and Turkey, as the basis for our discussions. The chapter also took note of the fluidity of Europe's borders and political movements, and the multispeed movement in the direction of democracy. In the next chapter, I build from this platform to explain contemporary Europe in terms of the legacies of key events from the twentieth century. Such a framework is necessary to understand many of the important elements of European politics today.

Notes

1. In general, when we refer to *states,* we are discussing territorial units with sovereignty, legal recognition, a government, and a population controlled by laws. Although not technically correct, the terms *state* and *country* can be interchangeable.

2. Gerard Delanty, *Inventing Europe: Idea, Identity, Reality* (Houndmills: Palgrave Macmillan, 1995). For a helpful animated map of Europe over the centuries, see Nick

Routley, "How the European Map Has Changed over 2,400 Years," *Visual Capitalist,* October 28, 2021, https://www.visualcapitalist.com/2400-years-of-european-history/.

3. The word "Balkan" loosely translates from Turkish as mountain. For historical maps of Europe, see Euratlas-Müssli, "History of Europe," http://www.euratlas.net/history/europe/index.html.

4. Robert Sapolsky, "This Is Your Brain on Nationalism: The Biology of Us and Them," *Foreign Affairs* 98(2), 2019: 42–47; see also Ernest Gellner, *Nations and Nationalism* (Ithaca: Cornell University Press, 1983).

5. Milada Anna Vachudova, "Populism, Democracy, and Party System Change in Europe," *Annual Review of Political Science* 24, 2021: 1–28; see also Madalina Calance, "The Resurgence of Nationalism in the European Union," Centre for European Studies Working Paper 4(1), 2012: 24–34, https://www.econstor.eu/bitstream/10419/198153/1/ceswp-v04-i1-p024-034.pdf.

6. Alexander Wendt, *Social Theory of International Politics* (Cambridge: Cambridge University Press, 1999).

7. James Burnham, *The Machiavellians* (Chicago: Gateway, 1943), p. 252.

8. Thomas Christensen, Knud Erik Jørgensen, and Antje Wiener, "The Social Construction of Europe," *Journal of European Public Policy* 6(4), 1999: 528–544; see also Thomas Christensen, Knud Erik Jørgensen, and Antje Wiener (eds.), *The Social Construction of Europe* (London: Sage, 2001).

9. Gabriel A. Almond and Sidney Verba, *The Civic Culture: Political Attitudes and Democracy in Five Nations* (Princeton: Princeton University Press, 1963), pp. 13–15; see also Gabriel A. Almond and G. Bingham Powell, *Comparative Politics: A Developmental Approach* (Boston: Little, Brown, 1966).

10. Gabriel A. Almond, Russell J. Dalton, and G. Bingham Powell Jr. (eds.), *European Politics Today* (New York: Longman, 1999), chap. 2.

11. Thomas Denk, Henrik Serup Christensen, and Daniel Bergh, "The Composition of Political Culture—A Study of 25 European Democracies," *Studies in Comparative International Development* 50(3), 2015: 358–377.

12. World Bank Data, "Land Area (Sq. Km.)," https://data.worldbank.org/indicator/AG.LND.TOTL.K2.

13. United Nations, "Department of Economic and Social Affairs: Population" (New York: United Nations, 2022), https://www.un.org/en/development/desa/population/publications/database/index.asp.

14. Russia's Far Eastern Federal District has a population of more than 6 million.

15. Besides Turkey, other candidate countries for EU admission are Albania, North Macedonia, Montenegro, and Serbia. Moldova and Ukraine submitted formal applications for EU membership immediately following Russia's invasion of Ukraine in February 2022. In a largely symbolic gesture, the EU advanced both to candidate status in June 2022.

16. United Nations Economic Commission for Europe, www.unece.org.

17. United Nations Department for General Assembly and Conference Management: Regional Groups of States, https://www.un.org/dgacm/en/content/regional-groups; also Worldometers, https://www.worldometers.info/geography/how-many-countries-in-europe/.

18. Gergana Noutcheva, Karolina Pomorska, and Giselle Bosse (eds.), *The EU and Its Neighbours: Values Versus Security in European Foreign Policy* (Manchester: Manchester University Press, 2013).

19. The name is the "English Channel" in English; the French simply refer to it as La Manche, the channel, or the sleeve. Conversely, the Channel Islands are known in French

as Les Isles Anglo-Normandes. Scientists estimate that the channel physically appeared only about 8,000 years ago. In terms of technicalities, the term *the United Kingdom* includes Great Britain (England, Scotland, and Wales) and Northern Ireland. For ease, I will use the UK and Britain interchangeably, and note that in this usage "Britain" also includes Northern Ireland.

20. Union for the Mediterranean, https://ufmsecretariat.org/.

21. Paul Kubicek, *European Politics,* 3rd ed. (Abingdon: Routledge, 2021), chap.1. See also Anthony Pagden (ed.), *The Idea of Europe: From Antiquity to the European Union* (Cambridge: Cambridge University Press/Woodrow Wilson Center Press, 2002).

22. Council of Europe, https://www.coe.int/en/web/portal/46-members-states.

23. World Bank Data, "Population in Total," https://data.worldbank.org/indicator/SP .POP.TOTL.

24. See the Country Profiles section at the end of the book for further details.

25. Thucydides, *The Peloponnesian War* (Harmondsworth: Penguin, 1972).

26. Niccolò Machiavelli, *The Prince* (New York: Norton, 2020), p. 46.

27. Martin Wight, *Power Politics* (London: Pelican, 1979), p. 137.

28. For coverage of the core factors in this sweep of European history, see Walter C. Opello Jr. and Katherine A.R. Opello, *European Politics: The Making of Democratic States* (Boulder: Lynne Rienner, 2009).

29. Andreas Wimmer, "Why Nationalism Works: And Why It Isn't Going Away," *Foreign Affairs* 98(2), 2019: 27–34.

30. This defeat also contributed to the rise of the Paris Commune, one of the most radical movements in French history, the discussion of which still divides the left and the right in French politics.

31. For a discussion of many of these issues, see José M. Magone, *Contemporary European Politics: A Comparative Introduction,* 2nd ed. (Abingdon: Routledge, 2019), chap. 2.

32. Adolf Hitler, *My Struggle* (London: Paternoster Library, 1938), pp. 247, 252.

33. Opello and Opello, *European Politics*.

34. European Union, "European Neighbourhood Policy and Enlargement Negotiations: Accession Criteria," https://ec.europa.eu/neighbourhood-enlargement/enlargement -policy/glossary/accession-criteria_en.

35. The railways also necessitated having a common timetable on which the trains would run, so this changed time from being set in localities on a national basis, to an internationally accepted time in the 1880s based on London (Greenwich Mean Time).

36. There are twenty-four official languages in the European Union.

37. Mark Leonard, *Making Europe Popular: The Search for European Identity* (London: Demos/Interbrand, 1998), p. 17.

38. European Commission, "European Neighbourhood Policy and Enlargement Negotiations: Chapters of the Acquis/Negotiating Chapters," https://ec.europa.eu /neighbourhood-enlargement/policy/glossary/terms/chapters_en.

39. The term *lingua franca* means an intermediary or bridge language used to communicate. Historically, it literally meant "language of the Franks," or language that West Europeans used in trade across the Mediterranean and the Middle East. It then comprised a mixture of Greek, French, Portuguese, Spanish, Arabic, and Turkish. The language was used for centuries. Today, English has taken its place as an intermediary language.

2

Critical Legacies of the Twentieth Century

IT IS A TRUISM TO SAY THAT EUROPE POSSESSES AN INCREDIBLE WEALTH of documented history, and many major events have shaped the continent. It is impossible to attempt a complete, or even a partial, history of Europe and its politics in this concise book. However, to be able to understand and explain the nature of contemporary European politics, it is important to touch on some key historical events and themes. The first chapter provided an exploration of broad historical (and geographical) factors that help us to understand the development of Europe. In this chapter, the specific focus are the legacies of the twentieth century. This is not an exhaustive examination, but it highlights events of the twentieth century that are important to our comprehension of European politics and society today.

To facilitate this inquiry, this chapter breaks down into chronological and thematic sections. First, it considers Europe at the turn of the twentieth century and its rapid descent into World War I, which lasted from 1914 to 1918. Second, it looks at the initial optimism of the 1920s, and how the extreme nationalism of the 1930s undermined this, leading to the outbreak of World War II. Third, it examines the Cold War era in Europe, chronicling the important developments from 1945 until the early 1990s. Fourth, it discusses the same period after World War II to 1990, but focuses on the rapid decolonization exercises undertaken by West European states, considering the societal impact of these changing policies.

The fifth section also begins after World War II, but focuses on the development of the European Union, starting with the proclamation of the Schuman Declaration in May 1950. Finally, the book examines Europe in the post–Cold War era after 1990, looking especially at the transformation of the former Soviet satellite states in Central and Eastern Europe. This brings us into the twenty-first century and provides a basis for the analyses in subsequent chapters.

The Early Twentieth Century: 1900–1919

Europe was arguably at the height of its power and "civilization" immediately prior to the catastrophe of World War I beginning in 1914. West Europeans had carved up Africa at the Berlin conference in 1884 without any African input. Germany had quickly amassed colonies for their "place in the sun," even though they had focused their energies initially on building up the German state and had eschewed colonization. The British Empire stretched across the world where "the sun never set," seemingly at the zenith of its powers after the six decades of stable growth under Queen Victoria, despite some misgivings after the unsteadying performance during the Boer War in South Africa from 1899 to 1902. France, similarly, possessed a global empire and had pride in its status. The Russian and Austria-Hungarian Empires, though not global, appeared at face value to be stable and functioning, notwithstanding the jarring maritime defeat of Russia by Japan in the war of 1905. Confident in their complete superiority and beneficence, none of these colonial powers paid attention to the damage inflicted by them on those they occupied.

The major European powers, with others from outside the continent in attendance, managed to negotiate some helpful agreements during the two Hague peace conferences of 1899 and 1907. These agreements centered on the peaceful settlement of disputes, the laws of war, and the potential for disarmament. Allied to the growth of European trade, the free movement of people across the continent, and a seeming "golden age" for Europe, the Hague conferences offered a perception of a strong, confident, somewhat unified, and peaceful Europe. This all quickly crumbled within a decade. German reluctance to have its powers abridged limited the Hague treaties, especially in terms of maritime forces, and displayed the country's instincts to increase its influence. A chemical weapons ban did not hold during World War I, nor did any hope for disarmament. The scheduled third Hague conference became a casualty of the outbreak of war, and never took place.

Historians struggle to explain why and how Europe quickly turned on itself in 1914. Rigid military alliances and the jingoistic belief that the war would be short-lived and successful helped propel countries to war. Few foresaw the stalemate that ensued, the trench warfare, and the carnage with the widespread use of the machine gun, the tank, and chemical weapons. The futility of this war still reverberates around Europe, and most small towns and villages house a memorial to their dead. Some 2 million people or more died from each of the countries of France, Germany, Russia, and Turkey. The fact that Europe slid into another major war two decades later provided a core impulse for the creation of the European Union. Besides this, two core legacies of the war are important to note.

First, the intervention of the United States into the war in 1917 was a telling moment in the ebbing influence of Europe, as well as its inability to police itself. Whereas in the past, alliances between European states had tipped the balance in favor of one group or another, in World War I the powers fought each other to a stalemate. US president Woodrow Wilson blamed European power politics and secret treaties for the war, and saw an opportunity to recalibrate and reform Europe through his Fourteen Points for Peace announced in January 1918. Many of these points called for self-determination of peoples in Europe (though not in European colonies), as well as the restoration of prewar boundaries in Belgium and France. The calls for self-determination led to the creation of "new" countries in CEE, including Czechoslovakia, Poland, and Yugoslavia, as the Austria-Hungary and Ottoman Empires broke up. The fact that the war had started with the assassination in Sarajevo of the Austrian heir to the throne, Archduke Franz Ferdinand, and his wife by a disgruntled Bosnian Serb nationalist, was an indicator of the tensions within that empire.

Second, dissent inside Russia, highlighted by the first revolution of 1905 prompted by the country's naval defeat to Japan, broke to the forefront of life because of the pressures brought about by the war. German assistance to Vladimir Lenin and other revolutionaries helped them toward a successful revolution in 1917, and Russia's quick exit from the war. The Russians ceded their interests in the Baltic to Germany in March 1918 and, with the later collapse of Germany, the states of Estonia, Latvia, and Lithuania were able to maneuver their way to independence in 1920 over German and Soviet intransigence with military help from Britain, France, and Poland. The subsequent implementation of communism, and the massive industrialization programs undertaken by Lenin's successor, Joseph Stalin, kept Russia largely out of mainstream European politics for two decades until it played a decisive role in World War II, and then developed its own empire in CEE until 1990.

The Versailles peace conference of 1919 was a mix of optimism and realism.[1] The creation of new states appealed to democratic and nationalist tendencies, but did not guarantee economic or political success, as people soon discovered. Germany emerged from the war in reasonable shape. Its core remained more or less geographically intact, although it relinquished Alsace-Lorraine back to France and demilitarized that border along the Rhine.[2] In addition, a sizable section of Eastern Germany separated from the remainder of the country to provide the newly emergent Poland access to the sea through the corridor to Danzig (Gdansk). The forcible reoccupation of the Polish corridor (and Poland along with it) would be the formal cause of World War II in September 1939, though many other earlier events contributed.

The Interwar Period and World War II: 1920–1945

The interwar years started relatively brightly. The League of Nations, based in Geneva, established a quasi-global institution for the first time, and promised assistance in conflict resolution.[3] Germany offered hope of stability and reform, with its first attempt at democratic government within the Weimar Republic. Germany's inclusion back into mainstream Europe seemed complete at the Locarno conference in 1925, when it accepted its new western borders with Belgium and France and the demilitarized zone, and guarantees of ever-lasting peace in Europe were assured. All the major powers in Europe, along with the United States, reinforced such optimism in 1928 by signing the General Treaty for the Renunciation of War (otherwise known as the Kellogg-Briand Pact, or the Pact of Paris), essentially renouncing war as an element of national policy. Partially because of this agreement, and as a way to consolidate peace, German war reparations halted. Nevertheless, the strands of unrest across the continent continued to build.

The remainder of Europe did not initially feel the impact of the Russian Revolution, partly because Lenin and Stalin were busy consolidating internal power and restructuring economic production within, but there appeared to be a tangible impact on workers' disaffection across Europe, and the fearful, retaliatory actions of government. Strikes and political strife became commonplace. Notable was the British General Strike of May 1926, centered on support for coal miners, and the continuing economic strain that forced Britain off the gold standard in September 1931. Economic turmoil and hyperinflation in Germany during the mid-1920s allowed Adolf Hitler and his Nazi Party to take advantage of these and other issues to capture power in Germany—albeit initially through constitutional means in January 1933.

The consolidation of fascism in Germany and Italy (under Benito Mussolini), the general strengthening of right-wing governments across much of Europe, and the impact of the Spanish Civil War in 1936–1939 in splitting European political opinion (as well as devastating Spain), were ominous features. This civil war pitted the Nationalists (backed by Italy and Germany) against the Republicans (backed by the USSR and volunteers from across Europe and the United States), with about 500,000 people losing their lives.[4]

Recession, inflation, and spiraling economic nationalism decreased stability, with no real international financial mechanisms available to bring any respite. The League was powerless and often unwilling to intervene, partly hamstrung by the political machinations of its dominant players, France and the UK.

With hindsight, and in real time for some observers, the events of the 1930s hurled Europe inexorably toward war. German expansion into Austria through the Anschluss in 1936, and its annexation in 1938, was one factor. British "appeasement" of Germany, in essence by sacrificing western Czechoslovakia to Germany in the Munich Agreement (or Betrayal) of September 1938, did nothing to stem the tide of war or Hitler's desire to correct the perceived injustice of the Versailles agreement. Germany absorbed most of Czechoslovakia in March 1939, and Germany's invasion of Poland in September 1939 finally triggered World War II. The German-Soviet Nonaggression Pact signed in August 1939 facilitated this invasion, as it promised Soviet neutrality in exchange for its control of eastern Poland and the Baltic states. This neutrality ended with Germany's invasion of the USSR in June 1941 in Operation Barbarossa, and the USSR became tied in an uneasy alliance with the others fighting fascism. Never has the expression that "your enemy is my enemy, therefore we are friends" been more apt.

The German-Soviet war is one of the largest and most brutal military conflicts in history—a war inside of World War II, and one that Russians still complain they get insufficient credit from the West for fighting. The death toll on Germany's Eastern Front was tremendous, with over 20 million fatalities.

Box 2.1   Europe and the League of Nations

The absence of the United States from the League of Nations allowed Europeans to dominate its business, especially Britain and France, which continued to see the League in terms of their own national interests. English and French were the League's official languages. Germany entered the League later in September 1926, six years after its founding, and left in 1933 soon after Adolf Hitler took power because the League refused to condone plans for German military expansion. The League did nothing during the Spanish Civil War in the 1930s since neither Britain or France wanted to antagonize any of the combatants, who they hoped would become allies. Besides mild sanctions, Italy invaded Ethiopia (Abyssinia) without cost. The League evicted the Soviet Union in December 1939 after its invasion of Finland, but this was already after the start of World War II and the effective collapse of the League, even though the USSR did not enter the war until Germany's attack on the country in June 1941.

Leningrad (today's St. Petersburg), was laid siege to for twenty-nine months, with several million fatalities. The eventual "liberation" of the east left cities such as Warsaw and Berlin (over 1 million died in the taking of Berlin) destroyed, and left the liberating Red Army in control of much of Central and Eastern Europe. The assistance of US forces coming from the west and south helped turn the tide against Germany, and ended the war in Europe in May 1945. The decisiveness of US and USSR intervention again underlined the inability and weakness of the traditional powers of Europe to solve their own problems.

Germany controlled much of continental Europe in 1940, including its nemesis of France, which was managed under the Vichy government of collaboration. This was perhaps the culmination of the power and growth of the German Empire since its beginnings in 1871. Save for the geographical good fortune of the English Channel, it seems inevitable that Germany would have occupied the UK also.[5] The sheer dominance of Germany, combined with its callous murder of about 6 million Jews in the Holocaust, led to postwar efforts to contain its power, by occupying forces as well as by a novel experiment in European cooperation—eventually becoming the European Union. Besides neutral Ireland, Portugal, Spain, Sweden, and Switzerland, the war decimated Europe. Those fortunate enough to survive the war faced a destroyed transportation structure, with bridges, roads, and railways in a serious state of disrepair. Many German cities were little but rubble. Millions of Europeans struggled to find food and shelter. It was in this context with the vivid memory of the war that policymakers set out to try to reconstruct Europe.

Cold War Europe: 1945–1991

Wartime agreements between the UK, the United States, and the USSR sealed the distribution of power within Europe for when the war concluded. Winston Churchill, Franklin D. Roosevelt, and Joseph Stalin met in Yalta (Crimea) in February 1945 and agreed to divide Germany after the war into four sectors (the three signatories plus France). The USSR would have influence over Poland, but promised free elections there. At Potsdam, just outside of Berlin, the three countries met again between July and August 1945. Harry S. Truman replaced Roosevelt who had died in April, and midway through the conference, Clement Attlee replaced Churchill, who had just lost the national election in early July. The three leaders finalized plans for the distribution of four zones of control in Germany. In addition, Poland and Germany shifted westward some 150 kilometers across the map of Europe to provide the USSR a greater territorial buffer on its western flank, with Germany losing one-quarter of its pre-1937 territory, mostly to Poland. Soviet territorial expansion also came at the cost of Czechoslovakia and Hungary, and this allowed the USSR to border those countries for the first time.[6] All agreed on the demilitarization of Germany, with its leaders put on trial for war crimes. The USSR gained a "sphere of influence" over most of Eastern Europe including the Baltics. Stalin almost immediately broke his promise to hold free elections in the region by purging governments and installing his own pro-Soviet leadership.

The agreements over Germany were adhered to in the immediate aftermath of the war, in that the Soviet army withdrew from western sectors of Berlin to pass those on to British, French, and US forces; likewise, the US forces that had liberated western Czechoslovakia withdrew to allow Soviet forces to take hold. Cooperation quickly broke down, however, over the administration of Germany, symbolized by the Soviet blockade of Berlin in 1947–1948, and the decision in the West to unify the three allied sectors of Germany into one. The Truman Doctrine of March 1947 offered support to Greece and Turkey, which were attempting to resist Soviet-supported communist takeovers, but this assistance was available for any country in Western Europe to resist Soviet influence. The Marshall Plan (technically the European Recovery Program) announced in June 1947 by the US secretary of state, George Marshall, promised economic assistance to all of Europe, but the Soviet-influenced Eastern Bloc countries quickly rejected the aid, thereby reinforcing the division of Europe. The creation of the West German state and the North Atlantic Treaty Organization in 1949 consolidated the Cold War division of the continent. NATO provided a US guarantee of military protection for any member attacked by the USSR. The future of Europe now lay in the hands of "occupying superpowers," the United States and the USSR.

This sense of weakness was not lost on the former dominant powers of Europe—notable also in the rapid decolonization of the British and French empires—and they began to look for ways to reassert themselves. Britain's path was to tie itself further to the United States, but other countries looked to a European solution. West European countries were required to establish the Organisation for European Economic Co-operation (OEEC) in 1948 as a mechanism to distribute US funds through the Marshall Plan. This pattern of cooperation led six countries (Belgium, France, Italy, Luxembourg, the Netherlands, and West Germany) to seek further partnerships, and they established the European Coal and Steel Community (ECSC) in 1951. This pooling of resources in strategic commodities provided political, economic, and strategic elements to their cooperation, and hinted at a way forward in European cooperation.

The hardening of the Cold War during the 1950s was evident in such things as the creation of the USSR's Warsaw Treaty Organization (or Warsaw Pact) in

1955—a reaction to West Germany entering NATO—and the Soviet army's intervention in Hungary a year later to suppress its uprising. The Hungarians believed, wrongly, that NATO forces would intervene to help, but there was little incentive for the United States to embark on a war with the USSR for the sake of a few Eastern European countries. The US strategy of containment, first espoused by US diplomat George Kennan in 1947, meant attempting to prevent Soviet expansion, but not necessarily to roll the USSR back. Events outside of Europe during the 1950s, in Korea and Vietnam, exemplified the tense relationship between the superpowers, and the building of the Berlin Wall in 1961 consolidated the rigid separation of the two halves of Europe.

The Berlin Wall came to symbolize the division of Europe after World War II, and the real tensions that existed within Europe. Initial plans by the victorious powers (the UK, the United States, and the USSR—and later France) to manage occupied Germany jointly after 1945 soon collapsed in acrimony, and by the end of 1949 two separate German states existed. Berlin, however, proved more problematic, as it encompassed four sectors, and was more than 100 miles inside of East Germany. The USSR made efforts to squeeze out the other powers from Berlin in a blockade of the city in 1948–1949. Over the 11 months that road and rail transit was blocked, the United States organized 200,000 flights into West Berlin, bringing much-needed supplies to its citizens. Unable to break US will, the USSR relinquished the blockade in May 1949, just a month after the signing of the NATO agreement.

In the late 1950s, West Berlin became a relatively easy access point for several million citizens of East Germany (the German Democratic Republic [GDR]) and other CEE states to flee to the West. And so on August 13, 1961, without warning, construction began of a concrete wall 87 miles, or 140 kilometers, long to encircle West Berlin. Ostensibly to prevent West German reactionary forces tampering with the successful revolution in East Germany—the Berlin Wall's official name was the Anti-Fascist Protection Wall—it aimed to stop East Europeans fleeing to the West. It came to symbolize the oppression that took place across the communist states of CEE, and the efforts that the East German state would make to keep citizens under control and inside the East.

At the beginning of the 1970s, West German chancellor Willy Brandt's Ostpolitik, or Eastern Policy, promoted a loosening of tensions in Europe whereby West Germany started the slow process toward mutual recognition of East Germany, the USSR, and other CEE countries. The extent to which Brandt's work was considered bold and visionary won him the Nobel Peace Prize in 1971. One sign of success achieved in 1973 was when the two German states became members of the United Nations. This rapprochement was still relatively low-key, as the USSR's aggressive invasion to put down the Prague Spring of domestic

---

Box 2.2   Twentieth-Century Germany: Changing Locations

The map of Germany changed many times during the twentieth century (and, for the record, a number of times during the nineteenth century too). A consolidated empire began the 1900s, a result of the unification of the country for the first time in 1871. After World War I, Alsace-Lorraine was lost to France, and the Polish Corridor to the international port of Danzig (Gdansk) cut off a section of Eastern Germany from the rest of the country. In the 1930s, Germany reoccupied the demilitarized zone to the west, and the Anschluss with Austria combined the countries in 1936, with Austria fully annexed into Germany in 1938. Germany took over western Czechoslovakia in 1938 (the small Slovak state remained nominally independent, though essentially a German client state under the clerical fascist leadership of Monsignor Jozef Tiso) and added western Poland to the geographical boundaries by 1939. Alsace-Lorraine reverted to Germany. Following World War II, the occupying powers split Germany into two countries in 1949, and it lost considerable land in the east to Poland.[a] It also relinquished Königsberg on the Baltic Sea to Russia, which named the land Kaliningrad after the Russian revolutionary, Mikhail Kalinin. Germany's eastern border moved about 100 miles west, and today remains on the Oder-Neisse Rivers. Germany also lost its acquired territories in Austria and Czechoslovakia, as well as ceding Alsace-Lorraine back to France. The shifting back and forth of Alsace-Lorraine makes Strasbourg a symbolic city of French-German and wider European cooperation today, and it is home to the Council of Europe and one of the homes of the European Parliament. Both East Germany and West Germany became members of the United Nations in 1973. In 1990, the two countries reunified, with the capital of Germany back in Berlin, but the postwar boundaries remained intact.

Note: a. Some sites of the 1936 Berlin Olympic Games are today in Poland. Currently, Berlin is only about 50 miles (80 kilometers) from the Polish border at Frankfurt Oder and Slubice. Slubice on the Polish side of the Oder River was part of Frankfurt and Germany prior to 1945.

---

reforms in Czechoslovakia in 1968 showed its determination to maintain its grip on Eastern Europe. The final settlement of the postwar status of Germany would have to wait until the Cold War itself ended.

The Loss of Empires and Decolonization: 1945

Already discussed in the previous chapter were the brutal manner in which European countries sought colonies around the world, and the arrogant way in which Europeans exploited those colonies for financial gain within a burgeoning global capitalist system. For all the talk of European civilization, grandeur, and moral superiority, we cannot hide the brutality and racism with which colonies and their citizens were treated (nor the long periods involved in slave trading). How were European countries coping in a postcolonial, postindustrial, postprime condition?

The impact of the two world wars severely undermined Europe's abilities to hold on to their colonies. Many colonies were lost much earlier, such as the Portuguese and Spanish colonies in the Americas, and the British colonies in the United States. The two world wars, however, combined with open US opposition, undermined the military and economic ability of European countries to keep colonies, leading to a rapid period of decolonization.[7] This led to a loss of prestige, a loss of overseas income, a need to rethink global strategy, and a reckoning with how to deal with the resultant domestic issues, notably the angst felt in European political systems and the many immigrants who came to Europe from former colonies.[8] In addition, the return to their home country of many of those citizens who had been involved in the overseas colony presented challenges in adapting to the end of empire.[9] Tellingly, this did not lead to much internal reflection about the merits of colonialism and the damage caused by these endeavors around the world, nor did it completely end European influence over what were to become former colonies, as most of them struggled to develop.

Independence granted to India (and Pakistan) by the British in 1947 was probably the landmark event so soon after the end of the war, as India had been the most prized and lucrative colony, the "jewel in the crown." Independence gathered pace to many countries across Asia and North Africa, though as France's war of attrition in Algeria in the 1950s displays, not always without cost. The French loss in Vietnam in 1954 provided major repercussions beyond France, and led to US involvement. The Anglo-French debacle during the Suez Crisis in 1956 over Egyptian nationalization of the Suez Canal was another major turning point in the decline of European authority in the region, underlined further by the UK's withdrawal from its Middle East policing role in 1967. Such a vacuum led to the increasingly active role played by the United States in that region.

British and French decolonization was sometimes orderly, though the rapid diminishing of their prestige and power played out dramatically on the political stage for decades, arguably still to today. One obvious example is the collapse of the French Fourth Republic in the 1950s, and the assumption of power by Charles de Gaulle in a new Fifth Republic in 1958. The UK retaliated through vicious repressions against independence movements, particularly in Kenya and Malaya, unsettling the colonial power. For France and the UK, maintaining a partnership of former colonial possessions, their Commonwealths, helped to soften the blow, as did the continuance of important economic ties. These organizations offer some tangible benefit of continuing influence in the world for Britain and France, though this is becoming increasingly nebulous, especially for Britain. Both countries also maintain their seats on the United Nations Security Council, so this gives them a degree of status perhaps matching their nuclear-based military and economic strength, and so the stature of these two countries is mixed.[10]

Just as France and the UK have had a tough time adapting to their lessened role in the world postdecolonization, so these issues have become ones for the EU itself to consider. What should be the role of the EU with those countries with an ex-colonial relationship? Are there obligations to help these former colonial territories? Are there trade advantages that could accrue to Europe in maintaining privileged linkages to large swaths of the world?

I will now discuss briefly the main European countries involved in decolonization after 1945, and consider some of the social and political implications of this decolonization. Even though Scandinavian countries and Austria-Hungary, for example, were involved in empires, these were primarily Europe based, so I will not discuss those here. Similarly, Germany lost its colonies at the end of World War I, and so did not face the same sorts of issues.

Belgium

Belgium's colonization was limited to two countries during the twentieth century, and clearly driven by the ambitions of King Leopold. Belgium's rule over Congo for six decades stands as one of the most brutal in history (no mean feat), with an estimated 10 million Congolese losing their lives.[11] The country gained its independence suddenly and ill-prepared in 1960 but plunged immediately into civil war. It has continued to be one of the most unstable and poorest countries in the world as the Democratic Republic of Congo (DRC), even though it has incredible mineral resources. The other colony was Rwanda that, like Congo, was absolutely poverty stricken and unstable at independence in 1962, and plunged into one of the worst genocides of recent history in 1994.

There is little positive one can say about Belgium's colonization or decolonization, and the national embarrassment has prompted Belgium to advocate strongly for development assistance to these and other developing countries. The spark of the Black Lives Matter movement in 2020 led to widespread calls to remove statues of Leopold and other colonialists from cities in Belgium, and more of a reckoning with the country's colonial past. Congolese living in Belgium point to the continuing racism that they face in Belgium, a country with a significant right-wing populist, anti-immigrant movement.

France

The French strategy of integrating colonies, and colonial elites, into the fabric and mentality of France made decolonization a greater existential crisis than for most other Europeans. Struggling from German occupation and the Vichy government during World War II, along with desire to resist the subjugation of ideas from the Anglo-Saxon world, the demise of colonialism was quick. During the 1950s, France suffered a significant defeat and exit from Vietnam in 1954, a humiliating withdrawal from the Suez Canal after a military incursion (with Britain and Israel) in 1956, and an ongoing civil war in Algeria that led to the collapse of the French government in 1958.[12] This culminated in the withdrawal from all sub-Saharan African colonies en masse in 1960.

France's relations with Algeria were among the most significant of all colonial relations. France had involvement with Algeria for centuries when it was within the Ottoman Empire, but it was not until 1830 that France took direct control over the colony. French settlers migrated to take over prominent positions controlling Algeria, and the country became an integrated territory as part of France. Algerians never accepted French rule, and continual clashes were met by increasing levels of French force. These tensions contributed to the collapse of the French government in 1958, after which Charles de Gaulle orchestrated a path to independence by 1962, seen as a betrayal by most French settlers in Algeria.[13] Native (Muslim) Algerians had their French citizenship taken away. Official French government documents on Algeria had remained mostly classified as too sensitive, until President Emmanuel Macron announced a slight loosening of restrictions in March 2021.[14] This decision angered the military and many on the far right politically, and it is likely that new information about Algeria can only add to tensions within France. The issue became a major political topic in the 2022 presidential and parliamentary elections. In January 2022, to assuage and woo the far right, Macron apologized for the suffering caused to French colonists by the withdrawal from Algeria. The Algerian population in France remains its largest immigrant community with about 500,000 residents, just slightly higher than the numbers for the Moroccan community.

Unlike other European powers, however, France maintains an active economic (and military) presence in some of its former colonies, notably in West Africa, where its troops have been involved in fighting perceived Islamic extremism in former colonies such as Chad and Mali (though France indicated a withdrawal from Mali in 2022). France continues to have a significant presence around the world in its remaining territories, many of which are small islands in the Atlantic, Indian, and Pacific Oceans (e.g., Réunion). Many people from its former colonies now live in France, where successive governments welcomed them. Fluency in French and respect for the culture were strong attributes, whereas the color of skin was less important. To this extent, France officially continues not to consider the ethnicity of its citizens. In recent years, populists have gained political strength in their opposition to such widespread migration, notably the National Rally. Tensions with Muslim communities are widespread in the country, especially as the government maintains its pursuit of secularism and opposition to multiculturalism. Various terrorist incidents have inflamed these relations, and made conditions especially fraught in the early 2020s.

Italy

Italy's twentieth-century colonial history is relatively limited, similar to Belgium. Its main territories were Libya and Eritrea/Somaliland in Africa, with additional land taken in the 1930s as Benito Mussolini tried to embellish his fascist credentials, but this was quickly lost before the end of World War II. As such, there is less migration from its colonies than for either France or Britain, though problems continued in Libya with the continued presence of Italian settlers.[15] Political tensions do arise from largely illegal migration out of Libya (not just Libyans, but Africans from throughout the continent), and this has contributed to a populist racist backlash in Italy, especially in the richer northern regions, where the majority of migrants settle.

The Netherlands

The Netherlands was a global trading power in the 1600s with colonial territories around the world. Many of these were lost in subsequent centuries to Britain in particular, but also to other European countries, and so by the twentieth century relatively few territories remained Dutch. One of the principal countries to gain independence in 1949 was Indonesia, and the Dutch gradually relinquished their influence in the Caribbean, though they still retain Aruba, Curacao, and Sint Maarten. With centuries of global trading history, and possessing a relatively deregulated economy, the Netherlands received significant numbers of migrants. The initial toleration for such communities has waned, partly because of the dense population of the country, and populists on the far right have agitated for stricter immigration laws.

Portugal

Portugal is another country with significant global colonial possessions, having been one of the first to travel outside of Europe in the spice trade (and later slavery), with many of its colonial possessions linked to those trade routes. Many of those territories were lost to other colonial powers or, as Brazil, to independence in previous centuries. After World War II, Portuguese governments made significant efforts to hold on to their colonial possessions, leading to long wars of attrition in places like Angola and Mozambique. The collapse of military government in Portugal in the 1970s helped those two countries to independence—though not peace as long civil wars continued in both—in 1975. Portuguese settlers returning to the homeland provided difficulties for the government in terms of resettlement and jobs. China took back Macau from Portugal in 1999, leaving only a couple of small islands close to Portugal as territories.

Portugal is one of Europe's "oldest" countries with similar borders held for centuries. It is physically peripheral in the far southwest of Europe, so somewhat separated from trends elsewhere in the continent. It is also one of the poorest countries in Western Europe, so not a huge magnet for migrants, except for those who speak Portuguese. As such, the country has fared relatively well in its handling of migrants, especially those from its former colonies, and has not faced the populist backlash common elsewhere. It was only in 2019 when a populist anti-immigrant political party gained prominence and, even then, it remained marginal in Portuguese politics.

Spain

Spain's colonial zenith was centuries ago, where its influence was concentrated in the Americas and the Pacific. Its control of these regions was primarily lost in the nineteenth century, leaving Spain with marginal territories in Africa in the twentieth century. Western (Spanish) Sahara was an acquisition of Spain at the 1884 Berlin conference, and remained in its hands until 1976. Since that time, Morocco has claimed control of the territory. Spain retains colonial coastal ports inside Morocco up to today; namely, Ceuta and Melilla. Spain's refusal to cede these ports does little to help its moral platform in its efforts to regain Gibraltar. As other European countries decolonized in the period after World War II, Spain was inward focused dealing with forty years of fascist government and social isolation.

Like Portugal, Spain has relative success in dealing with migration. Perhaps this links to its centuries-long ties to Islam, and more recently to the desire to promote tolerance after the brutality of the Francisco Franco regime. The beginnings of populism and far-right politics through the Vox party emerged nationally in 2020, but not to the levels found to the country's north.

The United Kingdom

Britain's experience was similar to France's in terms of a rapid decolonization after World War II. In some ways, though, it was more stunning as the British

Empire was so vast, with the physical territory of the islands of the UK accounting for about 1 percent of the landmass of the empire at its zenith. The UK also served as the hegemonic power of the global system for a century or more, a role France never possessed. Once India and Pakistan became independent in 1947, this gave rise to major pressures to decolonize elsewhere. Countries gained independence over a broader period than French colonies, after some minor attempts to prepare countries for that step. The pomp of independence ceremonies belied the fact that many colonies had to fight hard to gain their freedom. This transition also had a significant impact on the way in which British institutions dealt with former colonies, and how personnel continued to interact in their "mission" to assist them.[16]

Although the UK was less open to welcoming its former colonial citizens, the need to bolster its workforce, particularly in sectors such as the Health Service, led to significant numbers of migrants coming from the Caribbean and South Asia, clustering in certain cities and particular districts inside those cities. A racial backlash developed against these migrants, and this has been a constant political issue. In 1968, the prominent Conservative politician Enoch Powell gave his "rivers of blood" speech against immigration and multiculturalism, and this trend of thought remained prominent. The political and economic malaise of a postimperial Britain gave impetus to membership in the EU, and also provided grounds for the Margaret Thatcher revolution of the 1980s, but that still left questions as to the direction of the country.[17]

The harkening back to greater days of independence (from the EU) and empire allowed the Brexit movement and the UK Independence Party in the 2010s to obtain significant support by promoting a nationalist (white supremacy style) platform. Successive Conservative governments in the 2010s pursued policies to significantly reduce immigration, and promoted a repatriation program especially to the West Indies. This targeted many who had been in Britain living legally for decades, and only widespread public opposition put a stop to the policy. Although one could argue that Britain has modest success at multiculturalism, there is still significant racism and political tension as evidenced by large-scale protests in 2020 during Black Lives Matter protests. Some of these protests were targeted at the legacy of slavery in the UK, notably in terms of statues, and a couple of prominent companies, including Lloyd's, said they would consider reparations.[18] Protests over race continued, though, and this issue was again exacerbated following the departure from the UK (and the royal family) by the Duke and Duchess of Sussex with accusations of racism by the couple aimed at the establishment.[19]

The UK continues to have overseas possessions, which appear anachronistic today (similar to France), but are symbolic of the country's previous global status. Gibraltar and the Falkland Islands, over which Britain went to war with Argentina in 1982, are a couple to note, as is Hong Kong, which China took back through negotiations in 1997. For some critics, Northern Ireland is another part of a long "colonial" history that awaits a conclusion a century after Ireland (Eire) gained its independence from Britain.

The Development of the European Union: 1950

The political elites of Western Europe recognized several critical developments in the post-1945 environment. The trauma and destruction of World War II (and, for many, the memory of World War I twenty years before) provided an impetus for new types of political and economic policies. The reliance on US benevolence and security protection in light of European weakness and vulnerability, and the real (communist) threat from Soviet occupation of much of CEE, forced a reckoning in terms of new foreign policy options. Europeans' ability to control their own destiny suddenly appeared limited, and their global influence rapidly diminished. At this point of adversity, Robert Schuman, the French foreign minister, made a bold proposal in May 1950:

> World peace cannot be safeguarded without the making of creative efforts proportionate to the dangers which threaten it. The contribution which an organised and living Europe can bring to civilisation is indispensable to the maintenance of peaceful relations. . . . Europe will not be made all at once, or according to a single plan. It will be built through concrete achievements, which first create a de facto solidarity. The coming together of the nations of Europe requires the elimination of the age-old opposition of France and Germany. Any action taken must in the first place concern these two countries.[20]

Schuman's proposal centered on the pooling of coal and steel production for France and West Germany and others who wished to join, helping to build coordinated economic production as well as limit one country's ability to expand unilaterally its military program.

This European Coal and Steel Community provided the opportunity for six West European states to begin to pool their economic resources and build some political space for themselves, in addition to answering the tough question of how to deal with West Germany.[21] Rather than subjugate the country, as had been the initial tendency immediately after the war, there was a need to rebuild the country quickly to stand on the front line against the Soviet army. The ECSC also offered a mechanism of control over the renewed militarization of West Germany—just in case.[22]

The relative success of the ECSC led to efforts to provide a common defense force or army for Western Europe, but that failed in 1954 due primarily to the desire to keep such a strategic area under national control (this is something with which the EU struggles yet today). Talk of creating a European Political Community also foundered for similar reasons. These failures led the six partners into more limited fields of technical and economic cooperation, notably the peaceful European Atomic Energy Community (Euratom) and the European Economic Community (EEC) in 1957.[23] The EEC provided a broad-based scheme to open up the six national markets by reducing barriers to trade, but there was little inkling in 1957 of how diverse and expanded this organization would become.

The constant themes of the EU since the 1950s have been "widening" and "deepening"; that is, searching for a balance in terms of adding more member countries while building a deeper level of integration across a wider number of issues, moving to an economic union and a possible political union. Notably, military cooperation has not been a high priority, preferring to rely on NATO. The nature and role of the EU have engaged theorists for decades, debating the various pathways and potential endgame of the EU. The proponents of intergovernmentalism see the EU as a vehicle for member governments to pursue their rational goals, not letting go of their independence of action.[24] The functionalists see the EU as a way to build integration slowly through the sharing of important economic tasks and goals, thereby promoting integration. The neo-functionalists believe that such economic cooperation will spill over into other areas of cooperation, notably in the political and security domains. The supranationalists see the EU developing into a form of federal superstate, a "United States of Europe," and see this as the goal of an "ever closer union." We can use all these insights to understand the character of Europe today and the status of the EU vis-à-vis the member countries, as well as the relationship of the EU with wider Europe.

Successive British governments remained aloof, upset by the challenge the new organization appeared to pose to sovereignty, and confident in their country's ability to maintain its "splendid isolation" from the continent of Europe. Within six years, however, the UK realized its need to be on the inside of this new European institution. The resistance of French leader Charles de Gaulle to British membership, unsure that this was genuine Europeanness or just British (and US) aims to subvert the EU, left Britain outside until its successful third formal application, with eventual membership in 1973.[25] Western Europe's economic jostling between the EEC (the "inner six") and the European Free Trade Association (founded in 1960, and initially known as the "outer seven" [EFTA]) during the 1960s hinged on the model of cooperation to be followed. EFTA, led by Britain, supported a loose intergovernmental association, whereas the EEC promised much closer ties. In the end, the EEC offered the better economic prospects, and when Denmark, Ireland, and the UK joined the EEC in 1973, that made the organization the undisputed economic bloc of Western Europe. EFTA continues today, with Iceland, Liechtenstein, Norway, and Switzerland as members, with a post-Brexit Britain signing a free-trade agreement with EFTA members (minus Switzerland) in July 2021.[26]

Hopes for economic growth remained somewhat unfulfilled into the 1980s. Stagflation and unemployment racked EEC members, and competitiveness at a global level slumped. Talk of the potential demise of the EEC was widespread until the European Commission president, Jacques Delors, embarked on a major reform plan for Europe, the Single European Act of 1986, whose goal was to remove all barriers to trade by 1992.[27] This success led to further progress with the 1992 Treaty on European Union, or Maastricht Treaty, which promised further integration in foreign policy, justice and home affairs, and the establishment of a European currency, the euro.

Box 2.3   Evolution and Nomenclature of the European Union

The European Union has possessed several names marking its gradual evolution. With the Treaty of Rome in 1957, the European Economic Community, often referred to as the Common Market, came into being alongside the European Coal and Steel Community and the European Atomic Energy Community. These operated as somewhat separate organizations until 1967, when they became part of the European Communities. As a centralized organization took shape, this became known as a singular European Community, The 1992 Maastricht Treaty on European Union began the change of name to European Union, although the European Community remained as one of the three pillars (along with Common Security and Foreign Policy, and Justice and Home Affairs). These three pillars remained somewhat separate until the Treaty of Lisbon signed in 2007 formalized the name as the European Union for all the operations within it. This symbolized the movement from the early (and easy) days of a free-trade area to the more "advanced" features of a quasi-economic union. Rather than bounce back and forth with varying titles in this book, I use the name European Union to discuss the organization since the 1950s. As can be seen, the EU has continued to change and expand in members (from six to twenty-eight, then twenty-seven members) and in the scope of its operations. The original six members in 1957 were Belgium, France, Italy, Luxembourg, the Netherlands, and West Germany. In 1973, Denmark, Ireland, and the UK joined, and in 1981 Greece also joined. Portugal and Spain joined in 1986, and Austria, Finland, and Sweden in 1995. The largest growth of ten additional countries took place in 2004, bringing in Cyprus, Malta, Estonia, Latvia, Lithuania, Poland, Czech Republic, Slovakia, Slovenia, and Hungary. Bulgaria and Romania joined in 2007, with Croatia joining in 2013. The UK left in 2020.

The European Union, formed officially under the Maastricht agreement, sought to streamline and improve decisionmaking in the Treaty of Amsterdam, signed in 1997, and the Treaty of Nice, signed in 2000. Neither treaty fulfilled the wish or need to make the EU decisionmaking machinery more efficient, partly because of differing perspectives of national members. With the fall of the Berlin Wall in 1989, the EU quickly realized the immense importance of reaching out to the liberated countries of CEE to bring them into the Western fold. Aid and trade programs were hastily constructed, and negotiations leading to membership in the EU began. These negotiations were based on the 1993 Copenhagen Criteria, which established key steps for these countries to achieve to obtain EU membership. Core elements of these criteria included democratic government, an open and functioning capitalist market, and the ability to absorb and implement all the EU laws contained in the *acquis communautaire.*

The biggest enlargement of the EU took place in 2004, bringing in ten new members primarily from CEE (see Box 2.3). Cyprus had many centuries of alternating Greek and Turkish control, but the British seized control in the nineteenth century and made it a formal colony in 1925 after the collapse of the Ottoman Empire. After independence in 1960, conflict between Greeks and Turks continued. Following a military coup d'état in Greece in 1974, Turkey invaded the island and it has been partitioned since then. The EU decided to admit only the Greek sector of two-thirds of Cyprus, angering Turkey.

Bulgaria and Romania joined the EU in 2007, with Croatia added as the EU's most recent addition in 2013. For the first time in more than a century—or arguably for the first time in history—the majority of European countries aspired to a similar form of government in democracy, and were drawn together willingly (rather than by force) in a single economic partnership promoting free trade and open borders. Most of the European countries remaining outside of the EU aspired to eventual membership, with the major exception of Russia. We cannot understate the significance of this cooperation in contrast to centuries of war and hostility within Europe, although the important geopolitical implications of EU enlargement were complex and not all positive.[28] With a long-term perspective on European history, however, we should not perceive the EU to be permanent automatically, but this is more the present status of European relations.

With the EU riding a wave of optimism in the new millennium, the leaders launched a plan in 2003 to create a European constitution, a single document to bring together the peoples of Europe into a tighter political and social identity. This constitution would also help to streamline, codify, and expand on existing treaties signed within the EU (especially where Nice and Amsterdam had fallen short), and to provide political leadership by having a European president (president of the European Council) and a European foreign minister (high representative for foreign and security policy). Agreed to by European member states in 2004, the constitution was defeated in referenda in France and the Netherlands in 2005, and was likely to have been defeated in other national referenda if they had taken place. Never had the distance between the political elites and the populations of Europe appeared so large, an indication of popular opposition to the encroachment of the EU into the lives of everyday citizens and their national perspectives.

Not content to see the constitution die in such a manner, the document was retooled, the word "constitution" dropped, and the modest goals of the revised treaty sold to the European public. The EU Reform Treaty, known widely as the Lisbon Treaty, was signed by member governments in Lisbon in December 2007. Irish voters rejected this version in June 2008, and so modifications again took place to assuage the nationalist fears of an EU growing too powerful. The Lisbon Treaty finally obtained Irish approval in a second referendum in 2009 and, with other countries not risking their own referendum, it went into effect in December 2009. Subsequent crises surrounding the global recession and Greek debt, immigration and refugees, and the Brexit vote of 2016 left little time for any major treaty revisions in the subsequent decade.

Post–Cold War Europe: 1991 and Onward

The death of the hard-line Soviet premier, Leonid Brezhnev, in November 1982 after eighteen years in control opened slightly a door of opportunity in the rest of Europe. This was not evident until the coming to office of Mikhail Gorbachev in March 1985, following the short terms of office of two ailing leaders, Yuri Andropov and Konstantin Chernenko, each of whom ran the country for just over a year before their death. Gorbachev offered new possibilities in relations with the outside world. The effective bankruptcy of the USSR, and the disastrous repercussions of the April 1986 Chernobyl nuclear explosion, forced a path of economic and political reforms. His ideas of glasnost (openness and transparency) and perestroika (economic reform) gained ground, and in negotiations with Western leaders, particularly US president Ronald Reagan, reforms in Russia took place and international tensions eased. Gorbachev's unwillingness to use Soviet force to maintain control over CEE encouraged protests across the region, ultimately leading to the dismantling of the Berlin Wall by protesters in November 1989. The sudden fall of the Berlin Wall took much of the threat and tension out of Europe, and symbolized the transition of power and the new opportunities for Europe.

Why was the fall of the Berlin Wall so significant? In place for almost thirty years, few if any observers contemplated its end in 1989, despite widespread protests across the CEE. Gorbachev's acceptance of the need to change Soviet policy toward the CEE states indicated that the USSR was unlikely to step in to prevent the ouster of Soviet-backed governments across the region, and would allow the Berlin Wall to fall. Once that process had begun, however, Gorbachev seemed powerless to prevent these forces of change breaking apart the Soviet Union itself in 1991 into its constituent ethnic parts, although that had never been his intention.[29] In the meantime, the four formal occupying powers of Germany and the two German states (the Four plus Two) finalized agreements, and the reunification of Germany took place in October 1990.

Russia itself then went into a decade of democratic transition and institutional reform, led by President Boris Yeltsin, as well as a tailspin of self-doubt and bitterness. The Soviet Empire and control of large areas of CEE had collapsed in the space of six years, one of the most dramatic and rapid collapses of any empire in history. Into that void stepped Vladimir Putin, appointed in 1999 by Yeltsin as Russian president, who went on to win his first presidential election in March 2000. Putin's goal increasingly was to rebuild the prestige and influence of Russia globally, and especially in bordering countries with a reconstruction of the former Soviet Empire. For Putin, control over Ukraine became a key factor, doing everything possible to keep that country out of the EU and NATO. His inability to prevent Ukraine's westward drift directly led to Russia's military incursions in 2014 and 2022.

Despite the exuberance across CEE in the early 2000s at the collapse of Soviet control, these countries were in poor shape. Subservient to Soviet demands and economic strategies, their economies were stunted and performing poorly, much worse than their Western neighboring states. Economic reform, fresh strategies, and foreign investment needed to change the country's trajectories.[30] Political reform hastily took place, with new constitutions and elections bringing in democratically elected leaders for the first time since the 1930s, or for some the first time ever. Recriminations against outgoing communist leaders took place, but could not overwhelm movement forward. Security concerns were also important, as many sought protection from Russia within NATO.[31] The Czech Republic, Hungary, and Poland joined NATO in 1999, with seven other CEE states joining in 2004. As mentioned earlier, there was a parallel march to membership in the EU, with most of the same countries having joined by 2007. CEE transformed dramatically within a decade or so, but the economies of the region still needed much more improvement.

The EU and CEE

In the post–Cold War era of the 1990s, EU programs rapidly expanded into the transition economies of Central and Eastern Europe. CEE states attracted

Box 2.4   Czechoslovakia and the Velvet Divorce

Czechs and Slovaks have a long and illustrious history in the geographical center of Europe. One of Europe's oldest universities, Charles University, began in Prague in 1348, and the city was a center of the Holy Roman Empire, which survived for a thousand years until its dissolution in 1806. In the nineteenth century, the territories were contained within the Austrian-Hungarian Empire, though treated somewhat differently. After World War I, the independent country of Czechoslovakia was created and flourished, as a leader in industrialization and democratization (though the western half, the Czech part, was predominant). By the mid-1930s, the country came increasingly under the gaze of Adolf Hitler. Rather than fight to defend the country, Britain and France acquiesced to Hitler's demands under the "Appeasement" agreements of 1938 ("peace in our time," as British prime minister Neville Chamberlain claimed), and Czechoslovakia was occupied by Germany. During the next seven years, Germany separated Slovakia from the Czechs, and administered the land as two distinct countries.

Near the end of the war, the United States liberated western Czechoslovakia (including Plzen), but as part of the postwar bargain, turned over control of the whole country to the USSR. The occupation was particularly hard on the Czechs, who were more economically advanced and more democratic than most other countries in CEE. Attempts to promote economic and political liberalization, notably in the Prague Spring, ended by crushing Soviet occupation in 1968. However, massive political protests within the country, allied to corresponding events across Europe, eventually brought the country's liberation in 1989 in the Velvet (relatively peaceful) Revolution. The Czechs and Slovaks now were unhappy partners in a liberated country, with the Slovaks feeling particularly resentful of the perceived economic advantages and superior aspirations of the Czechs. Not wanting to be second-class citizens in their own country, the Slovaks pushed for partition. In a remarkably peaceful separation, the two countries split in the Velvet Divorce of 1993 and became separate countries, both eventually gaining entry into the European Union in 2004. While the Czechs deepened their democracy, grew their economy, and gained recognition as "Eurorealists," the Slovaks struggled a little to entrench their own democracy, and lagged a little behind the Czechs in economic performance. In 2019, according to the World Bank, Czech GDP per capita stood at $23,494 whereas the Slovak figure lagged at $19,266.

large-scale loans and investment from West European governments and businesses. One major EU program was the Poland and Hungary: Assistance for Restructuring Their Economy (PHARE); symbolically, the word *phare* in both English and French means lighthouse or beacon.[32] This program, partly managed by the Organisation for Economic Co-operation and Development (OECD), expanded through the 1990s to include assistance to virtually all the former communist countries across the region in preparing them for EU membership. The EU gradually phased out the funds after these states achieved membership, in the accession rounds of 2004 and 2007. Many Western businesses moved into CEE to take advantage of relatively skilled, but low wage, workforces. Continuing reforms in Central Europe made these countries more attractive for investment, and economic transformation geared them toward accelerated membership in the EU.

Countries such as the Czech Republic, Hungary, and Poland made quite rapid transformations and increased trade with the West, whereas others further to the East moved more slowly. But membership in the EU was the ultimate goal for these countries, and this required adoption of significant political and economic policies. These included improved governance, better oversight of the economy, privatization, and a reduction of corruption. As many in the West feared a rapid influx of workers from Eastern Europe, some EU members placed limitations on the acceptance of CEE labor. Agricultural subsidies were also a huge issue for existing members of the EU. Long drawn-out negotiations took place to haggle over what subsidies to allow CEE states, and how to prevent these payments from undermining existing subsidies paid to Western European farmers. For Russia, however, EU membership was never in consideration, and so that country did not have to perform to any external (EU) standard. This is one factor helping to explain the rapid divergence of Russia from the remainder of CEE, and some of the problems faced by the Russian transition.[33]

Transition Economies of CEE

Although all economies are constantly in some form of change or transition, the term *transition economy* describes former socialist countries in transition to capitalism. Even before the collapse of Soviet rule in CEE in the late 1980s, many economies were experimenting with some form of reforms. The Soviet army vigorously suppressed Czech reforms in 1968, and this action slowed reforms across the region for a decade or more. In the 1980s, however, attempts to maintain the socialist systems provided some innovative economics, led by Gorbachev's Soviet reforms of perestroika after 1985. These attempts to reform socialism failed, and in the end contributed to its downfall.

During the height of the Cold War, the economic systems of CEE were coordinated in the Council for Mutual Economic Assistance (CMEA). The CMEA was a system established to allow Soviet control and exploitation of the satellite economies, all in the name of socialist partnership. These command economies operated on production quotas, and suppressed initiative by workers or managers. Products did not need to meet any quality performance standard, as the command system guaranteed markets and sales; and traditional notions of supply and demand did not exist, as the government fixed the prices and often stamped them directly onto the product itself. Governments produced a handbook of prices that dictated the "market." On the positive side, the government guaranteed jobs for life, and employers provided a strong welfare and support system.[34]

In the late 1980s, this economic system came crashing down with the collapse of communist rule, unable to maintain any form of competitiveness with the rest of Europe or the outside world. Plans to integrate these economies into the West came quick, but were problematic. Most of these CEE companies were uneconomic, uncompetitive, and grossly overstaffed. Skill levels in any form of management or capitalistic endeavor were largely nonexistent. Many companies had outdated equipment and machinery, and some had significant environmental issues connected to them. As Western companies looked around for which companies to buy or absorb, due diligence was virtually impossible, as there were no reliable annual reports or company books to assess.

In Germany, for example, the government established a state body, the Treuhandanstalt (Treuhand, or "trust agency"), to handle the absorption of about 8,500 East German businesses into the reunified country. Most businesses went cheaply at a nominal price, and some fell victim to asset stripping despite requirements that this did not occur. Workforce redundancies were widespread and large, with workers over forty years of age generally left to face long-term if not permanent unemployment. Opportunities for the younger generation, when educated, were much more open.

This pattern was common across the rest of Eastern Europe and Russia, with a significant difference. Unlike in Germany where the West German government put money and its prestige into tackling these issues, in other countries these economic resources were not present. Privatization took a variety of paths in these countries, with voucher and shock therapy being paths to liberalization.[35] As most citizens in the CEE did not have money to buy shares in companies, the government issued vouchers to them to use in company purchases. This system generally did not work, as people did not understand their use and often sold them at minimal cost. Companies tended not to come into the hands of large numbers of shareholders, but rather into a much smaller group of people who became immensely rich.

In Russia, the absence of any laws to manage the new economy in the early 1990s accentuated the problems and meant that anything and everything was by default "legal." Russian companies, especially in the energy sector, came under the control of a handful of oligarchs, whose power and wealth the Yeltsin government tolerated in return for their support. It was only under Putin after 2000 that the government brought these oligarchs under political control. Those who towed the Kremlin line and supported Putin kept their wealth; those who did

---

Box 2.5   The Challenge of German Reunification

The two German states served as proxies for the United States and the USSR in the Cold War. The different levels of economic performance and social liberties between the two German states contributed to large-scale defections from East to West, with Berlin one of the largest exit points. The German Democratic Republic built the Berlin Wall in 1961 to halt these defections, and it became a symbol of communist oppression for almost thirty years. The tearing down of the Berlin Wall in November 1989 came as a shock to all observers, but symbolized how brittle the control over communist countries was in reality. Over the forty years of official separate existence (1949–1989), the two German states had become different entities—in ideology, attitude, wealth, social policy, and skills, though not language. The challenge was how to put the two countries back together, how to reunify Germany. One technical, yet important, issue was the legality of reunification. As part of the settlement from World War II, the occupying powers of the United States, the Soviet

Union, Britain, and France had to themselves "allow" reunification, but the West German government faced the difficult task in how to absorb the GDR. West German Chancellor Helmut Kohl made the decision to treat both countries at face value as "equal," unifying the countries (and currencies) at parity. Huge investments—around $100 billion a year for the next decade—were needed in Eastern Germany to bring it up to a physical standard of the West, and vast sums were needed to improve education and workforce standards. Today, the task is not yet complete, and lingering differences in social attitudes remain. In many ways, the GDR was fortunate to have West Germany to invest these large sums of money, as other countries across CEE made much slower economic and social transformations. Germany has made the transition back to being the continent's wealthiest country, its largest in terms of population (certainly within the current EU membership, though behind Russia and Turkey), and arguably the EU's de facto leader.

---

not, the government hounded out of the country, imprisoned, or killed. The Russian "Wild East" gradually stabilized under control by the government and by organized groups or mafia, who brought a form of discipline to the economy, and who often had connections to the state security services.[36]

The transformation of CEE has been quite remarkable, given the basic absence of experience in or knowledge of Western economic practices. Between 1990 and 2018, seven CEE countries surpassed growth of 500 percent in their GDP, with Poland leading the pack with 788 percent growth.[37] The boom in MBA programs in the region helped to provide the trained business leadership that these countries needed, along with an important transition in economic mindset. However, it is still fair to say that these countries lag somewhat in economic indicators after almost two decades in the EU and with significant investment made—their GDP per capita data are still below Western counterparts. For example, the World

Bank reports the average EU GDP per capita income (2019 figures) to be $34,913, with the highest figures for Luxembourg ($114,704) and Ireland ($78,661), with France at $40,493 and Germany at $46,445 at the heart of the EU figures. In contrast, the highest-performing CEE were much lower, led by the Czechs at $23,494, with both Hungary ($16,731) and Poland ($15,692) reasonably close, but with Bulgaria still showing economic duress at $9,828.[38]

Even with reunification in Germany, differences between West and East Germany continue today, with earnings in the former East standing at 88 percent that of the West.[39] Some unfavorable political events and higher levels of corruption give the EU some qualms, especially with Bulgaria, Hungary, Poland, and Romania. Most telling is the poor economic performance of potential candidate countries, where the same 2019 figures have GDP per capita at $5,353 for Albania, $6,022 for North Macedonia, and $7,411 for Serbia. Nevertheless, considering the status and condition of these countries just thirty years ago, the transformation has been remarkable, and in no small measure helped by the European Union.

Notable Legacies

How can we sum up the impact of these legacies on contemporary Europe?[40] All countries are shaped by the events of history, but in the context of Europe the historical legacies are vital to understand and explain the present. In this section, I isolate and summarize six major legacies of the twentieth century that shed light on contemporary Europe, but acknowledge that there are many more.

The legacy of fascism and communism is the first. Although Europe has had its share of authoritarian governments up into the twentieth century, the totalitarian governments of Germany and the USSR were significantly different in their use of repression and technology to control their populations. The end of World War II brought a halt to fascism in Germany and Italy, but not to the ideology. Although slow to grow, neofascist movements have become much stronger in recent years, in a variety of guises and countries. Although it is sometimes difficult to pin the neofascist label on many of these ultraconservative or populist parties, it is clear that in countries such as Austria, Belgium, France, Italy, and Switzerland, there has been significant growth in these movements, often aided and abetted by Russia, coalescing around issues of immigration and opposition to a centralized European superstate, the EU.

Soviet repression and control of Eastern Europe lasted for less than fifty years, but its impact on the political and economic development of those countries has been significant. Although they made major strides in implementing democracy (though in recent years Hungary and Poland have appeared to slip backward), their economies are taking longer to catch up to their Western European colleagues in the EU. Most CEE countries were in economically disadvantageous positions vis-à-vis their Western neighbors for centuries prior to communism, but central planning, the recovery of war reparations, and dictation from Moscow had a devastating impact in the postwar era. A final point to make about the legacy of communism is that of its impact on Western Europe, helping to bring erstwhile antagonists together and to forge a common strategy within the EU.

Building on this point, the second legacy is the creation of the EU itself. Besides the pressure and fear of communism pushing West Europeans together, there is the legacy of multiple wars within Europe throughout the centuries, culminating in the cataclysmic world wars of 1914–1918 and 1939–1945. With the increasing sophistication and deadliness of military technology, it is doubtful whether Europe could have withstood (or will withstand) another major war, and this awareness prompted visionary and pragmatic leaders across the continent to push for détente. This appeared to be the only hope for the salvation and security of Europe, and its ability to maintain its role and influence in the world. This awareness contributed to the absolute shock and horror at the major conflagration between Russia and Ukraine in 2022, potentially dragging NATO and the whole of Europe into a wider catastrophe, including a possible nuclear war.

The third legacy concerns the continuing strength of nationalism and subregional identity within Europe, despite (or possibly because of) the growth of continental unity. The importance of national culture and language has not necessarily diminished under the EU, and is potentially resurging in the shape of widespread populist movements often in direct opposition to the EU. Brexit is a good example of this based on a major claim for national identity, anti-immigration, and "independence" from Europe, but there are other examples across Europe. We are also witnessing increased subnational or subregional identity, perhaps because the decline of any realistic external threat to Europe after the end of the Cold War has made the nation-state less central in political life. One could also suggest an erosion of state powers because of the increasing influence of the EU bureaucracy, as well as the EU's attempts to bolster democracy—including subregional democracy—through the policies of the EU Committee of the Regions. Examples abound from Scotland to Corsica, from the Catalan and Basque regions to the former Yugoslavia. The historical significance of regional cultures and language/dialect had been subsumed somewhat in the centralization of power within European states—both Western and Eastern— and on many occasions had been forcibly repressed (Spain with Catalonia, or

England with the Welsh and Irish), but this revival indicates something of a weakening, or perhaps maturing, of the European state system.

A fourth key legacy to consider is European involvement in countries and regions around the rim of the European continent. Today, doubts linger about whether Russia and Turkey fit the definition of being European partly because of their failure to embrace democracy, but the interactions with these countries over the centuries have been intense. The influence of the Ottoman Empire can still be seen and felt in the Balkans; likewise, the influence of Russia on the Baltic states (current EU members) and on Georgia and Ukraine (potential EU members) is significant. Turkey's agonizingly long quest for membership in the EU is simply another chapter of this long and, at times, difficult relationship.

Other near neighbors also have had long relationships with Europe. The countries of North Africa, notably Algeria and Morocco, have had extended associations with France, and the presence of large African communities in France (and Italy and Spain) are a testament to that legacy, with these communities often living in the shadow of racism and discrimination. Europe's association with the Middle East stretches back to biblical times, and then to the Crusades, and more recently to the nineteenth-century imperialism conditioned by political and economic imperatives. Europe's influence there waned at the end of the twentieth century as the United States took on the role of external moderator, and the countries of the region exerted their economic muscle and control over their oil supplies. The legacy of this region, however, remains strong in Europe in countless political, social, and economic ways.

At a more global level, the fifth legacy of overseas empires and conquests provide numerous and significant issues. The Portuguese Empires in Africa, South America, and Asia; the Spanish in Africa (still, in enclaves in Morocco) and South America; the Dutch in the Caribbean, Africa, and Asia; the Belgians in Central Africa; the Danish in the North Atlantic; the French and British across the world. Such legacies can be seen in the cosmopolitan nature of European communities today, the historical trade legacies, the EU trade partnerships and programs, and all sorts of other bilateral and multilateral associations. The strain of warfare during the twentieth century weakened all these states' capabilities to hold on to their colonies, and post-1945 we witnessed decolonization on a massive scale. This has changed the nature of European relationships with former colonies, though there remain many elements of potential friction and tension.

The final legacy to address here is that of the historical development of each country and region of the continent. At times, the distinctiveness of Europe can be masked by talk of a European "community" of nations, or a shared history or shared sense of development. This commonality may be present at some macro or abstract level—the shared experience of World War II, for example—but there are many factors keeping Europeans apart. What exactly could be said to be the common cultural trait of Europe? We could certainly not say language or religion, nor necessarily political experience, philosophy, or ideology. We could not argue that there is a common vision of Europe for the future, based on some common legacy imbued to all Europeans.

Conclusion

This chapter shows the degree to which many core political issues facing contemporary Europe are legacies from events of the twentieth century. To some extent, these are legacies affecting the whole of Europe, and so there is a common connection here. However, we should not overemphasize a single European experience or consciousness, despite the impact of the EU on its twenty-seven members, and keep in mind the differing cultural, economic, and political influence of twentieth-century developments across countries and regional groups. The experience of Bulgaria, Russia, or Turkey, for example, is not typical of a West European state. The legacy of colonialism is different for each of the colonial powers of Europe, and that legacy is not particularly relevant to those countries that did not possess an empire. All these factors, nevertheless, contribute to what is modern Europe.

Over the following chapters, we look more closely at the machinery of government and the structure of institutions across Europe. We begin in the next chapter with an overview of European constitutionalism and political structures.

Notes

1. Versailles was chosen to assuage the memory of the declaration there of the German Empire in 1871.

2. Germany had taken Alsace-Lorraine from France after the war of 1870.

3. The United States never joined the League, despite President Wilson being the driving force for the organization. Britain and France remained constant, but other major powers came and went.

4. The author George Orwell volunteered to fight for the Republicans, and covered events in the war in his book *Homage to Catalonia*. Ernest Hemingway covered the war as a reporter, and actively supported the Republicans. His book covering the war is *For Whom the Bell Tolls*.

5. Germany did occupy the British territories of the Channel Islands in June 1940. German efforts to cripple the Royal Air Force in the 1940 Battle of Britain were unsuccessful, and this prevented a major German land and sea invasion.

6. Michael G. Roskin, *The Rebirth of East Europe,* 3rd ed. (Upper Saddle River, NJ: Prentice Hall, 1997).

7. Martin Thomas, Bob Moore, and L. J. Butler, *Crises of Empire: Decolonization and Europe's Imperial States,* 2nd ed. (London: Bloomsbury, 2015).

8. Miles Kahler, *Decolonization in Britain and France: The Domestic Consequences of International Relations* (Princeton: Princeton University Press, 1984).

9. Ron Eyerman and Giuseppe Sciortino (eds.), *The Cultural Trauma of Decolonization: Colonial Returnees in the National Imagination* (Cham: Springer/Palgrave, 2020).

10. Christopher Hill, "Powers of a Kind: The Anomalous Position of France and the United Kingdom in World Politics," *International Affairs* 92(2), 2016: 393–414.

11. Crawford Young, *Politics in Congo: Decolonization and Independence* (Princeton: Princeton University Press, 1965).

12. Anthony Clayton, *The Wars of French Decolonization* (Abingdon: Routledge, 2013).

13. Todd Shepard, *The Invention of Decolonization: The Algerian War and the Remaking of France* (Ithaca: Cornell University Press, 2006).

14. Constant Méheut, "France Eases Access, a Little, to Its Secrets," *New York Times,* March 10, 2021.

15. Pamela Ballinger, "Colonial Twilight: Italian Settlers and the Long Decolonization of Libya," *Journal of Contemporary History* 51(4), 2016: 813–838.

16. Sarah Stockwell, *The British End of the British Empire* (Cambridge: Cambridge University Press, 2018).

17. See, for example, Will Hutton, *The State We're In* (London: Vintage, 1996). See also in a similar vein, Anthony Sampson, *The Changing Anatomy of Britain* (London: Hodder and Stoughton, 1986).

18. Mark Landler, "Two Prominent British Firms Say They'll Pay Reparations for Slavery," *New York Times,* June 19, 2020.

19. Benjamin Mueller, "Royal Rift Reveals Britain's Underbelly: A Very Big Silence Around Race," *New York Times,* March 12, 2021; Zoe Williams, "The Family Arsenal," *The Guardian Weekly,* March 12, 2021.

20. Robert Schuman, French foreign minister, "The Schuman Declaration," May 9, 1950, Robert Schuman Foundation, https://www.robert-schuman.eu/en/declaration-of-9-may-1950.

21. Belgium, Italy, Luxembourg, and the Netherlands joined France and West Germany as the founding members of ECSC and the European Union.

22. For a detailed history regarding the development of the EU, see Jonathan Olsen and John McCormick, *The European Union: Politics and Policies,* 6th ed. (Boulder: Westview, 2017); Brent F. Nelson and Alexander Stubbs (eds.), *The European Union: Readings on the Theory and Practice of European Integration,* 4th ed. (Boulder: Lynne Rienner, 2014); Desmond Dinan, *Origins and Evolution of the European Union,* 2nd ed. (Oxford: Oxford University Press, 2014); Desmond Dinan, *Ever Closer Union: An Introduction to European Integration*, 4th ed. (London: Red Globe, 2010); T. R. Reid, *The United States of Europe: The New Superpower and the End of American Supremacy* (New York: Penguin, 2004).

23. Sherrill Brown Wells, *Pioneers of European Integration and Peace 1945–1963: A Brief History with Documents* (Boston: Bedford/St. Martin's, 2007); see also Pascal Fontaine, *Jean Monnet, a Grand Design for Europe* (Luxembourg: European Communities, 1988).

24. For a helpful discussion of intergovernmentalism and the other theories, see Andrew Moravcsik, *The Choice for Europe: Social Purpose and State Power from Messina to Maastricht* (Ithaca: Cornell University Press, 1998), especially chap. 1. See also Olsen and McCormick, *The European Union,* chap. 1.

25. De Gaulle's presidency ended in 1969, so his departure facilitated British entry into the EEC.

26. European Free Trade Association, "EEA EFTA States Sign a Free Trade Agreement with the UK," July 8, 2021, https://www.efta.int/Free-Trade/news/EEA-EFTA-States-sign-free-trade-agreement-UK-524641#:~:text=On%208%20July%202021%2C%20the,the%20United%20Kingdom%20(UK).&text=The%20agreement%20also%20contains%20substantial,change%20as%20well%20labour%20law; for EFTA, see https://www.efta.int/.

27. George Ross, *Jacques Delors and European Integration* (New York: Oxford University Press, 1995).

28. Christopher Hill, "The Geo-Political Implications of Enlargement," Working Paper RSC no. 2000/30 (Florence: European University Institute, 2000); see also Rawi Abdelal and Kimberly A. Haddad, *A Wider Europe: The Challenge of EU Enlargement,* 9-703-021 (Cambridge, MA: Harvard Business School, 2003).

29. Stephen White, "The Context of Russian Politics," in M. Donald Hancock, Christopher J. Carman, Marjorie Castle, David P. Conradt, Raffaella Y. Nanetti, B. Guy Peters, William Safran, and Stephen White (eds.), *Politics in Europe,* 5th ed. (Washington, DC: CQ Press, 2012), chap. 6.1.

30. David Pinder (ed.), *The New Europe: Economy, Society and Environment* (Chichester: Wiley, 1998).

31. Zbigniew Brzezinski, "A Plan for Europe: How to Expand NATO," *Foreign Affairs* 74(1), 1995: 26–42.

32. European Parliament, "Briefing No 33: The PHARE Programme and the Enlargement of the European Union," https://www.europarl.europa.eu/enlargement/briefings/33a2_en.htm.

33. Vladimir Popov, *A Russian Puzzle: What Makes the Russian Economic Transformation a Special Case*, Research for Action Paper 29 (Helsinki: United Nations University/World Institute for Development Economics Research, 1996).

34. Roskin, *The Rebirth of East Europe.*

35. Robert Kennedy and Amy Sandler, *Shock Therapy in Eastern Europe: The Polish and Czechoslovak Economic Reforms* (Cambridge, MA: Harvard Business School, 1999); see also from a major proponent of shock therapy in Russia, Jeffrey D. Sachs, "Russia's Struggle with Stabilization: Conceptual Issues and Evidence," *Proceedings of the World Bank Annual Conference 1994* (Washington, DC: World Bank, 1995).

36. Gideon Lichfield, "Having It Both Ways: A Survey of Russia," *The Economist* (Special Survey), May 22, 2004.

37. Statista, "Percentage Growth in GDP in EU Countries from Central and Eastern Europe Between 1990 and 2018," https://www.statista.com/statistics/1066050/cee-real-gdp-growth/.

38. World Bank, "GDP Per Capita (Current US $)—European Union," https://data.worldbank.org/indicator/NY.GDP.PCAP.CD?locations=EU; see also Brilliant Maps, "European GDP Per Capita in 1990 Compared to 2016," January 30, 2018, https://brilliantmaps.com/european-gdp-per-capita-1990-2016/; see the Country Profiles section at the end of the book for more details.

39. Kate Connolly, "Stark Divides Persist, 30 Years After Reunification," *The Guardian Weekly,* September 25, 2020.

40. Ian Kershaw, *The Global Age: Europe 1950–2017* (New York: Viking, 2019).

3

Foundational Structures of the Political Arena

THE CORE FEATURES OF EUROPE'S POLITICAL DEVELOPMENT WERE DIS-
cussed in the previous two chapters, and so I now turn to a focus on the manner
in which governments operate across the continent. Governmental institutions
within Europe display a wide variety of structures, rules, and operating practices,
linked in part to respective histories and cultural traditions. We can anticipate this
in a group of forty or more countries with a diversity of history, culture, and size.
Britain, with arguably almost a thousand years of relatively steady evolutionary
political development without a successful invasion into the country since 1066,
does not have the same political structures as a freshly minted country, such as
Croatia, or even a refurbished one, such as Russia. Nevertheless, there are commonalities across the institutions of European governance that make such a comparison workable and worthwhile, without being too oversimplified.

Democracy is a central concept underpinning the structure and nature of government in Europe, even though the full nature of this differs by country.[1] How
do the institutions of each country operate? In what ways are the separation of
powers between branches of government organized? How firm is a constitution
in the setting of rules for government actions? How do legislatures operate? How
do executives—presidents, chancellors, prime ministers—operate within the
political arena? How do judiciaries and surviving monarchies fit within the existing political realms?

The interplay of institutions at the local, national, and European levels provides a complex environment of overlapping and, at times, conflictual political
powers. These relationships are not static, especially in terms of the evolution of
the European Union's constitutional role and its impact on its member states.

Change is also marked, however, in the political development within the more recent constitutions of Central and Eastern Europe, which have about thirty years of operation behind them. We look first to the nature of constitutions, and then move on to consider how governments organize in terms of features such as federalism or unitary structure, parliamentary or presidential systems, and unicameral and bicameral chambers. Our primary concentration is on countries, but I end the chapter with a consideration of the organizational structure of the EU. In the next chapter, I examine the ways in which governments perform in terms of the role of executives, legislatures, and judiciaries.

Constitutions

A constitution lays out and organizes the structure of government and the powers allotted to each branch of government, and provides an overview of a country's ideals and beliefs, including protections for individuals and their human rights. To Americans, the US Constitution of 1787 is a sacrosanct written document shaping life and politics, though with continuing (and increasingly bitterly divided) interpretation by the US Supreme Court. To most Europeans, this perception of a written constitution is unnecessarily rigid, even though support for constitutionalism is widespread. For the United Kingdom, the constitution is not a codified document, but consists of statutes, precedents, and long-standing political practices or "constitutional behavior" dating back to the Magna Carta of 1215 and the Bill of Rights of 1689. Many refer to the Magna Carta as the birth of democracy and the start of the limitation of absolute rule. Neither claim is completely correct, though the Magna Carta did provide some check on the power of the king by prominent traditional leaders, and helped to begin the concept of control over the king's spending. Some in contemporary Britain would prefer a written constitution to clarify rules and roles, and check executive power. Others prefer the flexibility that an unwritten constitution provides. There is considerable debate regarding the pros and cons of a codified constitution, and there is little consensus on the need.

For the French, constitutions are convenient documents for particular eras, but are open to change. After all, France is currently in its fifth republic since the 1789 revolution, with many more regimes and at least fourteen different constitutions. The constitution of the French Fifth Republic emerged primarily to suit Charles de Gaulle's political situation in the late 1950s, but has remained more or less constant since then. Opponents may rail against the constitution as giving too much power to the president but, once candidates win the presidency, their zeal for constitutional reform tends to recede.

A similar situation is present in Russia, where the post-Soviet constitution emerged in turbulent times, reflecting differences between then president Boris

Yeltsin and the Russian Duma (parliament), which led to the Duma's impeachment of Yeltsin. These tensions led Yeltsin to send tanks to attack the Duma in October 1993 in a show of force, and allowed Yeltsin to shape the constitution—somewhat along French lines—to favor the presidency over the prime minister when it finally went into force in December 1993. The fluidity of this document was evident, however, once Vladimir Putin relinquished the presidency because of term limit restrictions, and yet effectively ran the country as prime minister in 2008–2012 before returning to the presidency. Putin was successful when he sought to amend the constitution to his favor in July 2020 via a referendum, and this change enables him potentially to have two further elected terms as president. This could allow him to serve as president until 2036, a concept toward which there is some opposition in Russia, spearheaded by Alexei Navalny and his supporters.

Constitutions in other European countries have similarly been born out of necessity and circumstance. The German Basic Law, approved in May 1949, initially served only West Germany, and came about after the collapse of the Four Power Agreement on Germany following World War II.[2] The constitution displayed the influence of US occupying forces in having components of the US political system incorporated (e.g., bicameralism, federalism, and judicial review), but it also pulled ideas from the Weimar Republic, notably the adoption of a parliamentary system. With German reunification in 1990, the Basic Law became the constitution for the whole of Germany.

In Spain, the civil war in 1936–1939 wiped away the country's constitutional framework, and the country lived under the military rule of Francisco Franco until his death in 1975. Franco conceived of plans for a peaceful transition to a full democracy in Spain after his death, including not only a constitution but also the reestablishment of the monarchy (known as the Crown) with King Juan Carlos, something that Franco had played a major role in destroying in the 1930s. The constitution passed a parliamentary vote in October 1978 and a national referendum in December 1978 with over 91 percent support, and became the law at the end of 1978.

Franco's fellow officers appeared less enamored by democracy and the constitution, with a small group attempting a coup d'état in February 1981. King Juan Carlos acted strongly against the coup, and this averted any real conflict. Continuing military unrest led to another coup attempt in October 1982, but on this occasion intervention against the plotters took place several weeks before the coup date, and few problems ensued. A similar story unfolded in neighboring Portugal after the overthrow of the fascist government in April 1974 in the Carnation Revolution. A coup attempt in November 1975 was unsuccessful, and a new constitution was approved in April 1976.[3] The constitution itself came under fire for being overtly antibusiness, and major reforms occurred in 1982 and 1989.

Box 3.1   Turkey's Constitution

The Ottoman Empire's first constitution appeared in 1876, but with the breakup of that Empire following World War I, Turkey promulgated its first constitution in 1921. Since then, three constitutions superseded that; namely, in 1924, 1961, and the current constitution passed in 1982 and ratified in a referendum. This constitution has already received nineteen amendments, with the most significant coming after a 2017 referendum. This changed the structure of Turkey's political system from a parliamentary to a presidential one. The ruling Justice and Development Party forced through the change in a referendum widely condemned for irregularities to benefit its leader and the prime minister, Recep Tayyip Erdoğan, who concentrated his power in the new role of president, as well as continuing to act as prime minister.

Across CEE, the collapse of communism and Soviet control led to the need to write new constitutions in the early 1990s. Legislatures approved new constitutions during 1990–1992 in Bulgaria, Croatia, the Czech Republic, Estonia, Lithuania, Macedonia, Romania, Slovakia, and Slovenia, with subsequent membership as confirmed democracies in the Council of Europe.[4] Constitutions took shape influenced by local histories and cultures, as well as by political preferences, but none of them reintroduced a monarchy. Seven of the twelve CEE states adopted unicameral legislatures. Poland took a little longer in discussing its transition, and only finalized its constitution in 1997 after a referendum. The Poles decided on a unitary, semipresidential system (similar to France) with a bicameral legislature—the lower house (Sejm) utilizes proportional representation voting, whereas the upper house (Senate) adopted a first-past-the-post system.

The Distribution of Political Power

Europe possesses a diversity of political systems for what is essentially the geographical distribution of state power—that is, how and where political decision-making power resides in different parts of government at the central and the regional levels. Options for the distribution of power include the formation of federal and unitary institutional systems, and legislative bodies with unicameral or bicameral structures. In addition, there are examples of devolution of power, and power-sharing arrangements in divided countries, which do not neatly fit into the traditional categorization. Furthermore, the development of EU political institutions with certain powers has added to the complexity of decisionmaking for its members. I now discuss the relative merits of each of these systems, with examples to illuminate.

The Federal Model

A federal system, with shared powers between the central and regional governments, is present in Austria, Belgium, Germany, Russia, and Switzerland. This political structure helps to maintain the balance between strong regional identities and the federal center, helped by bicameralism at the national level (discussed below). This system is particularly helpful in a divided country, such as Belgium, where a complex history has left Dutch- and French-speaking parts of the country hostile to each other and delicately balanced, sometimes incapable of forming a national government. Belgium was a unitary state until it officially became federal in 1993 as a way to manage its increasingly hostile regions. The country divides into three main regions. The northern region is Flemish (Dutch speaking) and the southern region is Walloon (French speaking), while the third region around the capital city of Brussels includes both languages. The role of Brussels as a more neutral buffer region between the other two gains strength by serving as the headquarters of the EU. There is also official recognition of German as a national language, for a small number of German speakers in the east of the country.

Germany possesses a well-defined federal system of sixteen states or *länder,* which have national representation in the Bundesrat, the federal second (upper) house. The founding of the German Empire in 1871 had required a semblance of federalism to assuage the various royal families that now amalgamated into a greater Germany. Although Adolf Hitler swept away this system in the 1930s, it returned in postwar Germany partly as a way to offset any centralizing tendency. After reunification in 1990, the sixteen *länder* comprise ten regions from West Germany, five from East Germany, and Berlin as the capital.

In Switzerland, similarly, a federal system helps to hold together a diverse population separated by religion and four national languages—French for about 20 percent of the total population, German for 64 percent, Italian for 8 percent, and Romansh. The country also divides roughly evenly between Protestants and Catholics. The 1848 constitution moved Switzerland toward federalism, where power is shared by a relatively weak central (confederation) government, twenty-six cantons (or regions), and through these to 2,300 communes. The principle of subsidiarity pushes as many decisions as possible to the local commune level, although the national population also exerts significant direct control through referenda on numerous policy decisions. In contrast, Russia witnesses the greater consolidation of power at the federal center of Moscow. Austria also is a weak federalist system that increasingly operates like a unitary system.

Box 3.2   Russia's Federalism

Russia is the world's largest country physically, and with significant regional and ethnic distinctions appears to be an obvious example of the utility of federalism. Under the constitution, Russia has eighty-five federal administrative regions, or "subjects" as they are officially called. They represent their interests in the Council of the Federation, the country's upper house, to which they each send two representatives for five-year terms. They have significant authority in their own right to handle local issues. However, as part of the centralization of power under Vladimir Putin, these regions have seen their independence eroded, and they have come increasingly under the control of the Moscow central government. One such measure was the ending of direct elections for their regional leaders, with appointment by the president (Putin) to replace these. The lower house, the Duma, contains 450 directly elected representatives from across the country, who sit for five-year terms. The United Russia party, which affiliates with Putin, dominates the Duma, and it held on to its super majority after elections in September 2021.

The Unitary Model

The majority of political systems in Europe are unitary, where a central government makes the core, important decisions for the country. This does not preclude governments from having some shared powers at state, county, regional, or city levels, but the predominant capacity for decisions and financial control rests centrally in country capitals.[5] Unitary states vary in size, with many of Europe's largest countries being unitary. Unitary states can be unicameral or bicameral in terms of their central legislature, and I examine these terms in more detail below. France is a good example of a bicameral unitary system, where core decisionmaking and budgetary power rests with the central government in Paris. This includes policies such as school curriculum, where the central government organizes it uniformly for all the schools in the country. Sweden is a unicameral unitary system, which centralizes its main governmental decisionmaking in the hands of the central government in Stockholm. Although smaller countries tend to have unitary systems—naturally enough, perhaps, microstates such as Andorra, Liechtenstein, and Monaco are unitary—this is not automatic (as federal Belgium exemplifies), nor is it the case that larger countries are automatically federal. The decision normally rests on historical and cultural factors.

Even in these unitary systems, however, there is the possibility of the devolution of some decisionmaking authority to regions. Such action is often in response to regional pressures, and this devolution helps to contain pressure for further splits. Spain and the UK offer examples of such devolution in different degrees. In the UK, the British government has tried to hold off calls for independence in Scotland and Wales by allowing referenda on the topics and by shifting considerable decisionmaking to local assemblies. In Scotland, the local assembly has power to pass laws on a range of topics, including agriculture, education, the environment, health, and law.[6] After Britain's exit from the EU, such an arrangement seems insufficient for many in Scotland, where support for remaining in the EU is high, and calls are growing for another referendum to bring about complete independence.[7] In Spain, the Madrid government has conceded significant local autonomy to seventeen regional autonomous communities, but this has not been sufficient for many Catalans, who continue to promote full independence through referenda. In 2017 Catalans proclaimed their independence, but the Spanish government rejected this, and in October 2019 Spain's supreme court sentenced nine prominent Catalan political leaders to prison for sedition. This issue is far from settled.

War, or at least significant internal disunity, has shaped other changes in unitary states and their decisionmaking capacities. The federal state of Yugoslavia, for example, broke into multiple unitary (and ethnic) states in the 1990s after the end of the Cold War. The state of Cyprus maintains Greek and Turkish governments in a divided island, and Northern Ireland possesses a complex array of power-sharing arrangements forged under the Good Friday Agreement in 1998. The status and future of Northern Ireland is again in flux after the UK's departure from the EU, as Northern Ireland clings to its open trade border with (EU member) Ireland, undermining its membership in the (non-EU) British Isles.

The Stability of European Political Systems

An important issue to consider when looking at the constitutional framework and political structure of European countries is the extent to which they bring stability, which is a positive quality, supplemented by popular support and general respect for democratic traditions. Are European states "strong" in the sense of stable and viable, as opposed to fragile? The Fund for Peace offers an annual index by which we can measure stability across countries and over time.[8] The index analyzes twelve cohesion, economic, political, and social indicators to measure the relative stability or fragility of states, such as the level of factionalized elites, group grievance, economic performance and inequality, respect for human rights and the rule of law, and state legitimacy. In its 2021 report, the world's most stable country was Finland. In fact, the five Nordic countries were in the top seven countries in the world, with Switzerland and New Zealand the other two; fifteen of the twenty most stable countries in the world were European. Turkey received the poorest score ranking in Europe at 57 (the lower the number, the more fragile a state is), followed closely by Russia at 74, indicating political and social difficulties in those two countries. In contrast, Finland stood at 179.

The index is a useful tool to help us compare the resilience of European countries and the support of their citizens. It increases our awareness of countries that are relatively stable, and those that are struggling within their political system. Besides the poor ranking of Turkey and Russia, the index also highlights the difficulties faced by many Balkan states as they create patterns of policy behavior in their relatively new countries. Understanding how the relative performance of a country changes over time also provides a sense of the dynamism of European societies.

European Union "Federalism"

For many supporters, the goal of the EU is to form a federal superstate (or supranational) state, a true United States of Europe. This goal has supporters and detractors across the continent, often in disagreement about what exactly is the goal, or the degree to which a federation is possible. We can trace the concept back to the discussions of the early 1950s, where many of the founders of the EU supported tight integration, in contrast to the ideas of British leader Winston Churchill, who spoke of union in Europe but simply in terms of interstate cooperation. Despite the unsuccessful attempts to form political and defense unions in the early 1950s, the core idea of an "ever closer union" was part of the preamble to the Treaty of Rome in 1957. This expression remained in subsequent treaties as the EU expanded its operations. Detractors within the EU could see this as vague enough to accept, but this issue continued at the heart of the debate about the future of the EU—what exactly is "an ever closer union"? We can see this debate in the 2000s with the unsuccessful attempts to forge a European constitution, even though there were steps forward in the more successful efforts to promote common foreign and security policies for all EU members.[9] After his election in France in 2017, President Emmanuel Macron strongly promoted the idea of a federal Europe (with France as a key driver), partly in juxtaposition to the impending departure of Britain from the EU. Calls for some sort of federal Europe continue, and EU institutions such as the European Commission and European Parliament remain quite central to the goal of shaping a European political identity.

In contrast, many Europeans, in terms of governments and populations, do not share the desire for federation and, if anything, would like to see even less centralizing power by the EU than is present currently. Many view the EU institutions as undemocratic, as the regular European citizen votes only for the European Parliament, and then not really in a capacity as an embryonic European government. Although European courts nominally have final decisionmaking authority over national courts in some areas, it is difficult to argue with conviction against the viewpoint that national governments still hold predominant authority, and that any likelihood of a full European federation looks remote.

The EU has helped to dilute members' decisionmaking capacity in some areas, notably over economic policy within the single market and with the euro, and with an increasing range of political, economic, and social policies managed by the European Commission, which I discuss further in Chapter 7. Some think the EU role has weakened the state, and has helped the rise of subnational centers of decisionmaking, such as the increasing powers of some groups calling for greater autonomy inside of the UK and Spain.[10] The EU's Committee of the Regions has contributed somewhat to the improved status of these subnational political entities by providing them a venue to promote their identity. The Covid-19 pandemic in 2020–2022 further underlined the weakness of EU federalism and continental policy, when countries reverted to national health policy decisions and closed borders to other Europeans to navigate their way through the crisis. The EU itself initially responded slowly and poorly to the pandemic, ceding decisionmaking to member governments and illuminating the weakness of any EU claims to greater continental management.

Separation of Powers

Although we can trace the idea of possessing different branches of government back to philosophers such as Aristotle and John Locke, we normally ascribe the initial concept of three branches of government and the separation of powers between them to Baron de Montesquieu. Writing in the 1740s primarily about the British system of government, his ideas translated for the first time into a constitution in the United States in 1787.

All political systems in Europe today operate on a separation of powers model, though the relationship between legislatures, executives, and judiciaries differs significantly across European countries. This differentiation can be explained by the type of institutional structure used in a country (e.g., a parliamentary or semipresidential system), as well as by the level of freedom allowed to the legislature and judiciary by the executive. Coalition governments also require greater power sharing or veto powers over legislation, and so promote additional elements of checks and balances. Political systems with a weaker level of democracy, such as Hungary and Poland, also display less separation of power. We look in detail at these three branches of government and their operations in the following chapter. First, though, we need to clarify the manner in which the political structures operate, and we begin with the parliamentary system, which is the predominant system of government in Europe.

Parliamentary Model

Separation of powers is to a certain extent limited in parliamentary systems, where the political party or coalition of parties with majority control of the legislature also forms the executive branch. The parliamentary system is the one used by the majority of European countries. In the UK, for example, the prime minister heads the executive branch, but gets that position by his or her control of the legislative branch, in this example the House of Commons. In Germany, the chancellor leads the executive by virtue of his or her control of a majority in the first chamber, the Bundestag. In a parliamentary system, the head of government does not gain office through a direct election, but controls government by being the leader of the majority party or coalition of parties. Despite this, there is normally considerable emphasis in national elections on who could potentially lead the government, a trend sometimes referred to as the "presidentialization" of parliamentary elections.

Power is "fused" or "concentrated" in parliamentary systems as the executive sits in the legislature and controls it by possessing the majority in that legislature. This is especially the case in European legislatures where tight party discipline can consistently deliver the necessary votes to pass legislation. This makes parliamentary systems quite effective in lawmaking as executives can impose discipline on the voting of their party members, even though coalition governments may find this difficult at times and require greater bargaining across diverse groups.

Most European political systems are parliamentary in nature (or include an element of parliamentary organization in a hybrid system), with the fusion of power between executive and legislative branches, and with limited judicial review of decisions available (with a notable exception of Germany). This lack of a complete separation of powers can appear to be somewhat antidemocratic, and parliamentary systems are open to abuse or, put more neutrally, political leaders have the ability to promote forceful policies with minimal constraints. Elections are the major method of changing the political landscape and leadership, as normally there are no term limits on leaders. For example, Tage Erlander served as Swedish prime minister uninterrupted from 1946 until 1969, and Helmut Kohl in Germany served as chancellor from 1982 to 1998. The benefits of this political structure are that governments can govern by having reliable majorities (or solid coalition majorities) in the legislature. Accountability of government is relatively clear, and it is easier for voters to apportion blame for failed policies, even though coalition governments can lead to blaming others and the undermining of accountability. Coalitions can also contribute to separation of powers, as groups must contest with each other to make policy.

Parliamentary systems require that the executive possesses the majority of support within the legislature. At times, executives can lose this support, especially in a coalition of a number of ruling parties, and a "no-confidence" motion carried by the legislature can force the government to resign. This can lead to a number of outcomes depending on the country, but often leads to new elections. Such elections can threaten the jobs of those in the legislature, as many junior politicians cannot be guaranteed to return, and so the threat of new elections can temper the desire of the legislature to carry through a no-confidence vote. Countries such as Belgium, Italy, and the Netherlands provide many examples of governments forced out, and this can be destabilizing for the country and can make it extremely difficult to make policy. Indeed, according to one study, from 1945 until 2019, the average life span of a government in Italy has been just over one year. Since 1990, the life span of governments in Bulgaria, Lithuania, and Poland has been just under two years. Sweden, which has many minority governments, defies prediction with an average life of government at over four years since 1945.[11]

Voting governments out, without any clear idea what to replace it with, is not ideal. To counter this, countries such as Germany have the policy of "constructive

Box 3.3   The Swedish Parliamentary System

Sweden has a unicameral parliamentary system with a constitutional hereditary monarch. The prime minister takes their position with a majority vote in the Riksdag (technically avoiding receiving fewer than 175 negative votes in a parliament of 349 members). The prime minister forms the executive branch with twenty or so cabinet ministers appointed by the premier. The unitary political system has twenty-one counties or administrative units. National elections take place every four years. Sweden is one of a few European countries where minority governments are common, where the prime minister does not control a majority in the Riksdag, but can obtain a majority of votes when needed to remain in office. Although ruling with a minority appears precarious, the Swedish political system operates in a stable manner even with a minority government. The official head of state is the monarch, but this is a purely ceremonial role since 1975. Unlike in other countries, the Swedish monarch does not nominally select the government, does not formally sign government programs into law, and is not commander in chief of the armed forces.

no-confidence." Here, the legislature can remove the executive, but if it proves impossible to form a new government, then the old executive comes back. Unpopular government is perhaps better than no government at all. Even in Germany, though, new elections are often the better option to obtain the input of citizens. Other European countries to adopt this model include Belgium, Hungary, Poland, Slovenia, and Spain. One notable exception where no-confidence votes cannot remove the leadership is Switzerland, as part of its power-sharing framework.

One final characteristic to note about parliamentary systems is the presence of two executives. I discussed above the role of the executive in terms of the head of government, or the political leader in the legislative body, who is in control of domestic and foreign policies. Parliamentary systems also possess a ceremonial leader, a head of state, who normally has some important tasks including meeting with foreign dignitaries and signing legislation. This role exists within strict nonpoliticized parameters under the eye of the head of government, and is of less significance than the political executive leader. In many European countries, such as Belgium, the Netherlands, Spain, Sweden, and the UK, a constitutional monarch fills this ceremonial role. Of the remaining countries, half directly elect through a national election the ceremonial leader (or president), such as in Austria, Finland, and Ireland. In Finland, for example, the president can hold two six-year elected terms, and has the constitutional right to lead in matters of foreign policy, a residual role from Finland's former status as a semipresidential system. In the other half, such as Germany, Hungary, and Italy, an indirectly elected president holds the position, appointed often by votes of regional governments. The term *president* should not be confused with the presidents we see in mixed semipresidential systems, who do have executive authority.

Mixed Semipresidential Model

A true presidential system and separation of powers model, along the lines of the US political system, is not present in Europe with the exception of the rather unusual systems of Cyprus and Turkey. In the Republic of Cyprus (the Greek-speaking sector), a directly elected president holds both governmental and ceremonial authority, though this does not extend to the northern third of the island under Turkish control.[12] Turkey possessed a parliamentary system until 2017 when a contentious referendum ushered in a presidential form of government to consolidate power for Recep Tayyip Erdoğan, as mentioned earlier in Box 3.1. Both Cyprus and Turkey, then, are forms of a pure presidential system.

Other countries follow a form of government recognized as hybrid or semipresidential, with slight differences in application.[13] These systems combine aspects of presidential and parliamentary systems, with normally a directly elected president in addition to a prime minister, who operates within a parliamentary structure. In this system, there are two political leaders or executives rather than one being more ceremonial, with the president having the more powerful position. In France, this hybrid came about in the 1958 constitution because of Charles de Gaulle's desire for strong presidential leadership (himself), but his somewhat reluctant deference to the tradition of French parliamentary governance. The president is in a much more powerful role than the prime minister, who the president selects, and the National Assembly has a much weaker role to play than most legislative bodies in Europe. The president is directly elected to office every five years (formerly seven), but the prime minister remains in office by preserving majority support in the National Assembly.

Lithuania, Poland, Portugal, Romania, and Russia also utilize the semipresidential model of government. In Portugal, for example, direct elections select the president for a five-year term, and the president appoints the prime minister and cabinet. The president also has the ability to dismiss the prime minister and the parliament. Portugal has a unicameral legislature, in which deputies hold four-year elected terms, and the prime minister is the leader of the majority party or coalition in that body. In Russia, the president and prime minister (chairman) both serve six-year terms. The president gains office through a direct election, whereas the prime minister receives an appointment by the president and does not have to be a member of the Duma. The president also has the ability to remove the prime minister and the cabinet. The constitutional framework has received constant "adjustments" in the past twenty years as a way to maintain the continuing dominance of Vladimir Putin.

This hybrid system opens up possibilities of competing centers of power, when a president and prime minister (and parliament) represent opposing political parties, a system often referred to by its French term of *cohabitation*. The hybrid, then, exhibits more possibilities of a separation of power between branches of government, but can also often witness the different branches of government controlled by the same political party, as in France and Russia in 2021.

Bicameralism

Many legislatures in Europe are bicameral in nature, especially those with a federal political system, such as Austria, Germany, and Russia. Unitary systems, such as Britain, France, and the Netherlands also have two chambers. The norm in such systems is to have a more powerful, directly elected lower chamber, and a less powerful, indirectly elected or appointed upper chamber. Italy, however,

Box 3.4   Poland's Semipresidential System

Poland is a unitary, bicameral political system where direct elections select a president every five years. Elections for the legislative body are every four years, and the prime minister is the leader of the majority party or coalition. The president and prime minister jointly appoint the cabinet. The prime minister sits in the lower house (Sejm) where proportional representation elections select the 460 representatives. Parties must pass a 5 percent threshold for membership, though national minority parties receive an exemption. The prime minister can be removed through a vote of no-confidence, but this is a constructive vote where a new prime minister must be agreed on or otherwise the former returns. The upper house or Senate has 100 members elected directly by plurality, first-past-the-post elections. Both houses need to pass a law, though the Sejm has the ability to override a veto by the Senate.

is an example where both houses have equal powers, whereas Poland provides an example where the people directly elect both houses (though via different types of elections to provide a different composition of representatives). In Germany, the two houses are equal in matters concerning federal legislation that directly affects the states, normally about 40 percent of business.

The benefits of a bicameral system are purportedly that deliberations by two dissimilar bodies provide better representation and superior legislation in the long term, even though passing such legislation is often more difficult and potentially time consuming in the short term. As the second (upper) house does not generally face direct elections, an argument is that it can reflect more carefully on the merits of legislation, rather than come under pressure from popular sentiment and the need to face an electorate on the issue. In federal systems, one of the houses (normally the upper house) provides representation for each federal region. Upper houses, in general, have only limited ability to hold up legislation approved by the lower houses. In contrast to the United States, prestige and power normally rests in the directly elected lower houses of European political systems, where the executive resides.

In the UK, the upper house was unelected until the House of Lords Act of 1999, and primarily represented the landed aristocracy—a throwback to history rather than democracy. Today, hereditary peers elect their fellow peers (so an indirect or limited election) to a limited number of seats, whereas other members achieve appointments for life (technically by the monarch) to represent various groups, such as successful businesspersons, former leading politicians, and others deemed worthy, either in what they have accomplished or what they have donated to a political party. The House of Lords has the capacity to amend and potentially delay legislation, but cannot override the more powerful House of Commons, where the prime minister and cabinet sit.

In France, a unitary bicameral system, the primary house is the National Assembly, where deputies contest direct elections (second ballot, or runoff, system) every five years. The upper house or Senate contains members indirectly elected by local governments across France as well as by overseas territories. Often serving rural areas, the Senate generally tends to possess a more conservative or right-of-center disposition as well as a slower time frame of deliberation. The Senate term in office is six years, with half the members facing election every three years. The Senate president is first in line to take over the running of the country if the president becomes incapacitated. The National Assembly, however, is the more important branch of government where the prime minister sits, and which can ultimately override the Senate.

Germany is a bicameral, federal system. The Bundestag is the first (and not technically the lower) chamber in which the chancellor and cabinet reside, and members have direct elections every four years. Membership is at least 598, as the number can fluctuate above that minimum depending on the outcome of the election. The second house is the Bundesrat, where sixty-nine members represent the interests of the sixteen *länder*. The state governments select representatives to pursue the states' interests, and there is not a set time limit to hold office. These representatives also hold positions in their state government, and so must represent their state's interests rather than their own. Often they work in their home state, so they send others to represent their interests in the Bundesrat. Each state receives votes based on their respective population, and each state votes as a bloc. States have a range of votes from three to six depending on their population size. The Bundesrat's support is required for constitutional and other major issues, but is not required for all legislation. Policy matters tend to be coordinated and consensual whenever possible between the two houses.

Unicameralism

There are twenty-six states in Europe with a unicameral national legislative body. The list includes all five Nordic countries and others such as Bulgaria, Croatia, Greece, Hungary, and Ukraine. As expected, all European microstates are unicameral, as is the European Parliament, which is possibly less expected. Unlike in national systems, the European Parliament possesses considerably less powers of decisionmaking, although these powers have increased in recent years, especially since the Treaty of Lisbon. A unicameral legislature streamlines legislative decisionmaking, and the executive is composed of members drawn from the majority party or parties in this assembly. Arguably, one legislative body makes for a more effective and efficient policy process, with clearer transparency, though with fewer checks and balances. It works well in unitary systems, and in smaller countries, both geographically and demographically. Unstable coalition governments, however, can still derail the system.

As an example, in Norway there are 169 members in the Storting, or General Council, where direct elections take place every four years. During the twentieth century, Norway split the Storting into a quasi-bicameral system, operating in two allied chambers. The government abolished bicameralism in 2007 as unnecessary, and instituted a pure unicameral system.

Constitutions and Veto Players

One approach to understanding the way in which constitutions operate is to consider their structure in terms of allowing groups to oppose or veto policy. In bicameral systems, some constitutions allow for the equal power of both houses, so legislation needs greater consensus to pass. In Germany, as mentioned above, on federal or constitutional issues, both houses hold equal powers and so must work together to find common ground. In contrast, where one house is clearly stronger, such as with the House of Commons in the UK (or similarly in France with the National Assembly), there is less need to push for consensus, and so less opportunity for the ability of groups to veto policy. Even within the House of Commons itself, one party tends to dominate agenda setting and has less need or interest in seeking greater consensus outside of its party. The term *majoritarian* describes this.[14]

In unicameral systems, especially where there are coalition governments, we can also witness the need for governments to seek wider consensus on policy alternatives, where groups can exert significant veto power on policy. This need to push to consensus can vary, with Nordic countries and the Netherlands tending to be more consensus oriented. Some constitutions build in the need for consensus, as explained below.

This idea of veto players links to an earlier concept of consociationalism, or strong consensus democracy, which focused on a power-sharing format of government in deeply divided societies. Developed initially by the political scientist Arend Lijphart, this model looks at how competitive elites can be brought together to overcome deep cultural, ethnic, or religious differences to share power, normally utilizing a proportional representation type of election and allowing a veto over policy to each elite group.[15] In Switzerland, for example, a cabinet of seven ministers comprises leaders of the major parties, where the leader of government (the president) rotates among these members on an annual basis. Decisions need consensus with groups holding a veto over implementation. Public intervention is possible on most topics through a national referendum, although decisions by referendum do not protect minority interests.

Another good contemporary example of this concept is in Northern Ireland. Although a part of the UK, Northern Ireland has some ability to make policy at the local level. Northern Ireland began its existence in May 1921 after the South (Eire, or Ireland) gained independence from the UK, although the factors contributing to these divisions had been in play for centuries. The Protestant majority in the North wanted to remain part of the UK, fearing the dilution of their interests in a majority Catholic Ireland, and so the six counties of Northern Ireland split from the rest of Ireland. Conflict erupted in the 1960s in Northern Ireland as the Protestant majority clung to their power, challenged by the increasing assertiveness and calls for justice among the growing Catholic minority. Both sides militarized, and hostilities between militant factions brought widespread casualties, 3,500 deaths, and a breakdown of the local (Stormont) government, requiring direct control from London.

After three decades of unproductive efforts, the Good Friday Agreement (or Belfast Agreement) of April 1998 helped to broker peace and a power-sharing arrangement between the major parties. The electoral system changed to a proportional representation system, with a cabinet representing the parties, and the right to veto action that groups opposed. This worked well until a breakdown occurred in 2017, and the country limped on without a government until the British and Irish governments reached an agreement in January 2020. The fallout from Brexit and the UK's departure from the EU broke the fragile balance. Tensions rose and riots broke out in April 2021.[16] Unionists, predominantly Protestant, fear a potential dismemberment from the UK, as a border is now in place between Northern Ireland and the remainder of the UK, despite promises to the contrary by the British government. Nationalists, predominantly Catholic, seek to preserve the open border with the South. Their party, Sinn Fein, won a narrow victory in elections in May 2022 for the first time, increasing tensions between the groups. Both sides hold veto power over future policy and the status of Northern Ireland. Ongoing attempts by the UK government to change the terms of the Brexit arrangement with the EU regarding Northern Ireland add to the instability.

European Union Constitution and Separation of Powers

The development of the EU since the 1950s is significant in terms of the institutions created and the number of member states that belong. Rising from an initial membership of six, the EU today comprises twenty-seven members, with several other countries in the candidate stage. Although Britain's departure in January 2020 was the first major reversal of membership (Greenland also withdrew in 1985), some still hope for the EU to grow to around thirty members, with Serbia and Montenegro the current candidate frontrunners. In terms of its institutional growth, the EU has expanded into many new areas of policymaking and has strengthened the role and capacity of its institutions. These institutions, however, are quite distinct from what we see in European states, although we can try to argue a separation of powers between them.

These institutions, initially, possessed little authority and handled EU business simply as an extension of member governments. Since its inception, and through various treaty agreements discussed in Chapter 2, the EU has adapted to become much broader in scope. Today, we can debate the extent to which the institutions have taken on a "European" character of their own, something distinct from the twenty-seven member governments. This relates to the level of supranationalism within the EU. Can we see a federal Europe developing with its own distinct institutional structures and powers?

A major effort to build a federal Europe came with the plan to create a constitution, as mentioned in the previous chapter, and this exercise helps to illuminate the underlying tensions and difficulties of the European experiment. Launched as a proposal in 2003, the constitution aimed to be important at several levels.[17] The constitution planned to pull together and simplify for popular consumption all the disparate agreements and treaties into a more uniform and streamlined "statement of intent" for Europe. As Europeans gained a greater clarity regarding the mission of the EU, the constitution would serve as a unifying and simplifying document around which European citizens could rally and be educated—a constitution that could be read in a pamphlet or put on a wall in a poster. The actual constitution document, in reality, stretched to 474 pages, in rather typical EU style. Once the average European understood how vital the EU was to European life, this would stimulate further and enhanced European cooperation, based on the rationale of the ever closer union. This is how the EU elite perceived it.

An initial draft developed by the constitutional convention proclaimed Europe to be a "Christian" continent—and supposedly the EU an organization of Christians. Even though opposition led to the dropping of this idea, it pointed to a fundamental difficulty regarding agreement over what the EU actually is and stands for.[18] In the end, the constitution merely stated in its preamble the following: "DRAWING INSPIRATION from the cultural, religious and humanist inheritance of Europe, from which have developed the universal values of the inviolable and inalienable rights of the human person, freedom, democracy, equality and the rule of law."[19]

Many feared the increasing strength and scope of the EU, and interpreted the idea of a constitution to mean that the sovereignty, power, and independence of national governments would suffer under the growing omnipotence of Brussels. To offset this idea, Article 1.5 of the constitution stated: "The union shall respect the equality of Member States before the constitution as well as their national identities, inherent in their fundamental structures, political and constitutional, inclusive of regional and local self-government. It shall respect their essential State functions, including ensuring the territorial integrity of the State, maintaining law and order and safeguarding national security."[20] Whatever the common perceptions, the constitution was defeated in national referenda in France and the Netherlands, and this halted its forward movement.

Resourceful as always, the EU and its member states switched tack, dropped the contentious idea of a formal constitution, and sought modest enhancements through a new treaty. This Lisbon Treaty, signed in 2007, hoped to clarify and strengthen the leadership of the EU by establishing two new positions. These were a president of the European Council, and a newly configured high representative of the Union for foreign affairs and security policy (foreign minister), serving also as the vice-president of the European Commission. This treaty was itself defeated in a referendum in Ireland in 2008, leading to further watering down, rewording, and public education on the merits of moving Europe forward. When this revised treaty came up for voting in 2009, of the 27 members only Ireland put this to a (second) popular referendum. All the other countries took the slightly safer route of deliberating in national parliaments.

With the successful passage of the Lisbon Treaty, a slightly stronger European-wide institutional structure emerged. The first president of the European Council was Herman Van Rompuy (Belgium), and the president in 2022 is Charles Michel (Belgium). The first high representative after Lisbon was Catherine Ashton (Britain), and the office holder in 2022 is Josep Borrell (Spain). These appointments result from intense governmental backroom deals, rather than by popular vote or national parliamentary vote. I discuss the impact of these changes of institutional structure below, but can say that they have been minimal. As a quick side note to avert too much confusion, we need to be aware that there are numerous presidents in the EU—of the Council of the European Union, the European Council (a presidency), the European Commission, the European Parliament, the Court of Justice of the European Union, and the European Central Bank, to name the more important institutions.

In reality, there is no simple document to lead us to the guiding principles and policies of the EU, but as mentioned in the previous chapter there is a large body of laws known as the *acquis communautaire* ("what has been acquired by/of the community"). The *acquis* provides the body of some 30,000 legal agreements guiding European economic and social policy and democracy, and its acceptance and implementation is a core requirement of all current and potential EU members. The *acquis* currently has 35 chapters or sections, running to more than 100,000 pages (different lengths in different languages).[21] These chapters include topics such as freedom of movement, competition policy, fisheries, justice, and the environment. The full implementation of all the *acquis* into national law and policy challenges even the wealthiest and most organized of states. It is impossible to consider ordinary European citizens wanting to wade through the *acquis* to gain a better appreciation of the EU; hence, the initial allure of the idea of the constitution. How to capture the essence of the EU in a short document and captivate the imagination of Europeans with it remain a challenge.

I discussed earlier in this chapter the separation of powers as it relates to national governments, but the concept of separation of powers at the EU level is rather complex and less clear-cut. The task of the judicial branch rests somewhat with the Court of Justice of the European Union and other European courts, with significant powers of judicial review. The legislative power is, arguably, present in the European Parliament, though this institution has struggled to have the same capacities as legislatures at national levels. It has gained, however, increased legislative capability over the past two decades, especially following the Lisbon Treaty, and is beginning to have some powers comparative to a national legislature. Discerning who holds executive powers is a little difficult, compounded by a different conception of separation of powers; namely, that between national governments and the presence of a "European" government. Several institutions share executive power; namely, the European Council and the Council of Ministers representing the member states on the one hand, and the European Commission representing "Europe Union interests" on the other.

Although member states ultimately hold the upper hand in this decisionmaking relationship, this can vary. On aspects of trade, the European Commission tends to hold more of the executive power, whereas on matters of foreign policy, the member states predominate. The term *pooled sovereignty* hints at the attempt to sort out and share executive powers, often underlined by qualified majority voting on issues, but the amount of sovereignty that states agree to pool depends on the issue at stake. Increasing efforts by the European Parliament to gain a more important seat at the table to share execution of policy complicate the situation. A clearer sense of the interrelationship of these institutions and their respective powers will become evident, hopefully, as I discuss the institutions in more depth in subsequent chapters. There are dozens of EU institutions (hundreds if we include the less well known), and I do not plan to study them all, or even most of them, in great depth. I focus on the primary institutions, and provide an indication of the breadth of other specialized bodies.[22] I also consider a number of other international institutions on the European continent, such as the Council of Europe, but these are primarily intergovernmental and have little capacity to act beyond what member countries explicitly allow.

Conclusion

This chapter focuses on the broad organizing political structures of European states. For a relatively small and compact continent, there is wide disparity in the manner in which governments operate. Although most states pursue democracy as a guiding principle (with exceptions noted), there are many distinct ways in which states organize themselves to pursue this goal. I discussed differences between federal and unitary states, and bicameral and unicameral systems, but need to end with a reminder that no system is necessarily superior to another. All reflect national culture and historical development, as well as the size and relative diversity of the country. Each country is unique in its political structure, but I attempted to pull together some broad comparative pointers to explain what takes place. Building on this foundation, the next chapter looks at the specific ways in which governments operate, filling in more detail about the organization of the three branches of government.

Notes

1. Eric Maurice, "European Democracy, a Fundamental System to Be Protected," Robert Schuman Foundation Policy Paper, no. 578, December 1, 2020, https://www .robert-schuman.eu/en/doc/questions-d-europe/qe-578-en.pdf.

2. The four powers were the United States, Soviet Union, the United Kingdom, and France.

3. Before the constitution of 1976, Portugal had promulgated different constitutions in 1822, 1826, 1838, 1911, and 1933.

4. OECD (Organisation for Economic Co-operation and Development), "Constitutions of Central and Eastern European Countries and the Baltic States," SIGMA Paper no. 2 (Paris: OECD: 1995), https://doi.org/10.1787/5kml6gf26mvk-en.

5. We should not confuse unitary with unicameral or bicameral political systems. Unitary systems can possess one house (e.g., Sweden) or two houses (e.g., France).

6. The Scottish Parliament, "About the Scottish Parliament," https://www.parliament .scot/visitandlearn/12506.aspx.

7. The population of Scotland voted to remain in the EU in the 2016 Brexit referendum after declining independence in a 2014 referendum. The Scottish government in June 2022 scheduled another referendum on independence for October 2023, but the UK

government refused to approve it. The UK Supreme Court is to deliberate on the constitutionality of this referendum in October 2022.

8. The Fund for Peace, "Fragile States Index 2021," https://fragilestatesindex.org/.

9. European Union, *Ever Closer Union: The Legacy of the Treaties of Rome for Today's Europe* (Brussels: General Secretariat of the Council, 2017), https://www.eui.eu /Documents/Research/HistoricalArchivesofEU/ADG/Ever-Closer-Union-catalogue.pdf.

10. Liesbet Hooghe and Gary Marks, *Multi-Level Governance and European Integration* (Lanham, MD: Rowman and Littlefield, 2001).

11. Paul Kubicek, *European Politics,* 3rd ed. (Abingdon: Routledge, 2021), p. 155.

12. Cyprus Profile (Nicosia), "Government and Politics," https://www.cyprusprofile .com/page/country-information/politics.

13. Maurice Duverger, "A New Political System Model: Semi-Presidential Government," *European Journal of Political Research* 8, 1980: 165–187.

14. Catherine E. De Vries, Sara B. Hobolt, Sven-Oliver Proksch, and Jonathan B. Slapin, *Foundations of European Politics: A Comparative Approach* (Oxford: Oxford University Press, 2021), chap. 11.

15. Arend Lijphart, *Patterns of Democracy: Government Forms and Performance in Thirty-Six Countries* (New Haven: Yale University Press, 1999); or the earlier Arend Lijphart, *Democracy in Plural Societies: A Comparative Exploration* (New Haven: Yale University Press, 1977).

16. Rory Carroll, "Peace Under Fire," *The Guardian Weekly,* April 16, 2021.

17. European Parliament, "The European Constitution," https://www.europarl.europa .eu/Europe2004/textes/2005-01-10-brochure-constitution-en-v02.pdf.

18. Srdjan Cvijic and Lorenzo Zucca, "Does the European Constitution need Christian Values?" *Oxford Journal of Legal Studies* 24(4), 2004: 739–748.

19. Official Journal of the European Union, *Treaty Establishing a Constitution for Europe*, C310, Vol. 47, Brussels, December 2004, http://publications.europa.eu/resource /cellar/7ae3fd7e-8820-413e-8350-b85f9daaab0c.0005.02/DOC_1.

20. Ibid., Art. 1.5.

21. European Commission, "European Neighbourhood Policy and Enlargement Negotiations: Acquis," https://ec.europa.eu/neighbourhood-enlargement/enlargement -policy/glossary/acquis_en.

22. European Union, "Institutions and Bodies Profiles," https://europa.eu/european -union/about-eu/institutions-bodies_en#other-eu-institutions-and-bodies.

4

Leaders,
Leadership, and
Governing Institutions

IN THE PREVIOUS CHAPTER, I CONSIDERED THE BROAD ORGANIZATIONAL and constitutional structure of governmental systems in Europe, looking at aspects of the separation of powers, parliamentary structures, federal and unitary systems, and bicameralism and unicameralism. I also attempted to explain the developing European Union institutions within the context of separation of powers and decisionmaking. In this chapter, I focus on the actual institutions through which countries govern, looking in turn at legislatures, executives, and judiciaries, providing examples of different operations across the continent. Although my emphasis is on national governments, I also include a short comparative discussion of the role of EU institutions.

Legislatures

Legislatures in Europe come in a variety of names, structures, and capabilities, but their unifying common theme is their role in deliberating on and passing legislation. Some legislatures, such as those in France and the United Kingdom, have long histories through which their functions have evolved. Others, such as those in Central Europe and Russia, have operated for much shorter time spans, in reality for only two or three decades. Legislatures also differ in terms of whether they are unicameral, with power concentrated in the one chamber, or bicameral, where policy needs to pass through two distinct chambers. Within the parliamentary framework, as discussed in the previous chapter, the legislature and the executive link or fuse together, as an executive in parliamentary systems is part of the legislative body.

Given these ties to the executive, it is a fair question to ask whether legislatures have much independence, or even importance, in modern European political systems. With limited powers to set the political agenda, and with party leaders normally able to exert strict party discipline, legislatures more often than not are reactive institutions to ideas shaped by party leaders and executives, and not the true deliberative bodies we sometimes portray them to be. Of course, legislatures can at times bark and bite, such as when coalition partners need to come together on a particular policy option, but even then the executive tends to be the more important element. Legislative independent powers also weaken as a country becomes less democratic, such as we see in Russia or Turkey, or increasingly in Hungary and Poland, where they become simply rubber stamp agencies for the executive. There is also evidence that legislatures ceded their authority to executives across Europe in initial efforts in 2020 to combat the Covid-19 pandemic.[1]

Core Roles of a Legislature

One core role of a legislature is the ability to pass a budget, and control of the purse played a central role in the evolution of parliamentary powers. In the UK, for example, the evolution of the role of Parliament linked to the monarch's need to leverage money in taxation from the people, from the time of the Magna Carta in the thirteenth century to the present. Legislatures are also involved in the day-to-day debate and sharpening of other legislation, but they can also cede power to the executive in terms of their being in session for only limited periods of the year. Legislatures also do not always have the powers to initiate legislation, as that prerogative tends to rest with executives. In many ways, then, most legislatures are reactive institutions, responding to prompts from the executive branch.

Another important role of a legislature is to monitor, elect, and hold accountable the executive. As I have already discussed, this is difficult with the fusion of power in a parliamentary system, where tight party discipline can hold members in check—often enforced by senior party members in the executive. Voting on potential laws is one way to pass judgment on executive policies, though it is unusual for executives to lose such votes in a parliamentary system, unless they are in a relatively weak coalition, or even a minority government. In semipresidential systems, the president faces little accountability as he or she sits largely outside of formal legislative control, answerable to the people in national elections.

Accountability, or at least potential embarrassment, of the executive often comes through official questions by the legislature under parliamentary procedure. The executive normally receives these questions in writing, but at times chambers have the ability to call the executive before them for public grilling. Finland and Germany provide good examples of question time for government leaders and ministers, whereas in France, even though the system exists, it is barely used. The European Parliament (EP) has the ability to question the president of the Commission in monthly meetings. The best known example of this is Prime Minister's Question Time in the UK—though other government ministers face the House of Commons also—but this tends to be more theater and testing the abilities of the minister rather than anything truly productive in terms of gaining information or government concession. Party discipline normally allows for soft questions from the leader's own party, so the grilling tends to come from the opposition parties. The confined nature of the UK House of Commons heightens these confrontations, with seating for only about two-thirds of the members on benches, and with political parties facing each other across a narrow divide of a symbolic two sword lengths (about thirteen feet, or four meters). Throughout most other legislatures, politicians sit in horseshoe formations, somewhat less adversarial in nature, though not automatically any more efficient.

Several other important roles of a legislature are worthy of note. Legislatures help to provide a forum for debate as well as education about the important issues within society, even though the important part of building legislation normally takes place in committees. In this way, they help to simplify complex issues into major talking points and, through political parties, provide guidance to citizens as to how they should view these issues. Voting to pass bills into law offers a mechanism to resolve disagreements within society, even though issues are rarely resolved in any permanent basis and are open to re-litigation with a change of party control after a subsequent election. Legislatures work to shape and construct perceptions within society.

Legislatures are also important for their role in representation. This includes the representation of ideas and policies that exist within society, as well as regional differences of opinions. As we saw with bicameralism, a key aspect of a second chamber is to provide a different type of representation within the legislature, often based on regional sentiments. The idea of representation also embraces the need of a legislature to reflect the diversity of people within a society—represent the ideas of women, minorities, and different social classes. In these areas, legislatures often perform poorly as they tend to contain male elites by default without active intervention to bring change. Increasingly, we see the introduction of gender quotas in elections, such as in Belgium, France, and

Greece, where women gain greater opportunity to compete in politics.[2] Legislatures also have the ability to exert influence over other political bodies, notably with their role in electing judges or monitoring other government committees.

Women in Legislatures

In a historical perspective, women have played a limited role in legislative bodies, linked to the fact that laws prevented women from running for office and women began to receive the vote in parts of Europe only in the early twentieth century. No country in Europe has equal representation for women, though many countries have witnessed a slow and steady increase in female representation. Nordic countries have around 40 percent female representation. Iceland currently tops the European list with 47 percent female representation in parliament, though twelve other European countries have 40 percent or higher.[3] The lowest-performing European country, with only 14 percent female representation, is Hungary, ranked 147 in the world. Although a small number of countries have legislative quotas for women, such as Italy, the majority of countries operate a voluntary system for the selection of women candidates for political parties.[4] This ensures that traditional sexist barriers for advancement of women in European politics remain. As many countries operate proportional representation elections with candidates listed by their parties, it would not be difficult to boost the numbers of women candidates on a list, but this is a slow process.

In the European Parliament, the situation is more positive. In the first EP direct elections in 1979, women won 15 percent of the seats, but by the EP election in 2019, this figure sat at just under 40 percent. Eleven EU states had some form of gender quota for the EP elections, with countries such as Belgium, France, and Luxembourg requiring 50 percent representation for women and the others 40 percent. The European Parliament agreed in May 2022 to require all countries to have 50 percent representation for candidates, but it was unlikely that national governments would endorse this unanimously as required for implementation.[5]

Minority Groups in Legislatures

A definition of what an *ethnic minority* is can prove difficult in many European contexts, as is the question of whom to count as such. Generally, the term refers to groups who are different to the majority of citizens by way of immigrant status, religion, ethnicity, or other key distinguishing feature and who wish to maintain and promote this distinction. Groups of ethnic minorities fared poorly in the 2019 EP elections, registering only about 5 percent of the EP's composition.[6] Representation of minorities and minority issues in parliaments across Europe is generally poor, a fact underlined by the widespread Black Lives Matter protests in 2020.[7] In France, collecting data on ethnic minorities is illegal, but an unofficial count had 6.35 percent of the National Assembly as ethnic minorities after the 2017 election. This was a marked improvement on the 2 percent of representatives before the election.[8] In Germany after its 2017 elections, ethnic minority representation in the Bundestag stood at 8 percent of the total, up from 6 percent before the election.[9] Following the British general election of 2019, 10 percent of members of Parliament came from ethnic minority groups, whereas the figure for the opposition Labour Party stood the highest at 20 percent.[10] These numbers remain low overall across Europe, indicative of the challenges facing governments in terms of handling minority issues.

The European Parliament

The European Parliament, based in Brussels, Luxembourg, and Strasbourg, has evolved in character and function since its formation in 1952 as the Common Assembly of the European Coal and Steel Community. It became the EP in 1962, comprised of members appointed by national governments. The first direct elections to the EP took place in 1979, and have occurred every five years since then. There are currently 705 seats in the EP, roughly distributed among members according to population size (the largest size of the EP was 751 seats pre-Brexit).[11] Although members must win in nationally based elections, once elected they sit in the EP not by national affiliation but by political inclination. Socialists from Denmark, for example, sit alongside socialists from Portugal. The powers of the EP have gradually transformed from virtually nonexistent to considerable shared decisionmaking and lawmaking with the European Council. The EP has broad powers to approve (though not nominate) members of the European Commission, including its president, and to review the Commission's performance. The EP has less influence over areas guarded more closely by national governments, such as defense and foreign policy, though it is involved in voting on major matters of trade treaties.[12]

It is probably fair to say that the EP is increasingly becoming a strong European institution looking out for and with oversight over EU interests, as well as the ability to vote on most EU policy. EP representatives, however, tend to win election to look after national interests in the EU, and these national concerns and issues rather than a pro-European vision can undermine the performance of the EP. A good example of this is in the UK, where some delegates elected to the EP actually belonged to parties hostile to the EU itself, such as the UK Independence Party (UKIP). In 2014, UKIP won the EP elections in

Britain with 28 percent of the national vote, calling for Britain's departure from the EU. In 2019, the similarly right-wing populist and anti-EU party, the Alternative for Germany (Alternativ für Deutschland [AfD]) in Germany, won 11 percent and fourth position in the EU elections. Elections to the EP take place according to national electoral models rather than any overarching European model (though they must be proportional), and they take place on different days according to national norms, although within a confined time limit of a few days for all of them.

The EP is the only directly elected institution within the EU, and so has a claim to be the antidote to the "democratic deficit," the relative absence of democratic institutions across the organization. The EP also claims to be the mouthpiece of Europeans, where other EU institutions seem aloof and distant to the populace. This is a little deceptive because few Europeans tend to care about the exploits of the EP, and turnout at European elections is lower than at national elections. Viewpoints of citizens tend to be reflected more in national governments, which are represented in Europe at the Council of the European Union and European Council level, and so the "who best speaks for Europe" question is a complex one. The EP has been able to leverage its claims to do this over the years into a stronger policy role in relation to the other institutions of the EU.

Unlike its partner institutions, which have their operations in Brussels, the EP operates in three main locations. Its core business and meetings increasingly take place in Brussels, at the heart of European operations, but one week a month everybody hauls off to Strasbourg for plenary sessions—along with files, translators, secretaries, and so forth. A further complication is that much of the administrative support for the EP is in Luxembourg. This is clearly inefficient, but highly political, and the chances that the French government will relinquish the EP presence in Strasbourg any time soon are slim. As throughout the EU, juggling the interests of twenty-seven member countries is difficult, especially concerning a legacy or founding member such as France (or Luxembourg).

The EP elects its own president for a single term of two and a half years. The president chairs sessions of the parliament, and represents the EP to other EU organizations as well as overseas. The president signs most laws and the budget on behalf of the EP. There is an agreement between the two major political groups in the EP that the president should rotate between them, moving from center-right to center-left every thirty months. This normally holds because these two largest political groups combine their votes for the nominated candidate. The vast majority of EP presidents have been citizens of the largest or the original member countries. Besides one term for a Pole, West European countries have provided the previous EP presidents. The current president, Roberta Metsola, elected in January 2022, is the third woman to hold office and is Maltese.

Executives

Executives, whether prime ministers, chancellors, or presidents are responsible for the execution or carrying out of policy. This includes responsibility for the development of policy, shepherding laws through parliament, and the enactment and implementation of policy through large government bureaucracies. In a traditional parliamentary system, there are not direct elections for executives, although leaders normally will have to win a seat as an individual candidate, or in proportional representation elections through a high ranking on a party list. Rather, executives in parliamentary systems obtain their positions through leadership of the parties winning the most votes in legislative elections, or controlling the winning coalition. In semipresidential systems, the president normally selects the prime minister, who must gain the majority support of the legislature.

The executive branch is also comprised of a group of ministers responsible for various policy areas, and this "cabinet" of ministers is accountable to the public for their policies and actions. This effort to produce collective responsibility or solidarity means that ministers hold responsibility for everything the government does, even if the policy in question has little connection with an individual minister's scope of responsibility. Those ministers who cannot accept responsibility for all policies often need to resign from the government.

Cabinets or Councils of Ministers

The exact composition of executives differs across Europe. All have a head of government, who has the title such as prime minister or chancellor (see the Country Profiles section at the end of the book for specific national titles), and this leadership position provides some entitlement for selecting colleagues to serve in the government. These are normally senior members of the same political party or closely affiliated or coalition partner. The cabinet is often a critical place for bargaining over and vetoing potential policies, and tends to reflect political power and its limitations. Switzerland offers a more codified example of this bargaining process. It has an established system in place to guide the selection of the cabinet, and this includes both winners and losers at the election as a means to maintain the balance between various language and interest groups within the country. This is more government by committee than most other European countries, and the cabinet concept promotes more consensual government.

Each country has different rules about who is eligible to serve as ministers in the government. The majority of members are officials who have won election, but many countries enable nonelected persons to serve, or as in France, require politicians to resign their elected position once asked to serve within the government. In Britain, executives are composed of members from both Houses of Parliament, including unelected members of the House of Lords, though by tradition the prime minister can come from only the House of Commons.

The cabinet or council of ministers is a critical decisionmaker in most European countries, and it guides the affairs of government. A cabinet comprises senior political figures, who barely conceal their ambition and are often rivals to the prime minister or chancellor, so it can be a difficult task balancing such powerful political forces. In coalition governments, the majority in Europe, cabinet membership is the result of deliberative and sometimes painstaking negotiation between the coalition partners, often with important positions passed to key allies (and at times facilitated by the head of state). Such positions, through careful balancing and weighting, take into account the size and importance of the relative coalition partner. In Germany, for example, one tradition is to make the leader of the main coalition partner the vice chancellor, nominally second in line and able to take over the government if the chancellor becomes incapacitated. In the Netherlands, a similar procedure allows a senior coalition partner to be the first deputy prime minister. Another possibility is to enable a coalition partner to take over the prestigious foreign affairs portfolio.

Although herding strong-willed and ambitious politicians is never an easy task even in one's own party, probably the greatest challenge to governmental cohesion is in maintaining coalition governments. Here, different political parties cooperate and often need each other to obtain political power. Tensions can easily surface between the factions within the executive, and coalitions can fragment. At times, the weakest coalition partner can drive the government—the tail wagging the dog—if the government needs its support to remain in office. This can pull the government away from its traditional policy spectrum, implementing policies favored by a small group in society, so putting the government under increasing strain. Such balancing among portfolios again helps us to understand broader policymaking in many countries, and the ability of groups to check or veto others. This trend is not necessarily negative, however. Coalition partners can push for greater environmental initiatives, or increased rights for women and minorities, policies that would perhaps be more difficult to launch if a dominant party did not need a coalition ally.

Minority Government

An interesting feature of the parliamentary system is minority governments, which are common in Scandinavia. Here, a political party or coalition cannot command a majority, but remains in office as a minority with the support of

---

Box 4.1 Coalitions and Political Instability in Italy

Balancing the differing coalition partners in the cabinet can lead to significant political instability and the fall of governments as they fail to maintain majority control of the legislature. Italy is an excellent example of the difficulties in maintaining a government. Only one government since 1989 lasted its full term of five years (Silvio Berlusconi). Italy has had almost seventy governments since the end of World War II. Recent problems in forming government link to the rise of populist parties, such as the League and the Five Star Movement, and the constant jostling for advantage in the Italian political system. Three different governments in the period 2019–2021 highlight continuing instability. The president of Italy officially has the task of calling on politicians to try to form a government, which then must obtain majority support in the parliament. A new government cobbled together a coalition under Mario Draghi in February 2021, with an uncertain though hopeful future.[a] This government collapsed in July 2022.

Note: a. Jason Horowitz, "Italy's New Leader Outlines Recovery, Appealing for Unity and Sacrifice," *New York Times,* February 18, 2021.

---

other parties on particular issues. This takes place where often no other political party or coalition can muster a majority, or where parties do not wish to threaten their reputation as junior members of a coalition. Such a system requires considerable skill in balancing priorities among parties, seeking common ground on issues, and carefully balancing the membership of the cabinet. Normally holding a fresh election is the way to try to move to a majority government, but such minority governments can remain in office for long periods. Since 1945, more than half of the governments in Denmark, Norway, and Sweden have been minority governments. In recent decades, governments in Denmark, for example, have survived on average for one to two years, and sometimes shorter. Estonia has had six minority governments since its emergence from Soviet control in 1992. Even the British government, normally touted as one of strong party dominance and stable government (and not proportional representation elections), has operated with minority governments in 1974, 1977, 1997, and 2017–2019. There were minority governments in eleven European countries in 2020.

Semipresidential Executives

A similar issue may be present in hybrid or semipresidential governments, with features of both presidential and parliamentary systems. It is quite possible to have a president representing one political party, and a prime minister from a different party and ideology, what is known as *cohabitation*. This cohabitation is potentially fraught with difficulty, as the executive contains divergent political interests, which pull it in different directions and can veto policy options. Unlike in coalition government, there is no unifying interest in joining forces for the sake of governmental survival, and there can be strong interests in undermining the other branch of government. In France, for example, the president can select the prime minister, but this person must have the support of the National Assembly—and only the assembly can formally remove the prime minister, although the president can informally pressure the prime minister to resign. France has had several periods of cohabitation, in 1986–1988, 1993–1995, and 1997–2002. During cohabitation, parliamentary processes may become more significant, as the strength of the presidency is undermined. Following a referendum in 2000, France reduced the length of the president's term from seven to five years in 2002, and this brought presidential and parliamentary elections into the same year, so reducing the chance of cohabitation. In other examples, Portugal had a government of cohabitation after 2016. Poland had cohabitation after 2007, whereas Romania has had successive cohabitation governments over the past twenty years.

In the absence of compromise, the government may achieve little, and countries need to wait until the next election cycle to see whether a new constellation of political forces emerges. A tempting, though somewhat inaccurate analogy, is in the US presidential system, where the president from one political party might need to coexist with a legislature controlled by another party, such as occurred during the last six years in office of Presidents Bill Clinton and Barack Obama. Though the political fallout and deadlock may be similar, the big difference in the European hybrid or coalition systems is that these competing forces are all *inside* the executive, thus making government cohesion quite challenging.

Women Executives

Women political leaders in Europe as a subset of executives remain the exception rather than the rule, although there is an increasing record of accomplishment as head of state or head of government. In some large European countries, such as Italy, Russia, and Spain, there has never been a woman head of government or head of state. France has had two women prime ministers, but no woman president. Edith Cresson remained in office for one year in 1991. President Emmanuel Macron appointed Élisabeth Borne as premier in May 2022 to bolster his party's chances in the June parliamentary elections. The center-right Gaullist party (Les Républicains) chose a woman presidential candidate, Valérie

Pécresse, for the first time ever in 2022, although she only managed to win 4.7 percent of the vote in the first round of the April 2022 elections. Poland has had two women prime ministers, similar to the UK, where Margaret Thatcher dominated an era as prime minister for eleven years after 1979. Thatcher was the first woman to be elected prime minister of a European country, and set out to change the nature of British society, promoting policies of neoliberalism and weakening the powers of organized labor. Her legacy in the UK still divides the country, needless to say, with supporters and opponents alike. Theresa May was less polarizing, but had a difficult period in office during 2016–2019 at the height of the Brexit crisis, which effectively led to her ouster. Germany has had only one woman chancellor, but Angela Merkel proved to be the longest-serving head of a European government in recent times, serving from 2005 as chancellor until her retirement in December 2021.

Iceland was the first European country to elect a woman president in 1980, Vigdís Finnbogadóttir, and she served as president for sixteen years. Mary McAleese served a notable fourteen years as president of Ireland between 1997 and 2011. Gro Harlem Brundtland is worthy of mention for winning three separate terms as prime minister of Norway. Finland appointed the

---

Box 4.2   Angela Merkel, Chancellor of Germany

Angela Merkel was the longest-serving woman head of government in Europe. She grew up in East Germany (with Polish ancestry), is a chemist by training, and began her career in politics after the 1989 reforms. She served as leader of the Christian Democratic Union (CDU) from 2000 to 2018, and chancellor from 2005 until 2021, when she decided to step down. She was the first woman chancellor of Germany, and she wielded considerable influence leading Europe's strongest economic power. This translated into Merkel's influence over the EU and its policy, and observers considered her the leading voice supporting international institutions and the Western Alliance during the Donald Trump presidency in the United States. Successful and well respected inside and outside Germany, Merkel suffered criticism over certain policies, notably over her unwillingness to challenge Russia for its actions; Germany's initial reaction in 2020 to the Covid-19 pandemic; and her handling of EU policies on immigration, debts, and the Greek crisis. A period of uncertainty and transition existed in 2022 after her departure, worsened by the Russian invasion of Ukraine that put pressure on the new, seemingly unprepared government of Olaf Scholz.[a]

Note: a. Constanze Stelzenmüller, "The Singular Chancellor: The Merkel Model and Its Limits," *Foreign Affairs* 100(3), 2021: 161–172.

youngest ever woman, Sanna Marin, to serve as prime minister of any country when she took office in December 2019. She was thirty-four years of age when she became premier, and the third woman to hold that post. A majority of Finnish cabinet members were also women, including three other women in their thirties. In fact, of the five Nordic countries in February 2022, four of them had women leaders, with Norway being the exception.[13] Of the three Baltic states in 2022, both Estonia and Lithuania had women prime ministers, with Estonia also having a woman president. The current EU Commission president, Ursula von der Leyen, is the first woman to hold this position, but she complained about problems of blatant sexism in a meeting with the Turkish president in April 2021.[14]

Despite such cases as heads of government and heads of state, women remain far from equity in European politics. Outside of Scandinavia, it is more of an exception for women to serve as a head of government. One notable exception in the cauldron of Balkan politics is the prime minister of Serbia, Ana Brnabic, in office since 2017, who is openly lesbian. It is arguably a little easier to win an election to be head of state, where the position is often more ceremonial than political. I also should state that having a woman political leader does not necessarily mean that the leader supports women's issues, or that a particular style of government is to be expected. One criticism of Thatcher was that she did little to support women in society. The more important factor at stake, perhaps, is the liberal feminist idea of equity, and that women should simply have equal opportunity to serve and represent as men in the highest echelons of politics.

Monarchies

Monarchies might appear to be anachronistic in today's democratic Europe, but they continue to thrive, albeit with significant constitutional constraints. There are currently eleven constitutional monarchies in Europe, and they serve as the (unelected) head of state.[15] Specific powers vary from country to country. Perhaps the most famous constitutional monarch is in the UK, where Queen Elizabeth II has ruled for seventy years since February 1952, the longest-reigning monarch in recent European history (Louis XIV ruled France for seventy-two years through much of the seventeenth century), and the longest-reigning woman monarch in world history. Though large on pomp and circumstance, constitutional provisions tightly bind and limit the monarch's real powers. The prime minister scripts her annual speech to Parliament that sets out the legislative agenda for the coming year. Her Majesty's courts and armies are hers only in name. Although the monarch has the technical ability to veto legislation, this has not been instituted in the UK since Queen Anne in 1707—indeed, such an action today would prompt an immediate constitutional crisis.

Although the British respect and tolerate the monarchy, support would be quickly undermined if the monarch actually became "political" in public, though her advice to ministers in private is enriched by her long experience. More criticism is made of the amount of state funding that the upkeep of the monarchy and various palaces cost, but increased tourism, lobbying overseas for trade, and a role in national stability may offset this cost. The occasional wayward trajectory and scandal surrounding other members of the royal family—such as the allegations against Prince Andrew in 2022 for having sex with a trafficked minor—are often causes of criticism. Similarly, there is the apparent mistreatment of "outsiders" after marrying into the royal family, such as with Princess Diana in the 1990s, and with Meghan Markle, the Duchess of Sussex, in the early 2020s.

Other monarchies in Western Europe tend to possess lower profiles than that in the UK. Monarchs in the Netherlands and Sweden have less formal roles than in the UK, and are less opulent in their approach to governance. In Belgium, the monarch has the tricky role of rising above the squabbling political divisions within the country to provide an element of national unity. In microcountries, such as Liechtenstein and Monaco, monarchies still exert influence. In Spain, the need for the monarchy to provide social cohesion and unity in a potentially divided country was so important to the outgoing fascist leader General Francisco Franco that he reinvented the monarchy that he had dissolved during the 1930s civil war. The king of Spain helped to strengthen the new democracy of Spain post-1975, particularly in the early years, but ongoing corruption charges against King Juan Carlos dogged his later years, leading to his abdication in June 2014 and self-exile from Spain to the United Arab Emirates in August 2020.

In countries with constitutional monarchies, the influence cast by the royal family tends to be more social than political. They are usually at the pinnacle of the social order, a relic of social class and divisions that continue to have some resonance today. In the UK, an award by the queen is still worthy of receipt and provides social recognition. Other monarchies of Europe succumbed during violent periods of their history. In France, the 1789 revolution put an end to the royal family, though there was a short-term reversal to monarchy during the mid–nineteenth century. Other monarchies, such as in Austria and Russia, were pushed aside during World War I, and the spread of communism across Central and Eastern Europe ended most other monarchies in those regions. In their place today are often ceremonial presidents, such as in Germany, where their powers are also constrained by constitutional provisions. There is relatively little enthusiasm for the return of monarchies in these countries.

Box 4.3   Monarchs and Microstates

The small states, or principalities, of Andorra, Liechtenstein, and Monaco have a long history of political change and territorial influence by larger neighbors. With democracy and territorial inviolability as key tenets of Europe today, one can assume that these microstates will remain intact, though never be sure. Each state is wealthy, densely populated, and with long life expectancy. Each has a long-standing tradition of monarchy, though increasingly tempered by constitutional safeguards. Liechtenstein has had a monarchy since the country's inception in 1719. The House of Grimaldi has ruled Monaco since 1297, though with interludes of foreign occupation. Andorra is a shared principality and has had that designation since 1278. The country is sandwiched in the Pyrenees between France and Spain, and has joint monarchs, or coprinces, in the form of the Bishop of Urgell (in the Catalan part of northeast Spain) and the president of France. Even though France is not monarchical, then, its president serves as a joint monarch of Andorra.

Government Administrations or Bureaucracies

The word "bureaucracy" has negative connotations and makes one think of bloated and inefficient workforces. Although these ideas are widespread in Europe, figures suggest a much smaller workforce. According to the EU, the share of workers in government compared to the total workforce has remained constant at about 16–17 percent over the past twenty years. Sweden, Denmark, and Finland (in that order) have the highest number of people in government administration, at around 25–30 percent. Norway, as a non-EU member, is comparable. In contrast, the perception of Germany is as a strong administrative state, but it has the smallest government workforce of any EU member at about 10 percent of its total workforce. In Britain and France, bureaucrats tend to be more generalist, with the ability to move from one department to another, whereas in most other European countries administrators are more specialized and compartmentalized, and so lack mobility.[16]

Another underlying theme of executives is the balance of power between elected ministers and unelected career administrators. Unlike in the United States where the top administrators are politically appointed, throughout Europe senior bureaucrats are normally lifetime careerists, supposedly politically "neutral" in their role and advice given to ministers. Some countries, such as Hungary and Poland, have increasingly moved to political appointments. Given that ministers do not necessarily have experience in their cabinet positions, and on average may stay three to four years in that role, they are often dependent on the expert knowledge and advice of their administrative counterparts. The principal-agent concept speaks to the problem of politicians maintaining control over their advisers. Bureaucrats have the opportunity to shape policy to their interests, to slow down the implementation of policy to which they might disagree, and in a worst-case scenario hang on and slow policies until a successor politician comes into office. It is arguably better for the development of sound policy to listen to the opinions of these seasoned administrators but, conversely, the elected politicians are there to pursue a policy mandate irrespective of the opinions and biases of the careerists.

This relationship can be bitter at times. We can see the spate of complaints seeping out of Whitehall in the UK by senior civil servants unhappy that their advice was spurned and ignored by the Labour governments of Tony Blair and Gordon Brown, but also by the more recent Conservative governments of David Cameron, Theresa May, and Boris Johnson. In France, a similar tension often exists with the *énarques*, the cadre of officials trained at the elite École Nationale d'Administration (ENA) in Strasbourg, although here the blending of government ministers and bureaucratic officials is more complete. Unlike with bureaucracies in other countries, the ENA has provided a stream of government officials and politicians since its foundation in 1945 by Charles de Gaulle. This includes four presidents and eight prime ministers. This sense of entitlement and elitism along with their almost total grip on government led President Macron, himself an ENA graduate, to threaten to disband the institution in 2019 as a response to popular protests.[17] Following continuing protests and with an eye on the 2022 elections, Macron followed through with his threat and the ENA closed in December 2021.

At the other end of the spectrum, a shortage of skilled government personnel along with low salaries can undermine the ability of executives to develop and implement sound policy. For example, some CEE governments can find it difficult to attract high-quality administrative personnel into government because of much better and higher paying opportunities in business or in the EU bureaucracy. The highest average salaries for officials, as perhaps expected, are in Nordic countries at an average of €4,000 a month, whereas they are €500 in Bulgaria, €600 in Romania, and €700 in Hungary. Even when we take into account relative purchasing power and the different costs of living, the differences are quite large.[18]

The Council of the European Union

The Council of the European Union is a key decisionmaker within the EU and forms part of the executive.[19] Normally referred to simply as "the Council," or informally as "the Council of Ministers," the Council represents the twenty-seven member states at the ministerial level, and thus is critical in shaping the policy and direction of the EU. The Council has deliberated in Brussels since its establishment in 1958. The Council is also the location where key votes on European policy take place, often by qualified majority vote (QMV), but also by simple majority vote or unanimity depending on the issue.[20]

The actual representation on the Council differs depending on the issue at hand—agriculture ministers, for example, show up for discussions on agricultural policy, or transport ministers on transportation, and so on. There are, in fact, ten different councils, and these meet as needed depending on the issues under discussion. These are:

1. Agriculture and Fisheries
2. Competitiveness
3. Economic and Financial Affairs
4. Education, Youth, Culture, and Sport
5. Employment, Social Policy, Health, and Consumer Affairs
6. Environment
7. Foreign Affairs
8. General Affairs
9. Justice and Home Affairs
10. Transport, Telecommunications, and Energy

The power of the Council rests with its key decisionmaking and treaty signing capability, although the European Parliament increasingly shares some of this capability. Ultimately, though, the EU is not going to move forward on any major policies without the Council's approval. How voting takes place between twenty-seven national governments is a contentious topic and agreements on voting powers are difficult to reach. In the past, every time the EU expanded, another round of debate on voting powers ensued. In essence, the Council previously weighted voting capacity by population size and economic strength of a country, with Germany getting the most votes and Malta the least. The Lisbon Treaty changed and simplified voting to be a combination of a single vote per country, linked to general population size.

Decisions based on simple majority are normally routine procedural votes (e.g., approving an agenda) requiring fourteen positive votes. Decisions requiring unanimity are often sensitive issues, such as foreign policy, justice and home affairs, membership in the EU, financial issues of the EU, and citizenship. Most decisions take place under QMV, where a positive vote requires 55 percent of member governments in support plus the representation of at least 65 percent of the EU's population. Blocking minorities can prevent the adoption of policies, and for a blocking minority to succeed a vote needs at least four countries representing 35 percent of the EU population. This prevents small countries always blocking policy. For example, the four countries of Malta (0.11 percent of the EU population), Luxembourg (0.14 percent), Cyprus (0.20 percent), and Latvia (0.43 percent) could agree to block a policy but comprise less than 1 percent of the EU's population, so the current policy prevents this. Conversely, France, Germany, Italy, and any other country comfortably pass the threshold to block policy.

Despite the principle of QMV, the reality exists that if a government makes this a serious issue and refuses to go along with policy, then oftentimes the policy goes back to renegotiation. This is especially the case if one or more of the larger countries are in opposition. This hierarchy or pecking order within the Council normally includes France and Germany, and to a lesser extent Italy (and formerly the UK). Without their agreement, it is difficult to imagine policy moving forward. Overall, the goal of the Council is to forge consensus wherever possible.

With the constant shifting of representatives and issues through the doors of the ten council(s), the General Secretariat (GSC) of administrators and civil servants is an important body for organizing and facilitating the work of the Council. Also of great importance is the Committee of Permanent Representatives (better known by its French acronym of COREPER).[21] These are normally career ambassadors, who represent the interests of the home governments, and advise on policy to the Council as a whole as well as to their national governmental ministers. COREPER ambassadors reside permanently in Brussels—in contrast to ministers making up the council(s)—and so provide significant influence on European policy and decisions from the shadows and margins of the Council. There are also more than 150 working groups existing within the Council, specializing on a wide variety of issues and advising on these to the Council.[22]

Given the complexity of the work of the Council, along with the European agenda as a whole, control over the management of the Council, including the chairing of sessions, rotates among member countries on a six-month basis. This six-month oversight is the presidency of the Council.[23] This presidency provides countries with an opportunity to emphasize areas of interest to itself, and nominally speak for the interests of Europe on a global stage. Though somewhat equitable, problems have emerged with this system. Larger countries are better equipped with skilled personnel to handle these tasks than smaller countries with limited diplomatic resources. Similarly, larger countries representing the EU likely hold more sway on the world stage than do smaller states.

To counter some of these problems, the Lisbon Treaty moved away from a single country presidency managing distinct six-month periods to a trio of three members sharing the load and helping to provide greater continuity to policy. The trio plans a longer-term EU strategy over an eighteen-month period, enabling each country holding the six-month presidency to focus on specific issues selected. The trio of the presidency for July 2020 to December 2021 was Germany, Portugal, and Slovenia. Once Slovenia's term ended, the next trio for January 2022 to July 2023 was France, the Czech Republic, and Sweden. These trios are already in place up to 2030, with the goal of keeping together each trio of three states to work with each other again in the cycle, attempting to provide a little more continuity to EU policy.

The European Council

The European Council is the organization comprising heads of state or government of the twenty-seven EU member countries.[24] Initially, political leaders met as needed to outline the basic direction of the EU, but given this important role, these meetings were more formal after 1975. The European Council did not come into existence as a formal institution until after the Lisbon Treaty in 2007. Included in its membership is the European Council president as well as the president of the European Commission. It meets two to three times each year, or as needed (and in recent years it has met more frequently, such as eight times in 2019 and 2021, and ten times in 2020), to set out broad outlines and agendas, as well as to drive hard bargains over potential and real roadblocks to cooperation. Alternatively, obstinate heads of government can resist and derail policies favored by the majority of governments here. This is a forum for the classic backroom deal, the all-night session, the arm twisting and cajoling—all before the mandatory group picture and bland communiqué. The European Council is not a pond of equal size fish, and talks and lobbying for support tend to flow out from the partnership of the two largest countries, France and Germany.

The European Council does not vote on or ratify EU treaties, so it is not a formal part of that legislative decisionmaking machinery (even though it is clearly important in framing the strategy for what can or cannot become law). Given that it contains national political leaders who are used to leading policy formulation in their own countries, the Council's deliberations have become increasingly dominant in helping to shape policy.[25] It does have a specific role to play, however, in several important issues and votes, notably in electing the president of the European Council.[26] In addition, it proposes the president of the European Commission and appoints the high representative for foreign affairs and security policy. The European Council also appoints the members of the Commission as well as the executive board of the European Central Bank.

The other major role to outline is that of the European Council president. Before the Lisbon Treaty, the president was more of an informal player, but since 2009 the president's position is transparent and significant.[27] Elected for a two-and-a-half-year period (renewable once) by the European Council sitting as heads of government, the job of the president is to manage European Council meetings and to represent the EU in a diplomatic role. The president is normally someone with a high level of experience in national government, and to date all have served as their country's prime minister. The current president, elected in December 2019, is Charles Michel, former prime minister of Belgium.

The European Commission

The European Commission is another major arm of the EU institutional apparatus, with an important caveat in that the Commission does not vote on policies and has no formal role in treaty approval. This should not undermine its importance, as it has the central power to propose EU legislation, and the key role in implementing policy.[28] It is also the main watchdog over members' adherence to the treaties. The Commission first appeared in 1958, following the amalgamation of the three commissions (ECSC, Euratom, and EEC) after the Treaty of Rome. The Commission is a series of appointed individual commissioners who manage aspects of policy, much like a cabinet of a national government (called here the *college* of commissioners), but the term also refers to the 32,000 administrators who work within the Commission. The Commission is also broken down into thirty-three Directorates-General and twenty-two Executive Agencies to manage commission business, with examples of these units including Agriculture and Rural Development, Competition, and Justice.[29]

The Commission is the official diplomatic representative of the EU, with missions around the world and attached to main international organizations, such as the EU missions to the United Nations in Geneva and New York. The Commission, rather than national governments, represents the EU at the World Trade Organization. When the EU was smaller, EU commissioners were drawn from every country, with the "big four" (France, Germany, Italy, and the UK) getting two commissioners each. As the EU evolved to twenty-seven members, this became unwieldy, and discussions ensued to reduce the size of the Commission. This proved politically difficult, as all members wanted representation in the Commission, and so the Lisbon Treaty confirmed that all members would have one commissioner.

National governments nominate their commissioner, who is often a prominent national political figure. Commissioners gain approval from national delegations in the Council, but also need approval by the president of the European Commission as well as by the European Parliament. At no point do these commissioners need approval from the populations of Europe. Once appointed, commissioners promise to relinquish national ties and interests, and promote the interests of "Europe" and the EU broadly defined.

A core element of the Commission's activity focuses on trade and the single market, of which the Commission acts as the custodian. The Commission is responsible for the promotion of harmonization of policy across the EU, and the support for liberalization of that market. The Commission decides whether companies are abiding by the rules of the market, and has the ability to levy large fines on those that do not. As part of its goal to encourage competitiveness, the Commission rules on whether company mergers are allowable, or whether they venture more toward monopoly. This power is exerted on all companies that wish to do business in the EU market, whether European or foreign.

Some of the largest Commission cases (and fines) have dealt with US technology companies operating in Europe, with Apple, Google, and Microsoft being the most noteworthy, but not the only ones. For example, the eventual 2010 merger of Oracle and Sun Microsystems, two other US-based technology companies, was held up for eight months while the Commission deliberated its impact on competition in the European market. Perhaps the Commission's most prominent case was the 2016 fine of $14.8 billion (€13 billion) against Apple for evading its full payment of taxes to Ireland, which allegedly had set illegally the corporate tax rate at about 1 percent to lure Apple. An EU appeals court struck down the fine in July 2020, but this case could continue to the European Court of Justice.

Tensions naturally surface within the European executive between the interests of national governments, represented by the Council, and the guardians of the interests of Europe, represented by the Commission. While all these bodies suffer from a democratic deficit, the Council, at least, comprises representatives of nationally elected governments. The Commission is completely unelected, and commissioners often unknown, and yet they wield considerable power. These "faceless bureaucrats" or *Eurocrats* of the Commission are often those pushing for greater European integration, and this frequently runs them afoul of public opinion in many countries. There is shared power at the center of Europe, but ultimately in any test of wills, the national governments win out.

The role of Commission president began in 1958, and today the president serves for a five-year term. The European Council appoints the president, who must also gain the approval of the European Parliament. Without such approval, the European Council must select another candidate. Following this appointment, the Council and the president select members of the college of commissioners, who also must obtain parliamentary approval. The Parliament also has the ability to remove the whole Commission including its president, similar to the idea of a no-confidence vote in a national parliament. The nomination of the president takes place just following the EP elections, and the nomination should reflect the outcome of those elections. This is an attempt to bring some democratic input into the Commission, which lacks direct legitimacy in the eyes of many Europeans.

The Commission president directs the work of the Commission and has oversight over the work of the commissioners, as well as the ability to allocate portfolios. The president is the main diplomatic representative of the Commission, and arguably the leader of the European initiative. The current president, Ursula von der Leyen, the first woman to hold this position, served as German defense minister before starting this role in December 2019, and her term expires in October 2024. The position is renewable.

Many other important EU institutions carry out practical and important functions in liaison with the Commission. These include the European Investment Bank, based in Luxembourg, which provides funding for projects, and the European Ombudsman, based in Strasbourg, which intervenes on behalf of whistleblowers or those who feel unfairly treated within the EU organization. In addition, the EU has fifty-one agencies, specializing in a wide variety of issues, with headquarters scattered across the continent.[30] Examples of these agencies are: the European Agency for Safety and Health at Work (EU-OSHA), based in Bilbao; European Border and Coast Guard Agency (Frontex), based in Warsaw; European Environment Agency (EEA), based in Copenhagen; European Police Office (Europol), based in The Hague; and European Union Intellectual Property Office (EUIPO), based in Alicante. All these agencies provide high-level, professional fact-finding and research input to the main EU institutions in Brussels, as well as help monitor and implement policies in their respective areas.

Judicial Systems

There are many different judicial systems across Europe, reflecting historical tradition and development. These systems tend to divide into two. There is a system based on common law and precedent, exemplified by the UK (excluding Scotland) and Ireland, where law is not only made from legislation, but also through interpretation by the courts. The second operates with codified law (often called Napoleonic, dating from 1804 in France, though the Romans used a similar type of legal system in their empire), such as found across much of continental Europe, where less interpretation of the law is the norm, and reliance is on a rational, defined set of laws less open to interpretation. The Russian Civil Code follows a similar logic. Legal systems across Europe also operate in different ways, from the preference for jury trial in the UK to trial before judges in much of Europe, or in terms of the powers of individual prosecutors to pursue potential criminals, such as found in Belgium and Italy.

Judicial Review

At the constitutional level, the power of judiciaries in maintaining a separation of powers also differs. Although Austria founded its judicial review system after World War I, perhaps the Federal Constitutional Court of Germany, based in Karlsruhe, provides the strongest example of judicial review in Europe, where the court reviews government decisions and policies for their constitutionality. The two federal houses elect judges for twelve-year, nonrenewable terms, with votes to some extent based on party composition in those houses. The court is split into two branches of eight judges each to facilitate business (one court for basic litigation, the other for more political issues between the branches of government), but the full court is needed for major (constitutional) opinions. In France, constitutional review takes place in a Constitutional Council, established in the 1958 constitution, after approval by the legislature but before the president signs a policy into law. Former presidents have the ability to sit on this court, and appointees are often prominent politicians. The nine appointees serve nine-year nonrenewable terms, with a third replaced every three years. The president along with the presidents of the Senate and National Assembly each get to select three members. In an addition to checking the constitutionality of legislation, the court also is the country's official location for the approval and dissemination of election results. Similar constitutional courts exist across most of Europe, including Russia and Turkey, although their powers (and independence) vary from country to country.

In France and Germany, many of the cases coming to the court originate from opposition politicians, rather than through the legal system. For example in France, a petition from sixty (opposition) politicians within the National Assembly or Senate automatically places a case with the Constitutional Council. Most other countries in the continent do not allow such structured review, but still maintain judicial independence. In Sweden, for example, judicial review takes place in a decentralized manner by local courts, as there is no national constitutional court. Interestingly, none of the other four Nordic countries possesses a national constitutional court.

In the UK, debate on judicial reform began in 2003, and brought action with the introduction of a supreme court in October 2009 outside of the traditional confines of the House of Lords, which served as an appellate body.[31] The court has grown in stature over the past decade, and has taken over the appellate role of the House of Lords. It remains the highest court of appeal for civil and criminal cases (though not in Scotland for criminal cases). The court made a bold move in declaring actions in temporarily closing parliament by Boris Johnson in 2019 as unconstitutional. It is uncertain whether this will lead to the widespread ability to challenge acts of Parliament for their constitutionality, as the court does not nominally possess the power to usurp the long-standing tradition of the sovereignty of Parliament. The monarch appoints the twelve judges on the advice of the prime minister and a selection committee, and there is compulsory retirement at the age of seventy.

The limited nature of constitutional review in many European systems indicates something of a weakness of the concept of separation of powers between executive, legislative, and judicial functions of government, although more countries are attempting to develop their policies on review. The independence of judiciaries from political meddling is widely entrenched, although some countries, such as Italy, claim to have politically inspired judges. The recent attempts by the national governments in Hungary and Poland to weaken the independence of their judiciaries brought opposition within those countries as well as from the EU. In Poland, for example, the ruling Law and Justice party changed the law to allow the government to fire justices if they involved themselves in "politics," and the government increased its control over the country's constitutional court. The EU responded with threats, including the possible eviction of Poland from the EU, though the EU has been unsuccessful in changing Polish policy to date. There are attempts to use European courts implementing European treaty law to force Hungary and Poland to change their policies.[32] An initial ruling by the Court of Justice early in 2022 offered an avenue to the Commission to withhold funds to recalcitrant member countries. The European courts continue to rule on the constitutionality of EU policies as well as actions taken by any of the EU's twenty-seven members. In a country such as Russia, the central government, and President Putin in particular, heavily influence the judiciary.

Ombudspersons

The concept of an ombudsman (or person) developed in Sweden, when the 1809 constitution created the office. Today, the title of the office across Europe is normally ombudsman. The idea was to have an independent official investigate complaints against government agencies, as Swedes had complained against the deposed monarch. The office resides within the parliamentary structure, and is not a judicial role, although its results are similar to a form of judicial inquiry or review.[33] This system has worked well in Sweden, and today there are several ombudspersons working on an increasing number of issues. These include consumer protection, the safeguarding of children's rights, and greater equality in society. With little binding power, the acceptance of such reports requires a high level of respect and democracy within the government system.

Other Nordic countries adopted the ombudsperson system after World War II, and this is an important feature of their model of government and accountability. In addition, the EU introduced the ombuds office in Strasbourg as part of the 1992 Maastricht Treaty on European Union. The European ombudsperson, as mentioned earlier, is responsible for the protection of individual rights against maladministration by institutions of the EU.[34]

European Courts

The Court of Justice of the European Union (CJEU), informally known as the European Court of Justice (ECJ), is the highest court within the EU.[35] It serves as a supreme court for Europe with the ability to interpret and enforce EU law, as well as to strike down laws deemed unconstitutional and against treaty law. It can supersede national courts in judgments over EU treaties and law. Based in Luxembourg since the court's establishment in 1952, the ECJ is essentially two courts. National governments appoint the judges to both courts for six-year renewable terms. Judges rule, however, as they see best for Europe, rather than follow a nationalistic perspective. The CJEU is comprised of twenty-seven judges, one from each member country. This court handles major issues relating to treaty law and the smooth operations of EU institutions. The General Court comprises two representatives from each country, and handles specialized issues related to treaty implementation, such as policies on competition, trade, and agriculture. This court began operations in 1988 to help with the overall workload, and changed its name after the Lisbon Treaty of 2009 from the Court of First Instance.

At the civil level, the European Court of Human Rights, based in Strasbourg, is technically outside of the realm of the EU. It is an integral part of the Council of Europe, and its main charge is to protect the Council of Europe's European Convention on Human Rights. This convention is a central part of the Council's raison d'être, and was adopted in 1950 as one of the initial actions of the Council. In place for more than seventy years, the convention attempts to protect the individual rights and freedoms of European citizens, including the prohibition of the death penalty and torture.[36] It is the main court of appeal for civil cases, and is the final level of appeal above national courts for such civil cases, although its ability to enforce implementation of decisions over intransigent national governments is limited. The court is comprised of forty-seven members, essentially one for each country member, with each judge appointed for six-year terms, renewable. To date, no member has been suspended or expelled for actions against the convention, though Greece and Turkey received temporary suspensions from the Council for military incursions into politics, and Russia in 2000–2001 for its military actions in Chechnya. The Council also suspended Russia in 2022 following its invasion of Ukraine.

With the development of these international courts, we are beginning to see the development of European-wide institutions establishing the authority to take some legal decisions away from the national level. However, outside of narrow legal decisions within the EU, these courts do not displace the significance or jurisdiction of national courts.

Conclusion

Europe possesses an interesting variety of institutional structures across its forty-plus countries. Although many differences exist, we can see the importance of parliamentary and semipresidential procedures in organizing political life. Within these broad categories are various important distinctions— federal and unitary, parliamentary or semipresidential, unicameral or bicameral. We can see some semblance of similarity across the continent, and this chapter examined these in terms of the roles of legislatures, executives, and judiciaries. Within the EU27, and those countries associated with the EU in Western Europe, a commitment to democracy remains a paramount element of government, though this is under challenge across the continent in many ways.

Despite some commonality in parliamentary democratic institutions, there are significant differences in terms of the respect held for these institutions nationally, as well as how these political systems operate in terms of the political processes. I turn to an examination of these competitive processes in the next chapter, focusing on the contested nature of elections, political parties, and interest groups.

Notes

1. Emmanuel Cartier, Basile Ridard, and Gilles Toulemonde (eds.), "The Impact of the Health Crisis on the Functioning of Parliaments in Europe," Robert Schuman

Foundation Policy Paper, December 15, 2020, https://www.robert-schuman.eu/en/doc/ouvrages/FRS_Parliament.pdf.

2. Catherine E. De Vries, Sara Hobolt, Sven-Oliver Proksch, and Jonathan B. Slapin, *Foundations of European Politics: A Comparative Approach* (Oxford: Oxford University Press, 2021), chap. 7.

3. World Bank, "Proportion of Seats Held by Women in National Parliaments (%) May 2022," https://data.worldbank.org/indicator/SG.GEN.PARL.ZS?name_desc=false; also IPU Parline, "Monthly Ranking of Women in National Parliaments: May 2022," https://data.ipu.org/women-ranking?month=5&year=2022.

4. International Institute for Democracy and Electoral Assistance (IDEA), "Gender Quotas Database," https://www.idea.int/data-tools/data/gender-quotas/database.

5. Rosamund Shreeves and Nessa Boland, "Women in Politics in the EU: State of Play," European Parliamentary Research Service, PE 689.345, March 2021, https://www.europarl.europa.eu/RegData/etudes/BRIE/2021/689345/EPRS_BRI(2021)689345_EN.pdf.

6. "Minorities Still Lack a Strong Voice in New European Parliament," *Reuters*, June 14, 2019, https://www.voanews.com/a/4959282.html.

7. David de Groot, "EU Legislation and Policies to Address Racial and Ethnic Discrimination," European Parliamentary Research Service, PE 690.525, May 2022, https://www.europarl.europa.eu/RegData/etudes/BRIE/2021/690525/EPRS_BRI(2021)690525_EN.pdf.

8. Romain Houeix and Françoise Marmouyet, "Diversity Gains Ground in France's New-Look National Assembly After Vote," *France 24*, June 21, 2017, https://www.france24.com/en/20170621-france-diversity-gains-ground-new-look-national-assembly-after-legislative-election.

9. Mara Bierbach, "Who Makes Up the New Bundestag?" *Deutsche Welle (DW)*, October 24, 2017, https://beta.dw.com/en/germanys-new-bundestag-who-is-who-in-parliament/a-41082379.

10. "Election 2019: Britain's Most Diverse Parliament," *BBC News*, December 17, 2019, https://www.bbc.com/news/election-2019-50808536.

11. European Parliament, "Number of MEPs to Be Reduced After EU Elections in 2019," June 13, 2018, https://www.europarl.europa.eu/news/en/press-room/20180607IPR05241/number-of-meps-to-be-reduced-after-eu-elections-in-2019.

12. For an overview of the EP, see European Union, "European Parliament," https://europa.eu/european-union/about-eu/institutions-bodies/european-parliament_en.

13. "Number of Prime Ministers in the Nordic Countries by Gender as of November 2021," *Statista*, February 2, 2022, https://www.statista.com/statistics/1085918/prime-ministers-in-the-scandinavian-countries-by-gender/. Sweden gained its first woman premier, Magdalena Andersson, in November 2021.

14. Michael Birnbaum, "'Would This Have Happened If I Had Worn a Suit and a Tie?': EU President Ursula von der Leyen Denounces Sexism in 'Sofagate' Incident," *Washington Post*, April 26, 2021, https://www.washingtonpost.com/world/europe/von-der-leyen-sexism/2021/04/26/5b2738dc-a6b1-11eb-a8a7-5f45ddcdf364_story.html.

15. Countries with some form of constitutional monarchy in Europe are Andorra, Belgium, Denmark, Liechtenstein, Luxembourg, Monaco, the Netherlands, Norway, Spain, Sweden, and the United Kingdom. (As a theocratic city-state, Vatican City is not included.)

16. Tim Bale, *European Politics: A Comparative Introduction,* 4th ed. (London: Palgrave Macmillan/Red Globe, 2017), pp. 78–87.

17. "Why Emmanuel Macron Wants to Abolish ENA, France's Most Elite College," *The Economist,* May 4, 2019.

18. "Share of Government Employment Nearly Stable," European Union, Eurostat, https://ec.europa.eu/eurostat/cache/digpub/european_economy/bloc-4d.html.

19. For a discussion of the institutions of the EU, see Herman Lelieveldt and Sebastiaan Princen, *The Politics of the European Union,* 2nd ed. (Cambridge: Cambridge University Press, 2015).

20. European Union, "The Council of the European Union," January 31, 2022, https://www.consilium.europa.eu/en/council-eu/.

21. (Le) Comité des représentants permanents.

22. Council of the European Union, "Council Preparatory Bodies," https://www.consilium.europa.eu/en/council-eu/preparatory-bodies/.

23. Council of the European Union, "The Presidency of the Council of the EU," https://www.consilium.europa.eu/en/council-eu/presidency-council-eu/.

24. Council of the European Union, "The European Council," https://www.consilium.europa.eu/en/european-council/.

25. Jean-Guy Giraud, "The European Council: A Self-Proclaimed 'Sovereign' Off the Rails," Robert Schuman Foundation Policy Paper, no. 574, October 13, 2020, https://www.robert-schuman.eu/en/doc/questions-d-europe/qe-574-en.pdf.

26. Council of the European Union, "The Role of the European Council in Nominations and Appointments," https://www.consilium.europa.eu/en/european-council/role-nominations-appointment/.

27. Council of the European Union, "The President's Role," https://www.consilium.europa.eu/en/european-council/president/role/.

28. European Parliament, "Fact Sheets on the European Union: The European Commission," https://www.europarl.europa.eu/factsheets/en/sheet/25/the-european-commission.

29. European Commission, "How the Commission Is Organised," https://ec.europa.eu/info/about-european-commission/organisational-structure/how-commission-organised_en.

30. European Union, "Institutions and Bodies Profile," https://europa.eu/european-union/contact/institutions-bodies_en.

31. The Supreme Court (UK), https://www.supremecourt.uk/index.html.

32. Eric Maurice, "Protecting Checks and Balances to Save the Rule of Law," Robert Schuman Foundation Policy Paper, no. 590, April 6, 2021, https://www.robert-schuman.eu/en/doc/questions-d-europe/qe-590-en.pdf.

33. M. Donald Hancock, "Sweden: Where Is the Power?" in M. Donald Hancock, Christopher J. Carman, Marjorie Castle, David P. Conradt, Rafaella Y. Nanetti, B. Guy Peters, William Safran, and Stephen White, *Politics in Europe,* 5th ed. (Washington, DC: CQ Press, 2012), pp. 455–456.

34. European Union, "European Ombudsman," https://europa.eu/european-union/about-eu/institutions-bodies/european-ombudsman_en.

35. Court of Justice of the European Union, https://curia.europa.eu/jcms/jcms/j_6/en/.

36. Council of Europe, "The European Convention on Human Rights," https://www.coe.int/en/web/human-rights-convention/home. The Council of Europe has made available a simplified summary of the European Convention on Human Rights for popular consumption; see Council of Europe, "European Convention on Human Rights

(Simplified Version)," https://www.coe.int/en/web/compass/european-convention-on-human-rights. On a personal note of privilege, the court banned corporal punishment in UK public (government-funded) schools, taking effect in 1986, though a little late to benefit this author. Students in private schools could receive corporal punishment until 1998. The terminology can be confusing because private schools in the UK are commonly referred to as "public" schools.

5

Groups and the Contest for Power

ALTHOUGH WE MAY THINK OF EUROPE AS HAVING A LONG HISTORY OF democratic representation and institutions, this is actually not the case through much of the continent. The vast majority of women, for example, could not vote until the twentieth century, as late as 1944 in France and 1971 in Switzerland. Germany had a brief affair with democracy in the early 1920s in the Weimar Republic, but did not fully embrace democratic government until the 1950s (in West Germany), and as a unified Germany not until the 1990s. Portugal and Spain had military rule and nondemocratic forms of government until the overthrow of fascism in the mid-1970s—with democracy consolidated by their membership in the European Union in 1986. Greece suffered a coup d'état in April 1967, with military rule continuing until 1974, and EU membership allowed in 1981. Russia began to tinker with ideas of democracy only in the late 1980s and early 1990s under Mikhail Gorbachev and Boris Yeltsin, and then gradually reversed this trend after 2000 under Vladimir Putin. Much of Central and Eastern Europe began to implement democratic principles only in the early 1990s after the end of Soviet control, and some of these states are barely democratic even today.

This chapter analyzes the participatory frameworks of Europe—primarily elections, political parties, and interest groups—illuminating the similarities and differences of structures and activities. It also assesses the limitations of democratic participation in a number of countries. At a basic level, we can argue that most European countries share a common underpinning of democratic ideals, but that these play out in very different ways. We have elections, political parties, and interest groups across the continent, but all these take quite different

115

forms depending on the country in question. Likewise, the ability of minorities to influence public policy differs by political system, as do the role of the media and the extent of corruption. In addition to the various national structures, there is a layer of EU elections, political parties, and interest groups for the EU27, and these complicate issues of participation. History and political culture also play important roles in shaping attitudes toward democratic government.

Socialization, Culture, and Political Participation

Socialization considers the methods by which we learn about our society, and culture implies the values and beliefs that we hold. Much of the pioneering work on the importance of culture came from Gabriel Almond, as discussed in Chapter 1. Political culture links to our understanding of social constructivism, which shapes our perception of the political environment. These are never easy concepts to consider, and can vary depending on our level of focus. Is there a single political "national" culture in Belgium, for example, or multiple cultures etched by divisions between Flemish and French subcultures, or by the fractured political landscape of numerous political parties and, in particular, the strong voice of the far right? Can we talk of a homogenous British political culture as surging Scottish and Welsh nationalism and identity undermine the dominance of Englishness, and as Northern Ireland deals with its own significant soul-searching for a common political mind-set and potential unification with Ireland? We can see the complexity of identity in the former Yugoslavia, as numerous states struggle to consolidate their own identities and institutions, along with entry into the EU.

At the national level, we can ask questions regarding the strength of a common political culture in the light of regional, ethnic, linguistic, religious, gender, or class distinctions. Attempts made by the EU to create some sort of non-threatening yet viable European political culture complicate the issue, and try to cement support across the continent for the institutions and the concept of the Union. Creating citizens of Europe, who embrace a pan-European political outlook and belief system alongside national and subnational ones, has proved difficult to date, and offers the prospect of multiple political identities.

Democracy prides itself on allowing for participation and choice by individuals in the political process, but there is a wide divergence of activity. For most Europeans, their only substantial form of political participation is voting in a national election and, even then, more than one-third of voters generally do not participate. Local government and European elections fare much worse in terms of voter turnout, apathy, and levels of interest, often helping to skew results in favor of extremist agendas. European Union elections tend not to focus on European policy issues, but rather reflect national issues and performance, to support or punish national political actors, or to judge the relevancy of the EU to the individual country and its citizens. These EU elections rarely reach 50 percent voter turnout, even when they are held only every five years.

Participation in other aspects of political life besides elections varies on the issue and by country. Antiwar rallies, such as against the 2003 US and British invasion of Iraq, or protests against recession and budget cuts can often put tens of thousands of people in the streets, but such intensity is difficult to maintain for any length of time. The impact of such protests vary, though rarely are they effective in changing government policy.[1] One major exception to this are the rallies that took place across CEE in the late 1980s in protest against their communist governments. In Poland, for example, the Solidarity trade union, based in the Gdansk shipyards, was instrumental in building opposition to the central government. In Czechoslovakia, protests in the Velvet Revolution at the end of 1989 included up to half a million Czechs in the streets. Leaders of these opposition movements, namely Lech Wałęsa in Poland and Václav Havel in Czechoslovakia, both went on to become the founding president of their respective country after the collapse of Soviet control.

Box 5.1   The Human Freedom Index

This index, published annually by the Cato Institute (United States) and the Fraser Institute (Canada) uses seventy-six indicators to compare the level of freedom of citizens across the world. These indicators include the effectiveness of the rule of law, freedom to practice religion, the openness of civil society, and the free movement of people. It can be used as a brief, shorthand way to consider the relative openness of society and the ability of people to participate politically, as well as an indicator of the level of democracy. In the 2020 Human Freedom Index report, the highest-ranking European country is Switzerland in second place (New Zealand tops the list). All five Nordic countries score in the top 20, with Denmark leading the pack at fourth. Spain (29), Italy (31), and France (33) appear slightly lower on the index, indicating some social dislocation within their societies. Poland (45) and Hungary (49) score even lower, underscoring the movement away from democratic norms in both countries. A huge gulf exists, however, between these and Russia (115) and Turkey (119), where authoritarianism has displaced any semblance of democracy.[a]

Note: a. Ian Vásquez and Fred McMahon, *The Human Freedom Index 2020: A Global Measurement of Personal, Civil, and Economic Freedom* (Washington, DC: Cato Institute/Vancouver: Fraser Institute, 2020), https://www.cato.org/sites/cato.org/files/2020-12/human-freedom-index-2020.pdf.

Elections

The holding of regular, freely contested elections within a universal electorate is a critical element of democracy. Such elections developed slowly in Europe, and were evident in a few countries in the nineteenth century, albeit without women having the vote. These elections helped to stave off domestic unrest and political instability, and modestly shrank inequality. For example, in France and Germany, extension of the franchise to men took place immediately following the uprisings of 1848. In contrast, Sweden expanded the franchise to men only in 1909.[2] In Britain, the extension of the franchise to increasing numbers of men through the Reform Acts of 1832, 1867, and 1884 transformed the country away from simply a landowning elite in control.[3] Such extension of the vote was rarely easy, and required significant political pressure, as Box 5.2 illuminates.

Box 5.2   Peterloo, Chartists, and Suffragettes in the UK

The evolutionary nature of the UK political system belies the fact that the extension of the franchise proved difficult, with major obstacles and violence often occurring. A landmark event was the Peterloo massacre in St. Peter's Field, Manchester (home to the Industrial Revolution), in 1819, where about 60,000 gathered to seek greater political representation, and where 18 protesters died at the hands of military personnel sent to disperse them. Named as a play on words after the 1815 Battle of Waterloo, Peterloo indicated the long road ahead to win the franchise and political rights for the (male) working class. The struggle continued despite widespread government repression, and a People's Charter promulgated in 1838, calling for such things as universal male suffrage, secret ballot elections, equal distribution of districts based on population, and annual elections. The chartist movement per se faded in the 1860s, though not the desire for reform nor the government's opposition. Many men received the vote in 1867 (though it was 1918 before all men received the vote), and secret ballots were the norm in elections after 1872. The idea of women receiving the vote had received some support among chartists, but it was after the 1860s that a movement led by women emerged to promote suffrage. Initially non-violent, their calls faced outright opposition by government, and the suffrage movement, in response, became more activist by the turn of the century. Their protests at Parliament, Buckingham Palace, and sporting events continued to face government resistance, and arguably alienated some support. It was not until after World War I—and women's important roles in that war—that social norms changed to enable women to vote. Initially, this was for property-owning women (such women had actually received the franchise in the Isle of Man in 1881), but with the success of this, all women received the vote in 1928. Similar sets of events were common across most of Europe as women struggled for political recognition.

Following World War I, more countries adopted democratic elections, especially in newly constituted countries such as Czechoslovakia and Poland. Increasing authoritarianism during the 1930s, however, undermined elections in some of Europe's largest countries as fascism took hold, especially in Germany, Italy, and Spain. When Germany invaded in 1938, Czechoslovakia was the last remaining democratic country in CEE. After World War II, elections became a central plank of public policy in Western Europe, reinforced by the EU and its policy to admit only democracies into its membership. One of the earliest examples of the power of elections was in the UK with the ejection of war leader Winston Churchill in the national elections of July 1945, less than two months after the war in Europe ended (and before the end of the war in Asia). Across CEE, however, fair elections fell victim to manipulation by the Communist Party of each country. Rigged single-party elections became the norm for decades until the 1990s, when these countries were able to develop their own party structures and electoral systems. Their initial elections were monitored closely with the hope that democracy could quickly take root in the region, and indications were that these early elections were relatively free.[4] Elsewhere, Portugal and Spain, notably, also suffered in their democratic growth because of the continuation of fascist governments until the 1970s.

Elections are at the core of democratic life, giving citizens the exercise of a degree of control and accountability over their elected representatives. Admittedly, this can be quite limited control as elections happen at infrequent intervals, and the influence that citizens hold at times other than elections is perhaps minimal. Elections take place at local, national, and European levels, although the turnout is largest at national elections. Some countries, such as Belgium and Luxembourg, have compulsory voting, so their turnout is normally around 90 percent of the eligible population. But voting turnout in other countries is generally in the 60–70 percent range for national elections, and considerably lower for local and European elections. The 2019 EU parliamentary elections had an average voter turnout of 50.66 percent, the highest turnout since 1994, though this average masked low turnout in countries such as Slovakia (22 percent) and the Czech Republic (28 percent).[5] There is uncertainty about what actually drives people to vote in Europe. Besides obvious motivations, such as economic interest, there also appears to be some residual influence of factors like class identification and religion.[6]

There are numerous national distinctions in the management of elections to the extent that every country possesses a unique system.[7] The electoral systems, however, tend to boil down to different permutations of two main models. They are the single-member, single-district system (first-past-the-post [FPTP]) typical of the UK, and the multiple member (multiple winner) proportional representative system typical of the majority of European countries. There are also hybrid models with combinations of these two, such as in Germany, Italy, and Russia. Electoral systems help to influence the number of viable political parties competing in each system, as Maurice Duverger, a French political scientist and politician, initially explained in the 1950s, although political culture and strategic voting are also factors.[8] I outline the main features of each system, with examples below.

Single-Member Districts

The single-member, single-district system provides a single winner in each electoral district based on a plurality of votes won, or a first-past-the-post system. The main example of this system in Europe is the UK (although not including Northern Ireland), and there are similarities to the electoral system in the United States.[9] In the UK, the country has 650 electoral districts, with one winning candidate emerging from each with a simple plurality. It is quite common for the losing candidates to possess a majority of the combined votes, with the winning candidate often possessing only 30–40 percent of the vote.[10] Although not strong from an equity or representative standpoint, this electoral system reduces the number of parties likely to win because the more established parties tend to hold an advantage. This system also reduces the likelihood that new national parties can develop. The result usually is a single party in control of the government, normally with representation larger than their percentage of the vote, arguably making policy formulation somewhat easier without the need for coalitions.

In the December 2019 UK general election, for example, the Conservative Party won a sweeping victory, but the figures show how their vote received inflated gains. Of 650 total seats in the House of Commons, the Conservatives received 43.6 percent of the vote, and yet received 365 seats (or 56.15 percent of the total seats). For the losing Labour Party, the inverse occurred, in that the party received 32.2 percent of the vote, but only 203 seats (or 31.23 percent of the total seats). The Liberal Democrats suffered, as usual, in being the third party by receiving 11.5 percent of the vote, but only 11 seats (or 1.69 percent of the total seats). For the Labour and the Liberal Democrat parties, receiving widespread support across the country but coming in second or third in each district won the party nothing. Conversely, for the Scottish Nationalists, having their vote concentrated in Scotland was beneficial in their ability to win these local races. They converted 4.4 percent of the total UK vote into 52 seats (or 8 percent of the total seats).

A variation on this FPTP system is in France, where two consecutive elections, or a double ballot, take place. The first election serves as a form of primary election, where all candidates take part to reveal their relative strength. If a candidate wins 50 percent or more of the vote (a majority), then there is a declared winner without a second vote, though this does not happen often. Otherwise, any candidate with more than 12.5 percent of the vote can go forward, but normally the top two vote getters move into a second round of voting, allowing the winner then to always obtain a majority of the votes. The double ballot takes place in presidential elections and in elections for the National Assembly.[11] The French system tends to limit the number of parties that win and are therefore represented in government, even though unlike the UK (or the United States) the country often has more than two viable political parties.

Proportional Representation

A drawback to the plurality model is that those people who vote for losing candidates are true "losers"—even if they form a majority of the electorate, they gain no representation. The proportional representation (PR) system attempts to tackle this issue by having a system of multiple winners inside of an enlarged electoral district. Forty countries—the vast majority—inside Europe use some form of PR elections, including all European Parliament

---

Box 5.3   The French Presidential Elections of 2017 and 2022

In the French presidential election of 2017, eleven candidates stood in the first round on April 23. The two top vote recipients, Emmanuel Macron (Republic on the Move [La République en Marche!]) and Marine Le Pen (National Front) went on to the second ballot on May 7. Macron won the second round with 66.1 percent of the vote to Le Pen's 33.9 percent. This recorded a significant victory by Macron, and so strengthened his legitimacy, even though in the first round he had beaten Le Pen by less than 3 percent (24.01 percent to 21.3 percent). Turnout in the first ballot was 77.7 percent, and for the second 74.6 percent. The elections for the National Assembly followed the presidential elections about a month later (June 11 and 18). Although this election also resulted in a resounding victory for Macron's (new) party, turnout for the two elections was only 48.7 percent and 42.6 percent.

In the 2022 presidential election, Macron and Le Pen again topped the first round on April 10, separated by less than 5 percent of the vote. In the second round on April 24, Macron won 58.5 percent of the vote to Le Pen's 41.5 percent, a much closer margin than in 2017, reflecting the increasing influence of far-right voters. The voting turnout, however, was the lowest in presidential elections since 1969, pointing to widespread disillusionment with French politics. Macron's Ensemble! coalition lost its absolute majority in the June 2022 National Assembly elections.

elections.[12] This system links the proportion of votes received to a proportion of seats awarded in the national legislature, though each country has variations on that theme. The primary method of counting is the D'Hondt method, named after the Belgian mathematician, Victor D'Hondt, who designed the system in 1878. Although complex, this method minimizes the number of votes left aside in the calculation of proportionality.

Many countries have a minimum "threshold" of votes that a party must receive nationally to gain any representation—as an example, this is 5 percent for a number of countries, including Croatia, Czech Republic, Estonia, Germany, Hungary, Poland, and Russia. For some countries, such as Germany and Serbia, ethnic minority parties have the threshold waived. In Poland, the threshold waiver also exists for ethnic minority parties, but there is an 8 percent threshold for coalitions, so three different thresholds are in effect. This is only for the lower house, or Sejm, because elections to the upper house, the Senate, utilize FPTP. These different electoral systems for the two houses led to different parties gaining control of them after the October 2019 elections.

The Netherlands has no threshold, so with 150 seats in the lower house, the House of Representatives, a party needs only 0.67 percent of the vote to get a representative elected. The country divides into twenty electoral districts, with twenty separate lists of candidates. There were thirteen parties represented in the Dutch House of Representatives after the 2017 general elections. Even with a threshold of 4 percent, Sweden had eight parties represented in its unicameral Riksdag following the 2018 national elections. In Sweden, the country divides into twenty-nine electoral districts, with elections following a distinct procedure. Voters have the choice of three colored ballots, with the purpose to vote strictly for the party list, to provide preferences to the party list, or to write in one's own candidate. In the past, voters selected their preferred ballot in public, and challenges went to the EU to overturn this. Sweden changed procedure in 2019, with the selection of the ballot now taking place in secret.

The net effect of all these slightly different systems is to put more parties into the winning arena, therefore enabling a greater number of parties to gain representation in the national legislature. While creating an arguably more democratic and representative system, the downside can be a splintered political system with multiple smaller parties leading to the need for coalition government. Another issue is the weakening of an individual candidate's relationship to voters, as votes tend to link to party lists and not to individual candidates. About 75 percent of European elections use this simple PR system, with a closed list of party officials, or with an open list where voters rank party officials or add other names. Senior members of the party place themselves at the top of the list, increasing their chances of election. In Switzerland, electors rank the candidates in the list rather than the parties, though this is something of an exception. Two countries, Ireland and Malta, use a more complicated single transferable vote (STV) system, where electors designate their candidates by preference and, once a candidate receives sufficient votes for election, then votes shift to second or third choice candidates. This makes sure that those elected have the widest popular support within society.

Hybrid Mixed-Member Elections

Seven European countries use a hybrid model, where some seats are allocated by FPTP, and others on the basis of PR. In Germany, we see the standard model where half of the seats in the Bundestag are allocated to each of the two electoral systems (electors have two votes, one for a candidate, and the other for a party). This combines the practical need for limited numbers of parties for easier governing, but caters to a greater sense of representation of the diversity of public preferences and allows for the growth of new parties. This two-vote system helped the rise of the Green party in the 1980s and the rapid rise of the far-right Alternative for Germany party after it was founded in 2013. The number of members in the Bundestag can differ slightly as numbers round up to accommodate the PR-elected candidates. This mixed-member system split on a fifty-fifty basis is also in use by the Welsh and Scottish Assemblies, and by the Russian Duma.

Other countries offer a similar kind of mixed-member system, notably Andorra, Hungary, Italy, Lithuania, North Macedonia, and Ukraine. In these systems, however, there is less effort to link the results of the first vote when calculating the PR allocation, but rather the PR allocation adds to whatever result the first vote produces. This can lead to exaggerated power of the winning party, as we see in Hungary with the Fidesz party. In addition, the split is usually not fifty-fifty, but each allocation varies by country. In Italy, for example, the Chamber of Deputies allocates seats with 37 percent from the first (FPTP) vote, and 63 percent from the second (PR) vote. In Hungary, the allocation for FPTP is 53 percent.

Referenda

A referendum is a mechanism used at times in many European countries to seek the opinion of the public on a particular issue. Referenda can be in regional or local elections, but here I focus on referenda at the national level. These votes can be binding or nonbinding depending on the country's laws. Switzerland uses referenda frequently to handle national issues, more so than other European countries. Three national referenda took place in Switzerland during 2018, for example, and two additional referenda occurred in February 2020. In September 2020, Swiss voters approved a plan to provide at least ten days of paid paternity leave, and turned down a proposal to close their borders to EU citizens.[13] Three referenda took place in March 2021, including a controversial ban on the wearing of the veil in public. This passed with 51 percent of the vote, and was opposed partly because of the fear of the impact on Middle Eastern tourism to the country.[14] In February 2022, a referendum succeeded in banning advertising of cigarettes to minors. The primary reason for so many referenda in Switzerland is that the population can call a referendum by way of a petition, with 50,000 signatures needed for an optional referendum, and 100,000 needed for a mandatory or constitutional referendum (out of a total national population of 8.5 million). This makes Switzerland something of a quasi-direct democracy (Liechtenstein follows a similar pattern of referenda-driven policy), and helps to maintain a more open framework of government pulling together strong, disparate language and cultural groups.

France and the UK have used referenda occasionally, but few political parties support the concept. The UK undertook a referendum in May 2011 potentially to change the electoral system to a proportional representation (alternative vote) system. This was heavily defeated, so the single-member system survived (although Britain was required to use a PR electoral system in European Parliament elections when it was an EU member, and PR is used in Northern Ireland). Austria (in 1978) and Sweden (in 1980) held referenda regarding the future of nuclear power in their countries. Austria turned down the option, whereas the results of Sweden's nonbinding referendum were more inconclusive and did not change official policies. On abortion rights, the predominantly Catholic microstate of San Marino overwhelmingly approved abortion rights for the first time in a referendum in September 2021.

In the past, some EU members have put major political initiatives to the vote, most notably regarding membership in the EU and the proposed European constitution. When ten countries joined the EU in 2004, all of them except Cyprus (due to its internal political problems) held a referendum on membership, a condition laid down by the EU itself. On the issue of the European constitution, four countries (France, Luxembourg, the Netherlands, and Spain) held referenda in 2005, with only Luxembourg and Spain voting in favor. The tendency to have these European initiatives voted down by European populations led to national parliaments preferring to handle these issues. Studies show a consistent divergence in support for the EU between elites (high) and citizens (low), with the smallest gap in Belgium, Luxembourg, and the Netherlands.[15] In 2009, for example, only one country's citizens (Ireland) voted on the Lisbon Treaty, and the other twenty-six countries decided against testing the public will, for fear of a veto. For the Treaty of Nice, Ireland had rejected the treaty in a referendum in 2001 before narrowly approving it in a second referendum in 2002. Ireland approved abortion rights in a referendum in May 2018. Norway and Switzerland each held two referenda on entry into the EU, which all failed. In light of Russia's invasion of Ukraine, however, Danes chose in a referendum in June 2022 to reverse their long-standing refusal to take part in EU Security Policy.

Germany, in contrast, has limited grounds for a referendum at the federal level, partly with an eye on the manipulative use of populism by Adolf Hitler in his rise to power. The provisions for a referendum include changing the constitution and changing the status of the territory of the *länder*. Germany did not hold a referendum on any of the major treaties within the EU, nor did it hold one regarding reunification in 1990, even though this action essentially changed the constitutional framework of the country. A handful of referenda have taken place within states, but this is not the preferred manner of political operation. Political culture has shaped this position along with a fear of the manipulation of popular opinion, as had occurred under Hitler. Belgium and the Czech Republic are examples of countries with no mechanism for a national referendum, although the EU required the Czechs to hold one on EU membership in 2003.

Box 5.4 Britain and Brexit

One of the most renowned and contentious recent examples of a referendum is the UK's vote to leave the European Union in June 2016 (the EU Membership Referendum).[a] Prime Minister David Cameron promised a referendum on the topic if his Conservative Party won the 2015 general election, which it did. He hoped to use the referendum to silence the Eurosceptic wing of his Conservative Party. Although all the "established" parties supported the remain camp, a strong (and controversial) campaign by the leave camp and the UK Independence Party led to a narrow victory by 51.89 percent to 48.11 percent with a turnout of 72 percent of the electorate. Cameron immediately resigned, and his successor, Theresa May, unsuccessfully tried until 2019 to forge an agreement on the terms of EU departure with the EU itself and the British Parliament. Her failure forced her own resignation, and her successor, Boris Johnson, finally managed to gain agreement, and Britain officially left the EU in January 2020. This, however, marked only the start of Britain's bitter divorce settlement, as several years of negotiations take place to finalize all the terms of the new relationship, including the status of Northern Ireland.

Note: a. Britain held a previous referendum to remain in the EU in 1975. On that occasion 67 percent voted to remain. Greenland, an autonomous territory of Denmark, is the only other country to vote to leave the EU, and this was via a referendum in 1982.

European Parliament Elections

Elections to the European Parliament take place every five years, and follow each country's national electoral model—different systems on different days, but the elections are contained to a three- to four-day period. Prior to 1979, national governments appointed members to the EP. These often were already members of their national parliament, and they considered the task of serving on the EP more a welcome distraction than a heavy responsibility. In an attempt to make the EP more meaningful and connected to European populations, direct elections started in 1979.

European elections tend to reflect national issues and tensions, and the country's relationship with the EU, rather than be contests over European issues per se. There is little coordination among parties across the continent, and so we tend to see twenty-seven distinct national elections rather than a single European election. All elections take place on a PR basis, as required by the EU, but each country selects its own type of PR procedure. In Britain, such elections allowed small groups to gain representation in the European Parliament where they were unable to make that breakthrough in the British Parliament (under a FPTP system). Ironically, these parties often were hostile to the existence of the EU, and promoted a distancing of the UK from the EU project from within the EP. The country was divided into twelve multimember electoral districts for the elections, with Northern Ireland, Scotland, and Wales being their own district and England taking the remaining nine.

In the EP elections of May 2019, Britain took part even though it was negotiating a departure from the EU. Following its departure in January 2020, its seventy-three seats in the EP were reallocated, with twenty-seven redistributed to other countries and forty-six seats held back for future member states. This action reduced the EP size from 751 to 705 members.[16] Each country followed its own nationally approved method of election, with seats distributed roughly by population. For example, of the total 751 seats in the EP prior to January 2020, Germany had the most with 96 seats, whereas Spain had 54 seats, and at the other end Malta had 2 seats. Average voter turnout across Europe in 2019 was 50.66 percent as mentioned above, which was a significant uptick on the previous two elections that saw turnouts of 42 percent in 2009 and 2014. The 1979 EP election, the first popular election, was the only one to surpass a turnout of 60 percent to date (61.99 percent), albeit with only nine countries involved.[17] In general, however, national elections in Europe attract a higher turnout than EP elections.[18]

Political Parties

Democracy often hinges on the number and vitality of political parties represented in the national system, giving expression to diverse political viewpoints.

Belgium and the Netherlands, for example, have a significant number of parties represented in the national legislature, far more than a country such as Britain, but this reflects more about the nature of the electoral system than about democracy per se. In the 1990s immediately after the fall of the Berlin Wall, countries in CEE each had dozens of political parties represented in national legislatures. In Poland, for example, sixty-nine parties contested the 1991 elections, with twenty-nine gaining seats in the lower house. These parties often represented individual politicians, and displayed an early yet evolving sense of democracy in these countries. Today, they all have far lower numbers of political parties, but again this should not automatically be viewed negatively in terms of participation in the system, rather than as a maturation of political life in the region.

Political parties normally reflect divisions or cleavages within society, so representing social or economic divisions. Traditionally, parties divided on a left-right political axis, influenced by religious and urban-rural factors. This structure is less evident today as new political parties emerge that do not easily fit an ideological pigeonhole.[19] Emerging sets of issues contributing to political factionalism focus on debates over materialism and postmaterialism, by considerations of the impact felt by globalization (winners and losers) due to the country's insertion into the global capital system, and by a growing competition between those favoring green alternative policies as opposed to those promoting a more autocratic or populist agenda.[20] Other factors to consider are the aging of the European population and their changing needs, and the growth of migrants in societies with their slowly increasing political voice (and, of course, the resultant opposition to that voice).[21]

The traditional distinction between political parties and interest groups normally hinges on the argument that the goal of political parties is to control government policy through winning an election: Interest groups merely aim to influence government policy and the policy of political parties. Although this distinction can seem somewhat arbitrary—for example, green, feminist, or populist parties often blur the line between party and interest group—it is helpful for us to distinguish one type of political unit from the other. Parties also tend to aggregate or coalesce issues into a combined platform, whereas interest groups tend to focus on a single issue or cluster of issues primarily linked to their main purpose and rationale. This is especially the case in most European political systems, where two, three, or four main parties dominate the country's politics, irrespective of the total number of parties present. A PR electoral system, however, has the effect of encouraging a multiplicity of parties to form and fight, and so lessens the need for aggregation of issues as parties can remain smaller and more focused on their preferred issues. This also creates a broader spectrum of political parties than in a two- or three-party system.

Some countries display relative stability in their political party structures. For example, the UK's Labour and Conservative Parties have dominated the political landscape for decades. This masks important events in Britain, however, such as the rise of a viable third party, the strength of nationalist parties, particularly in Northern Ireland and Scotland, and the rise of alternative parties, such as the UK Independence Party in the EP elections. In Germany, we see two prominent parties in the Christian Democrats and the Social Democrats, but also the presence of important third parties that are often coalition partners. The Greens and the Free Democrats, for example, joined the Social Democrats in a coalition government in December 2021. We also see radical insurgent parties, such as the Alternative for Germany. In France, mainstream parties regularly morph in terms of name or direction, as they link more often to personalities than in Germany or the UK. For example, the most successful party in the French national elections of June 2017, The Republic on the Move (La République en Marche!), formed as a political vehicle for Emmanuel Macron only in 2016.

The rise of green parties has been quite prominent across Europe. In Germany, as mentioned, The Greens (Die Grünen) have taken a coalition role in both national and *länder* governments. Strong (extremist) right-wing parties have also become much more common, such as in Belgium, France, and Italy, or as in Austria where the Freedom Party has been a coalition partner in government. In CEE, all the political parties (with the exception of the Communist Parties) formed post-1990, and there is still some fluidity in terms of their structures and platforms. Party discipline tends to be quite strong across most political systems, as one's political career depends on adherence to the party goals and rules, especially during PR elections when a career depends on having a name placed on the electoral list.

An important point to stress is the decreasing interest of citizens in formally joining a political party. Almost universally across the continent, membership of political parties is on the decline. Austria appears to have the highest membership in political parties at about 17 percent, but France, Germany, Sweden, and the UK register less than 4 percent membership.[22]

One way to begin our discussion of political parties is to consider them in terms of the traditional labels of party families on the left, center, and right. Although this can be oversimplistic and misleading, it is still helpful to provide a starting framework for analysis. The terms *left* and *right* evolved from the French Revolution in 1789, when the radical groups in the National Assembly seeking change clustered in solidarity to the left of the presiding officer, whereas the conservatives and nobles grouped themselves to the right. This framework helps us to get a useful comparative overview of European political parties. I then go on to discuss other political parties that reflect recent political divisions.

Parties of the Left and Center-Left

The spectrum of political parties differs across the continent, influenced by national culture and issues, and by the nature of each electoral system. It is possible, though, to discern some commonalities. Communist Parties of the (far) left have been present in mainstream politics for decades, though they have struggled a little to find a new identity after 1989. Until the 1980s, Communist Parties in France and Italy were strong; in Italy, the party often received 30 percent of the vote in national elections, before it splintered and resplintered after 1990. In France, the French Communist Party (PCF) became a coalition partner in the national government during 1981–1984 and again from 1997 to 2002, but it has weakened since. On reunification of Germany in 1990, the Communist Party in former East Germany retained some influence under its new name of the Party of Democratic Socialism (PDS), but then merged with other socialist groups in 2007 to form The Left (Die Linke) party. In the 2017 federal elections, The Left won 9.2 percent of the total votes, securing representation in the Bundestag as the fifth-largest party, but slumped to less than 5 percent in the 2021 elections. Communist Parties in other CEE states fell quickly from their position of total dominance after 1989, but remnants are still present across the continent.

Since 1945, some of the most successful political parties in national elections across Europe have been social democratic parties of the moderate or center-left. These parties, which consistently have formed governments, include Social Democrats and socialist or labor parties in countries such as the Czech Republic, France, Germany, Spain, Sweden, and the UK. Although their traditional views on state intervention in the economy have moderated in recent years, their support of social welfare is the strongest driver of their political identity. All promote trade union rights, social safety nets, public education, strong health care protections, and minority rights.

Political trends did not favor the moderate left during the 2010s, as far-right populism gained strength, and conservative politicians pushing neoliberalism gained favor. For example, across CEE by 2020, no social democratic government remained in power.[23] Furthermore, social democratic parties in Britain, France, and Germany witnessed severe electoral reverses during the 2010s and in Italy and Spain remained important players only in coalition with other parties.[24] The Social Democrats (SPD) in Germany reversed that trend in September 2021 as it took the largest share of the vote and became the major partner in a coalition government. In Portugal, António Costa's Socialist Party unexpectedly won an outright majority in national elections in January 2022. In the Nordic bloc, social democratic parties remain important players, but their importance has also declined in recent years. However, Norway reversed this trend in September 2021 when the Labour Party ousted the conservatives.

Parties of the Center

In contrast to social democrats, parties at the center of the ideological spectrum tend to be among the smallest in Europe, though often critical in terms of playing a role in government coalitions. These parties tend to support laissez-faire, neoliberal economic policies of limited government intervention and free trade, and to promote greater freedom of individual action and responsibility.[25] Perhaps the best example of this type of party is the Free Democratic Party (FDP) in Germany, which has served as a partner in government coalitions on and off since 1949, but normally only winning around 10 percent or less of the national vote. In some elections, the FDP failed to pass the 5 percent threshold and so could not gain representation in the Bundestag. The party returned to government as part of the ruling coalition following the 2021 elections with 11.5 percent of the national vote.

In the UK, the Liberal Democrats formed in 1988 as a partnership of the long-established Liberal Party and the much newer Social Democratic Party, a splinter group of the Labour Party. The Liberal Democrats served as a coalition partner in the national government in 2010–2015, when they gained 23 percent of the vote and fifty-seven seats (under FPTP, translating into only 8.7 percent of the seats in parliament) in the 2010 election. The result left the Conservatives without a working majority.[26] Once the Conservatives regained a working majority, they jettisoned the coalition.

The most recent resurgence of the political center is perhaps in France, with the 2017 victory of Emmanuel Macron sweeping him to the presidency and his party, La République En Marche!, to control of the National Assembly. Macron has worked actively to reinvigorate the center inside the EU through the Alliance of Liberals and Democrats for Europe (ALDE), which became Renew Europe after the 2019 EP election.[27] One of his closer partners is Mark Rutte, premier of the Netherlands, whose party, the People's Party for Freedom and Democracy (VVD), has controlled the government coalition since 2010, and won a sweeping victory for its fourth term in March 2021.[28] As a further example, the Centre Party in Finland serves as a member of the government coalition.

Parties of the Right and Center-Right

The Conservative and Christian Democrat parties of the right of the European spectrum are established parties of government across a range of countries. Such parties have controlled government, or government coalitions, over the past decade in countries including Croatia, Germany, Greece, Hungary, Italy, Poland, Spain, and the UK, and they form the largest group (the European People's Party [EPP]) in the EP. More pro-business and promoting traditional values, "stability," "order," and minimal state intervention, these parties have succeeded in capturing the support of many Europeans across the continent.[29]

The Christian Democratic Union (CDU) stands as one of the most important political parties in Germany, and alongside its ally the Christian Social Union (CSU), has had long periods in office. Notable examples include the government of Helmut Kohl between 1982 and 1998 as well as the government of Angela Merkel between 2005 and 2021. The CDU had a poor showing in the elections of 2021, however, even though it came in second just behind the SPD. In the UK, the Conservative Party has also led with long periods in government office, notably during the governments of Margaret Thatcher and John Major from 1979 until 1997, and then under successive leaders from 2010 to present. In Spain, the conservative People's Party controlled government between 1996 and 2004, and again from 2011 to 2018.

Parties of the Far or Radical Right

The parties of the center right have struggled at times to maintain an identity separate from the parties of the extreme right, who support antimigrant, anti-EU, law and order, and pro-nationalism or nativist policies.[30] These populist parties of the radical right have grown significantly in the past decade, notably in Austria, Belgium, France, and Italy, often eating into the support of the center-right parties, but also pulling support from the center-left. The UK Independence Party proved to be influential in its opposition to the continued membership of the country in the EU, and in shaping the Brexit referendum result in June 2016. The party won the largest share of the vote in the 2014 EP elections, promoting a platform against membership in the organization. Following their success in the 2016 referendum result, and facing internal squabbles, the party declined with its mantle taken up in 2018 by the Brexit party. Both UKIP and Brexit had a common link in the leadership of Nigel Farage. The Brexit party scored the highest vote in the 2019 EP elections, again underscoring the determination to leave the EU. The party renamed itself Reform UK in January 2021.

Parties considered initially conservative have moved to the right and become less democratic, such as the governing parties in Hungary (Fidesz) and Poland (Law and Justice). The drift rightward by Fidesz led by the populist Viktor Orbán contributed to its departure from the EPP in March 2021.[31] This shift helped to draw support away from a radical right party, Jobbik (Movement for a Better Hungary), which won close to 20 percent of the vote in the 2018 national elections and became the country's second-largest party. Orbán and Fidesz won a sweeping fourth term in office in national elections in April 2022. Other populist parties have grown rapidly and challenged traditional conservative parties on the right. These populists garner support through anti-immigrant and anti-EU platforms, and gained considerable representation in recent national elections.

One of the largest and best-known far-right parties is the National Rally in France (known as the National Front before 2018). Founded in 1972 under Jean-Marie Le Pen, the party gradually worked toward more mainstream respectability, pushing an anti-EU, anti-immigrant, and anti-NATO policy. The party caused a shock by making it to the runoff stage in the 2002 presidential election, and did so again under the leadership of Le Pen's daughter, Marine Le Pen, in the 2017 and 2022 elections. In these runoff elections, the party suffered a heavy defeat as other parties coalesced to defeat the far right. In the run-up to the 2022 national elections, the National Rally struggled a little as other parties of the right also took up anti-immigrant platforms. The most prominent presidential challenger to Le Pen on the far right was Éric Zemmour, a CNews TV pundit, who espoused extreme anti-Semitic and anti-immigrant views (despite being of Jewish and Algerian descent). Zemmour came in fourth in the first round of the April 2022 elections with 7.1 percent of the vote.

Other significant far-right parties include the League in Italy, the Sweden Democrats, and the Alternative for Germany. The League (before 2018, the Northern League) is a separatist party in northern Italy that calls for increasing regional autonomy within a federal framework, and is especially opposed to redistributive policies toward the south of the country. The League took part as a coalition government partner from 2000 to the present, and was the largest party in Italy during the 2019 EP elections. The Sweden Democrats have grown in importance more recently, with the party finally passing the 4 percent threshold to enter the parliament in 2010, scoring 5.7 percent of the vote in national elections. In 2018, the party was the third-largest in national elections, gaining 17.5 percent of the vote. In Germany, the Alternative for Germany has a more remarkable growth. Founded only in 2013, the AfD scored 12.6 percent of the vote in the 2017 federal elections, making it the third-largest party in Germany, but dropped a percentage in the 2021 elections. Its opposition to mainstream

German policies and to the EU led to the German government controversially proposing security surveillance against it as an extremist and nondemocratic organization in 2021.

The rise of these and other far-right parties is a critical trend in European politics. We can also point to the growth of the Finns Party in Finland, the Swiss People's Party in Switzerland, or Italy's M5S. In Greece, the Golden Dawn party rose to prominence following the Greek financial crisis in 2009, and became the third-largest party in the 2012 elections. It declined during the decade, not winning any seats in the 2019 elections, and essentially disappeared in 2020 following the conviction of its leadership for criminal activity. Virtually all countries of Europe now have viable parties pushing a nationalist, anti-immigrant agenda. Portugal and Spain appeared to have remained outside of this trend, but the far right began to see success in these countries after 2019. In Spain, the Vox party jumped into prominence in November 2019 placing third in Spain's national election, pushing to crush separatist movements such as in Catalonia and opposing immigration.[32] In January 2021, a radical right politician, André Ventura, placed third in Portugal's presidential election, marking the rapid emergence of the far-right Chega party.[33] Chega also placed third in the country's national elections in January 2022.

These parties gain support from each other across Europe, and there is considerable evidence of Russian support to many of them. Their continuing growth and influence across the continent appears steady, especially as they tap into right-wing social movements, and they are likely to retain importance as potential coalition partners in government in many countries.[34] There is no guarantee of this status, however, as the loss of power by the populist Czech premier, Andrej Babis, in elections in October 2021 show. At this stage, most operate within the democratic framework, though whether they support the wider principles of democracy and inclusion is uncertain, certainly not with regard to migrant communities.

Other Political Party Groupings

With widespread proportional representation elections, there are many smaller political parties in European politics that fall outside of a tidy left-center-right political axis, but that can exert influence and that reflect some of the more recent cleavages in European politics. One set of parties that are most notable are the green parties. Perhaps the best known are the Greens in Germany, which served as partners in previous national coalition governments, and joined the government coalition again in December 2021. Smaller green parties are evident in most countries across the continent, especially in Western and Northern

Europe, where the greens tap into the postmaterialism of citizens. Green parties in Belgium, Finland, Ireland, the Netherlands, and Sweden have also served as coalition partners in government.

Regional parties are also prominent in many countries, promoting policies of importance to a particular region. These include Catalan and Basque parties in Spain, or the Scottish Nationalists and the Welsh Plaid Cymru in the UK. In Bosnia and Herzegovina, the political landscape comprises a significant number of ethnic Bosnian (or Bosniak) and Serb parties. Italy has almost forty identifiable regional parties, though most are small, and similarly Spain has over fifteen such parties. These regional parties can legitimately function within the parameters of democratic politics or can drift toward great extremism. Special interest parties are also present in many countries, though they are often small. Parties representing pensioners or older citizens are present in more than a dozen European states, such as the 50Plus party in the Netherlands. Feminist parties exist in a handful of states, such as the Feminist Initiative in Sweden.

Parties in the European Parliament

Political parties at the EP display a similar spectrum of interests and representations to parties at the national level. As discussed above, elections to the EP take place every five years, with the next elections slated for May 2024. Although there are literally dozens of different national parties elected to the EP, the parties join broad coalitions in the EP, sitting by ideology rather than national identity. Parties of the center-left and center-right are the largest groupings traditionally, but these fluctuate with each EP election. Extremist parties of the right and left are present, and tend to hold common views hostile to the EU, even seeking its dissolution. In the EP after the 2019 elections, the 705 members of the EP sit in seven major groupings.[35] The largest groups are the center-right European People's Party (187 seats), the center-left Progressive Alliance of Socialists and Democrats (147 seats), and the centrist Renew Europe (98 seats). The next-largest grouping is Identity and Democracy (76 seats), with a far-right and Euroskeptic agenda.

Interest Groups

Interest groups are important societal actors, and their activities provide a common avenue to promote political involvement. Many groups in Europe are well organized and permanent, with established paths to influence the political system. Interest groups in Europe, however, mimic less the role of political action committees in the United States, which blatantly serve to funnel large amounts of money to political parties and agents. The European pattern of interaction is not as focused on funneling finance, as most countries and the EU have strict limits on financial contributions to parties. National and EU political leaders and the allied bureaucracies, nevertheless, are heavily involved in working with lobbyists and, despite clear ethical mandates, much questionable activity takes place. We look in more detail at some specific areas of interest group activity here, although Chapter 6 discusses more aspects of these social issues, notably regarding peace movements, feminism, and lesbian, gay, bisexual, transgender, and queer/questioning (one's sexual or gender identity) (LGBTQ) groups.

Trade Unions

Trade unions remain influential, though arguably their powers are diminishing in many countries from what they were twenty or thirty years ago. Membership has subsided across much of Europe, except in Italy where there has been a resurgence. Nordic countries remain the highest in terms of union membership, with Denmark, Sweden, and Finland all registering more than 70 percent of workers belonging to unions (Norway stands at around 50 percent).[36] Here, labor unions play a significant collaborative role in shaping national public policy, working conditions, and wage rates.

Farmers' organizations remain quite strong, despite the fact that there are now relatively few farmers in Europe, especially in the western countries of the continent. French farmers are notorious for their ingenious protests and their influence over French and European agricultural policy, and yet French total unionization stands at only around 8 percent of the workforce. On average, unionization across the EU's twenty-seven members stands at about 23 percent of the workforce. With growing neoliberal policies across the continent, the influence of labor as a core interest group has waned.

Business Groupings

Business groups are prominent lobbyists across Europe, normally with close access to governments. At the European level, action is coordinated through the powerful Confederation of European Business, known as Business Europe, which comprises national members from all EU members and seven nonmember European countries, including Norway's Confederation of Norwegian Enterprise and the UK's Confederation of British Industry.[37] Based in Brussels, Business Europe has extensive relations with the European Commission and European Parliament, and can shape and influence EU policy to favor business interests.

They wield much more influence than workers' organizations. There are an estimated 15,000 lobbyists, and up to 5,000 or so interest groups, attached to the EU that lobby on behalf of their specific interests.[38]

Most countries have one organization representing business issues nationwide, but Germany has two. These are the Federal Association of German Industry (BDI), which promotes the interests of large German industry, and the Confederation of German Employers' Association (BDA), which provides a voice for all other companies in the country. These business interests play an important role in shaping German government policy, and in turn EU policy itself.

Religious Groups

Religious interest groups remain strong, especially in countries such as Germany and Italy, where they maintain close ties to political parties. Religious issues also continue to cast influence over public debate in countries such as Ireland and Poland, where debates about abortion rights and LGBTQ rights are prominent. The influence of the Orthodox Church in Greece and Russia remains strong, and in Russia in particular it is seeing a renaissance, especially with its vocal support of Russia's invasion of Ukraine in 2022. Much of the decision-making about religion takes place at the national level, and so lobbying tends to focus there. The Lisbon Treaty, however, through its Article 17 allowed the EU to consider religion in terms of its overall policymaking, and this opened EU institutions in Brussels to increased lobbying from religious organizations.

Environmental Movements

Of growing importance in recent years have been green and environmental movements. These tie to increasing postmaterialism in developed societies, but also link to the fear of the impact of climate change. These groups are most prominent in supporting sustainability across economic sectors, including renewable energy and recycling. In some countries, such as Germany, the Greens have converted themselves into a strong and viable political party, but mostly their role has been pressuring governments to take more account of environmental issues. Vast numbers of other interest groups, lobbies, and nongovernmental organizations, including business lobbies, cover the whole spectrum of political life.

These groups not only are active at the national level, but often are heavily involved in trying to shape European legislation in the EU, primarily engaged with the Commission and the Parliament. This system is still evolving, but lobbyists are becoming a more prominent part of the European legislative landscape in Brussels. All these groups contribute to the development of a nascent Social Europe, often unwittingly, through lobbying at the European level.

One of the more fascinating cases of environmentalism is that surrounding a young Swede, Greta Thunberg, who began to protest climate change as a high school student in a one-person demonstration outside of the Swedish parliament in 2018. Through social media, Thunberg's actions reverberated not just across Europe, but worldwide, as she met with heads of government and addressed the United Nations. Thunberg brought attention to modes of transportation as a feature of climate change, and helped to spur even greater emphasis on sustainable methods of public transport. Her influence continues.

The Media

The print media have a long tradition of involvement in political life across the continent, aiming to keep politicians honest if possible. In most countries, newspapers represent various strands of the mainstream political spectrum, though during the period of communism, this was not the case in CEE. The newspapers themselves often reflect powerful owners and their own personal political stances. Examples today of the control exerted by Rupert Murdoch in the UK, or Silvio Berlusconi in Italy, show that often the media are not as "free" as some think or hope. The *News of the World* tabloid scandal in the UK in 2011 offered insights into how powerful the Murdoch brand had become in considering itself to be above the law. Accused of a series of phone hackings and facing a backlash of opposition, the newspaper closed down, only for a successor to form quickly under Murdoch to take its place. In Italy, former prime minister Berlusconi owned more than 80 percent of all national media channels, an obvious conflict of interest still legal in that country, and leveraged that power to become prime minister.

The power of television has led to greater governmental regulation and often involvement in this industry. However, the satellite and digital revolutions in recent years have led to an explosion in the number of television stations available, and the range of information provided. Much of this proliferation centered in the entertainment and sports arenas, but news coverage has also expanded dramatically. Inside of four years of existence, for example, the right-wing channel CNews owned by the billionaire Vincent Bolloré became France's largest news network, and a launch pad for Éric Zemmour's run for president in 2022.

One area that has not progressed in any significant way is pan-European media. This is largely to do with language, but also links to broader cultural values. The obvious lack of a single unifying European language makes it virtually impossible for media to carry across the continent, although the use of English as a lingua franca has enabled some publications to try; for example, the *Financial Times* touts itself as Europe's business daily newspaper, and the *Economist* seeks a similar niche market. *Le Monde Diplomatique*, a monthly, attempts to straddle the European market with French, English, German (and Kurdish), Greek, Italian, Norwegian, Portuguese, Russian, Spanish, and Turkish editions, as well as editions in other less used languages, such as Albanian and Hungarian.[39] Some media have a European market, but offer different language versions to fit national markets; the TV channel aimed at the youth, MTV, fits this model. Many online-only media sites also attempt multilingual coverage.

Knowledge about what is going on across Europe has heightened, but it is difficult to argue that this has created a greater sense of Europeanness. Peoples' attentions still primarily focus on what transpires at a national level, and interest gets piqued primarily if an event has an impact on their national environment. Many countries, such as Germany and Spain, have powerful regional media, so one cannot even think of dominance at the national level.[40] The vast majority of Europeans read or hear little about neighboring European countries, and often what they do hear is sensational or derogatory, or sometimes prone to xenophobic tendencies. The political scandal that sells in the media is essentially politics at the national level, and the same occurs for sports. As we have already mentioned, many people follow the European Champions League in football/soccer across Europe, but this does not create a European identity. Rather, it promotes national, or even sub-national, interest and pride at the expense of Europe.

Technology has enabled many changes to take place in European media. The internet allows multilingual sites to be available to any viewer at relatively minimal cost. Access to non-European media offers anyone willing to seek out alternative viewpoints that opportunity. The growth of social media sites—such as YouTube, Facebook, and Twitter—allows alternative channels of information flow to those previously considered dominant. In the same vein, any government attempt to control the flow of information through social media has become that much more difficult. The EU continues to act to prevent monopolization of the flow of information through social media, and there are ongoing actions against "big tech."

Globalization has had an impact on the media and the flow of information in Europe, and the internet is today a vital provider of news. The ability to obtain information from almost any source is something of a liberating factor, especially as most countries of Europe purport to allow free media. The delivery of a vast amount of information through the medium of English, including outlets such as the BBC and CNN, as well as written business media such as the

Financial Times, also offers the prospect of a common European transnational media, at least for those with the ability and willingness to access their news in English. It is difficult to find a true pan-European source of news and information besides the EU itself or EU-focused multilingual think tanks, and language issues will continue to make this the case. Short of translating into multiple languages—or all the EU languages as the official European website has to do—it is difficult to foresee the development of a Europe-wide media network, and likely that national and language-based sources will continue to dominate.

The organization Reporters Without Borders compiles a World Press Freedom Index, based on the ability of journalists to go about their business without government intervention and threats. In its 2022 index, thirteen of the twenty best countries for journalists to carry out their work are in Europe, with the top five countries being Norway, Denmark, Sweden, Estonia, and Finland, The UK (24), France (26), and Italy (58) all exhibited some constraints in the freedom of journalists to operate, although Hungary at 85 showed the pressures placed on journalists there by its increasingly far-right government. At the end of the spectrum, Turkey (149) and Russia (155) again show the extent to which they are far apart from the traditional democratic norms of most of Europe, with high levels of hostility displayed to prevent a free press.[41]

One final area to mention concerns the important aspect of trust in the media. This varies widely across Europe. In a Eurobarometer survey taken in early 2021, there was a remarkable difference in the level of trust toward media. Highest levels of trust came in Western European countries, with Belgium, Luxembourg, and the Nordic countries registering more than 70 percent trust in media sources, and the Netherlands topping the list at 80 percent. Conversely, countries in CEE had much smaller numbers of people trusting the media, with Bulgaria (30 percent), Hungary (36 percent), and Poland (42 percent) among the lowest. Interestingly, as an indication of its rather poor political environment, Spain registered only 34 percent trust.[42] Trust in the Austrian media took a hit in October 2021, when revelations that the right-wing chancellor, Sebastian Kurz, had bribed media for favorable coverage forced his resignation.

The Military

The history of Europe over the centuries is one interwoven with the centrality of its militaries. The twentieth century witnessed two world wars fought on European soil, and tens of millions of casualties, as we saw in Chapter 2. However, that century also consolidated the trend toward civilian control over the military. Exceptions to this rule are notable, such as the continuation of military rule in Portugal and Spain until the mid-1970s, or the rule of the generals in Greece after the 1967 coup. Wars flaring across the former Yugoslavia in the 1990s, or between Russia and Georgia in 2008, or between Russia and Ukraine since 2014 highlight that limited war in Europe still exists, but also show that civilian administrations do control their militaries. Militaries exert considerable influence in lobbying civilian governments to promote military interests, such as new weapons programs. Business groups also support such lobbying, as they are interested in supplying the military with those weapons. Most countries have prestigious military institutes to train their leaders and to promote ethical principles and belief in civilian control. Examples of such institutes are ESM Saint Cyr in France, and the Royal Military Academy Sandhurst in the UK.

The rise of the EU has led to a valid question: Does every member country need its own national military? According to national governments, the answer is yes. The bigger area of debate is how to coordinate these national forces at a European level. Should they be coordinated through the US-backed North Atlantic Treaty Organization, whose members historically were from Western Europe, but which is gradually absorbing members from the former communist bloc, much to the chagrin of Russia? Or should they be coordinated through a European defense agency, and gradually be integrated into a single European force, intrinsically though not explicitly aloof from the United States?

Significant differences of opinion exist on this issue, with many of the newer EU members reluctant to break ties to US security protection. There is increasing coordination across the militaries of the EU, however, and this is likely to increase in the future—though not automatically to the detriment of the United States and NATO. The post–September 11 wars in Afghanistan and Iraq also exemplify these tensions. The war in Afghanistan received broad European support, and took place as a NATO operation. The intervention in Libya in 2011 was also a NATO operation. In contrast, the US-led war in Iraq in 2003 led to bitter criticism in many European capitals, particularly in Berlin and Paris, and divided many European governments from the United States, and Europeans from each other. Russia's invasion of Ukraine in 2022 had the dual effects of strengthening EU military cooperation and bolstering unity within NATO, aided by the surprising request of neutral states Finland and Sweden to join the organization. The war underscored the continuing dependence on NATO to deter further Russian incursions elsewhere in Europe.

EU Committee of the Regions

Two other interest groups related to the EU and European politics more generally deserve a mention. The Committee of the Regions (CoR) represents regional opinions from European members and provides advisory opinions to the European Council and Commission.[43] Established in 1994, the CoR members receive appointments for renewable five-year terms by the Council, and must be representatives (ideally elected) of local or subnational groups inside of member countries. There are 329 total members, with numbers roughly reflecting national populations. France, Germany, and Italy have the largest representation with twenty-four members each, down to Malta having the least at five. The CoR serves as something of a pressure valve for local identity, allowing regional opinions a voice and opportunities to lobby Brussels. As a purely advisory body, however, the CoR produces little traction on issues that national governments oppose. It elects its own president to chair meetings for two-and-a-half-year terms.

EU European Economic and Social Committee

The European Economic and Social Committee (EESC), like the CoR, is a similarly nonbinding organization representing the opinions of civil society in terms of social and labor groups, as well as employers.[44] With numerical representation similar to the CoR, the EESC has representation across three groups of members: employers, workers, and civil society (known as Diversity Europe). Although some observers think the committee is somewhat redundant given the plethora of advisers and specialists across EU institutions, the Lisbon Treaty confirmed its place and importance in EU deliberations, even though the EESC is only advisory.

Conclusion

Political participation in Europe takes place at various levels, in complex patterns. As a continent of primarily democratic governments, there is relative freedom to organize interest groups and engage with and in political parties. These freedoms become more constrained the further east one goes in Europe, and in countries such as Belarus and Russia (and Turkey), these are particularly limited. Elections tend to be relatively free and fair (with similar exceptions) without the overt corruption and influence of blatant vote buying found in other parts of the world. This is not always perfect, however, as we can see with the limited media freedom in Italy, or in the questionable political practices in Hungary and Poland.

Perhaps the greatest deficit of democracy is at the European level, notwithstanding the presence of the EP. The sense of distance that most Europeans feel from what takes place in the EU raises questions regarding whether it can ever become a European government. The rise of populism with its overt nationalist and anti-EU agendas display eroding support for the EU, and an underlying support for national prominence. The issues that provide the underlying fabric to European politics and society are the focus of the next chapter.

Notes

1. I discuss these issues in more depth in Chapter 6.

2. Daron Acemoglu and James A. Robinson, "Why Did the West Extend the Franchise? Democracy, Inequality, and Growth in Historical Perspective," *Quarterly Journal of Economics* 115(4), 2000: 1167–1199.

3. UK Parliament, "The Reform Acts and Representative Democracy," https://www.parliament.uk/about/living-heritage/evolutionofparliament/houseofcommons/reformacts/.

4. *Elections in Central and Eastern Europe: A Compendium of Reports on the Elections Held from March Through June 1990* (Washington, DC: Commission on Security and Cooperation in Europe, 1990).

5. European Parliament, "2019 European Election Results," https://europarl.europa.eu/election-results-2019/en/turnout/.

6. Tim Bale, *European Politics: A Comparative Introduction,* 4th ed. (London: Palgrave/Red Globe, 2017), pp. 201–214.

7. David Farrell, *Electoral Systems: A Comparative Introduction,* 2nd ed. (London: Red Globe/Palgrave Macmillan, 2011). See also Michael Gallagher and Paul Mitchell (eds.), *The Politics of Electoral Systems* (Oxford: Oxford University Press, 2008).

8. Maurice Duverger, *Political Parties: Their Organization and Activity in the Modern State* (London: Methuen, 1954).

9. Technically, Belarus is the only other country in Europe to have a simple first-past-the-post system, but that is not a functioning democracy as the failed August 2020 presidential election indicates.

10. The winning political party can have barely more than 40 percent of the national vote. In a so-called landslide victory for the Conservative Party in the December 2019 elections, the party won only 43.6 percent of the national vote. In election victories in 2010 and 2015, the party scored only 36 percent of the national vote.

11. Normally, the presidential elections are two weeks apart, whereas the National Assembly elections are one week apart.

12. Michela Palese, "Which European Countries Use Proportional Representation?" *Electoral Reform Society,* December 26, 2018, https://www.electoral-reform.org.uk/which-european-countries-use-proportional-representation/.

13. Noele Illien, "Swiss Voters Approve Law Mandating Paternity Leave," *New York Times,* September 28, 2020.

14. Nick Cumming-Bruce, "Swiss Narrowly Approve Ban on Face Coverings," *New York Times,* March 8, 2021.

15. Herman Lelieveldt and Sebastiaan Princen, *The Politics of the European Union,* 2nd ed. (Cambridge: Cambridge University Press, 2015), pp. 118–119.

16. European Parliament, "Redistribution of Seats in the European Parliament After Brexit," January 31, 2020, https://www.europarl.europa.eu/news/en/press-room/20200130IPR71407/redistribution-of-seats-in-the-european-parliament-after-brexit.

17. Statista, "Voter Turnout in the European Parliament Elections in the European Union (EU) from 1979 to 2019," January 28, 2022, https://www.statista.com/statistics /300427/eu-parlament-turnout-for-the-european-elections/.

18. Daniel Stockemer and Andre Blais, "Voters and Abstainers in National and European Elections," *European Review* 27(2) 2019: 300–315.

19. Marco Lisi (ed.), *Party System Change, the European Crisis and the State of Democracy* (Abingdon: Routledge, 2019).

20. Ronald Inglehart, *The Silent Revolution: Changing Values and Political Styles among Western Publics* (Princeton: Princeton University Press, 1977).

21. Robert Ford and Will Jennings, "The Changing Cleavage Politics of Western Europe," *Annual Review of Political Science* 23, 2020: 295–314.

22. Markus M. L. Crepaz, *European Democracies,* 9th ed. (New York: Routledge, 2017), pp. 46–47.

23. Robert Anderson, "Social Democracy: What's Left in Central Europe?" *Balkan Insight*, March 26, 2020, https://balkaninsight.com/2020/03/26/social-democracy-whats -left-in-central-europe/.

24. Flavia Krause-Jackson, "Socialism Declining in Europe as Populism Support Grows," *Independent*, December 29, 2019, https://www.independent.co.uk/news/world /europe/socialism-europe-parties-populism-corbyn-left-wing-francois-holland-snp -a9262656.html.

25. Caroline Close and Emilie Van Haute (eds.), *Liberal Parties in Europe* (Abingdon: Routledge, 2019).

26. Richard Youngs and Camino Mortera-Martinez, "A Liberal-Centrist Vision for Europe?" Carnegie Europe, March 14, 2019, https://carnegieeurope.eu/2019/03/14/liberal -centrist-vision-for-europe-pub-78533.

27. Renew Europe held 98 of the 705 seats in the EP after the 2019 election.

28. Jon Henley, "Netherlands Election: Mark Rutte Claims Fourth Term with 'Overwhelming' Victory," *The Guardian,* March 18, 2021.

29. Richard Wilke, Jacob Poushter, Laura Silver, Kat Devlin, Janell Fetterolf, Alexandra Castillo, and Christine Huang, "Political Parties," *Pew Research Center,* October 14, 2019, https://www.pewresearch.org/global/2019/10/14/political-parties/.

30. Pippa Norris and Ronald Inglehart, *Cultural Backlash: Trump, Brexit, and Authoritarian Populism* (Cambridge: Cambridge University Press, 2019); see also Jasper Muis and Tim Immerzeel, "Causes and Consequences of the Rise of Populist Radical Right Parties and Movements in Europe," *Current Sociology* 65(6), 2017: 909–930.

31. Matina Stevis-Gridneff and Benjamin Novak, "Hungary's Ruling Party Breaks with Conservative EU Allies that Shielded It," *New York Times*, March 4, 2021; Paul Lenvai, *Orbán: Hungary's Strongman* (New York: Oxford University Press, 2016). (Subsequently titled *Orbán: Europe's New Strongman.*)

32. Martin Caparros, "Vox and the Rise of the Extreme Right in Spain," *New York Times,* November 13, 2019.

33. Katie Livingstone and Colm Quinn, "Was Portugal's Election a Breakthrough for the Far-Right?" *Foreign Policy,* January 26, 2021, https://foreignpolicy.com/2021/01 /26/portugal-presidential-election-far-right-breakthrough-ventura-rebelo-sousa/.

34. Manuela Caiani and Ondřej Cisař (eds.), *Radical Right Movement Parties in Europe* (Abingdon: Routledge, 2019).

35. European Parliament, "About Parliament: The Political Groups of the European Parliament," https://www.europarl.europa.eu/about-parliament/en/organisation-and-rules/organisation/political-groups.

36. Worker-Participation EU, "National Industrial Relations," http://www.worker-participation.eu/National-Industrial-Relations/Across-Europe/Trade-Unions2.

37. Business Europe, https://www.businesseurope.eu/.

38. Lelieveldt and Princen, *The Politics of the European Union,* chap. 6.

39. Le Monde Diplomatique, https://www.monde-diplomatique.fr/diplo/int/.

40. Bale, *European Politics,* chap. 7.

41. Reporters Without Borders, "Press Freedom Index 2022," https://rsf.org/en/ranking.

42. Standard Eurobarometer 94, Winter 2020–2021, Public Opinion in the European Union (Brussels: European Commission, 2021).

43. European Union, "European Committee of the Regions," https://cor.europa.eu/en.

44. European Union, "European Economic and Social Committee," https://www.eesc.europa.eu/en.

6

Social Issues and Challenges

AFTER EXPLORING THE GOVERNMENTAL STRUCTURES AND POLITICAL processes of European countries in previous chapters, our goal in this chapter is to consider the most important political issues that shape the fabric of society and underpin the basis for action and policy. To what extent is there a common set of social issues that all Europeans face and respond to similarly, or are all issues specific for a country? Do the citizens of Ireland, for example, face similar social issues to those in Romania? Could we argue that the political issues in Denmark are similar to those in Turkey? Do people in Europe, or at least those living in European Union member states, define themselves by a common agenda or shared set of ideas shaped by the EU? Peace? Welfare? Tolerance, or diversity? Do such ideas extend to prospective EU members, such as Serbia or Ukraine? Do citizens embrace the drive for a more unified European social identity, or are they happy not to go beyond their national, or subnational, identity?

Answers to these questions, of course, depend on the level of specificity utilized. To some extent, all issues are local and specific to a country, or even a region within a country. Specific cultures, histories, or populations, as well as the political system in which issues surface, all influence the nature and evolution of issues. In this light, we should be wary of overextending our comparisons, thereby potentially minimizing real differences. We should also try to avoid privileging a particular set of ideas, or a dominant narrative, about Europe, as postmodernists warn. Keeping such a micro-level and localized lens of observation, however, does little to help our comparative study or our understanding of broad trends across the continent, assuming they exist.

With these caveats in mind, then, we can cautiously move forward to explore the level to which we find commonality of issues across the continent. The EU creates some level of shared identity through its policies, which require member states to respond to a common set of stimuli. In turn, EU member countries have issues that require some sort of collective response at the EU level. These actions not only are trying to shape the identity and character of the Union itself, but also at times are attempting to fashion something much more elusive; namely, some kind of European societal identity. The relatively free movement of people around the EU, the efforts at integrating higher education, the plethora of European institutions, and the presence of euros in the pockets of many Europeans all help to translate into a sense of Europeanness, a feeling of collective belonging. The EU also provides nonmembers with a sense of being the "Other" or the outside group, often needing to react and respond to the policies and actions of the EU.

Many political issues and trends shape the character and fabric of European societies.[1] This chapter examines these issues, and judges the degree to which we see common processes and results across the continent, a topic introduced in Chapter 1. I assess the extent to which these issues promote individualistic national responses, but we can also see whether or not some sort of nascent European societal fabric is developing.

Language, Religion, and Culture

The multitude of European languages provides a cause for celebration of culture, and maintains discernible national entities divided by language across the continent, thereby diminishing somewhat the prospects for a complete European identity forming. Not only are there distinct national languages and dialects, but many countries are multilingual, bringing about their own distinct issues. The Swiss have appeared to be better than most at dealing with their four national languages, and have developed their own form of consensus government, as discussed in Chapter 3.

Belgium has a compromise government of two distinct halves, and uneasily coexists inside the geographical boundaries. Throughout history, the territory now occupied by Belgium was occupied by alternating forces—Romans, Spanish, Austrian, French, and Dutch, to name some of the main ones. The region was, and remains, bitterly divided by religion—Protestant and Catholic—and by language—Dutch and French. After the Napoleonic wars, the major powers, especially Britain, wanted this region to be something of a neutral zone and outside of the control of France. Initially put under control by the Netherlands, a nationalist uprising led to the breakup of the territory and the establishment of Belgium in 1831, a result crafted by the British. Today, Belgium is a federal country divided broadly between a Dutch-speaking Protestant north, and a French-speaking Catholic south. Brussels forms a mixed, third region. Political parties also divide by region and language. Bitter differences between these social and linguistic blocs makes government formation difficult. Belgium went 194 days without a government in 2007–2008 because of bitter wrangling between the two regions, but a breakdown of politics eclipsed this in 2010–2011 with a failure to agree on a national government for 541 days. Language and identity shape the Belgian political landscape.

Language and culture issues in other countries have accentuated the changing, possibly weakening, power of the state in Europe, such as in Spain with Catalans and Basques, or in Britain, with attempts to revive Welsh and Gaelic languages. In other countries, dialect is an identifying characteristic that tends to divide rather than unite, even if in subtle ways. Such issues are prominent in countries such as France (Parisian vs. the rest) and Germany (northern vs. southern, and Protestant vs. Catholic), but can also be seen in relations between English and Scots (or between those in southern and northern England), or Czechs and Slovaks (a factor in the dissolution of Czechoslovakia in the Velvet Divorce of 1993). Language and culture also played prominent roles in the changing map of Europe during the 1990s, particularly in the Baltics and the Balkans, bringing about new territorial units in their constituent linguistic and ethnic parts, though not always cleanly or peacefully. By one account, there are currently twenty-six countries in Europe with active separatist movements seeking some level of autonomy or independence from the country in which they reside.[2]

The continuing use of Russian by ethnic Russians in Baltic countries is a particularly acute issue, especially as these are only recently independent countries. In Latvia, for example, ethnic Russians make up about one-quarter of the population. Even more prominent is the strategic Russian enclave of Kaliningrad, territory taken from Poland by the USSR after World War II, which is sandwiched between Lithuania and Poland, and cut off by land (it was previously German) from the rest of Russia. Vladimir Putin claimed that common cultural ties made Ukraine an integral part of Russia rather than an independent country as an element of his justification for Russia's invasion in February 2022, a claim hotly disputed by Ukrainians.[3] As the war dragged on into the middle of 2022, Russia's more limited goal appeared to be control of Russian-speaking Ukraine and its resources, with land access through to annexed Crimea. There are fears Russia, if unchecked, could offer a similar explanation to try to create a land bridge through Lithuania or Poland (both NATO members) to Kaliningrad, which is only about 100 miles from Belarus.

Language creates significant operational issues at the EU level. Within the European Parliament, for example, protocol allows the use of all national languages. This provides a translation nightmare in the permutations of translating every language, and the influx of new members required an expansion of the Parliament chamber in 2004 to accommodate the interpreters. At the European Commission level in Brussels, French and English have been the main languages of operation, though Chancellor Helmut Kohl did attempt to make sure that German remained a working language in Brussels. With the influx of Central European states, English has now essentially become the main working language of the European bureaucracy, though not without some resistance, especially from France.

Religion played a major role in the historical development and politics of Europe, not least in terms of the original power of Catholicism and the Pope, the challenge of the Reformation and Protestantism, the influence of religion on government, and the all too numerous wars fought across the continent in the name of religion. Overseas, religion also helped shape or justify European conquests, such as with the Crusades across the Middle East, the Spanish conquistadores in Latin America, or the British carrying "the white man's burden" into Africa.[4] These issues were addressed in Chapter 1.

Today, religion still provides some influence on politics and society, notably in terms of Catholicism in countries such as Belgium, Ireland, Italy, Poland, and Spain. Here, Catholicism continues to exert influence over social mores and policies, though with caveats, as we see rising secularism. For example, Spain in 2010 moved toward policies recognizing gay marriage and approving abortion rights, against organized protests led by the Catholic Church. Ireland finally approved abortion in the thirty-sixth amendment to the constitution in September 2018, following a successful referendum with 66 percent approval to change the constitution. One can also see rising secularism in Poland where fierce debates on abortion rights take place. Scandals, especially concerning the abuse of children over the years by certain priests, damaged the status and following of the Catholic Church across Europe, and had a long-term effect on its institutional influence. Few political decisions hinge on religion, except perhaps for an occasional debate on abortion, or as in France, debates about the presence of crucifixes in public school classrooms, or the wearing of the hijab, as part of the broad policy of secularism. Throughout most of Europe, religious intervention can be something of a nonissue, such as in the widespread support for stem cell research. In some countries, notably Belgium and Northern Ireland, the division of the country between Catholics and Protestants is also a critical religious issue, even though it is not the sole reason for division.

One issue that has contributed to religious tensions in recent years, however, has been the growing presence of Islam within the borders of Europe. Many Europeans are opposed to the rising number of Muslims, and to changing fundamental beliefs to accommodate them. This unease is visible in France, where the government pushed through policies outlawing the hijab. In Switzerland, a referendum passed a ban on the building of minarets in November 2009, something similar to the debate in the United States in 2010 about the building of a mosque near the site of the Twin Towers in New York. A referendum in 2021 in Switzerland narrowly passed a ban on wearing the hijab. Hostility to Islam mixes with class and gender issues. Governments, such as in France, tend to promote the idea of assimilation, but policies tend to make that difficult, and many Muslims have little option but to live in their own communities, facing racism, high unemployment, and social exclusion. This does play out on an external stage in terms of Europe's ambivalent relationship with Turkey and its long-standing requests to join the EU. Similarly, Bosnia and Herzegovina has been an ongoing issue for the EU as it comes to grips not only with its Muslim communities, but also with a complex mosaic of ethnicities in the region. We can view Serbian threats of secession in 2022 from Bosnia and Herzegovina within this prism.

A final element of religion to note concerns the ongoing tensions between predominantly Christian Europe and those of the Jewish faith. Anti-Semitism has been an enduring force throughout European history, unfortunately, as discussed in Chapter 1. Those of Jewish faith played central roles in political and social life, despite discrimination, and in 1933 as Adolf Hitler came to power in Germany, it is estimated that there were approximately 9.5 million Jews in Europe. Two-thirds of these were in Eastern Europe, with the largest settlement of 3 million in Poland.[5] The Holocaust led to the death of an estimated 6 million European Jews, with more than 1 million others fleeing the continent. By 2020, the Jewish population of Europe numbered about 1.3 million, with two-thirds of those living in France, Germany, and the UK.[6] Even with such low numbers for the Jewish population today, there is increasing hostility and anti-Semitism, especially from populist movements across the continent.

As an example of culture, organized sport has a considerable history in contributing to the European way of life and displaying the continent's soft power. Home to the original Olympic Games of ancient Greece, the Games of the modern era were reinvented by Pierre de Coubertin, a French aristocrat, and began in Athens in 1896. The marathon distance was established as 26 miles and 385 yards (42.195 kilometers) in the 1908 London Olympics (confirmed in 1921), with the extra yards added to make sure the race finished in front of the royal box. Hitler used the 1936 Games in Berlin to show off the supremacy of the German race.

East Germany at the height of the Cold War also used sport to display the superiority of the communist system.[7] The 2012 London Olympics were a vehicle to display the soft power of the UK, as well as to sponsor the regeneration of decaying (postempire) areas of East London and its docklands. The 2024 Paris Olympics will try to heighten France's prestige in the global system.

Other major organized sports in their modern form began their life in Europe (there are debates as to the true origins of these sports), and are often run from European headquarters. These include sports such as soccer/football, rugby, golf, tennis, track and field, and cricket—with the latter primarily a game played by those with a shared past within the British Empire, now the Commonwealth. Some of these organizations have come under fire for corrupt practices, notably the Lausanne-based International Olympic Committee (IOC) and the Zürich-based International Federation of Association Football (known by its French acronym FIFA, the Fédération Internationale de Football Association, because it started life in Paris).

Although most European countries play these common sports, there is little to bind people together across national boundaries, although the EU has increasingly moved to get more involved in policymaking.[8] Sport may well be the extension of war by other means, a way to pit countries against each other. Rarely do Europeans come together as a team representing the continent—golf's Ryder Cup is one exception—and even then this does little to unify the European population, as I explained in Chapter 1. Focus and attention still rests with national teams, or else at a lower level with club teams. A game between Real Madrid and Barcelona is far more than simply a soccer/football game, but a display of intense regional pride, culture, and politics within Spain, drawing back to the Spanish Civil War. Spain's success in winning the FIFA World Cup in 2010 for the first time, primarily with a team made up of these two fierce rival club teams, laid hopes for greater national reconciliation beyond the soccer field, but this never materialized.

The presence of many more foreign players in European soccer teams has done little to diminish the symbolism of the team representing local people. At times, this primordial loyalty can attract the worst elements of society, and violence and racism at European games remains a thorny problem, notably in Italy. Many observers regard the (English) Premier League as the world's top league in terms of money and players, and provides significant soft and cultural power to Britain around the world. The Premier League's efforts to combat racism is a good example of their soft power, and when the teams returned to play after the Covid-19 break in June 2020, all the players wore "Black Lives Matter" across the backs of their playing shirts. All teams continued to "take the knee" before the start of a game as a sign of opposition to racism.

One other interesting aspect of European soccer/football is the Union of European Football Associations (UEFA), which contains fifty-five national associations. These include countries such as Armenia, Israel, Kazakhstan, Russia, and Turkey.[9] Although the average European supporter takes teams from these countries for granted in European competitions, this does not automatically transcend into acceptance of these countries as "European." One embarrassment for Europe's leading football teams came in April 2021 with the demise within forty-eight hours of a proposed European Super League of the top twelve or so teams. Opposition from national associations and from regular supporters against the "greed" of owners undermined the game's reputation, at least temporarily.[10] In an act of unity, however, both FIFA and UEFA banned Russia from European and global football competitions in reaction to Russia's invasion of Ukraine in 2022, and UEFA stripped Moscow of the right to hold the Champions League final in Moscow in May 2022.

Ethnicity and Race

Ethnicity refers to the shared experience and common understanding or religion of a given set of people, and so overlaps with the previous category. No European country today is monoethnic, though some have dominant ethnic groups. Ethnicity tends to become a political issue where multiple ethnicities within a country compete and where minority groups press for group rights and recognition. The breakup of the former Yugoslavia through civil war into ethnic component parts in the 1990s was often bloody, and was indicative of the potency of ethnicity, religion, and culture developed over centuries, even when (or perhaps because) these had been suppressed for five decades under communist rule. In addition to ethnic traits, the Croats are mainly Catholic, the Serbs and Macedonians primarily Orthodox Christians, and Albanians and many Bosnians mostly Muslim.

For Slovenia, bordering Austria and Italy, the transition was swift, and membership in the EU was gained in 2004. For others, the transition has been more difficult. Croatia was the most recent country to acquire EU membership, but that took until 2013, whereas Serbia remains tied up in ongoing negotiations. A significant outstanding issue concerns the status of Kosovo (see Box 6.1). North Macedonia faced problems with its development and EU membership, specifically with opposition from Greece until it changed its name. France vetoed its path to EU membership in October 2019, unhappy about the prospect of adding yet another weak country to the EU. Bosnia and Herzegovina, cobbled together after war in the Dayton Accords of November 1995, was teetering on collapse at the beginning of 2022 as the Bosnian Serbian leader, Milorad Dodik, threatened to withdraw the Serbian sector from all government activities.

Neighboring Albania, though not part of the former Yugoslavia, also has an uphill struggle to develop the EU standards required in the Copenhagen criteria. Cut off from the rest of Europe for several decades in the twentieth century by its communist leadership, which adhered to Beijing rather than Moscow, Albania remains one of the poorest countries in the continent.

Other challenges for ethnic recognition remain unresolved: the pressure on the United Kingdom by Welsh, Scots, and Irish; the undercurrents against Parisian rule by groups of Bretons and Corsicans; the more vocal opposition to Castilian rule by Basques and Catalans; the separatist sympathies of Kurds inside the Turkish state; and the breakup of the Soviet Union into a multitude of ethnic-based states. The common thread through most of these cases is how minorities seek to coexist with dominant majorities of different ethnic stock. Language and religion are also additional factors that can strengthen the sense of difference.

One has to be careful in concluding that ethnic representation is stronger in Europe than in recent generations. Ethnicity was perhaps just as strong, but it did not often face benign neglect or even benevolence from national governments until relatively recently, and then unequally across the continent. Several

Box 6.1   Kosovo

Kosovo is a region of the former Yugoslavia, which officially became part of Serbia in the 1990s based on a centuries-old claim to the territory. The Serbs fought one of their most famous battles there in 1389 against Ottoman Muslims, a war deep in Serb political folklore and culture (even though they lost). Kosovo's population today, however, is almost completely (90 percent) ethnic Albanian. After fighting broke out in 1998 leading to an intervention by NATO, the United Nations took control. War crimes tribunals found many Serb commanders guilty of war atrocities. Kosovo's Assembly declared independence in February 2008 from Serbia, which bitterly opposed such calls. The dispute went to the International Court of Justice, which unexpectedly found in favor of Kosovo's independence in 2010, naturally opposed by Serbia (and its longtime ally, Russia). Nevertheless, the EU remains divided on recognition of Kosovo as an independent state and there is little movement on recognition or EU membership, as Kosovo continues to be an unresolved and potentially explosive international issue. New war crimes indictments against Kosovo president, Hashim Thaci, in June 2020, further undermined hopes for a resolution. The issue also complicates Albanian and Serbian negotiations for EU membership.

factors explain the resurgence of ethnic identity, including the impact of glob-alization on the role of the state and culture. The EU transcends the state some-what, and offers active support of local cultures in the Committee of the Regions. The increased sensitivity to human rights also makes it more difficult to suppress minority cultures and ethnicities.

Perhaps the example of the worst discrimination against an ethnic group in Europe is what takes place against the Roma, or Romani, often referred to as gypsies or travelers. The Roma is a group of people, about 12 million strong, who came to Europe around the tenth century from India. Although often labeled as one group, there are distinct ethnicities within the Roma. Roma often migrate across the continent, and find discrimination wherever they go. Although their traditional home is in Bulgaria, Romania, and Turkey, they have little or no polit-ical stake in those countries. With free movement available and legal around the EU, they are technically free to migrate, but face increasing persecution and physical attacks. Much of this hostility to the Roma appears to be to appease right-wing groups, and has significant racist undertones. Italy declared a state of emergency in 2008 and expelled thousands of Roma. Denmark, France, and Sweden also organized widespread sweeps of Roma for deportation in 2010, and with little support or political representation, ongoing hostility to the Roma con-tinues across Europe.[11]

Allied to ethnicity, *race* refers specifically to the physical characteristics or attributes that people possess and cannot be hidden, with the most notable being skin color. The most obvious historical example of racism is the subjugation of other peoples through colonization, and their subsequent mistreatment. In con-temporary Europe, racism is widespread as decolonization and migration brought significant numbers of people to live and work in Europe. For many in Europe, the competition for jobs enabled race to be a factor in opposition. Dis-crimination and police hostility to certain racial groups are evident across the continent, with tensions often the highest in large cities where racial minorities congregate. The hostility is highest with Black migrants, especially those from Africa or the West Indies. Racism in sports, notably professional football/soccer emerged decades ago as individual Black athletes began to join teams. Today, there are large numbers of Black players, but racism and racist taunts remain high, notably in Italy. Some countries, such as the UK, have attempted to com-bat racism head on, but this has done little to remove racism from wider society.

The Black Lives Matter movement became widespread across the continent after 2020 (less so in Russia and Turkey). This included calls for the removal of vestiges of empire and slavery (notably statues) as well as for the improvement of living conditions for, and legal protection of, minorities. Police discrimina-tion based on race was a prominent target of opposition and protest. Race is an ongoing issue that few, if any, European governments are successful in resolving. Likewise, during the Covid-19 pandemic, the spike in hate crimes against those of Asian descent rose, and this is another sign of racism in the continent.

Social Class and Workforce Relations

It is difficult to generalize about issues of social class in Europe, especially as class distinctions are difficult to measure. Nevertheless, we can argue that class consciousness remains significant. Political parties across the continent still align themselves to some degree on issues of class, and marked differences of income are prevalent. Labor movements and unions, though generally declining in stature and becoming more cosmopolitan in nature, retain their social class orientation and wield considerable powers in many countries. The development of class relations in CEE has been shaped by decades of communist rule, but class identity across those countries is an important political variable. In Germany, despite three decades of unification, gaps exist in the East- and West-based mentality on myriad social and economic factors, but a social class identity plays a role.

Rigid hierarchies are less visible than in a previous age of empire. Titles mean less than before in countries such as France and Germany, whereas in Nordic countries, membership in the royal family brings little social distinction and less political influence. In the UK, royalty packs a social punch with its widespread support, but this is somewhat dependent on respect for Queen Elizabeth II, in office since 1952, rather than love for the royal family and the concept of royalty per se. Class distinctions remain quite strong in the UK, but are eroding somewhat. Much was made of the elitist social background of former British prime minister David Cameron in the runup to the 2010 national elections—he had been educated at the bastions of privilege of Eton College (a private high school established in 1440) and Oxford University—but it is unclear how this affected the election. Of course, privilege perhaps allowed him to get to the leadership position of the British Conservative Party. Boris Johnson, who became British prime minister in 2019, also is a product of Eton and Oxford, reinforcing this notion of class privilege.[12]

The growth of social mobility has had a significant impact on traditional class relations. Increasingly, labor mobility across Europe is undermining traditional class structures, as more non-nationals enter workforces. At times, these workers stratify as a new working class if they take up menial jobs, exacerbated by cultural, immigration, and racial factors. At the upper end of the social spectrum, the evolution of a more open European-wide employment pool also serves to undermine the traditionally rigid social spectrum, as "foreign" workers are less likely to fall into national social patterns and regimens. Good command of the local language (or English) is as likely a determinant of securing a job as social background.

The raw political power of organized labor within Europe is generally declining, as is membership in trade unions, although this is not to say that they do not have an important role to play within European economies. Governments across the continent have gradually challenged the unions in terms of undermining their ability to maintain their benefits and their role in making economic policies, part of the influence of a neoliberal trade philosophy. Sometimes this has been a brutal exchange, such as with the Margaret Thatcher administration in the UK in the 1980s, and other times this has been more gradual and modest, such as in the highly structured situation of Germany and Sweden. At times, it has been muddled and inconclusive, such as in France over the past decade, with efforts by the Nicolas Sarkozy and Emmanuel Macron regimes to come to grips with reform.

Trade unions in Europe grew up in the nineteenth and early twentieth century, when working conditions were generally poor. Organized to fight for basic rights, such as safety, decent working hours, and a fair wage, unions were embroiled in many significant political battles and strikes. In the post–World War II era, union rights in Western Europe became more widely accepted, helped by the growth of welfare programs and a more holistic view of society. In CEE, trade unions were also a significant part of mainstream political life, but normally as a pawn of a controlling Communist Party. In many Western countries, unions remained part of the decisionmaking process, such as in Germany with the codetermination process, where companies are required to establish works councils (largely comprised of unionists, but not exclusively) to sit side by side with management on a board to make policies for the company. In Sweden, unions were included in annual wage rate negotiations with business and government leaders. Of course, in Iberia prior to the mid-1970s, trade unions were under strict state supervision, and only gradually exerted independent influence after the demise of fascism.

Stagflation (economic stagnation and inflation) across Europe in the 1970s led some governments to consider radical changes to their economic structures, including attempts to make their economies more flexible. This meant reducing the influence of unions in shaping economic policy. Over the past two decades, this has become a common spectacle across Europe, as privatization and neoliberalism have forced confrontation with trade unions, which have generally seen their power diminish. In turn, the numbers of trade union members have shrunk fairly drastically over this period, and legislation preventing quick and easy strikes has become more widespread. Even in a country such as France, known for its confrontational union activities, membership in unions is now down to less than 10 percent of the workforce.

Despite these trends, support in principle for trade unions remains generally strong. The EU Social Chapter developed in 1969, for example, called unequivocally for the maintenance of trade unions and their right to strike. The EU has a Works Council policy that enables workers to develop collaborative policies and strengthen the representation of workers in companies across Europe.[13] The EU also provides significant levels of funding for retraining of workers in depressed areas. One tense area of labor relations involves the tenure of employment, and the ability of employers to lay off workers easily. In France and Spain, for example, it is extremely difficult to lay off workers, a feature that trade unions naturally support. Companies complain that they need the flexibility to lay off workers in lean times, but their inability to be able to do this makes them unwilling to hire new workers in good times. The Macron government in France attempted to change these labor laws, but was met with stiff resistance. This issue is essentially a national issue to decide on, and gradually governments are removing protections on workers' employment in the hope of becoming a more competitive environment for business.

Another area where labor regulations have changed is in shopping hours, although these remain national policies. Such hours have been extended, and now include Sunday shopping in many countries. One of the most resistant countries to the change was Germany, where most shops traditionally closed at midday on Saturday. These changes point to the increasing need for flexibility by labor unions, the prevalence of social change, and the increasing competitiveness of an open European market. Whereas shoppers near traditional borders can be mobile to take advantage of discrepancies in business laws and prices— between neighboring countries, such as many Swiss in the Geneva area choosing to shop in the considerably cheaper French supermarkets over the border— the much vaunted ability of workers to move freely across Europe has not become a significant trend in mobility.

Culture appears to be a stronger force than economics, as Europeans traditionally have not strayed too far from their place of birth for employment, let alone moved countries. At the end of 2017, the EU stated that only 3.8 percent of the EU workforce lived outside of their countries of origin, and a significant proportion of these were university graduates.[14] There are some notable exceptions, though, even predating the opening of the single market. Large numbers of Italian and Spanish workers moved northward to seek employment; retiring British and German workers tended to move south to seek out warmth in their golden years. Turkish and Yugoslavian emigration to Germany had little to do with European labor policy. One of the best examples of EU members taking advantage of mobility policies is the massive emigration of Polish workers into the UK since Poland joined the EU. At the time of the Brexit vote in 2016, there were an estimated 800,000 Poles in Britain, making Polish the second most common language in the UK. After Brexit, many of these Poles left. Overall, today, countries of CEE face a greater exodus of their skilled workforce, leading to a brain drain issue that governments find difficult to prevent.

The nature and role of trade unions in Europe are evolving, but we should not conclude that this is all negative for workers. Rising prosperity for many could make a case for less of a need for union protection. The EU still provides guarantees for workers' rights, and an attempt to level the playing field for all workers across the single market. But unions have had to adapt to the tough competitive business environments within Europe and outside, and have had to agree to liberalize worker practices and protections. Whether a happy balance has been found, or whether workers' rights will continue to be eroded, is certainly something to be watched for in the coming years.

Gender

Although many perceive Europe to have led the way in the promotion of democracy, voting rights, and equality (though only coming in the twentieth century), women have not fared as well as (male) rhetoric suggests. The first European country to provide women the vote was Finland in 1906 (although this was prior to its independence from Russia in 1917), followed by Norway in 1913, and Denmark and Iceland in 1915.[15] Women received the vote in the UK in 1928, after a long suffrage struggle, and in the land of liberty and equality—France—women did not receive the vote until 1944. In Switzerland, women did not have the vote until a referendum passed in 1971, but this was better than Liechtenstein, where women obtained the vote in 1984 after a referendum with only 51 percent support (a fraction better than defeated referenda in 1971 and 1973). Spanish women received the franchise in 1931, but lost the vote following the civil war and did not regain full voting rights until 1976 at the end of Francisco Franco's rule. Women in Portugal, similarly, did not obtain full voting rights until 1975.

Representation of women in political life today lags considerably, as previously discussed, with no country in Europe having parity for women's representation in the lower houses of national legislatures.[16] At a snapshot of May 2020, Sweden led Europe with 47 percent of women in its national legislature, closely followed by Andorra, Finland, Spain, Switzerland, and Norway all at about 40 percent. A number of countries languished in the low 20 percent range, including Croatia, the Czech Republic, Greece, Slovakia, and Romania. The poorest scoring countries inside the EU were Malta at 13 percent and Hungary at just 12 percent. Representation for women in the European Parliament has risen over time, rising from 15 percent after the first direct elections of 1979 to 40 percent after the 2019 election.[17] Overall within EU member countries, the average figure for women in national legislatures stood in 2021 at 32.7 percent, and many other challenges stand in the way of equality.[18] These issues of gender equity in political life are discussed in more depth in Chapters 4 and 5.

The glass ceiling remains fairly well established in the business realm also. The EU initiated a series of directives on equality of pay for women, but data suggest that remuneration still lags at around 84 percent of that of men.[19] For top-level management of European companies, women hold only around 10 percent of the positions. The EU proposed a plan in March 2021 to compel companies to reveal gender disparities in salaries paid to employees, but its future was uncertain as governments could block implementation.[20] In the areas of Europe previously under communist rule, one might intuitively expect to find a better picture, but that is not the case. In political systems with proportional representation systems, there has been some movement toward the development of women's political parties, or else toward parties that support women's issues. There has also been a significant growth of interest groups dedicated to the promotion of women's issues. This trend has helped to give greater voice to such issues, but much still needs to be done to promote the cause of women across the continent.

Attitudes toward women in politics vary across the continent, often influenced by political culture. The role of male political leaders is often an issue. Scandals in 2011 with Silvio Berlusconi in Italy, or with Dominique Strauss-Kahn in France (a former director-general of the International Monetary Fund), focused on the mistreatment of women by two powerful men, but also reflected prominent cultural norms regarding the gendered roles within these societies. Women continue to find it difficult to climb the political ladders, and sexism remains a prominent political factor. We are also aware of the continuing subjugation of women across all aspects of society, and the fight against that.[21]

Although there have been occasional significant roles for women in political life throughout European history—Queen Elizabeth I or Queen Victoria in the UK, or Joan of Arc in France—the integration of women into politics is essentially a feature of the past century. The extension of the franchise to women was a slow process, but that has not led to the equitable presence of women in the political or business arenas. Much can be made of the role of Margaret Thatcher in the UK, or Angela Merkel in Germany, but these are only two examples. Italy and Spain, to name just two countries, have never had women heads of government, a case similar for the majority of European countries.

Within the legislative bodies of Europe, the picture is relatively bleak. As discussed earlier, Nordic countries boast of some 40 percent of their legislative bodies being composed of women, but most countries lag far behind this figure. Women are able to obtain occasional ministerial positions in government, but remain underrepresented, and are less likely to hold the high profile and "harder" positions, such as defense or finance portfolios. The position is similar in business, where the glass ceiling has held back women from holding equitable positions of power in European companies.

The rise of the #MeToo Movement across Europe has helped to address these issues somewhat, although there is much yet to be done. In France, the #BalanceTonPorc ("out your pig") movement began in 2017 raising issues and debate, and put pressure on governments across the country to take the issue of sexual harassment seriously. This has made some limited progress, challenging deeply entrenched aspects of French (male) culture. Similar movements spread to Spain (#YoTambien) and Italy (#QuellaVoltaQue). The European Parliament pushed for policies to protect the workplace for members of the EP. In March 2019, the Council of Europe agreed on a definition of sexism, and called on all members to eliminate it within their societies through their program titled "Campaign Sexism: See it Name it Stop it!"[22]

Minority and LGBTQ Rights

Minorities have not fared well throughout European history. In a relatively wealthy and "enlightened" country such as the United Kingdom, the treatment of the Welsh, Scots, and Irish by the dominant English displays fairly brutal hostility for centuries—and just a little more decent today. The Austrian-Hungarian Empire had scant time or energy for Czechs, Serbs, or Slovaks, whom the Austrians considered inferior to them. Russians within the Soviet Union had little regard for Estonians or Ukrainians, a factor important in their contemporary relationship too. Basques had an exceptionally hard time living within Franco's Spain, and many are still struggling to find acceptance within the Spanish state. The Roma of Europe have always been demonized, wherever they have found themselves. So this "us versus them" mentality, or "Othering" of minorities, has a long tradition within the continent. European colonial exploits and slavery around the world showed contempt for Others was not only confined within Europe, even though at times countries colonized were physically and demographically larger than the parent (e.g., with Britain and India).

In contemporary Europe, minorities are significant factors in politics and society as they attempt to promote their identity and group benefits, directly through national politics as well as through international agencies such as the Council of Europe or, for EU members, the EU's Committee of the Regions. This is seen in many examples, such as Turkish and Kurdish minorities in Germany, largely emanating from an earlier guest-worker program. Islamic minorities in France, now with the largest population of Muslims within Europe (outside of Turkey), are also very active. In Britain, Asian and West Indian minority groups promote their interests, and we see African groups in Italy and Spain, boosted by the uprisings of the Arab Spring in North Africa. These groups raise significant political challenges over issues of assimilation, immigration, multiculturalism, and general culture, and in many places fuel the rise of right-wing extremist parties hostile to their presence. The massacre in Norway in July 2011 of about 100 young Norwegians by a right-wing extremist protesting the country's liberal immigration policies is a case in point.

Questions also arise about the manner in which minorities can obtain representation within their national political systems. The failure to receive adequate representation, either perceived or real, often creates a climate of hostility and protest as we have witnessed in recent years in France. The breakup of the former Yugoslavia, and the resultant civil war and continuing unrest in places such as Kosovo, with its tensions between Serbs and Albanians, highlight the potential devastation such differences can cause.

The free movement of people provision within the EU allows for the mobility of Europeans to work across the continent. This has resulted in relatively few people moving countries, and little political problem to date as of itself. However, in the future these trends could provide further minority issues. As we just mentioned, in the UK over the past decade the largest inward flow of people has been from Poland, only to be reversed following Brexit. One of the many concerns over Turkish membership in the EU is the fear that Turkish workers will "flood" the countries of Western Europe looking for work. But often the issue of minorities is not so much linked to culture as race. Italians worked for decades in northern Europe without too much difficulty, partly because they "blended" in with the majority in a physical sense. Today, tensions arise because of migration of people who are racially dissimilar and so physically "obvious." Abuse often falls on African migrant workers or refugees, largely because they cannot blend in physically. Political parties of the right, such as the National Rally in France, fanned such hostility, along with the economic recession in the 2010s and during the Covid-19 pandemic in 2020–2022. Today in Europe, we see the politics of fear and hate.[23]

Box 6.2 France and Intersectionality

I have discussed the growing tensions in France over the official state goal of secularism and the increasing social pressures to allow for a deeper reflection of true French society. Secularism is a critical goal for a society with a history of religious conflict, even though France today is predominantly Catholic.[a] The French government, led by President Emmanuel Macron, rails against US ideas of intersectionality in explaining how different communities face social problems, and where the intersection of gender, race, and social class can provide challenges for groups that a regular French person might not face.[b] These tensions are visible in issues such as wearing the hijab in public, or the place of religion in society, but they cut to the core of how France perceives itself as a society—or more accurately, how different groups in France perceive of themselves and France in different ways. These issues are exacerbated by official pronouncements against ethnic difference, and that all French people are essentially equal. This undermines any real attempt to address race or gender in France. Similarly, these issues are reinforced by a general angst over the future of France, and the common perception of the gradual decline of France, or *déclinism*.[c] Societal relations became more unsteady with rising pressure from women and the #MeToo movement, as well as by the activist stance in favor of minority rights by youth groups, particularly the National Union of Students in France. Riots in April 2021 showed that this is an issue that is not going to subside, and proved to be an integral part of the French national elections of 2022.[d]

Notes: a. William Safran, "The Context of French Politics," in M. Donald Hancock, Christopher J. Carman, Marjorie Castle, David P. Conradt, Raffaella Y. Nanetti, B. Guy Peters, William Safran, and Stephen White (eds.), *Politics in Europe,* 5th ed. (Washington, DC: CQ Press, 2012), chap. 2.1.
   b. Norimitsu Onishi, "In Simmering Race and Gender Struggle, France Blames US Ideas," *New York Times,* February 10, 2021.
   c. Rachel Donadio, "France's Obsession with Decline Is a Booming Industry," *New York Times,* February 3, 2017.
   d. Norimitsu Onishi and Constant Méheut, "Pushing Change, Student Union Touches a Nerve in France," *New York Times,* April 5, 2021.

The debate over assimilation and multiculturalism is an important one with which many countries are battling. Multiculturalism implies that minority groups keep much of their basic identity, and take a somewhat "separate" space within the country in which they live. In 2010, the British and German governments came to a separate realization that these policies had "failed" in that minorities were not taking on the national culture and characteristics as they should. These were hotly contested statements, but indicate a level of difficulty that European states are having with the treatment and "absorption" of minorities.[24]

Social equality for LGBTQ Europeans remains one of the more contentious social issues in Europe today, with stark differences held in different countries. Decisions on gay rights are handled at a national level, and a complete spectrum of policies can be witnessed across Europe. Sixteen countries, virtually all in Western Europe, allowed same-sex marriage in 2019, and a further eleven some form of civil union, mostly in southern Europe.[25] The Netherlands was the first country to legalize same-sex marriage in 2001, quickly followed by Nordic countries. Generally speaking, in northwestern Europe, more rights are available to LGBTQ groups. Iceland's former prime minister, Johanna Sigurdardottir, was the first openly gay head of government in Europe, and the world in fact. Elected to office in 2009, she married her partner of almost a decade when same-sex marriages became legal in Iceland in 2010. In Ireland, Leo Varadkar became the country's first openly gay prime minister (known as Taoiseach in Gaelic) in June 2017. The current prime minister of Serbia is openly lesbian.

Resistance to the promotion of LGBTQ rights is quite strong in largely Catholic countries, partly because of opposition from the Pope and Catholic Church. This partially explains Italy's reluctance to embrace same-sex marriage, but major exceptions are Portugal and Spain, which are much more progressive on such rights. As one goes eastward across Europe, opposition to LGBTQ rights grows. Most countries of former CEE and the Balkans oppose such rights, and quite often this opposition is written explicitly into the constitution. In Poland, a largely Catholic country, LGBTQ issues have become a defining position in national politics, running afoul of EU obligations, and where many local municipalities have declared themselves to be "LGBTQ-free zones."[26] Hungary has also enacted similar legislation.[27] Homophobia remains prevalent in countries such as Russia and Turkey, and in the latter gay men face the prospect of imprisonment for up to five years for committing consensual sexual acts.

Youth and Aging

There are many difficult problems facing a core group of Europe's youth, such as widespread unemployment, inner-city violence, political extremism (skinheads), and alienation. These are especially the problems of large urban areas, where jobs are hard to come by, and often compounded by large groups of disaffected immigrants. In the early 2010s during the global recession, in the age group of sixteen to twenty-four years old, the average unemployment across the EU members stood at 20 percent, whereas the highest unemployment rate in this age group was in Spain at 42 percent. In 2019 (before the Covid-19 pandemic), youth unemployment across the EU stood at 15.1 percent. This would not perhaps be quite as bad if this were temporary unemployment, but much of this is long term. Indeed, some segments of Europe's young population may never get a job.[28] This has significant political and social repercussions. Often immigrant groups are scapegoats for unemployment, and accused of "stealing" jobs from nationals. This has led to the growth of many extremist, anti-immigrant, populist movements and parties across Europe, to which young unemployed persons are attracted. Extremist groups are common in football/soccer gatherings across the continent, as attachment to the club is the main anchor of life. But massive unemployment within immigrant communities also causes tensions. Such problems are evident in the riots in France over recent years, where large numbers of migrant youth expressed their anger and outrage on the streets at discrimination, alienation, and few life prospects.

In response, the EU along with national governments has targeted these groups for investment and support. Major plans to promote jobs and education have been funded, and efforts to assimilate large immigrant communities into society have been sponsored. Apprenticeship and job training schemes provide a lifeline to many, though rarely is this sufficient for much labor mobility, except perhaps with workers from CEE moving into the lower paid jobs in the West. The EU launched its Youth Strategy in 2019 to promote civic engagement, inclusion, employment opportunities, and sustainability.[29]

Universities are involved in trying to provide more opportunities for young, educated workers. The growth of student numbers in universities has allowed more people the opportunity of a higher education, while programs such as the European Region Action Scheme for the Mobility of University Students (ERASMUS) finance students to undertake study in countries outside their own during their degree program. Besides promoting employment possibilities, this also has the rationale of developing a cadre of "Educated Europeans" who feel more comfortable working in different parts of Europe, thereby promoting the concept of integration and a shared European culture.[30]

At the other end of the age spectrum, some equally thorny problems exist: Europe is getting older. As life expectancy increases, and the size of families decreases or is flat, the proportion of the continent older than age sixty-five is steadily increasing. In 2020, this stood at one in five (19 percent) of the EU population, an increase of 2.5 percent over the previous decade.[31] Within the EU, the average life expectancy in 2017 stood at 80.9 years, with women at 83.5 years and men at 78.3 years, an average difference of 5.2 years. This average masks disparities between former CEE states and other EU members in Western Europe, as I discuss in more depth in the following chapter. For the Baltic states, Poland, Romania, and Bulgaria, the difference between female and male life expectancy stands at over 7.0 years, with Latvia having the biggest difference at 9.9 years.[32]

This graying of the population raises all sorts of challenges in terms of providing adequate pensions and healthcare, and questions about how the countries are going to be able to afford these costs. It has provided some of the justification for the opening of borders to significant numbers of migrant workers to maintain economic growth, though often with a populist backlash. It has also added to the political debate across the continent, and to the growth of political parties and interest groups focused on the issues of senior citizens. The provision of health care and prescription drugs for the elderly is another key political issue faced. The challenges from the Covid-19 pandemic in 2020–2022 highlighted these problems facing older people across Europe, with the fatality rate much higher than for younger populations. In April 2020, during the early stages of the pandemic, some 90 percent of deaths from Covid in the EU had occurred in those older than sixty-five years of age.[33] This trend continued into 2022.

During the transition from communism in CEE in the 1990s, the fate of those age forty and older was bleak. There were few if any prospects for employment and training, and the social provisions and safety nets of communism disappeared rapidly. The situation in these countries has improved somewhat, but social provisions for older people lag behind those of Western Europe.

Migrants and Refugees

Migration within the EU, in terms of Europeans working in other countries, is relatively uncontroversial and forms an integral part of the single market. Tensions arise, however, when the rules of free movement are suspended. This happened when France and Germany limited the movement of CEE workers after the 2004 enlargement, and seems likely to occur if the remaining Balkan states or Turkey join the EU. Although some element of racial animosity is present, these concerns against migration are largely economic, with the avowed goal of protecting jobs for nationals, albeit against the stated goals of the EU. This sentiment also underpinned the Brexit decision in Britain.

Migration by ethnically non-European, nonwhite groups, often from former colonies though not exclusively so, is far more controversial, although virtually always the perception of the number of migrants present in a country far exceeds the actual number present.[34] This has led to severe political issues and repercussions in countries such as Belgium, Britain, France, Germany, Spain, and Switzerland. These tensions occur for many reasons. These are often large groups that are culturally dissimilar to all around; differences in race, language, and religion often set these groups apart from the remainder of society; their inability to integrate fully into European society can make them permanent Others, despite often being second- or third-generation Europeans; the assumption that they take skilled jobs from nationals; and the perception (contradictory to the previous point) that these immigrant groups carry out largely unskilled and menial tasks, making them liable to social exclusion by the mainstream of society. Some migrants are undocumented, but often critics exaggerate this to bring hostility and suspicion down on the vast majority of legal immigrants. In 2019, less than 1 percent of the EU population was undocumented.[35] In the same year, only 4.9 percent of legal immigrants in the EU27 were from countries outside of the EU.[36]

According to OECD figures, those migrating to Europe are much more likely to have a tertiary education than not, and so these are predominantly skilled personnel.[37] Unlike the United States, European countries have relatively less experience at assimilation of large numbers of immigrant groups, and growing nativism, resistance, and the rise of right-wing nationalist parties are issues to face (the United States is not immune to these pressures). Unfortunately, political elites often find it easier to turn against migrants to score quick political points than to deal with such difficult problems.

The UK has tried for years to limit immigration from overseas, predominantly from its former colonies, such as India and Pakistan, and from the Caribbean. Opposition to immigration helped to fuel the Brexit movement, as promises of closing borders to immigrants wooed supporters to the leave campaign. A major scandal took place in 2018 over the "Windrush" generation. This generation included immigrants from the West Indies who came legally to Britain to work between 1948 and 1970, and who had permanent right of domicile.[38] Nevertheless, the government threatened many with deportation after 2012, and actually deported some as it tightened restrictions on these residents. When all this became public in 2018, the scandal forced the resignation of the home secretary, and forced the government to back down. Anti-immigrant sentiment remained high, especially with expectations prompted by the successful British exit from the EU in January 2020. The Covid-19 pandemic, however, displayed how dependent Britain is on migrant labor in large sectors of the economy. This is especially the case in the National Health Service, where 28 percent of doctors are from outside of Britain, and the pandemic raised questions about the efficacy of restricting immigration.[39]

Undocumented economic migrants continue to find their way into Europe, often through perilous routes across the Mediterranean, primarily into Spain, Italy, and Greece. The EU has forcefully increased its policing to try to keep such migrants out, preferring to turn them back before they reach European shores. It is unknown how many migrants have lost their life trying to get into Europe, and keeping them out of Europe is an issue that gets significant attention in this age of populism. Besides these migrants, there are also large numbers of refugees and asylum seekers attempting to find a home in Europe, either temporary or permanent. Normally, these refugees live and work in Europe pending the outcome of their cases, but occasionally they remain hidden in the shadow economy. As a way to avoid this and to deter refugees, the British government announced in April 2022 that all refugees would be sent to and held in Rwanda until processed.

The biggest crisis came in 2016 with millions of refugees from the Syrian Civil War. These refugees overwhelmed Turkey and Greece, and led to major turmoil within the EU in attempts to conjure a policy. Germany and Sweden took the lion's share of these refugees, with considerable political challenges by right-wing opponents, but the majority of EU countries took few or, as in the case of Hungary, simply refused to implement EU policy. In stark contrast, millions of Ukrainian refugees were welcomed into the EU following Russia's invasion in 2022, partly because this situation was deemed to be temporary. I explore these challenges to EU policy in more detail in the next two chapters.

Terrorism

"Terrorism" is a difficult word to use accurately, or without controversy—especially in today's world. Certainly, there is no single definition to which everyone would agree. Was European colonization across the globe a form of terrorism, state sponsored or otherwise? In the sense that *terrorism* means acts of violence against the political status quo, there has been terrorism in Europe for thousands of years. Over the past century, these acts have been prominent. One of the contributing factors to the outbreak of World War I was the assassination of the heir to the Austrian throne by a (terrorist) dissident on the streets of Sarajevo, then still part of the Austrian-Hungarian Empire. Was this an act of liberation? A similar question hangs over the Irish Rebellion in 1916, leading eventually to Irish independence and the partition of north and south. That ongoing issue led to a revival of action by the Irish Republican Army after 1968, and all sorts of atrocities by Protestants, Catholics, and arguably the British government, until a settlement became possible with the Good Friday Agreement in April 1998. The British official inquiry published in 2010 into the Bloody Sunday massacre that killed thirteen in Derry, Northern Ireland, in 1972 provides a dark picture of the activities of the British government and army against peaceful protesters.

During the 1960s and 1970s, radical Marxist groups in Germany (the Baader Meinhof Gang, though they called themselves the Red Army Faction) and Italy (Red Brigade) undertook violent actions against the state, targeting prominent political or business leaders, but never really managed to get much support. In contrast, ethnic groups fighting for independence, such as the Basque Homeland and Liberty group (Euskadi Ta Askatasuna, or ETA) in Spain, could claim some level of local support for their ideas, if not for their methods of action. Something similar is evident for the Chechnya separatists fighting Russia in the Caucasus, and the many violent bombings that have taken place in Moscow.

Attacks by Islamic militants on the United States in September 2001 led many to assume that similar attacks on European targets would follow. These did happen in Madrid in 2004 and London in 2005. Both attacks highlighted the vulnerability of public transport systems to attack, and the inability to prevent further actions in the continent. Since then, smaller-scale yet ongoing attacks have continued, particularly in Britain and France. In Paris, the Charlie Hebdo attack in January 2015 is a notable example, where twelve people died in an attack on a satirical newspaper that had published materials ostensibly denigrating Islam. The most deadly terrorist attack in France took place in Paris in November 2015, with 350 injured and 130 killed, of whom 90 died in the Bataclan theater. The following year, in July 2016, some 86 people died in Nice when a truck driven by a militant deliberately ran into civilians. Similarly, there are continuing incidents of terrorism in other European countries, frequently involving one or a small handful of militants attacking citizens. The militants themselves often proclaim frustration at the violent actions by the government at their expense, and have little option themselves but to resort to violence.

Other Social Movements

Social movements not connected to the state, and often at loggerheads with the state, have become increasingly influential in the political landscape of Europe. These movements tend to aggregate individuals and small groups into a common cause through mostly peaceful protest for a limited period. The Green movement, which began in Europe in Britain and Germany in the 1970s (though the first political organizations were actually in New Zealand), is a good example of this, though it has transformed itself into formal political parties in a number of countries. The broader environmental movement has in some ways moved beyond the Greens, and now encompasses various efforts by many political organizations to promote green living—whether through recycling, opposition to genetically modified food, fair trade towns, and action against climate change. These activities involve citizens who would not consider themselves to be green activists, but rather that they are taking into account concern for the environment in their daily lives.

Another broad social movement is the peace movement. Its initial growth began with the Campaign for Nuclear Disarmament (CND) in the UK. As a way to symbolize this movement, the peace symbol was designed in 1958, depicting the letters N and D (for nuclear disarmament) in semaphore. This symbol quickly spread across the world as a universal sign for peace. This disparate group of peace protestors opposed the presence of US cruise nuclear missiles in Europe in the early 1980s. After a lull, the invasion of Iraq in the Gulf War of 1991 reawakened the movement to protest these actions, and they were again active after the second invasion of Iraq in 2003. Although many perceive the peace movement in Europe to be anti-American, it is more accurate to say that protesters supported peace as a goal, and opposed only specific actions of US foreign policy, rather than the country or Americans in general.

Another important social movement is that within CEE in the 1980s, leading to the fall of the Berlin Wall in 1989. Peaceful protests against communism took place in many countries during the 1980s, perhaps best known by the Solidarity movement in Poland and the strikes in Gdansk. Their large size and popular mandate made it increasingly difficult for the governments to control the protests, especially as the Soviet Union made it known in the late 1980s that it would not intervene. The lack of support for, and legitimacy of, those governments enabled them to rot from the inside, and their rapid collapse (as well as that of the Soviet Union itself) took most observers by surprise. The physical breakup of the Berlin Wall by hundreds of thousands of people on both of its sides in November 1989 is perhaps the best visible example of the power of social action in this period.

A significant social movement erupted in France in October 2018 in protest to proposed economic, tax, and labor reforms by President Macron's government. The yellow jackets (*les gilets jaunes*) caused immense dislocation to transportation in France on an ongoing basis, and forced some concessions from Macron. The protesters initially had widespread support in France as they pushed their claims for greater economic justice, especially for those in rural areas, but violence muted that support. Issues had not resolved before the coronavirus took center stage and temporarily paused some of the protests. In May 2020, Black Lives Matter protests took place all across Europe, partly in support for the movement in the United States, but also in protest against racism in European societies.

European Identity

Analysts often like to compare a nascent United States of Europe to the United States of America, to show the similarities and differences of the two enterprises. This is a theme touched on in several chapters of this book. The United

States has some advantages in building a unified society, as we might expect with a sovereign state. A federal government has authority over the whole country, albeit with significant powers granted to state governments. A constitution has been in place for more than 240 years, and a single language, currency, and military along with free movement of people provide the country with a single, common framework. In contrast, the European continent has no central core of a shared language or undisputed central government, and mobility is nowhere near the extent of that in the United States, for both legal and cultural reasons. Many important European countries lay outside of the EU. Political culture at a national level appears to be predominant.

There are some issues, though, on which Europe shows more unity than we see in the United States. For example, Europeans appear more unified in their position on the death penalty (opposition) than do Americans, who remain divided on this issue. Religion and religious differences are less significant in a political or social sense in Europe than in the United States with its "culture wars." A few countries continue to debate abortion rights, and the rise of large Muslim populations challenge religious acceptance. There is also a social consensus on governments providing health and welfare benefits across Europe, much more so than the heated and divisive debates that take place over the Affordable Care Act in the United States. Incarceration and gun control, issues discussed further in the following chapter, also display rather stark differences in policy in Europe from the United States.

The whole concept of a European identity is rather amorphous. It is interesting to consider whether European identity today is becoming stronger or weaker, or whether national identity is in any way declining. Fears expressed by many Europeans that the Brussels bureaucracy was getting too strong—rather than European identity per se—led to the adoption of the concept of subsidiarity in the Maastricht Treaty on European Union in 1992. A rather complex concept, its key thrust is that decisionmaking should be made at the "lowest" or the most local level possible, or the closest to the people affected, so promoting the idea of local democracy. In effect, this means that wherever possible—and where the EU does not possess exclusive jurisdiction—local and subregional populations should have their unique qualities recognized, and decisions should not be made based on the assumption that there is some common European standard, outlook, or population. The treaty states that "the principle of subsidiarity is to guarantee a degree of independence for a lower authority in relation to a higher body. . . . It therefore involves the sharing of powers between several levels of authority, a principle which forms the institutional basis for federal states. . . . It rules out Union intervention when an issue can be dealt with effectively by Member States themselves at central, regional or local

Box 6.3   Albania's Attempt to Join the EU

Albania is currently one of seven states in negotiations to join the EU (the others are North Macedonia, Moldova, Montenegro, Serbia, Turkey, and Ukraine). I have discussed issues surrounding Turkey's application for membership, and questions about its European status. Four states sit in the Balkans with neighboring countries that are already EU members, and so raise less questions regarding their European credentials and bona fides. In the context of sharing European identity and a common set of issues, Albania nevertheless raises many questions. Its history aligns with the region, with Roman, Venetian, and Ottoman control over the centuries. The country finally gained its independence from the Ottoman Empire in 1912, though its independence was short-lived, as it was invaded by Italy and then by Nazi Germany during World War II. Unlike other neighbors after World War II, it chose a path of communism modeled on China after a break from the Soviet Union, and completely sealed itself off from the rest of Europe until the revolution of 1991. At that stage, Albania was one of the poorest countries in Europe, and set out on a path of political and economic modernization. More than half of its population are Sunni Muslims. It applied for EU membership in 2009, and was accepted to candidate status in 2014, but its political, economic, and administrative policies need greater alignment with those of the EU before Albania will be able to take up membership. As I show in the Country Profiles section at the end of the book, Albania is one of the poorest countries in Europe, with a GDP per capita of just $5,353 in 2019, and one of its most corrupt. Can it ever gain membership in the EU?

level."[40] The EU Committee of the Regions also validates this view of the supremacy of local culture over the pan-European, and the desire to promote democratic processes within the often less-than-democratic structure of the EU.

Subsidiarity implies an aspect of dual citizenship, or perhaps even triple citizenship. People can simultaneously hold multiple loyalties and attachments: to Europe, to their country, and to their local region.[41] Furthermore, as people increasingly move around Europe, it would be possible to add a fourth potential loyalty; namely, to the country in which one is living and working. There is perhaps even a fifth, where Austrians and Czechs, for example, perceive a specific "Central European" identity. When authorities require people to select primacy of one attachment over another is when tensions come to the fore. This is normally a policy pursued by national governments fearing the reduction of central authority. Here, those governments can mistake the support for regional identity as separatism, a difficult distinction to make sometimes. Is increasing Scottish nationalism a form of separatism to the British state? Is Catalan identity a challenge to the Spanish state? Is Kosovar identity a threat to the Serbian state? In such cases, identity and political linkages to the EU can help provide political space and courage to challenge the national government.

One area to make a strong case for a developing European culture is in business. National business styles do remain important, and national brands, marketing styles, and tastes are strong. The vitality of the single market and the increased trade and activity within it has developed, however, more of a common European standard and practice, normally harmonized through the widespread use of the English language. The importance of lobbying the European institutions in Brussels for favorable decisions on the single market has also brought a certain unity of purpose and practice to many businesses. The job market, at more senior levels of European companies in particular, is more open to Europeans of any background and culture, and so to some extent corporate transitions in the European market are bleeding over into the cultural realm. Such developments are helping to force executives to understand other European colleagues, in terms of language and culture, something that has not really been as important before now. The impact of EU business legislation increasingly centralized in one place— Brussels—also helps to create a sense of an emerging common business identity within Europe. I deal with these issues in more detail in the next chapter.

We should not overplay the EU hand here, however. Some countries, such as Iceland, Norway, Russia, Switzerland, Turkey, and the UK, remain outside of the formal orbit of the EU and promote full sovereignty, and so are not as drawn in by the European initiative as other states. Europe is composed of many national and regional identities and languages, with diverse and well-established histories and cultures. Shared local experiences have fashioned these identities, and they are unlikely to wither in the face of a new political experiment undertaken by the political elites of Europe—especially where force is not really an option. Indeed, the prism of national context and language translates, reports on, and filters the activities and nature of the EU. It is impossible to imagine how a single European language for common use could evolve under current scenarios. Many policies remain formulated by national governments.

Furthermore, even if we accept that there is some core, shared sense of Europeanness, the growth in numbers of non-Caucasian "Europeans" is challenging this, where people are first-generation immigrants, or else whose parents or grandparents were. Even though European, their sense of identity is perhaps different. So the cosmopolitan nature of many European countries is not simply because of the free flow of Europeans around the continent—though the impact of, say, Polish emigration to Britain in the 2010s should not be underestimated—but also because of migration from Europe's far-flung erstwhile empires, in addition to other countries. It is this migration that is most obvious for racial, religious, and other cultural reasons, and which raises the most angst in areas of Europe. Although Europe prides itself on its worldliness, it is a different thing if the world decides to move to live in Europe.

Conclusion

This chapter has outlined numerous social issues across the continent that form the fabric of European society. Many of these issues are interrelated or intersectional, where a person can feel the impact of race, class, and gender in their day-to-day life. These issues are also constantly evolving, and their impact is not uniform across Europe. So, is Europe heading toward a single society, a United States of Europe? Clearly not, as quite stark differences remain at many social levels between countries. However, there are signs of modest agreement on certain minimal social goals and other socioeconomic objectives, especially within the EU27. The EU Social Policy Network, established in 2014, lays out guidelines for equal treatment in the social realm across the members.[42] These include fair treatment for women, and the right of labor unions to organize. These plans partner with the Council of Europe's European Social Charter for all European countries, dating back to 1961, and the EU Pillar of Social Rights, launched in 2017.[43] The EU's single market cannot operate effectively if social conditions vary dramatically from country to country, as this could potentially lead to large movements of people to countries with much better social conditions. At its broadest level, we can see the goal as to narrow the socioeconomic gaps between citizens of East and West, and between North and South, within Europe, and to use various EU policies as a redistributive mechanism to achieve this goal.

What is the role of the state in shaping attitudes toward government and society within Europe? Does this role differ markedly across the continent? In terms of support for the EU itself, there are marked differences in the way national governments perceive and support the organization. Smaller states, in general, such as Belgium and Luxembourg, appear to embrace the organization. Some of the biggest states are, at times, not that supportive at all, especially if the EU is pursuing policies against their national interests. The role of the state to support national "civic pride" also differs significantly across the region. Pride in institutions of government, and probity of its officials, differs markedly. One area of consistency is in terms of the death penalty, which EU membership prohibits. This policy has strong support across the continent, in terms of governmental action and popular endorsement.

Membership in the EU arguably has something of a homogenizing effect on the member states, partly by the need for legal conformity to the *acquis,* but also in terms of the expectations that membership of the EU club places on countries.

This has clearly helped in terms of the socialization of former dictatorships, such as Portugal and Spain, as well as helping to mainstream and stabilize former communist states of Central Europe. This moderating influence of the EU will potentially help to stabilize future Balkan members, and perhaps in the distant future could have a modifying influence on a future Turkish membership, even though their economies currently fall short of the EU average. For those West European countries outside of the EU, we assume there are common goals regarding basic aspects of social policy.

We must recognize that national and subregional societal factors continue to shape distinct populations within the countries of Europe. These factors exert influence on defining particular patterns of government, economic policy, and social goals, and these are unlikely to blend into a single European pattern or outlook any time soon. Indeed, it is the espoused goal of the EU to preserve such local identities and patterns of government, to maintain local democracy. In this way, there will remain significant social homogeneity and heterogeneity within the continent. Such flexibility and duality are strengths and the reality of contemporary Europe. I continue this discussion of a broad European fabric underpinning policy initiatives into the next chapter.

Notes

1. For a broad discussion of many of these issues, see José M. Magone, *Contemporary European Politics: A Comparative Introduction,* 2nd ed. (Abingdon: Routledge, 2019), chap. 3.

2. William Outhwaite, *Contemporary Europe* (Abingdon: Routledge, 2017), p. 49.

3. Anna Reid, "Putin's War on History: The Thousand-Year Struggle over Ukraine," *Foreign Affairs* 101(3), 2022: 54–63.

4. Rudyard Kipling wrote, "Take Up the White Man's Burden" for Victorian Britain, but the poem became an important means to support US intervention in the Philippines in 1899. The burden was to raise up and civilize "inferior" people, rather than simply to exploit them. In France, there was a similar concept of *la mission civilisatrice.*

5. United States Holocaust Museum, "Jewish Population of Europe in 1933: Population Data by Country," https://encyclopedia.ushmm.org/content/en/article/jewish-population-of-europe-in-1933-population-data-by-country.

6. Harriet Sherwood, "Europe's Jewish Population Has Dropped 60% in Last 50 Years," *The Guardian,* October 25, 2020, published article based on results from the Institute for Jewish Policy Research, https://www.theguardian.com/world/2020/oct/25/europes-jewish-population-has-dropped-60-in-last-50-years.

7. Stephen Wright, "Are the Olympics Games? The Relationship of Politics and Sport," *Millennium: Journal of International Studies* 6(1), 1977: 30–44.

8. Osvaldo Croci, "Taking the Field: The European Union and Sport Governance," in Ingeborg Tömmel and Amy Verdun (eds.), *Innovative Governance in the European Union: The Politics of Multilevel Policymaking* (Boulder: Lynne Rienner, 2009), chap. 10.

9. Union of European Football Associations, https://www.uefa.com/.

10. Jonas Fleega, "Football's 'Super League'—An Own-Goal for EU Soft Power," *EU Observer,* April 23, 2021, https://euobserver.com/opinion/151638?utm_source=euobs&utm_medium=email.

11. Romeo Franz, "After 50 Years, Where Do Roma Rights Stand Now?" *EU Observer,* April 8, 2021, https://euobserver.com/opinion/151466?utm_source=euobs&utm_medium=email.

12. Of fifty-five British prime ministers to date, twenty-eight studied at Oxford University. Oxford University, "British Prime Ministers," http://www.ox.ac.uk/about/oxford-people/british-prime-ministers; a further fourteen prime ministers studied at Cambridge University.

13. European Commission, "Employment, Social Affairs and Inclusion: Employee Involvement—European Works Councils," https://ec.europa.eu/social/main.jsp?catId=707&langId=en&intPageId=211.

14. European Parliament, "Free Movement of Workers," https://www.europarl.europa.eu/factsheets/en/sheet/41/free-movement-of-workers.

15. Iceland was part of Denmark at this time, and did not become fully independent until 1944 (when Germany was occupying Denmark during World War II). Property-owning women in the Isle of Man, UK were the first women to receive the vote in Europe in 1881.

16. IPU Parline, "Global Data on National Parliaments," https://data.ipu.org/.

17. European Parliament, "Women in the European Parliament (Infographics)," https://www.europarl.europa.eu/news/en/headlines/society/20190226STO28804/women-in-the-european-parliament-infographics.

18. Ramona Bloj, "Women's Europe," Robert Schuman Foundation Policy Paper, no. 587, March 9, 2021, https://www.robert-schuman.eu/en/doc/questions-d-europe/qe-587-en.pdf.

19. European Commission, "The Gender Pay Gap Situation in the EU," https://ec.europa.eu/info/policies/justice-and-fundamental-rights/gender-equality/equal-pay/gender-pay-gap-situation-eu_en.

20. Monika Pronczuk, "EU Proposal Seeks to Close Gender Pay Gap By Requiring Companies to Reveal It," *New York Times*, March 5, 2021.

21. For example, see Germaine Greer, *The Female Eunuch* (New York: McGraw Hill, 1971).

22. Council of Europe, "Human Rights Channel—Sexism: See It, Name It, Stop It," https://human-rights-channel.coe.int/stop-sexism-en.html; also see Council of Europe, "Preventing and Combating Sexism," https://www.coe.int/en/web/genderequality/combating-and-preventing-sexism and https://rm.coe.int/cm-rec-2019-1-on-preventing-and-combating-sexism/168094d894.

23. Claudia Postelnicescu, "Europe's New Identity: The Refugee Crisis and the Rise of Nationalism," *Europe's Journal of Psychology* 12(2), 2016: 203–209, https://www.ncbi.nlm.nih.gov/pmc/articles/PMC4894286/.

24. Rita Chin, *The Crisis of Multiculturalism in Europe: A History* (Princeton: Princeton University Press, 2017).

25. Michael Lipka and David Masci, "Where Europe Stands on Gay Marriage and Civil Unions," *Pew Research Center*, October 28, 2019, https://www.pewresearch.org/fact-tank/2019/10/28/where-europe-stands-on-gay-marriage-and-civil-unions/.

26. Graeme Reid, "Poland Breaches EU Obligations Over LGBT, Women's Rights," *Human Rights Watch*, February 24, 2021, https://www.hrw.org/news/2021/02/24/poland -breaches-eu-obligations-over-lgbt-womens-rights#.

27. Benjamin Novak, "Hungary Further Expands Executive Power and Curtails Gay Rights," *New York Times*, December 16, 2020.

28. Eurostat, "Youth Unemployment," https://ec.europa.eu/eurostat/statistics-explained /index.php/Youth_unemployment#:~:text=In%20the%20EU%2D27%20in,youth %20unemployment%20rate%20of%2015.1%20%25.

29. European Union, "European Youth Portal," https://ec.europa.eu/youth/policy /youth-strategy_en.

30. European Commission, "Erasmus +: EU Programme for Education, Training, Youth and Sport," https://erasmus-plus.ec.europa.eu/. Desiderius Erasmus was a Dutch renaissance scholar, who engaged with Luther on the religious debates of Protestantism, and who passionately believed in the power of education.

31. Eurostat, "Population Structure and Ageing," https://ec.europa.eu/eurostat/statistics -explained/index.php/Population_structure_and_ageing.

32. Eurostat, "Life Expectancy at Birth in the EU: Men vs. Women," https://ec .europa.eu/eurostat/web/products-eurostat-news/-/DDN-20190725-1#:~:text=Life %20expectancy%20at%20birth%20in%20the%20European%20Union%20(EU)%20was,a %20difference%20of%205.2%20years.

33. European Centre for Disease Prevention and Control, "Coronavirus Disease 2019 (Covid-19) in the EU/EEA and the UK—Eighth Update," April 8, 2020, https://www .ecdc.europa.eu/sites/default/files/documents/covid-19-rapid-risk-assessment-coronavirus -disease-2019-eighth-update-8-april-2020.pdf.

34. The UN defines *migration* as when a person stays in another country for a year or more.

35. Alex Nowrasteh, "Illegal Immigrants in Europe," Cato Institute, November 15, 2019, https://www.cato.org/blog/illegal-immigrants-europe.

36. Eurostat, "Migration and Migrant Population Statistics," https://ec.europa.eu /eurostat/statistics-explained/index.php/Migration_and_migrant_population_statistics.

37. OECD, "Migration," https://www.oecd.org/migration/.

38. "Windrush Generation: Who are They and Why Are They Facing Problems?" *BBC News,* November 24, 2021, https://www.bbc.com/news/uk-43782241.

39. Hugh Alderwick and Lucinda Allen, "Immigration and the NHS: The Evidence," *The Health Foundation*, November 19, 2019, https://www.health.org.uk/news-and -comment/blogs/immigration-and-the-nhs-the-evidence.

40. European Parliament, "The Principle of Subsidiarity," https://www.europarl .europa.eu/factsheets/en/sheet/7/the-principle-of-subsidiarity.

41. Thomas Risse, *A Community of Europeans? Transnational Identities and Public Spheres* (Ithaca: Cornell University Press, 2010).

42. European Commission, "Employment, Social Affairs and Inclusion: European Social Policy Network (ESPN)," https://ec.europa.eu/social/main.jsp?catId=1135&langId =en.

43. Council of Europe, "The European Social Charter," https://www.coe.int /en/web/european-social-charter; and European Commission, "European Pillar of Social Rights," https://ec.europa.eu/info/strategy/priorities-2019-2024/economy-works-people /jobs-growth-and-investment/european-pillar-social-rights_en.

7

Public Policy Debates
and Agendas

THIS CHAPTER FOCUSES ON CORE PUBLIC POLICIES GENERATED BY THE countries of Europe, discussing areas of commonality and distinction between them. Governments involve themselves in the policy process to make policies in the "public interest" and for the "public good," though how governments define these often leads to dispute.[1] Countries possess a national style and scope that distinguishes their policies from those of other countries, but the European Union does have significant influence in helping to shape public policies for its twenty-seven members. Examples include policies surrounding the euro currency, or the EU's Common Agricultural Policy (CAP). This EU influence extends to nonmembers, such as participants in the European Economic Area, which need to be in harmony with such EU initiatives.

Complete homogenization does not exist, and coming to such a conclusion would ignore the many economic and social differences that exist across the continent. What we do identify is a system of multilevel policymaking in Europe, with the interaction and interdependence of the EU and national governments in policy initiatives, with the emphasis varying depending on the policy under review.[2] Furthermore, even though the EU is involved in many aspects of agenda setting and policymaking, with significant influence not just in Europe but globally, the actual implementation of policy is normally the responsibility of national governments.[3]

Some differences are evident in terms of how broad economic or social philosophy diverges from country to country—such as in variance in traditions of welfare programs, LGBTQ rights, or engagement with trade unions—but also how policies can change within each country over time, particularly with a change of government. Political culture influences policies, but so can the political party in power, the changing mood of the population, the condition of the economy and budget, and lobbying by various interest groups. Countries also must respond to external factors, such as increasing competition and global demand for its products, as well as policies instituted at the EU level. The true nature of economic and social policy in Europe, then, is complex. I balance these factors in this examination of national policies, focusing broadly on the economic and social arenas. Prior to specific analysis, however, I open with a discussion about the broader features of European public policy.

Common Objectives of European Public Policy

Are there common objectives of public policy that most European governments share and, if so, what are they? To answer this question, we can make a case that there are several common denominators of policy broadly shared by the majority of Europeans, even though the specific level of implementation or acceptance differs across the continent. These ideas include a belief in social democracy; broad support for relatively high public spending and progressive taxation; widespread support for welfare programs, health care, and other public services, especially for the less fortunate; and a general respect for the workforce. Turkey and Russia may be outliers in their reluctance to embrace fully some of these goals, with sectors of their populations more in support than their governments, but these ideas have widespread support across the continent. Support for some policies, however, has waned a little in recent years in parts of Western Europe under pressure from global competition, neoliberal economic ideology, recession, and increased debt, and some convergence of economic policies is discernible. Despite these policy changes, significant support remains for these concepts within European societies.

Social democracy is discussed here not so much as a political movement or party, but rather as a broad outlook on life. Within Europe, it implies that the government supports a wide range of social objectives through central funding. It also implies some attempt to minimize the inequalities within society through direct economic policies—higher levels of taxation and generous support for the unemployed and others needing assistance. The *welfare state* is a term aptly applied to most European countries, where state support for education and health care is substantial, and where the onus remains on the state to provide, rather than the private sector. Compared with other regions of the world, public spending is relatively high as a percentage of GDP, and covers large public works and subsidized transportation.[4] Higher education is also predominantly public, with a belief in open and relatively inexpensive access to it for those who are qualified. Attempts to undermine such programs face resistance, as we can see in austerity efforts by governments in Greece and the UK during the 2010s.

The Gini Index (or Gini coefficient) is a common mechanism to measure income or wealth inequality within and across societies, with the lower the score the less the inequality. Given the socialist background of CEE states and their relatively poorer economic performance, they score lower generally than their West European counterparts. According to the World Bank, Slovenia (24.6), the Czech Republic (25.0), and Slovakia (25.0) score the lowest of all EU members, and so reflect the highest economic equality within European countries. The EU's three Nordic members score between 27.3 and 30.0, similarly reflecting their policy preferences. The only real outlier within the EU is Bulgaria with the highest score of 41.3, which indicates a poor administrative structure rather than an ideological slant. Turkey's score of 41.9 is similar. The UK's score of 35.1 does reflect its more laissez-faire environment (and as a point of comparison, the United States scores 41.4).[5]

This embrace of social democracy came under some pressure and scrutiny in recent years and, in many countries, governments scaled back these policies. Privatization and competition policies strengthened the private sector, and lessened the role of the state. Budgetary problems diminished the state's ability to maintain such high levels of public spending, while efforts to attract foreign businesses led to pressures to lower personal and corporate taxation levels in many countries. Despite resistance, this erosion is evident even in such welfare-supporting countries as Germany and Sweden. As a result, inequality within countries has increased in recent years.

While this overall European philosophy of social democracy holds somewhat true at a macro level, it is evident that differences are present once one begins to focus on specific cases. Factors forge differences, such as the level of government intervention and the degree of social protection offered by the state. Although one can always make the case that all European countries are unique, this is not necessarily helpful for comparison. One way to approach this is to think in terms of broad economic models to explain diversity in the continent. For example, the Nordic model stresses economic openness, egalitarianism, and social protection as core features, as typified by Sweden. The Anglo-Saxon model exemplified by the UK and to some extent the Czech Republic promotes open and transparent markets, less government intervention, relatively less social protection, and a less integrated role in the economy for labor unions. The Rhineland model, linked to France and Germany, exemplifies a strong role for government, a degree of protection for national businesses, and an emphasis on social protection. Poland and Hungary perhaps fit here. The Mediterranean model, typified by Greece and Italy, promotes a central role for the state, high levels of social spending, high levels of debt, and a less flexible attitude to policy change. Like all frameworks, the broad ideas are helpful in distinguishing some differences, but falter when focusing on specific factors in each country, as well as various reforms undertaken.

One of the most important challenges in European political economy in the post–Cold War era was closing the gap between the countries of Western and Eastern Europe. As discussed in Chapter 2, the Cold War divided Europe not only physically but also in terms of political, economic, and social policies and development. Countries of CEE have changed considerably over the past thirty years, and I draw attention to these developments in subsequent sections.

The Economic Policy Arena

This section begins with an overview of the European economic arena, and then moves to consider some examples of specific national economic policies. In a subsequent section, we address the role of the EU in shaping policy alternatives on the continent. The World Bank provides an Ease of Doing Business Index (renamed the Business Enabling Environment in 2022), which provides a quantifiable score for how an economy performs in terms of its regulatory environment, as well as the ease with which someone could begin operating a company there. This index offers a view of how open an economy is and, to a certain extent, how effectively the economy functions.[6]

In the 2019 rankings, Denmark is the highest-ranked European country, coming in fourth in the world. Other top twenty in the world finishers are Georgia (seventh), United Kingdom (eighth), Norway (ninth), Sweden (tenth), Lithuania (eleventh), North Macedonia (seventeenth), Estonia (eighteenth), Latvia (nineteenth), and Finland (twentieth). It is worth noting that many of these economies are CEE states, identifying their need to be flexible in their business operations to attract investors and grow their economies. Although Germany ranks closely at twenty-second, Spain (thirtieth) and France (thirty-second) indicate less open economies, whereas Italy (fifty-eighth) and Greece (seventy-ninth) give some indication of problems of openness and transparency within their economies.

The World Economic Forum (WEF), a nongovernmental organization based in Geneva, offers an annual Global Competitiveness Index, where the WEF defines *competitiveness* as the set of institutions, policies, and factors that determine the level of economic productivity.[7] This index provides a perspective on which economies are performing at a high level in terms of efficiency. Inside the top ten global performers are five West European states: the Netherlands (fourth), Switzerland (fifth), Germany (seventh), Sweden (eighth), United Kingdom (ninth), and Denmark (tenth). In this index, CEE states fare less well, highlighting continuing problems in their productivity. Greece again struggles coming in at fifty-ninth in this ranking, but Georgia (seventy-fourth) and North Macedonia (eighty-second) display economic challenges not evident in the World Bank's rankings.

In terms of a broader perspective on economic and social development, we can also look at the UN's Human Development Index, which assesses human capacity rather than simple economic data. These factors include life expectancy, education and knowledge acquired, and the standard of living assessed by the gross national income per capita. According to 2020 data, eleven of the twenty highest-ranked countries in the world are European, with Norway topping the list. The five Nordic countries are in the top eleven globally ranked. In contrast, Russia (fifty-second) and Turkey (fifty-fourth) are slightly adrift of the rest of Europe. Serbia (sixty-fourth), Albania (sixty-ninth), and North Macedonia (eighty-second) again indicate the work needed to be eligible for entry into the EU.[8]

European economies, especially in Western Europe, tend to be postindustrial, where services account for about two-thirds of employment and income across the EU27, as well as other highly developed economies such as Switzerland and the UK.[9] Manufacturing declined steadily over the past two decades, as much production moved eastward across the continent in search of lower costs, and now often outsourced out of the continent into Asia. According to the World Bank in 2019, manufacturing accounts for about 14 percent of total EU GDP.[10] Of the EU total industrial production, Germany accounts for 28 percent, with Italy at 16 percent, and France at 12 percent. Germany's predominance in industrial production is a critical factor in shaping its political and economic policies. In a sector such as clothing, for example, the figures vary with Italy providing almost half of total European output.[11] Agriculture now accounts for around 4 percent of the total workforce of the continent, but often wields more influence and controversy than that figure would suggest. The further east one moves in the EU, the more manufacturing and agriculture still figure as predominant factors, and the transition to service economies causes tensions within the EU27.

Corporatism has a long history in Europe, dating back to medieval times when workers and small-scale businesses organized themselves into guilds to cooperate and work together. During the interwar period, corporatism gained a bad reputation because of the way that fascist Germany and Italy organized their economies, with business beholden to the government. In the 1960s and

1970s, support for neocorporatism increased, and this entailed the close linkage of business, trade unions, and government in the organization of the economy, often in joint decisionmaking with a common pursuit of the public interest. A notable example of corporatism is where these players come together to agree on a prevailing wage for labor, or on some important national economic policies. Corporatism is more successful when business and labor organize in their own umbrella organizations, as this facilitates dialogue and negotiation.[12] A national organization established to coordinate such negotiations also helps. However, corporatism has declined in significance since the 1990s in the face of growing support for neoliberal, or market-driven, policies.

The best working examples appear to come from smaller countries, and those with a higher level of social cohesion. Normally, those countries seen with successful corporatist practices include Austria, Norway, Sweden, the Netherlands, and Denmark. Although the UK attempted consensual decisionmaking in the 1960s and 1970s through the National Economic Development Council, this cooperative model disappeared under the government of Margaret Thatcher in the 1980s, and Britain has been unable and unwilling to rebuild such cooperation since. Similarly, France and Italy do not have institutions or the political culture to build such cooperation.

Business, Corruption, and Corporate Responsibility

It would be nice to consider that a postconflict Europe might also have found a way to be postcorrupt, but that is not the case. To be true, European countries score highly on international lists for being the least corrupt, though Russia and some CEE countries tend to fare less well. Bulgaria and Romania, members of the EU after 2007, are causing significant problems to the EU bureaucracy because of their continuing and endemic corruption. Corruption scandals surrounding political favors to business have rocked West European countries in recent years, notably in the UK, France, and Germany. In Italy, scandals surrounding Silvio Berlusconi's business practices and personal behavior involved corrupt practices, though mostly ignored from within Italy.

In Transparency International's 2020 Corruption Perceptions Index, fourteen of the world's least corrupt twenty countries are European. Tying as the world's least corrupt country is Denmark, followed in order by the following countries in the top twenty: Finland, Switzerland, Sweden, Norway, the Netherlands, Luxembourg, Germany, the United Kingdom, Austria, Belgium, Iceland, Estonia, and Ireland.[13] By way of contrast, Bulgaria, Hungary, and Romania all tied at sixty-ninth, indicating the wide disparity across EU membership. Russia at one hundred twenty-ninth again displays the wide gulf between it and the EU.

Part of the goal of the EU is to promote common standards across its membership, but it is difficult to legislate common practices for politicians, or common values for what is normal and acceptable behavior, as national cultural norms insert themselves. The Organisation for Economic Co-operation and Development, based in Paris, to which many of the largest European countries belong, has developed a series of rules and norms concerning bribery in international business, though countries do not always follow these.[14] The World Business Council for Sustainable Development, a nongovernmental organization based in Geneva, boasts 200 companies as members, and perhaps serves a wider group in terms of promoting good business practice and sustainability.[15] The European Commission has attempted to stamp out unfair practices in the marketplace, with record fines handed down to businesses in recent years, especially for collusion and price fixing. It is hardly likely that corruption will disappear completely within the EU. Not only companies are involved in corruption, however, but governments also. One example is the implication of the British government in dubious deals selling armaments to Middle Eastern governments, especially the Saudi government during the prime ministership of Tony Blair. Rather than face a government scandal in 2006, Blair closed down an official inquiry looking into the deals on the grounds of "national security."

Corporate responsibility has strong support on the continent, even though this does not necessarily make European businesses more responsible in their practices. The broad support for social democracy in most countries implies that businesses should pay more attention to social contract obligations and the

---

Box 7.1   Parmalat: Corporate Corruption

Parmalat, an Italian company based in Parma (home of Parmesan cheese and Parma ham) specializing in food and dairy products, was one of Europe's strongest companies until its collapse in 2003. Through various fraudulent accounting methods and offshore holding companies, it turned out that the company had huge hidden debts and that some of its leading officials had been involved in corrupt practices, with fifteen of them found guilty in court. Parmalat's accountants also came under fierce scrutiny for allowing such illegality to take place unnoticed. It was Europe's biggest bankruptcy at the time. The Parmalat case undermined the smugness of Europeans that the corrupt business practices exposed in the United States with the cases of Enron and Tyco around the same time could not possibly happen in Europe.[a]

Note: a. Ron Rimkus, "Parmalat," CFA Institute, November 29, 2016, https://www.econcrises.org/2016/11/29/parmalat/.

impact of business on the environment, or that there should be closer monitoring over such activities. The EU actively monitors business action and has had a corporate responsibility plan in place since 2011. The Commission defined *corporate responsibility* as the need to integrate "social, environmental, ethical, consumer, and human rights concerns into their business strategy and operations."[16] In a Commission report published in March 2019, the EU documented its progress in promoting good business practices and sustainability, in European countries and overseas, though much work remains to be done.[17]

One of the biggest problems facing the newer members of the EU, and some future aspiring members, has been to combat corruption in government and business to bring them into line with the mores and practices of business in Western Europe. Corruption in countries such as Bulgaria and Romania remains high, despite efforts by the EU to combat it. This frustration with the new members has made EU policy even tougher for aspirant members, such as Croatia and Serbia, to pass the corruption threshold of the EU. We should not underestimate corruption in Western Europe, however. Recent examples abound, such as the 2019 findings against Volkswagen for falsifying its emissions standards in the "Dieselgate" scandal, or the 2020 jailing of a former French prime minister, François Fillon, for embezzlement of government funds. In February 2021, a French court convicted Nicolas Sarkozy, a former president, of corruption and influence peddling and sentenced him to three years in prison.[18]

Employment Policies

Unemployment is an economic, social, and political issue. All governments fear the potential instability from having large numbers of workers in long-term unemployment, even though views of unemployment differ. Some recognize unemployment to be a fact of economic life, whereas others attempt to minimize it, either with strict labor policies that limit the abilities of employers to lay off workers, or through significant state intervention in terms of unemployment and training programs. A key driver of the EU from the 1950s (and with its predecessor organizations in the late-1940s) was an effort to revive the moribund, destroyed economies of postwar Europe, to ease unemployment and to divert workers' attention from the potential attraction of communism. Memories of the 1930s depression and labor unrest, including the rise of Hitler in Germany, seared into the minds of political leaders. In the 1970s and 1980s across Western Europe, economic malaise and stagflation led to a series of political initiatives to combat unemployment, including new energy put into the EU. The 1986 Single European Act partly aimed to remove barriers to trade and economic activity, thereby spurring economic activity and reducing unemployment. Special funding emerged from the EU to ease long-term unemployment in inner-city, rural, and rust belt zones.

In the years since the 2009 recession, unemployment has again become an intensely political issue. This is particularly the case for long-term (structural) and youth unemployment, often one and the same. By 2009, one in five people younger than age twenty-five was unemployed. In some countries, the figure was higher—for example, 37 percent younger than age twenty-five in Spain were unemployed. As the recession deepened, and governments had less money to spend on economic programs, unemployment worsened and led to widespread dissatisfaction. Street riots from Athens to London in 2011 were symptomatic of a growing alienation among the continent's youth and a sense that gainful employment would perhaps never be available. The prospects of a radicalization of the politics of many young people were evident, and yet most governments seemed to lack the capacity to break this trend. The rise of populism in many countries links to poor economic prospects. For example, the Alternative for Germany party rose quickly after its establishment in 2013 in the eastern regions of Germany tied to the poorer economic prospects in those areas.

The Covid-19 pandemic caused significant levels of unemployment and economic dislocation across all of Europe during 2020–2022. National economies all but shut down, and massive subsidies for the unemployed became the norm. Border closures also threatened the normal pace of business, and nationalism prevented the development of shared policies across the continent. Inflation and supply chain issues, exacerbated by Russia's invasion of Ukraine in 2022, caused further economic problems by mid-2022, especially as a European boycott of some Russian energy supplies raised prices significantly. These are issues that will reverberate across European economies for years to come, and may well have long-term or permanent damage to the continent's economic fabric.

Since 2000, all EU member states have had to provide legal protection and equal rights in employment to the LGBTQ community.[19] However, as discussed in the previous chapter, this hides significant differences in treatment of LGBTQ communities across Europe in terms of such things as the right to marriage. A lack of protections for these communities in the workplace appears to grow in CEE; countries outside of the EU27, such as Russia and Turkey, have poor records in terms of LGBTQ protections, and Russia provides no legal protection at all for these groups.[20]

Business Culture

The growth of the EU's influence over the European market has had an impact on companies in Europe, even if this has stopped short of creating what we could describe as "corporate Europe." The EU's regulatory embrace shapes areas such as competition policy, subsidies, investment, barriers to trade, and money—the euro for the majority of members—but national policy still holds sway over corporate taxation levels, value-added tax (VAT) rates, and stock listings, as well as in significant regulatory areas, such as pharmaceuticals. Although managers are increasingly mobile within Europe, national characteristics of managers remain prominent.

Shaped by the work of Geert Hofstede and others, considerable evidence exists to show how varied European managers remain in terms of culture, style, and decisionmaking.[21] Hofstede's work compares business culture on a variety of criteria, including power distance, uncertainty avoidance, and individualism. For example, British management style tends to be more open and flat, comparable to the US business model, whereas many continental styles are more likely to be hierarchical. Managers in Portugal and Spain favor collective and interpersonal management approaches, whereas Germany and Italy favor more masculine or achievement-oriented action, along with greater emphasis on the individual. Ronnie Lessem and Franz-Friedrich Neubauer developed a business model for different regions of Europe. For example, the West model, such as the UK, emphasizes pragmatism and free enterprise, whereas the South model, such as Italy, emphasizes humanism, feeling, and convivial relations. A North model, based on France, focuses on rationalism, professionalism, and bureaucracy.[22] Similarly, we can identify a particular style of Nordic management.[23] Although English is emerging as the lingua franca of European business, there is considerably less convergence in business style. The EU is helping to shape ideas around corporate social responsibility and ethics, but prevailing national norms and laws continue to be core factors in influencing corporate practice.

Gender issues also remain problematic inside corporate Europe, as noted in previous chapters. On average, women hold only about 10 percent of top management positions across Europe. There is considerable debate as to whether the EU should mandate equitable representation, but to date without action. Some countries have opted for their own quota policies, such as Norway (outside of the EU) that requires a minimum of 40 percent female participation on company boards. Equity in salary also lags in companies, and in the EU27 marketplace women receive about 84 percent of the remuneration of men doing similar work.

Telecommunications and Transportation

Significant restructuring of the telecommunications sector across Europe has taken place, partly prompted by the policies of the Commission since the 1980s to promote competition and privatization, but also accepted by national governments as important in their competitiveness across Europe and globally. Monopoly national phone companies have weakened or divided under deregulation pressures, with fierce competition welcomed from mobile phone providers. Nevertheless, national companies remain dominant in some countries. Deutsche Telekom is the largest telecom company in Europe, with sales in 2016 of €73.1 billion, followed by Telefónica in Spain with €52 billion.[24] There is considerable fluidity and competition within the European market.[25]

National governments retain control over transportation policy in terms of support for roads or rail, or specific transport infrastructures. However, to promote the interconnectedness of the European market, the EU provides support for European-wide transportation initiatives linking countries, whether in terms of road links, high-speed train routes, or airline and open skies competition. Infrastructure is generally better in West European countries, where significant national financing is available to promote transport routes. In CEE, such national support is less available, and the cost to upgrade rather prohibitive.

France has possessed high-speed train links (Train à Grande Vitesse [TGV]) since the 1990s, and this system is not matched by any other country in Europe. For small countries, such as Belgium or the Netherlands, such a high-speed network makes little economic sense, except as a spur to the French system. Some small European states, such as Andorra, Cyprus, and Iceland, have no railway system. The UK's train infrastructure has lagged behind its West European partners, despite deregulation and privatization. Plans for a high-speed network were unveiled for the first time in 2020, partly as a political ploy of "leveling-up" poorer regions by the government of Boris Johnson to assuage voters in the north of England. With the high cost of construction, as well as the many likely environmental challenges, the government scaled back plans in 2022 and the system will take decades to develop, if it ever materializes. A new rail line across London, the Elizabeth Line, did open in May 2022, albeit over three years late but just in time for the queen's seventieth anniversary jubilee. Spain and Portugal operate national trains on a different gauge from the rest of Europe; thus, after the 1990s they built new lines for trains crossing Europe. Britain had a similar issue, so it built a special line to connect with France once the Channel Tunnel opened in May 1994.

The airline industry is a sector dominated by national policies and airlines, where the EU has a limited role. For decades, national governments owned their national airlines, but today we see largely privatized companies. For example, British Airways became a private company in 1987. Air France had majority government ownership until 2004, and today the French government holds a 16 percent stake. Scandinavian Airlines System originally had 50 percent ownership by

Box 7.2   The Channel Tunnel

The (English) Channel has helped to distance the UK from continental Europe for centuries, especially in a political and cultural sense, even though that distance is a relatively short 21 miles (34 kilometers) at its narrowest. Historically, the only way to cross was by ship until commercial flights started in 1919, and then the hovercraft between 1970 and 2000. Although ships still carry passengers across the Channel in large numbers, the quicker route is by train via the Channel Tunnel. Such a tunnel had been contemplated before (Napoleon in particular considered building a tunnel in the early 1800s), but the rise of the EU and Britain's trade connections to continental Europe brought the opportunity forward.

The tunnel's construction took place between 1988 and 1994 by a private consortium, the Eurotunnel Group, with a final price tag of about £9 billion, twice the planned budget. The tunnel's length is just over 31 miles (50 kilometers). Three separate tunnels actually form the Channel Tunnel, one primarily for passenger trains, the second for freight, and the third a smaller service tunnel. The tunnel faced problems early on with technical and debt issues, but seems to be running more smoothly now. In 2017, the managing company changed its name to Getlink. Brexit requires changing the flow of traffic, with increased border management, customs, and controls, so this is likely another period of uncertainty for the tunnel in the present and near future, along with the uncertainty surrounding the Covid-19 pandemic.

the governments involved, but today that stake is down to just under 15 percent for the Danish and Swedish governments. One of the biggest developments in airline traffic in recent years is the growth of private, budget, no frills airlines, enabled by the EU's deregulation of air space in 1997 to allow airlines to fly anywhere in Europe. The four largest budget airlines in Europe are Wizz Air (founded in 2003, headquarters in Hungary), Ryanair (1984, Ireland), EasyJet (1995, the UK), and Norwegian (1993, Norway). These airlines are highly successful and carry millions of passengers to numerous destinations each year, but all suffered during the 2020–2022 Covid-19 pandemic, with EasyJet initially grounding its whole fleet.

One other interesting example of an Anglo-French governmental partnership was in building the Concorde, the world's first supersonic passenger jet. The Concorde flew commercially between 1976 and 2003, and although the flights were profitable, the governments could never recoup their investments. The opposite of the budget airlines, Concorde contained around 100 seats only for first-class passengers. With just twenty planes in the fleet, large expenses remained unrecoverable, and the environmental impact (particularly noise) was extensive. No other airlines besides British Airways and Air France bought the Concorde as part of their fleets. The downturn in the travel economy following the terrorist attacks in the United States in September 2001 put further economic pressure on the airline, following a well-publicized and filmed crash of a Concorde in July 2000, killing all onboard.

Many important transportation policies also take place at city level. Cities regulate traffic in terms of parking restrictions, or can levy surcharges to travel into the cities (governments control surcharges to use highways). Taxi services are normally under local regulations in terms of who can be a taxi driver and rates that are charged. The control London has over its black taxis is an example. Recently, cities have had to contend with new transportation issues, such as with the rise of Uber and Lyft. The City of London had ongoing legal battles with the US-based Uber, contributing to a short-term ban on Uber there, until a legal agreement allowed Uber into London again in 2021. Many cities, such as Amsterdam, Copenhagen, and Heidelberg, have opted to restrict vehicular traffic, particularly heavily polluting vehicles, and have adopted significant amounts of bike lanes in their cities. Public transportation systems, whether buses, trams, and underground trains, are also controlled at the local level.

The EU has worked for several decades on the promotion of a Trans-European Transport Network, attempting to link the various national transportation systems (and coordinate national policies) to promote the single market.[26] Key elements of the EU strategy include the overall reduction of carbon emissions from transportation in line with the EU's environmental program, and the promotion of transportation infrastructure to link countries across the continent seamlessly. The EU plans include all types of transportation, but with an important goal to try to get the bulk of, if not all, freight transportation in Europe on trains by 2050. As part of this goal, the EU has targeted the interoperability of trains across all the national systems of Europe as a critical element. Also important for the EU are efforts to promote consumer rights on transportation across the EU27. One current goal is to try to bring together companies across the continent to become a global leader in autonomous transport (driverless vehicles, etc.).

Taxation

Taxation policy remains very much a national decision, in terms of corporate and personal taxation levels. At the corporate tax level, countries can use low rates as an incentive to attract business to their region, a policy used well by Ireland to attract technology companies over the past two decades. The average corporate tax rate in the EU27 in 2020 was 21.3 percent (23.3 percent for the eurozone). This figure has slowly dropped since 2000, when the EU average was over 30 percent. There is a wide range of corporate tax rates, with France (33.3 percent) and Germany (30 percent) being among the highest, dropping to countries such as Bulgaria (10 percent) and Hungary (9 percent) among the lowest.[27] Efforts to create a minimum global corporate tax rate of 15 percent continued in 2022, with potentially a significant impact on European countries.

Personal tax rates also differ by country, and lower rates are used to attract qualified, high-earning workers. The top tax rate for the highest earners is around 60 percent of income, with rates, for example, in Belgium (60.2 percent), Portugal (61 percent), and Sweden (60.1 percent). The UK (47 percent) and Germany (47.5 percent) are in the middle range, scaling down to lower ranges in CEE, such as Hungary (33.5 percent) and Poland (39.5 percent). Among the lowest tax brackets are the Baltic states, such as Estonia (21.3 percent) and Latvia (21.4 percent).[28] The EU's common value-added tax, essentially a kind of sales tax, operates within a band established by the EU, but is still open to national decisions concerning the actual rate, and to some extent what gets taxed. The minimum VAT rate allowed by the EU is 15 percent, and the highest rate charged is by Hungary at 27 percent. Only five EU members charge a VAT rate below 20 percent.[29]

Employment laws are also national in conception. Some countries, such as France and Spain, protect workers' rights considerably, making it difficult for companies to fire them. This, arguably, also makes companies less willing to hire them in the first place. In France, changing this policy has been one of the highest priorities of the Emmanuel Macron government. The UK, in contrast, has a policy less protective of workers, where companies arguably can expand and contract more easily based on the demands of the marketplace. The EU is developing policies regarding discrimination and affirmative action in the workplace, though here national rules are still predominant.

Energy and Climate Change

European countries possess different profiles in terms of energy usage and policy, even though the EU provides some overall coordination of policy goals.[30] Historically, many relied on coal as a core energy provider, and the presence of this commodity in abundance partly helps to explain the early ability to industrialize in countries such as the UK, France, and Germany. In the UK in particular, coal miners held an almost mythic status as the foundation of a modern, industrialized state, and this helps to explain the social disruption of efforts by the Thatcher government in the 1980s to destroy, essentially, the power of the miners. In contemporary Poland, dependence on coal for energy and employment raises obstacles for a smooth shift away from fossil fuels, although there are plans to add nuclear energy.[31]

France focused its energy policies on nuclear energy as a way to build self-sufficiency, and has the highest dependence on nuclear power of any country in Europe, currently standing at 75 percent of its total energy. Plans were to scale this back to about 50 percent by 2035, but in a surprise move in February 2022, President Macron announced an expansion of the nuclear program with the construction of fourteen new reactors, along with other smaller nuclear plants.[32] The UK has also a heavy use of nuclear energy, though controversies exist around any conversation of extending nuclear power, and small reactors are likely at about 10 percent of the cost of a regular plant. In Germany, plans are to phase out the use of nuclear energy completely after 2022, as part of its environmental program. States are beginning to build their renewable energy capacities, but differ on the speed of implementation. Across the EU, the average stood at 19 percent in 2018, pursuing the EU goal of 20 percent by 2020. This rate may rise as a result of efforts to wean countries away from dependence on Russia for energy.

A similar stance is present in terms of environmental policies in general, such as recycling. National policies can differ, and some countries particularly in CEE lag behind the standards of the rest of Europe. There is, however, a common denominator, or basic level, to which all countries in the EU need to aspire. Negotiations regarding global environmental policy, whether through the Kyoto, Copenhagen, or Paris Agreement, take place with the lead by the EU rather than directly by individual member countries. Standards and targets are EU-wide, rather than simply national. For European countries outside of the EU, there is a variance in terms of their environmental programs. For countries such as Norway, Switzerland, and the UK, there is a high level of commitment to sustainability. Others, such as Russia, Turkey, and Ukraine, remain far from the EU benchmark. Russia, in fact, has much to gain from short-term climate change, as this would unlock greater energy resources in Siberia, and free up shorter transit passages across the Arctic Circle.

One widely used quantitative method to judge the comparative performance of countries in pursuing better environmental policies is the Environmental Performance Index (EPI) developed at Yale University in the United States. In the index's 2020 rankings, the top ten environmental performers are all European—indeed, twenty-three of the top thirty countries are European.[33] Denmark tops the list, but the non-EU members just mentioned are all in the top ten (Switzerland third, the UK fourth, and Norway ninth). Four of the five Nordic countries stand in the top ten, with Iceland a rather laggardly seventeenth.

The index highlights the disparities between the better-performing West European states and the less environmentally agile CEE states, such as Hungary (thirty-third) and Poland (thirty-seventh). Russia (fifty-eighth), Ukraine (sixtieth), and Turkey (ninety-ninth) again display the relative policy distance between them and the rest of Europe.

Russia is a significant supplier of energy to many European countries, especially in terms of liquefied natural gas (LNG). Germany, Italy, and Poland each receive about 50 percent of their LNG from Russia, with France and the Netherlands around 25 percent.[34] This gives Russia tremendous political and economic leverage to switch supplies on and off, and helps Russia maintain some influence. For the EU as a whole, about 30 percent of its oil supplies come from Russia. Germany, in particular, is heavily dependent on Russian energy supplies for about 63 percent of its needs, and this partly explained German reluctance to criticize sharply or impose meaningful sanctions on the Vladimir Putin administration.[35] The phasing out of nuclear energy in Germany after 2022 exacerbates its dependence on Russia. Nevertheless, the German government announced the termination of a second pipeline program, Nord Stream 2, in February 2022 as a response to Russia's invasion of Ukraine, just after the pipeline's completion at a cost of $11 billion. The EU announced in May 2022 a staggered reduction over two years of Russian oil supplies to the bloc, though Hungary remained exempt from this and Germany slowly phased in the program. A lack of alternative gas suppliers made a similar ban in this sector more difficult to reach. What is difficult to know is whether these actions are permanent whatever the outcome of the Russia-Ukraine war, or whether an end to the war will reopen energy lines from Russia.

The EU prides itself on its environmental activism, and has had a series of action programs in place over the past decades. The seventh Environmental Action Program (EAP) covered the period 2013–2020, and laid out specific targets for the EU as a whole to reach.[36] Built into these policies was a prior agreement from 2007, which set the 20/20/20 goals for 2020. These programs are a 20 percent cut in greenhouse gas emissions (based on 1990 levels), 20 percent of energy from renewables, and a 20 percent improvement in energy efficiency. Although these goals were binding on EU members, each country received flexibility regarding its own specific targets.[37]

Member governments agreed in 2014 to promote further binding goals for 2030, and these continue to push countries in a similar direction. By 2030, the agreement for the EU as a whole was to reach a 40 percent cut in greenhouse gas emissions (based on 1990 levels), a 32 percent utilization of renewables for energy, and a 32.5 percent improvement in energy efficiency.[38] Again, each country has flexible targets depending on its level of development and energy needs, but the overall goal is for the EU27 to reach the goals collectively as part of the European Commission's Green Deal, agreed to in 2019. By most accounts, the EU was close to meeting its 2020 targets, but required much more vigorous action to reach the 2030, or the 2050, targets.[39] In July 2021, the EU announced its Fit for 55 package, which aimed for a 55 percent reduction in greenhouse gasses by 2030, including a ban from 2035 on all petrol/diesel cars and trucks.[40] As a way to help meet the climate targets, the EU announced in February 2022 that some nuclear and LNG plants could be designated as sustainable. The highest greenhouse gas emissions per capita within the EU are from Luxembourg, Estonia, and Ireland.

Non-EU members, such as Iceland, Norway, and the UK, pursue environmental strategies aligned with the EU, working within the Paris Agreement. Norway plans to allow only electric car sales after 2025. The UK has embarked on what is the world's largest wind energy program on Dogger Bank in the North Sea, with 200 turbines each almost the height of the Eiffel Tower. For the first time in December 2020, the UK generated more electricity from wind than any other source.[41] Going east across Europe, however, there is less support for such environmental strategies, and Russia's record is not positive with major levels of pollution recorded during Soviet times, but with little positive movement today. As already mentioned, Russia stands to gain from some aspects of climate change.

Tourism

Tourism provides significant earnings, where national-based policies and strategies predominate in a partnership of government and business. The job of the EU is only to support and help coordinate the actions of member governments. Those countries with better infrastructure (transportation, hotels) tend to do better at attracting tourists than others, but the importance of national attractions to visit also shapes income. Europe is the world's leading tourist destination, accounting for just over half of the global total of visitors.[42] In 2018, some €782 billion contributed to EU GDP from tourism revenue, with an estimated 672 million tourists. Tourism accounts for about 10 percent of the EU's total GDP. The top five destinations for tourists are Spain, Italy, France, and Greece (in the EU), and the UK.[43] For a country like Greece, tourism provides a significant portion of the country's earnings, with about 10 percent of the workforce employed there. In 2018, tourism accounted for about 43 percent of Greece's total service exports.[44]

Box 7.3　Tourism and Venice

Most European countries absorb their tourist visitors with a smile. Italy is one of the world's biggest tourism destinations, and in 2017 tourism accounted for some 40 percent of services exports, 13 percent of GDP, and provided jobs for 14.7 percent of the Italian workforce.[a] Some cities struggle at times with the vast numbers of tourists they have to accommodate. A great example of the pressure of tourism in the modern age is Venice, where the city struggles to manage the volume of tourists who arrive each year, especially the large volume coming by cruise liner. This led to the growth of the No Big Ships interest group (No Grandi Navi) to ban large cruise ships from Venetian waters. The total number of tourists visiting Venice in 2019 topped 36 million (in comparison, the Vatican had about 10 million tourists in 2019). The main area where tourists congregate is only about 40 square kilometers. Tourist numbers have overwhelmed Venice's capacity to cope, and have led to major calls to reduce tourist numbers. The 2020–2022 Covid-19 pandemic essentially stopped tourism in Venice (and across Europe), and stimulated fresh calls to regulate tourism in the city and promote more sustainable practices. The city went ahead and banned cruise ships in August 2021. The city needs the earnings, but locals hope to balance this with some respect and breathing room for them in their own city.[b]

Notes: a. *OECD Tourism Trends and Policies 2020* (Paris: OECD, 2020).
　b. Paula Hardy, "Sinking City: How Venice Is Managing Europe's Worst Tourism Crisis," *The Guardian*, April 30, 2019.

The Evolving Role of the EU in Policymaking

Do countries shape EU policies, or does the EU alter the dynamic of national policymaking? To what extent has the emergence of the EU as a central actor altered the debates and transactions about public policy, even in nonmember countries? How is European public policy made, and by whom?

There is evidence of an emerging common economic and social philosophy embraced by EU members today, as discussed earlier. This philosophy explicitly ties to the Copenhagen Criteria for membership, in terms of the promotion of democracy and human rights, as well as the implementation of a capitalist open economy. The EU has helped to forge its own economic space since the 1950s to pursue common policies and objectives, with a central instigator in the Commission.[45] This EU market has also helped to bring together the previously disparate economic systems of Europe, notably with the East-West split in the continent during the Cold War era. The euro requires the nineteen member-states in the zone to pursue specific criteria prior to joining and economic policies that conform to standards established by the Commission and the European Central Bank.

The steady growth of EU institutions matches the increasing influence over, or interdependence with, European economic and regulatory policy. From its modest beginnings in forming a common market, the EU developed a single external tariff, and then moved to try to eliminate remaining barriers to internal trade in the Single European Act of 1986. The Treaty on European Union signed in 1991 promised to create the single currency, and a dozen countries implemented this within a decade. In all these actions, the EU influenced the shape of Europe-wide economic policies and had a substantial impact on the domestic economic policies of member states, through regulation and the force of the market. Some sectors—and some countries—remain sluggish in adopting change, especially in strategic areas such as telecommunications and banking. Rules regarding ownership of businesses also remain largely nationally focused, as do corporate and personal taxation rates.

The global recession after 2009 exposed some of the difficulties within European economies. What had appeared to be a strength of the euro in holding disparate countries together now arguably became something of a weakness, as countries with fiscal problems threatened to sink the whole eurozone. The most serious case was Greece, which required significant economic restructuring and financial assistance, but problems across the weaker members—Portugal, Ireland, Italy, Greece, and Spain (PIIGS)—caused serious drawbacks for the euro. A €750 billion bailout in 2010 helped to prop up the euro, but critical decisions about ongoing bailouts from the wealthier to the poorer members caused deadlock within Europe. A core issue was the extent to which Germany, as the eurozone's strongest member, was willing to continue assisting the poorer members. This still has not been fully resolved, and was evident again in 2020–2022 in the struggle to put together an EU Covid-19 aid package.

The Europeanization of Policy

The rapid changes within CEE political and economic sectors in the 1990s led to increased interest in the concept of Europeanization. To meet criteria for EU membership, the CEE states quickly adopted EU norms, regulation, and policies at the national level, something considered as the Europeanization of policy. This is essentially top down, where EU policies shape and integrate into national arenas, in particular through actions of the Commission. Although these actions are rather transparent in terms of CEE, the concept is widespread across the EU in seeing how European initiatives embed themselves into national policymaking, and how policymaking across Europe becomes more homogenous. Put simply, it is "the domestic adaptation to European regional integration."[46] Membership in the eurozone, for example, requires the acceptance of European-level policies and economic philosophies. Such Europeanization, however, also is evident across the spectrum of policymaking, even in terms of foreign relations as I address in the next chapter.

Some also consider Europeanization in a bottom-up manner, where member states help to shape EU policy though input and influence. The influence of the German government in continuing to shape policy initiatives of the euro—and most other EU initiatives—indicates how national concerns can mold EU policy. Similarly, euroskeptic national policies from countries such as the UK (when an EU member), Czech Republic, or Hungary help to shape European policies by limiting what the EU can adopt. It is also possible to see Europeanization in fluid ways as the intermingling of top-down, bottom-up, and horizontal mixing of ideas to create a distinctive set of EU policies.

Such differences of opinion over the scope and role of the EU in public policy have contributed to debates over the nature, speed, and goals of European integration, as well as to the limits of Europeanization.[47] Terms such as *multispeed Europe, Europe à la carte, variable geometry,* or *differentiated integration* have become commonplace in the discussions of Europe. All of these terms indicate a diversity of opinions about public policy, and point to the difficulty of getting complete agreement on all aspects of all EU policy by all twenty-seven members. To what extent can EU members select the policies they support and the areas in which they wish to cooperate, and when can they reject policies, or sections of policies? Can the EU be sufficiently flexible to allow countries to select programs in which to participate, to opt in or opt out? Can the EU be loose enough to have countries engaged at differing levels?

This debate is not simply on the public policy level, but extends to the wider debate about whether the prospect is Federal Europe or an "ever closer union," or just looser cooperation between groups of friendly, neighboring, trading states. This is a larger ideological debate, but constantly played out in a practical sense in the public policy arena. The UK provided an excellent example of such differentiated participation in the policies of Europe, attempting often to limit the supranational scope of policy and, when failing, opting out of elements of policy that it opposed. Such differentiation did not end with the UK's withdrawal from the EU in January 2020, but is evident in negotiations over what the UK-EU relationship will be in the coming years, and whether the UK gets to cherry-pick elements of its partnership. Such differentiation is noticeable in the bitter divisions in the implementation of EU migration policy post-2015, when some members simply have refused to follow what the EU has demanded. Irish and Swedish neutrality creates the necessity to opt out of aspects of the EU Foreign and Security Policy. The eurozone is another example, where eight EU members currently do not participate, and we consider this next.

Euro and Euro Area Policy

For the first thirty years of European cooperation, policy-makers focused on providing increasing areas for economic partnerships. The removal of trade barriers was a high priority, eventually leading to the Single European Act of 1986, and the completion of the single market by 1992. Although various tariff and other barriers fell, the problem remained that each member retained its own currency, providing significant transaction costs and risks. The Treaty on European Union, signed in Maastricht in February 1992, laid out plans to tackle this issue over the following decade. Through a European Monetary Union (EMU), currencies of those states planning to join the euro were linked together to help converge their economic cycles. Members needed to meet strict criteria for their currencies in terms of stability and debt, and these criteria were required to satisfy skeptics in Europe, and international currency markets. Many observers at the time believed that a strong currency was impossible to achieve, given the political calculations of most members.

Despite this negativity, the euro launched in 1999 for banking transactions, and in 2002 as a currency for citizens' daily use. The euro facilitates trade and tourism, and removes transaction costs linked to transferring fluctuating currencies. The introduction of the euro and the disappearance of national currencies are significant not only in terms of economics, but also because of the social and political ramifications. Removing the Greek drachma, the world's oldest currency dating back two millennia, or the French franc merely going back to the fourteenth century, or the deutschmark, the symbol of postwar German stability and prosperity, are important changes to national life.[48]

The European Central Bank (ECB), based in Frankfurt, is responsible for the euro and the wider financial stability of the eurozone and, to a certain extent, the EU as a whole.[49] Its location in Frankfurt was partly to calm German fears about giving up control of its currency to an international body, even though the bank aspires to be European in scope and not pander to specific national interests. The ECB began its operations in June 1998, after more than a decade of preparation for the launch of the euro the following year. The ECB aims to provide stability in the eurozone to promote jobs and economic growth, but that provides it significant control over monetary policy in the member states.

The euro area in 2022 comprises 342 million citizens inside nineteen EU members, and the euro facilitates economic transactions for those remaining outside the zone (e.g., tourists visiting several countries within the euro area).[50]

Despite short-term problems, notably the crisis over Greek debt, the bank has achieved considerable success in its management of the currency. The euro is a key reserve currency of the International Monetary Fund, and its stability belies the political undercurrents of dealing with nineteen member governments, and speaks to the importance of Europe-wide leadership. After three decades in existence, the euro is a clear success for European policymaking, and few consider its disappearance likely. Similarly, few consider the euro likely to attract all EU members to join the area, and so differentiation will continue in this important sector. The EU approved Croatia to join the zone in January 2023, but opposition to Bulgaria (2024) and Romania (2027) on the grounds of corruption and profligate spending make these negotiations difficult.

The head of the ECB is a president, whom the European Council appoints for an eight-year nonrenewable term. The current president, appointed in November 2019, is Christine Lagarde (France), former managing director of the International Monetary Fund. The president manages a governing council made up of the central bank governors of the nineteen eurozone members. The ECB has faced problems, notably in terms of maintaining the eurozone relations with the eight members outside of the zone (mostly states in CEE), but also in keeping financial discipline within the zone.[51] One of its most prominent cases was dealing with the economic collapse of Greece following the 2009 recession, while at the same time attempting to be European in outlook rather than simply reflecting German interests and imposing austerity measures. Dealing with the Covid-19 impact on the eurozone and the EU economies in general in 2020–2022 was also an issue that taxed the ECB, along with the high rate of inflation prompted by the economic dislocation of the Russia-Ukraine war in 2022.

EU Competition Policy

One of the key roles of the Commission is setting the regulatory framework and the rules of competition by which businesses operate within the single market. The goal is to promote competition and business within a well-functioning single European market, and so reduce the prospect of monopolies undermining such competitiveness inside of Europe. Merger and acquisition (M&A) activity within Europe has grown significantly, but this is always under the scrutiny and regulatory eye of the Commission (Competition portfolio) to make sure that competition within the market is not stifled.[52] M&As also come under national law, but the EU has the right to scrutinize large mergers, even if the companies are not European in origin. If companies wish to do business in Europe, then the EU must approve of their mergers.[53]

In countries such as France and Germany, it is difficult for hostile takeovers to be successful, especially from outside of the country, because of the ownership structure of the companies and the legal protections afforded to them. The French and German governments often express concern at the use of foreign sovereign funds—overseas money linked to governments—to take over strategic companies in their energy and telecommunications areas. Similarly, angst occurred in Sweden in 2010 when a Chinese company, Geely, (successfully) bid to take over the struggling national champion Volvo.

There is a balance to achieve in promoting national business champions, which may be too small to be globally competitive, and European-wide companies (e.g., Airbus) to challenge the big players on the world stage. Furthermore, true competitiveness may only come at a global scale, but the Commission must balance this against the potential stifling of other smaller (European) companies. The biggest cases recently have been in the role played by US-based technology companies, such as Apple, Facebook, Google, and Microsoft. These companies have faced significant scrutiny by the Commission, and often have received huge fines for their deliberate limitation of competition.[54] Such fines include $5 billion to Google in 2018, $2.7 billion to Google in 2017, $1.45 billion to Intel in 2009, $1.2 billion to Qualcomm in 2018, and $731 million to Microsoft in 2013.[55] These decisions by the Commission to fine US technology giants have received the ire of successive US administrations, but highlight the degree to which the EU is a global regulatory power.[56] Countries also implement allied competition policy, such as in Italy that fined Amazon $1.3 billion for antitrust violations in December 2021. In a parallel development, the EU implemented the General Data Protection Regulation (GDPR) in May 2018 as a way to regulate these companies' respect for data privacy. Facebook (Meta) received a fine of $270 million at the hands of the Irish government in September 2021 for breaking these rules.[57]

European companies have also faced fines by the Commission. In 2016, Daimler, MAN, DAF, and Volvo shared a €2.93 billion fine for rigging the price of trucks across Europe.[58] A similar group of countries faced EU action in 2020 for colluding over emissions tests for their vehicles. Such decisions are fraught with political considerations, and this is evident with the ongoing debates about whether or not to allow a Chinese company, Huawei, to provide critical technology to build telecommunications across Europe, thereby potentially taking a dominating role in this sector.

EU policy restricts the temptation at a national level to provide subsidies to companies in trouble, although subsidies have not disappeared from Europe. Any potential support must gain approval through the EU State Aid Rules, and obtain Commission approval. The EU wants little to no subsidies to take place to maintain fair and open competition in the single market. Debates and controversies continue, however, as to the extent of subsidies given to Airbus over the years in its efforts to compete with Boeing, which also receives subsidies in different ways from the US government. In an October 2019 judgment by the World Trade Organization, the WTO found that the EU had made illegal subsidies to Airbus over a decade or more. The WTO levied a $7.5 billion fine against the EU, with the equivalent retaliatory sanctions allowed by the United States.[59] Despite all these issues, some European companies have undoubtedly risen to global prominence on their own terms, such as BP, Nokia, Philips, and Siemens. Recent efforts focus on attempts to develop policy to control subsidies paid by foreign governments to foreign companies operating in the EU market.[60] Although this policy consultation continues the Commission's goal to promote an open market, it is probable that increasing fears of Chinese companies operating in the market are pushing these initiatives.

The goal of the EU is to promote research, development, and scientific innovation across the region. Over the past decade, the EU's goal was to encourage member countries to spend 3 percent of their gross domestic expenditure on innovation, but by 2020 EU members recorded just over 2 percent spending. The EU is aware of the great need for Europe to maintain such programs to remain competitive with other regions of the world.[61]

With the growing influence of Brussels as the policymaking center for business rules, there has been a substantial growth of the lobbying industry, representing European and non-European companies, as I touched on in Chapter 5. Lobbying, or interest representation as it is officially named, is a little more difficult than under a single national government, as European decisionmaking flows from a complex interplay of national governmental and EU administrative players, notably the Commission and the European Parliament, making it less easy to target potential lobbying efforts. The EU claims that the system is less open to financial incentives, such as political contributions, because there are fewer pressure points to bring financial largesse to bear within the EU. This is in contrast to national political structures, and also because of efforts at transparency within the EU institutions.

The EU launched its Transparency Initiative in 2005, and companies began to register with the EU in 2011 to lobby openly. In 2019, the European Parliament required its members to register all interactions with any lobbyists. This has not reduced the fear of unfair influence within the EU, but transparency and scrutiny are helpful. Much lobbying, however, continues to take place at the national level to influence European decisions (working through the Council), as such peddling is much more difficult for the EU to control.[62]

The creation of the single market helps to make competition and growth easier for European companies, although this is not equitable for all. Business regulations within the EU are extremely complex and open to change, and so even the largest companies can find it tough to keep up with the rules and regulations regarding commerce. Smaller companies are at a distinct disadvantage in that they often do not have the personnel or the expertise to stay on top of regulations, nor do they know exactly how to take maximum advantage of the opportunities of the market. This is especially the case for small- and medium-sized companies in the transition economies of CEE, and many British companies faced these hurdles in the post-Brexit environment.

The EU has significant cooperation in the pharmaceutical sector.[63] It has common rules for clinical trials inside countries, and has a body of rules, Eudralex, governing products. There are significant challenges, however, in developing common harmonized regulations and the distribution of drugs in all the EU's languages. The European Medicines Agency (EMA) is a centralized body approving the use of drugs across the EU, something akin to the Food and Drug Administration (FDA) in the United States.[64] During the 2020–2022 pandemic, this system faced considerable challenges as the EU struggled to maintain control over the approval of vaccines to combat the coronavirus, as well as the distribution of the vaccines. Its work came under pressure from Russian propaganda efforts to diminish support for the EU vaccine programs. Most notable was the UK-Swedish AstraZeneca vaccine, which had significant difficulties gaining approval initially, and then some adverse results forced its temporary removal. In April 2021, the EU sued the company for breach of contract in not supplying the vaccine according to its contract, and demanded the diversion of some UK supplies to the EU, but this was another example of EU problems in managing the pandemic.[65]

The EU Budget

The budget is a primary area to consider if we make an argument that the EU is growing in strength and influence to the detriment of member countries. Over recent years, however, the EU budget stood at about 1 percent only of members' gross national income, so not an excessive amount by any standard. I should also note that the vast majority of the EU budget spending is to promote projects within member countries through cohesion payments, such as support for agriculture and rural areas, regional development, and worker mobility and training. The budget comprises member payments, taxes collected on goods emanating from outside the EU, and a portion of VAT taxes collected by member states. The Council, Commission, and Parliament negotiate the budget in broad outline for six-year periods in advance, with the most recent completed period 2014–2020. Each year, the budget is finalized and detailed in terms of specific priorities within the broader parameters of the six-year plan. In the 2014–2020 budget, policies related to economic growth, rejuvenation of decaying regions, jobs, and agriculture accounted for almost half of the EU budget. Plans for sustainability took a further one-third. Areas such as security and administration (6 percent) were small elements of the budget. The budget for 2019 stood at €165.8 billion, which was similar to the annual expenditure in previous years of the budget.[66]

Negotiations took place in early 2020 regarding the six-year budget plan for 2021–2027. These talks were more contentious than usual because of the background of the coronavirus pandemic ravaging the continent, as well as the rather instinctive desire of member governments to get the best possible deal for themselves. A preliminary agreement came in July 2020 after four straight days of negotiation between governments, and this six-year budget agreement amounted to €1.07 trillion, including special relief to those hard-hit by the pandemic. For the first time, the Commission gained the right to raise money on capital markets for the EU budget. In addition to the budget, members reached an agreement on a package to provide coronavirus relief to countries, particularly to help with the economic dislocation (discussed below). The Council, Commission, and Parliament gave final approval over the second half of 2020, with the budget becoming operational early in 2021.[67]

One of the biggest issues concerning the EU budget is the competition between member countries, as well as which countries are net contributors to the EU, and which are net beneficiaries; that is, which countries pay more than they get out of the EU. This issue was one of the most important lobbying points made by the leave campaign during the Brexit referendum, with the outlandish (and untrue) argument that the UK was a net contributor of £350 million weekly to the EU (just over €400 million). The UK was, in fact, a net contributor to the EU in 2018, but only to the tune of €9,770 million for the year, less than half of what the Brexit leave campaign claimed. This put the UK as the second-largest net contributor behind Germany, which was a net contributor of €17,213 million. For right-wing opponents of Germany's "bankrolling" of the EU, this figure rankles. The other net contributors are all wealthy West European members.

Conversely, the main beneficiaries of EU budgetary largesse are countries of CEE, as well as the poorer members of Western Europe, such as Greece and Portugal. The top two net beneficiaries from the EU budget are Hungary (€5,029 million) and Poland (€11,632 million).[68] This fact added tensions to the ongoing disputes between the European Commission and twenty-five members of the EU on the one hand and Hungary and Poland on the other about the latter two's deviance from EU policies and democracy. Efforts to cut these funds to Hungary and Poland failed in 2020 as the two governments threatened to torpedo the whole budget, but increasingly there are attempts to limit such funds to recalcitrant members. The overall politicization of the budget process and the allocation of funds continue to undermine and stoke opposition toward the EU and its institutions, but no permanent resolution is in sight to improve this process as member countries diverge on policies and the role of the EU.[69] The European Court of Justice, however, made a major ruling in February 2022 that the Commission could withhold budget funds to recalcitrant members—namely Hungary and Poland—to promote democracy across the bloc.

Agriculture and Fisheries

The Common Agricultural Policy is perhaps the best-known and most contentious policy within the European arena, and is the largest item within the EU budget. Conceived in the Treaty of Rome in 1957, the CAP began programs in 1962. Core aims of CAP are to stabilize prices and production of agricultural commodities, and to help rural development across Europe. In its early days, many saw the CAP as a special provision for France and its farmers to maintain their support for the EU, and through the life of the program France remains the largest recipient of overall funds, and the continent's largest food producer (though the Netherlands is the EU's largest food exporter). For France, farmers, agriculture, and the rural lifestyle have a deep emotional appeal, even though only about 7 percent of its workforce are farmers. Greece and Ireland are the largest per capita recipients of CAP payments. These funds are broken into two types. The vast majority of funds go to farmers directly through the European Agricultural Guarantee Fund (EAGF), whereas a much smaller amount goes to the protection of rural development through the European Agricultural Fund for Rural Development (EAFRD).[70]

Over the first two decades, CAP consistently took more than 70 percent of the EU's total budget. Under fire from critics, notably the UK, the EU gradually reduced the amount of spending on CAP. In the 2020 overall EU budget of €168.68 billion, CAP took a 34.5 percent share of €58.12 billion, with an average of 37.8 percent over the life of the 2014–2020 budget. The criticisms of CAP centered on the cost in absolute terms, the overproduction of large amounts of subsidized food leading to such things as butter mountains in rented aircraft hangars, and the allegedly unfair distribution of funds to privilege certain countries, notably France, which remains the country with the overall largest agricultural economy. The membership of CEE countries in the EU in the 2000s led to careful monitoring of CAP funds, as many feared these new members could potentially drain the EU financially with subsidies. Although these states did receive significant benefits, they still lag behind West European EU members in the funding per capita they receive. Efforts to reform CAP will continue, but the EU succeeded in its overall goal of providing stable and adequate food in Europe.[71]

The Common Fisheries Policy (CFP) is another contentious EU policy, though not at the same level as CAP. The EU27 accounts for 3.3 percent of global fishing and aquaculture (fish farming), and ranks them as fifth in the world. The core goals of the CFP are to maintain adequate and sustainable fish stocks in EU waters, arrange for a quota system for EU member countries, and to manage fishing agreements with other countries for EU waters and around the world. Funds come through the European Maritime and Fisheries Fund (EMFF), and for the 2014–2020 budget, the total funds available over the six years were €6.4 billion. For the 2021–2027 budget period, the proposed funding is €6.14 billion.

Spain and Denmark are the EU's top two fishing producers, and Spain itself receives about 20 percent of all EMFF funds.[72] As China controls about one-third of the world's fishing industry, this is another area of ongoing tension in EU-China relations. One of the loudest voices of disgruntlement over the years, however, belonged to the UK, and the push to "take back control" over its fishing policies proved to be a critical emotive plank of the Brexit campaign. This was somewhat ironic given the small size of the British fishing fleet and that EU countries receive most of British exported fish. Negotiations remain to finalize the relationship of British fishing with the EU post-Brexit, but a naval spat between Britain and France in May 2021 over Channel Island fishing rights highlights the ongoing tension.[73]

Regional Development

Another area in which corporate Europe seems to struggle is in providing growth and opportunities in postindustrial regions—in the so-called rust belts. Revival of such regions often relies on government and EU largesse, rather than farsighted corporate investment, but partnership between the two sectors tends to bring better results. The revival of the docklands along the Thames in London, for example, was because of both government and private investment. The selection of the sites for the 2012 London Olympics occurred because of the prospects for economic rejuvenation of these areas, again with a mix of public and private investment.

The EU Regional Development Fund (ERDF) is significant and forms part of the EU's cohesion policy to bring economic development to the continent, especially to those areas lagging behind others. Started in 1975, the ERDF retains importance, and in the 2014–2020 budget received €200 billion in funds. Programs focused on the promotion of growth and jobs, especially in disadvantaged regions, as well as greater cross-border cooperation. In the 2021–2027 budget, the ERDF is likely to receive around €250 billion, and emphasize programs in promoting technology innovation and assistance to small- and medium-sized companies.[74]

Social Policies in Europe

The Council of Europe has a European Social Charter for all its members ostensibly protecting social and economic rights for citizens in the field of employment, social protection, welfare, and health. Originally signed in 1961, and provided a seventh update in 2015, the charter provides the legal basis for social protection across the continent, and is an important element of the Council's human rights portfolio, although these clauses are potentially difficult to implement when recalcitrant governments oppose and ignore them.[75] Nevertheless, the Council perceives this to be a social constitution for Europe, at least setting benchmarks for behavior by governments and the treatment of their citizens.

The EU adopted its own Charter of Fundamental Rights in December 1969 based on the Council of Europe's, and this provided a broad umbrella of goals along with the basic development of a social safety net for citizens. Included in the charter were such "rights" as to a fair wage, freedom of association and collective bargaining, health protection, equality of treatment for men and women, and safety at work. EU Social Policy has developed significantly since the 1990s, promoting labor and women's rights in particular, but offering leadership on a broad range of issues.[76] Despite this role, most social policy formulation for EU members remains at the national level, with governments unwilling to cede authority to the EU, and consequently EU policy has struggled to gain traction.[77]

Where the EU tries to develop some sort of social policy, it is reliant on the member countries to implement it, and is powerless when they do not.[78] For example, policies on LGBTQ rights and abortion emanate at the national level. Countries in CEE have historically had liberal abortion laws, partly stemming from their history of communism, whereas countries of southern Europe along with Ireland have had much stricter laws, shaped by the influence of Catholicism. Retirement age linked to pension benefit is also policy made at the national level. Retirement age in Europe ranges from sixty-one to sixty-seven years, according to the Organisation for Economic Co-operation and Development, though an outlier is Turkey where the normal retirement age is fifty-one for men and forty-eight for women.[79]

The cost to national governments of maintaining a broad range of social policies is high. According to the OECD, government expenditure on public social goods as a percentage of GDP is highest in Europe. The world's top twelve countries spending on the social arena are all European, topped by France at 31.0 percent of GDP, Finland at 29.1 percent, and Belgium at 28.9 percent. The average for the EU stands at 26.7 percent of GDP. Luxembourg tops the world on a per capita spending basis.[80] Efforts by governments to trim social protection measures normally face major opposition, such as we can see in recent years in countries like France, Germany (25.9 percent), and the UK (20.6 percent).

The Greek financial crisis after 2010 engendered huge protests when the government attempted to cut budgets in the social arena. Austerity policies also loomed large over the British general elections of the 2010s, which led Prime Minister Boris Johnson to promise massive new infusions of money into the social network, and especially the National Health Service, in the election of December 2019. The consensus that public spending is a good thing is widespread, but the debate centers on public good versus streamlined public expenditure. Governments are willing to nibble around the edges, but rarely are capable of drastic changes in public social policy.

Criminal Justice

Differences also are evident in other social areas, such as criminal justice. A country like the Netherlands has progressive laws in these areas, with prostitution and the use of soft drugs, for example, essentially legal. Most other countries have much tougher laws in these areas. Firearms policies also differ from country to country, with little common control exerted by the EU. The Swiss have one of the highest per capita ownership of guns in the world, but a low fatality rate in gun violence. The British police normally do not carry weapons, though they do have access to them if needed. Deaths from guns in the United States stand forty-eight times larger than in the UK per 100,000 people. Deaths from gun violence across the EU27 are low, with Austria registering one of the highest totals, but less than one-quarter of the United States per 100,000. One area of agreement across Europe is the abolition of the death penalty. This is required of EU members, but even Russia and Turkey have eliminated it.

Similarly, policies on incarceration differ widely across Europe. In terms of incarceration per 100,000 population, Russia leads Europe with a figure of 386, closely followed by Turkey at 329. These figures again point to Russia and Turkey as outliers within European policy. All CEE countries tend to have relatively high rates of incarceration, including the Czech Republic (202) and Poland (190). In contrast, West European countries have lower levels, with the UK at the upper level. Nordic countries have among the lowest levels, with Norway and Sweden standing at sixty, Finland at forty-nine, and Iceland at forty.[81] In terms of prisons for those incarcerated, only France and the UK have some private prisons, and these are for small numbers of prisoners, with the majority in government-controlled prisons. Across the EU, prisons are government controlled. Domestic violence is an area gaining scrutiny in Europe, especially during the 2020–2022 pandemic. Overall, estimates are that about 6–10 percent of women in Europe are the victim of domestic violence in a given year, and that one in four women will experience domestic violence in their lifetime.[82]

Health Care

Health care is a major policy area controlled at the national level. Public health care funded by the state is most common across the continent, although with national deviations. Cradle to grave protection is commonplace and a right for citizens, but the increasing cost of such provisions has led to strains to maintain the coverage, and differing national actions. In most Nordic countries, health care provisions are still wide-ranging, including generous policies on maternity and paternity leave. Even with recession and budgetary crises, governments have found it extremely difficult to challenge the prevailing support for expenditure on health care.

Quality of life indexes normally place most European countries as high performance, whether in terms of infant mortality, life expectancy, or literacy. The life expectancy in Eastern Europe and Russia lags behind Western Europe, though the collapse in figures immediately after the transition in the early 1990s has stabilized. In Russia today, the average life expectancy for a man is only sixty-eight years, according to the World Bank. In Western Europe, life expectancy averages above eighty years of age, whereas in many parts of CEE that figure can be as much as ten years less. Moldova and Ukraine are the worst in Europe, both recording average life expectancy of seventy-two years.[83] The highest life expectancy is in the microstates, notably Monaco, where based on wealth, health care, and diet, average life expectancy is eighty-nine years (see the Country Profiles section at the end of the book for more details). Overall, the European population is aging and declining, and these factors provide challenges for economic and social policy.

Obesity is a key factor in health care, but figures are mixed. According to the OECD, the average rate of obesity for their member countries is 19.5 percent of the adult population.[84] The best-performing European member is Italy, with a score of 9.8 percent, the only one under a 10 percent threshold. Switzerland, Norway, Sweden, the Netherlands, Austria, and Denmark all score below 15 percent of the adult population. Conversely, the UK (26.9 percent) and Hungary (30 percent) score the worst for obesity of OECD's European members, though somewhat behind the overall worst score of 38.2 percent for the United States. These figures indicate national cultures, food choices, and food policies, and these are all factors that shape the health systems of their respective countries.

Euthanasia remains a controversial topic in the continent, with Switzerland possessing the most liberal laws, thereby attracting so-called suicide tourists with terminal illnesses to the country. Most reaction within Europe to the Swiss policy is not one of condemnation, but rather efforts to regulate and organize this movement of terminally ill people around the continent. To date, three EU countries allow for euthanasia, namely Belgium, Luxembourg, and the Netherlands, but it is likely that more countries will join that list.

Maternity and paternity leave is available across Europe, but differs by country in terms of specific elements, such as payments, length of time allowed for both parents, and how much is mandatory in terms of the leave. The current EU minimum for paid leave across all members is fourteen weeks.[85] The EU's Disability Strategy established in 2010 sets common minimum standards for policy across the EU27, with countries able to promote other policies locally. The policy is currently under review by the EU, and new standards are expected.[86]

Abortion rights also differ markedly across Europe, though the majority of countries allow abortions on request or for broad social cause. Only five countries ban or strictly limit the ability to have an abortion; namely, Andorra, Liechtenstein, Malta, Monaco, and Poland. Early in 2021, Poland restricted access to abortion to the tightest of all EU members, bringing widespread protest within the country. Fifteen countries have a mandatory waiting period for an abortion. Despite the right to an abortion in much of Europe, there are increasing social pressures to limit this right.[87]

Education

Free education, stretching into the university level, is still common practice in much of Europe. Some countries, such as the UK, have introduced modest tuition fees at universities, but these are controversial. Many countries continue to provide free university education. Most universities in Europe are also state universities, and there is traditionally little support for the growth of private universities as seen in the United States. In the UK, for example, universities fall under the control of a central authority, though Scotland maintains its own universities and policies (and a distinctive membership in the Bologna Process).

University degree structures follow a common European model for bachelor's, master's, and doctoral programs within the EU's Bologna Process, but this does not shape the content of degree programs or other initiatives made at a national level. The European Higher Education Area (EHEA) within the Bologna Process contains forty-eight member countries, including non-EU countries such as Armenia, Liechtenstein, Russia, Turkey, Ukraine, and the UK. Programs for elementary, middle, or high schools remain in the hands of national governments, though in the case of federal systems, subnational governments often make policy. Attempts at broad cooperation in education across the EU take place within the European Education Area.[88]

As in the Social Pillar, a critical concern for the EU is minimizing unemployment in the continent, especially youth unemployment. Recognizing the centrality of member governments to control policy, the EU offers support in terms of youth education (Petra), language training programs (Lingua), vocational education (Leonardo), the Erasmus university exchange program, and overall efforts to promote sustainable employment.[89] One recent development is the European Solidarity Corps, founded in 2016 and patterned somewhat on the US Peace Corps or AmeriCorps, which allows young people the opportunity to volunteer or gain work experience in projects across the EU.[90]

Human Rights

The Charter of Fundamental Rights of the European Union, initially written in 2000, became mandatory for all EU members with the implementation of the Treaty of Lisbon in 2009. The charter is compatible with the Council of Europe's European Convention on Human Rights, which is a central element of the Council's operations and which entered into force in 1953, as discussed in Chapter 3. All members of the Council of Europe must ratify these human rights provisions for membership. The European Court of Human Rights oversees the implementation of the convention, although there are limits on how much enforcement capability the court has over recalcitrant members.

The core mission of the EU's human rights policy is to promote a common platform of promotion of rights across all the EU members, as well as to promote human rights globally. This links to the concept of the EU as a moral power in the world, something I discuss in subsequent chapters. The charter has common ideas and principles that we might expect to see in any similar kind of human rights document.[91] There are, however, some notable statements to highlight. Article 2, for example, states, "No one shall be condemned to the death penalty, or executed." Article 8 says, "Everyone has the right to the protection of personal data concerning him or her." Other articles also promote specific EU agendas, such as Article 37, which gives all Europeans a right to environmental protection.

Social rights in general have a contentious history within Europe as member countries (especially the UK) have often railed against EU involvement in areas considered to be under national control. Traditionally, the EU has put together broad aspirations, but needs to work with governments for their promotion. The European Pillar of Social Rights emerged from the Treaty of Lisbon, and gained the support of the main EU institutions in 2017.[92] The twenty articles of the pillar are aspirational, and not all EU members will implement them. They cover three broad areas; namely, equal opportunity and access to the labor markets, fair working conditions, and social protection and inclusion. Specific articles refer to secure employment, equal opportunities, work-life balance, and health care rights. Article 19 of the preamble sums up the limitations of the EU to implement such programs, however, and the continuing prevalence of member countries:

> The European Pillar of Social Rights respects the diversity of the cultures and traditions of the peoples of Europe, as well as the national identities of the Member States and the organisation of their public authorities at national, regional and local levels. In particular, the establishment of the European Pillar of Social Rights does not affect the right of Member States to define the fundamental principles of their social security systems and manage their public finances, and must not significantly affect the financial equilibrium thereof.[93]

The Covid-19 Pandemic and Health Policy

Health policy is an area where member countries hold prominence in policy-making, so the emphasis of EU action is to supplement and assist governments. One role that the EU has promoted is in cross-border health policy, helping to make sure that EU citizens can obtain health care wherever they are living or traveling.[94] Within the Commission, the health portfolio includes food safety, and there are efforts to promote EU-wide cooperation on other matters such as infectious diseases.

With the limitations to EU policy, the response to the 2020–2022 Covid-19 outbreak was primarily a national one despite calls for greater collaboration. Each country chose its own strategy to pursue, and many borders closed by government decision.[95] Although the EU helped facilitate ideas, dialogue, and protective equipment, and supported programs to develop a vaccine, its weaknesses were evident in the face of a pandemic, especially as citizens primarily turned to domestic leaders for policy guidance. It was only in May 2020 that the EU began to put ideas together to provide economic support. It is difficult to know whether the pandemic will reinforce national strategies, or if it will nudge countries toward more coordinated health policies going forward. The EU did finally agree to a coronavirus emergency fund of €750 billion in July 2020, but this was for mitigation of the economic problems caused by the virus, and not for the promotion of coordinated health policy.[96]

The pandemic hit Europe hard beginning in spring 2020, with Italy being the hardest hit initially but soon the pandemic had spread across the continent. The EU proved incapable of pulling together a common response, and each country developed its own strategy. Some countries completely closed down, such as Italy and Spain, whereas others such as the UK and Sweden reacted slowly and, in the case of Sweden, did little to change their way of life, with somewhat disastrous results. National strategies led to the closure of borders across the EU, and a completely uncoordinated response. Each country devised its own economic plans to try to ameliorate the impact of the pandemic on the workforce, and each country had its own schedule for reopening, including its plans regarding whether to introduce Covid-19 passports or not. Each country organized its own political response, with legislation passed through national parliaments, often at breakneck speed.[97]

By early 2022, vaccination rates across the EU varied significantly, with 70-80 percent of the population vaccinated in many Western states, down to around 30 percent in Bulgaria. The EU's initial failure to act collectively, and the swiftness with which governments resorted to national survival strategies rather than to the EU, raised many questions about the ability of the EU to promote strong continental strategies in the future.[98] When the EU did agree—for example, on a plan to ban the export of vaccines outside of its borders—this did little to elevate the EU in its moral leadership claims.[99]

Conclusion

This chapter covers important ground in terms of economic and social policy. Although the EU possesses a significant role in policymaking, national governments of the EU27 also continue to play a central role in large areas of important economic and social policy. Countries not part of the EU control their own policy initiatives. It is difficult to envisage a scenario where the EU could take over these areas in the future. Even though there is wide variance in policies formulated, we can see that the EU helps to provide a basic common denominator or minimum for policy and regulation, even though there is often a divergence between the more established countries of Western Europe and the newer democracies of CEE. Differences are often the starkest when Russia and Turkey are included in the discussion. The 2020–2022 pandemic caused severe disruption to the cooperative policymaking apparatus within Europe, and it is uncertain the extent to which governments will recalibrate their policies going forward. It is also unclear what the longer-term impact of the Russia-Ukraine war will be on European policy.

Political and policy differences across European countries remain significant, as to be expected. How governments work with each other, inside or outside of the EU, to broker agreements and maintain peaceful relations is of critical importance, and a discussion of these issues forms the basis of the next chapter.

Notes

1. Thomas Birkland, *An Introduction to the Policy Process: Theories, Concepts, and Models of Public Policy Making,* 5th ed. (New York: Routledge, 2020).

2. Ingeborg Tömmel and Amy Verdun (eds.), *Innovative Governance in the European Union: The Politics of Multilevel Policymaking* (Boulder: Lynne Rienner, 2009).

3. Anu Bradford, *The Brussels Effect: How the European Union Rules the World* (New York: Oxford University Press, 2020); Herman Lelieveldt and Sebastiaan Princen, *The Politics of the European Union,* 2nd ed. (Cambridge: Cambridge University Press, 2015), chaps. 8, 9.

4. For data on public policy spending, see the Country Profiles section at the end of the book.

5. World Bank, "Gini Index," https://data.worldbank.org/indicator/SI.POV.GINI.

6. World Bank, "Business Enabling Environment," https://www.worldbank.org/en/programs/business-enabling-environment.

7. Klaus Schwab (ed.), *The Global Competitiveness Report 2019* (Cologny/Geneva: World Economic Forum, 2019), http://www3.weforum.org/docs/WEF_TheGlobalCompetitivenessReport2019.pdf.

8. *Human Development Report 2020: The Next Frontier: Human Development and the Anthropocene* (New York: UN Development Programme, 2020).

9. European Commission, "European Semester Thematic Factsheet: Services," https://ec.europa.eu/info/sites/info/files/european-semester_thematic-factsheet_services_en.pdf.

10. World Bank, "Manufacturing, Value Added (% of GDP)—European Union," https://data.worldbank.org/indicator/NV.IND.MANF.ZS?locations=EU.

11. Eurostat, "Industrial Production Statistics," https://ec.europa.eu/eurostat/statistics-explained/index.php/Industrial_production_statistics#Overview.

12. Markus, M. L. Crepaz, *European Democracies,* 9th ed. (New York: Routledge, 2017), chap. 11.

13. Transparency International, "Corruption Perceptions Index," https://www.transparency.org/en/cpi.

14. OECD, "Anti-Corruption and Integrity Hub," https://www.oecd.org/corruption-integrity/.

15. World Business Council for Sustainable Development (WBCSD), https://www.wbcsd.org/.

16. European Commission, "Internal Market, Industry, Entrepreneurship and SMEs: Corporate Social Responsibility and Responsible Business Conduct," https://ec.europa .eu/growth/industry/sustainability/corporate-social-responsibility_en.

17. European Commission, *Corporate Social Responsibility, Responsible Business Conduct, and Business and Human Rights: Overview of Progress* SWD (2019), 143 (Brussels: European Commission, 2019), https://ec.europa.eu/docsroom/documents/34482.

18. Kim Willsher, "Former French President Nicolas Sarkozy Sentenced to Jail for Corruption," *The Guardian*, March 1, 2021, https://www.theguardian.com/world/2021/mar /01/former-french-president-nicolas-sarkozy-sentenced-to-three-years-for-corruption.

19. European Commission, "Legal Aspects of LGBTIQ Equality," https://ec.europa .eu/info/policies/justice-and-fundamental-rights/combatting-discrimination/lesbian-gay -bi-trans-and-intersex-equality/legal-aspects-lgbti-equality_en.

20. Council for Global Equality, "The Facts on LGBT Rights in Russia," http://www .globalequality.org/component/content/article/1-in-the-news/186-the-facts-on-lgbt-rights -in-russia.

21. Geert Hofstede, *Culture's Consequences: International Differences in Work-Related Values* (London: Sage, 1984); see also https://www.hofstede-insights.com/product /compare-countries/.

22. Ronnie Lessem and Franz-Friedrich Neubauer, *European Management Systems: Towards Unity Out of Cultural Diversity* (New York: McGraw Hill, 1994).

23. Martin Lindell and Jouko Arvonen, "The Nordic Management Style in a European Context*," International Studies of Management and Organization* 26(3), 1997: 73–91.

24. Statista, "Leading Telecommunication Operators in Europe by Revenue 2016," https://www.statista.com/statistics/221386/revenue-of-top-20-european-telecommunication -operators/.

25. European Telecommunications Network Operators' Association (ETNO), https:// etno.eu/.

26. European Parliament, "Fact Sheets on the European Union: Common Transport Policy: Overview," https://www.europarl.europa.eu/factsheets/en/sheet/123/common -transport-policy-overview.

27. Trading Economics, "List of Countries by Corporate Tax Rate: Europe," https:// tradingeconomics.com/country-list/corporate-tax-rate?continent=europe. The tax haven of the Isle of Man has a zero rate of corporate tax.

28. Elke Asen, "Top Individual Income Tax Rates in Europe," *Tax Foundation*, February 22, 2019, https://taxfoundation.org/top-individual-income-tax-rates-europe-2019.

29. European Union, "Your Europe: VAT Rules and Rates," https://europa.eu/youreurope /business/taxation/vat/vat-rules-rates/index_en.htm.

30. European Commission, "Energy," https://energy.ec.europa.eu/index_en.

31. Justin Worland, "The Art of the Green Deal," *Time,* November 2–9, 2020.

32. Liz Alderman, "France Announces a Vast Expansion of Nuclear Power," *New York Times*, February 11, 2022; see also World Nuclear Association, "Nuclear Power in France," https://www.world-nuclear.org/information-library/country-profiles/countries-a -f/france.aspx#:~:text=France%20derives%20about%2075%25%20of,this%20to%2050 %25%20by%202035.

33. Environmental Performance Index, "2020 EPI Results," https://epi.yale.edu/about-epi.

34. Josh Holder, Karl Russell, and Stanley Reed, "How Russia's Natural Gas Powers the Market in Europe," *New York Times*, February 17, 2022.

35. Julian Wettengel, "Germany and the EU Remain Heavily Dependent on Imported Fossil Fuels," *Clean Energy Wire*, March 14, 2022, https://www.cleanenergywire.org/factsheets/germanys-dependence-imported-fossil-fuels.

36. European Commission, "Living Well, Within the Limits of Our Planet," https://ec.europa.eu/environment/pubs/pdf/factsheets/7eap/en.pdf.

37. European Commission, "Climate Action: 2020 Climate and Energy Package," https://ec.europa.eu/clima/policies/strategies/2020_en.

38. Clémence Pèlegrin, "Economic Recovery and Climate: For Europe and the World, Two Battles to Fight at Once," Robert Schuman Foundation Policy Paper, no. 579, December 8, 2020, https://www.robert-schuman.eu/en/doc/questions-d-europe/qe-579-en.pdf; see also European Commission, "2030 Climate and Energy Framework," https://ec.europa.eu/clima/policies/strategies/2030_en.

39. European Environment Agency, "Overall Progress Towards the European Union's '20-20-20' Climate and Energy Targets," https://www.eea.europa.eu/themes/climate/trends-and-projections-in-europe/trends-and-projections-in-europe-2017/overall-progress-towards-the-european.

40. European Council, "Fit for 55: The EU's Plan for a Green Transition," https://www.consilium.europa.eu/en/policies/green-deal/eu-plan-for-a-green-transition/.

41. Jillian Ambrose, "Watts Up: Sea Change for British Wind Power," *The Guardian Weekly,* January 15, 2021.

42. Michal Roman, Monika Roman, and Arkadiusz Niedziolka, "Spatial Diversity of Tourism in the Countries of the European Union," *Sustainability* 12, 2020: 1–16, https://www.mdpi.com/2071-1050/12/7/2713.

43. Eurostat, "Tourism Statistics," https://ec.europa.eu/eurostat/statistics-explained/index.php/Tourism_statistics; European Parliament, "Fact Sheets on the European Union: Tourism," https://www.europarl.europa.eu/factsheets/en/sheet/126/tourism#:~:text=In%202018%2C%20the%20'travel%20and,to%20some%2011.9%20million%20jobs); see also European Commission, "Internal Market, Industry, Entrepreneurship and SMEs: Tourism," https://ec.europa.eu/growth/sectors/tourism_en.

44. OECD, "Tourism Trends and Policies 2020: Greece," https://www.oecd-ilibrary.org/sites/f3180e03-en/index.html?itemId=/content/component/f3180e03-en#:~:text=linklink%20copied!-,Tourism%20in%20the%20economy,total%20employment%20in%20the%20country.

45. Larry Neal and Daniel Barbezat, *The Economics of the European Union and the Economies of Europe* (Oxford: Oxford University Press, 1998).

46. Paolo Graziano and Maarten P. Vink (eds.), *Europeanization: New Research Agendas* (Houndmills: Palgrave Macmillan, 2007), p. 7.

47. Reuben Wong and Christopher Hill (eds.), *National and European Foreign Policies: Towards Europeanization* (Abingdon: Routledge, 2011); see also Eleanor E. Zeff and Ellen B. Pirro (eds.), *The European Union and the Member States,* 2nd ed. (Boulder: Lynne Rienner, 2006).

48. The € (euro) symbol emanates from the Greek letter epsilon, with two parallel lines to denote stability.

49. European Central Bank, https://www.ecb.europa.eu/ecb/html/index.en.html.

50. Euro members in 2022 are: Austria, Belgium, Cyprus, Estonia, Finland, France, Germany, Greece, Ireland, Italy, Latvia, Lithuania, Luxembourg, Malta, the Netherlands, Portugal, Slovakia, Slovenia, and Spain. Croatia should join in 2023.

51. Paul Wallace, *The Euro Experiment* (Cambridge: Cambridge University Press, 2016).

52. European Commission, "Competition Policy," https://ec.europa.eu/competition/.

53. European Commission, "Competition Policy: Mergers," https://ec.europa.eu /competition/mergers/overview_en.html.

54. Michael Newell, "Top 5 Largest Fines Levied on Tech Companies by the European Commission," *New Economy*, February 18, 2019, https://www.theneweconomy.com /business/top-5-largest-fines-levied-on-tech-companies-by-the-european-commission.

55. The fine of $14.8 billion to Apple in 2016 related to the avoidance of corporate tax, and an appeal against the fine was successful in 2020.

56. Bradford, *The Brussels Effect*.

57. Adam Satariano, "Ireland Fines Facebook's WhatsApp over Data Transparency," *New York Times*, September 3, 2021; see also European Union, "General Data Protection Regulation (GDPR)," https://gdpr.eu/tag/gdpr/.

58. MAN is the acronym for Maschinenfabrik Augsburg Nürnberg (Germany), and DAF for Van Doorne's Automobiel Fabriek (the Netherlands).

59. Office of the United States Trade Representative, "U.S. Wins $7.5 Billion Award in Airbus Subsidies Case," October 2, 2019, https://ustr.gov/about-us/policy-offices /press-office/press-releases/2019/october/us-wins-75-billion-award-airbus.

60. European Commission, "Commission Adopts White Paper on Foreign Subsidies in the Single Market," June 17, 2020, https://ec.europa.eu/commission/presscorner /detail/en/ip_20_1070.

61. Gauthier Van Malderen, "Europe Is Increasingly Innovative," Robert Schuman Foundation Policy Paper, no. 105, January 26, 2021, https://www.robert-schuman .eu/en/doc/entretiens-d-europe/ee-105-en.pdf; also European Union, "Research and Innovation," https://europa.eu/european-union/topics/research-innovation_en.

62. Corporate Europe Observatory, "Lobbying the EU," https://corporateeurope.org /en/lobbying-the-eu.

63. European Commission, "Public Health: International Cooperation on Pharmaceuticals," https://ec.europa.eu/health/international_cooperation/pharmaceuticals_en.

64. European Commission, "Public Health: Legal Framework Governing Medicinal Products for Human Use in the EU," https://ec.europa.eu/health/human-use/legal-framework_en.

65. Francesco Guarascio, "EU Demands Immediate Access to UK-Made Vaccines in AstraZeneca Legal Battle," Reuters, April 28, 2021, https://www.reuters.com/world /europe/eu-legal-case-against-astrazeneca-begins-brussels-court-2021-04-28/.

66. European Council, "EU Budget," https://www.consilium.europa.eu/en/policies /the-eu-budget/.

67. Anne Vitrey and Sébastien Lumet, "Multi-Annual Financial Framework and Next Generation EU: Review of an Unprecedented, Tumultuous European Budgetary Chapter," Robert Schuman Foundation Policy Paper, no. 575, October 27, 2020, https://www .robert-schuman.eu/en/doc/questions-d-europe/qe-575-en.pdf.

68. Katharina Buchholz, "Which Countries Are EU Contributors and Beneficiaries?" Statista, January 13, 2020, https://www.statista.com/chart/18794/net-contributors-to-eu -budget/#:~:text=Germany%2C%20topping%20the%20ranking%2C%20put,Greece %20(3.2%20billion%20Euros).

69. Olivier Marty and Damien Ientile, "Reforming European Economic Policies," Robert Schuman Foundation Policy Paper, no 588, March 23, 2021, https://www.robert -schuman.eu/en/doc/questions-d-europe/qe-588-en.pdf.

70. European Commission, "The Common Agricultural Policy at a Glance," https://ec.europa.eu/info/food-farming-fisheries/key-policies/common-agricultural-policy/cap-glance_en.

71. European Parliament, "Fact Sheets on the European Union: Financing of the CAP," https://www.europarl.europa.eu/factsheets/en/sheet/106/financing-of-the-cap.

72. European Commission, "Oceans and Fisheries," https://ec.europa.eu/fisheries/sites/fisheries/files/docs/body/pcp_en.pdf.

73. Mark Landler and Stephen Castle, "UK and France Call in the Navy, Sort of, in Channel Islands Fishing Dispute," *New York Times,* May 7, 2021.

74. European Commission, "European Regional Development Fund," https://ec.europa.eu/regional_policy/en/funding/erdf/.

75. Council of Europe, "The European Social Charter," https://www.coe.int/en/web/european-social-charter.

76. European Foundation for the Improvement of Living and Working Conditions, "Community Charter of the Fundamental Social Rights of Workers," https://www.eurofound.europa.eu/observatories/eurwork/industrial-relations-dictionary/community-charter-of-the-fundamental-social-rights-of-workers.

77. Olivier de Schutter, *The European Social Charter in the Context of Implementation of the EU Charter of Fundamental Rights* (Brussels: European Parliament, 2016), https://www.europarl.europa.eu/RegData/etudes/STUD/2016/536488/IPOL_STU(2016)536488_EN.pdf.

78. Ivor Roberts and Beverly Springer, *Social Policy in the European Union: Between Harmonization and National Autonomy* (Boulder: Lynne Rienner, 2001).

79. OECD, "Current Retirement Ages," https://www.oecd-ilibrary.org/sites/99acb105-en/index.html?itemId=/content/component/99acb105-en#:~:text=In%202018%2C%20the%20OECD%20average,are%20in%20Austria%20and%20Israel.

80. OECD, "Social Expenditure Database (SOCX)," https://www.oecd.org/social/expenditure.htm. See also EU data at Eurostat, "Social Protection Statistics—Social Benefits," https://ec.europa.eu/eurostat/statistics-explained/index.php/Social_protection_statistics_-_social_benefits. For other data, see the Country Profiles section at the end of the book.

81. Statista, "Incarceration Rate in Selected European Countries in 2021," https://www.statista.com/statistics/957501/incarceration-rate-in-europe/.

82. Sami Nevala, "Violence Against Women: An EU-Wide Survey," European Union Agency for Fundamental Rights (undated), https://rm.coe.int/1680591fd9; see also European Commission, "International Women's Day 2022: Commission Proposes EU-Wide Rules to Combat Violence Against Women and Domestic Violence," March 8, 2022, https://ec.europa.eu/commission/presscorner/detail/en/ip_22_1533.

83. World Bank, "Life Expectancy at Birth, Total (Years)," https://data.worldbank.org/indicator/SP.DYN.LE00.IN. The average across Western Europe is higher than in the United States (seventy-nine years), and even the entire EU area (eighty-one) surpasses the United States.

84. OECD, "Obesity Update 2017," https://www.oecd.org/els/health-systems/Obesity-Update-2017.pdf.

85. European Parliament, "Maternity and Paternity Leave in the EU," https://www.europarl.europa.eu/RegData/etudes/ATAG/2019/635586/EPRS_ATA(2019)635586_EN.pdf.

86. European Commission, "Employment, Social Affairs and Inclusion: Union of Equality: Strategy for the Rights of Persons with Disabilities 2021–2030," https://ec.europa.eu/social/main.jsp?catId=1484&langId=en.

87. Center for Reproductive Rights, "European Abortion Laws: A Comparative Overview," https://reproductiverights.org/sites/default/files/documents/European%20abortion%20law%20a%20comparative%20review.pdf.

88. European Commission, "European Education Area: Quality Education and Training for All," https://education.ec.europa.eu/.

89. European Union, "Education, Training and Youth: Supporting Quality Education, Training and Social Cohesion," https://europa.eu/european-union/topics/education-training-youth_en.

90. European Union, "European Youth Portal: European Solidarity Corps," https://europa.eu/youth/solidarity_en.

91. *The Charter of Fundamental Rights of the European Union*, Official Journal of the European Union, C326 (Brussels, 2012), https://eur-lex.europa.eu/legal-content/EN/TXT/PDF/?uri=CELEX:12012P/TXT&from=EN.

92. European Commission, "European Pillar of Social Rights," https://ec.europa.eu/commission/priorities/deeper-and-fairer-economic-and-monetary-union/european-pillar-social-rights_en.

93. European Union, "European Pillar of Social Rights," https://ec.europa.eu/info/sites/default/files/social-summit-european-pillar-social-rights-booklet_en.pdf.

94. European Commission, "Public Health," https://ec.europa.eu/health/policies/overview_en.

95. As a snapshot of divergent national policies in November 2020, see "Health Measures and Travel Conditions," Robert Schuman Foundation Policy Paper, November 6, 2020, https://www.robert-schuman.eu/en/doc/actualites/FRS_Health_measures.pdf.

96. European Council, "Covid-19: The EU's Response to the Economics of the Fallout," https://www.consilium.europa.eu/en/policies/coronavirus/covid-19-economy/.

97. Emmanuel Cartier, Basile Ridard, and Gilles Toulemonde (eds.) "The Impact of the Health Crisis on the Functioning of Parliaments in Europe," Robert Schuman Foundation Policy Paper, December 2020, https://www.robert-schuman.eu/en/doc/ouvrages/FRS_Parliament.pdf.

98. "Covid-19: How Europe Has Mishandled the Pandemic," *The Economist*, March 31, 2021.

99. Benjamin Mueller and Matina Stevis-Gridneff, "Italy Stops 250,000 Doses from Leaving Europe," *New York Times*, March 5, 2021.

8

The Pursuit of
Peace Within Europe

FOR MILLENNIA, INCESSANT WARS BETWEEN GROUPS OF EUROPEANS have shaped the continent in myriad ways. The factors bringing about such conflict and change have been European in nature primarily, yet the impact of these has not always been contained within the boundaries of Europe, as the two world wars of the twentieth century illuminate. Europe's ongoing relationship with the world beyond its borders is the subject of the next chapter. In this chapter, I address important factors that shape the cross-national relationship of European states, and use several examples to help assess foreign policy motivations. To what extent have European countries succeeded in converting "swords into plowshares" and transformed their relations to be essentially peaceful in nature, especially within the European Union? Could a major war or a new Cold War break out engulfing Europe again, as some feared Russia's attack on Ukraine in 2022 could do? What are the primary motivations of European countries in their relationship with each other?

Two events, both interrelated, changed the nature and trajectory of contemporary European foreign relations, and increased moves toward a shared or coordinated series of policies, especially for the members of the EU. The first event is the transition to the post–Cold War era after 1990. This enabled the emergence of a reunified Germany at the heart of Europe, a lessening of tensions between West and East Europe, an adaptation of the role of the North Atlantic Treaty Organization and US influence over Europe, and the prospects for a reintegration of Russia and its former satellites into the mainstream of Europe, including into NATO itself. National as well as European concerns could shape foreign policies after 1990, but not necessarily through the lens of the (global) Cold War.

The second event, enabled by the end of the Cold War, is the continued movement toward a shared or coordinated European foreign policy for EU members, shaped by the EU as a whole, and representing what arguably is for the collective good of the EU27, rather than that of individual countries. This Europeanization of foreign policy began in earnest in the 1990s, but had earlier strands and gained strength under subsequent agreements, notably the Lisbon Treaty signed in 2007. It is still very much a work in progress, with no guarantee of complete success.

This chapter addresses a broad range of issues concerning foreign policy. It begins by looking briefly at the nature of European relations over previous centuries, with European politics dominated by the policies of individual countries. I then turn to consider the changes brought to countries' foreign policies by the growing influence of the EU and, within that, the development of a Common Foreign and Security Policy (CFSP). The CFSP is by no means a finished product, and there is considerable latitude for countries to deviate in their policies, but I ascertain the extent to which it has helped to coalesce foreign policy goals around some common themes and in relations with European countries outside of the EU. One notable example is the EU's relative unity of approach toward Russia immediately following its invasion of Ukraine in 2022. To a considerable extent, foreign policy between EU members has become domestic policy, as governments operate within the EU policy space. The distinction between the domestic and foreign is increasingly blurred. This chapter looks beyond the EU to other international organizations operating within Europe to see the extent to which European governments are attempting to cooperate. It examines the foreign policy of borders, in terms of issues such as open borders, migration, and the policing of Europe's external borders. It then considers case studies of a number of countries to understand their foreign policy processes and the degree of similarity across those countries. Included are some prominent non-EU countries, notably Norway, Russia, Turkey, and the United Kingdom.

Traditional European Power Politics

The first two chapters of this book presented ideas explaining that wars have shaped and often dominated relations between European countries throughout history. No area of the continent escapes this description, although differences are worth noting. The dominant states change over time, even though the states of Western Europe in general have exercised more influence than those in Central and Eastern Europe. Brute military power and prominence in trade and banking gave states the tools to exercise influence. Other elements, however, proved useful, especially in terms of the factors that shape what we refer to as "soft power" today—language, culture, religion, innovation, and prestige. Drawing from the travels of the Venetian Marco Polo along the Asian Silk Road in the late 1200s through to contemporary relations, European countries chose to flex their collective muscles outside of the continent to provide wealth, strength, and advantage in the European arena. When possible, the distraction of pursuing conquest overseas served as a small safety valve on European rivalry within the continent. The nineteenth century was perhaps the last era when this was possible and, with little left to grab overseas, the full direct competition between European states on European soil returned fully in the two major wars of the twentieth century.

Diplomacy between European states was rudimentary and transitory, based on traveling envoys, until France developed the modern system of permanent embassies and diplomatic training in the eighteenth century. The first recognizable experiment in European collective diplomacy took place after the defeat of Napoleon Bonaparte and the French army in 1815 with the Congress, and subsequent Concert, of Europe. The interests of states coincided to maintain some semblance of stability in Europe and to prevent the rise of radical populist political forces. German (or rather Prussian-dominated) national interest in the 1860s effectively ended this cooperation as Germany sought to expand its influence within the European political theater.

The intensity of national interests within Europe's leading countries made diplomacy increasingly difficult to resolve tensions, and that failure is obvious with the breakout of World War I in 1914. The League of Nations in the interwar period did not prove to be particularly helpful for European diplomacy as the major powers were not present collectively or simply refused to limit their own national agendas. The League became a tool of British and French government interests, rather than anything operating for the benefit of the continent. World War II highlighted the prominence of national interest in the continent, and its destructive power, especially as used by Germany. Something new had to happen to avoid further hostilities across the continent, though the Cold War again reflects the divergence of interests across Europe.

European Union Foreign Policy

One mechanism adopted to change the dynamics of European countries' foreign policies was the birth of the EU, as discussed earlier. At its beginnings in the

1950s, this was hardly a game-changer as it included just six West European countries, although the participation of France and West Germany at the organization's heart provided hope. The foreign policy of even these six members still rested with national governments, and it was only in subsequent decades that the EU began to make inroads into shaping national foreign policy.

Three broad, overlapping approaches help us to evaluate European foreign policy (EFP), following the framework of Christopher Hill, Michael Smith, and Sophie Vanhoonacker.[1] The first is the ability to unite Europe internally to strengthen peaceful relations between the EU27. At the core of this cooperation is the relatively successful France-Germany partnership, with the addition of the core of Belgium, the Netherlands, and Luxembourg, along with Italy. This cooperation has become more difficult with the EU's enlargement from its original six members, as well as with the different perceptions of what EU identity actually means.[2] For supporters of the liberal intergovernmental approach, for example, the EU provides a mechanism for member states to benefit through negotiations and policy coordination, so "national governments have an incentive to cooperate where policy coordination increases their control over domestic policy outcomes, permitting them to achieve goals that would not otherwise be possible."[3] Domestic pressures and economic interests arguably shape rational choices by governments whether or not to pursue EU policy. A study of EU decision-making in the security realm concurred, concluding that "the EU will probably continue to muddle through, advancing certain policies at times and at others leaving them dormant."[4]

The second area to consider is the degree to which the EU27 coordinates itself to promote a coherent set of policies in the international arena and toward other countries. To what extent is the EU a major actor in a rapidly changing global arena? Is the EU an actor in its own right, something greater than the result of its component states? The third area concerns the "power" that Europe can exert in the world. This considers not only the potential economic or military (or hard) power of Europe, but also the concept of Normative Power Europe (NPE), which stresses the moral leadership, or soft power, of the EU.[5] Such a role contributed to the EU receiving the Nobel Peace Prize in 2012, as discussed in Box 8.1. NPE is contentious, and questions abound regarding the apparent moral leadership of the EU, and its self-identity as a coherent unit. Do non-Europeans view the EU in such a benevolent light and as a moral leader? Does the EU project "power" in the self-interest of member states rather than for an entity labeled the "Europe Union"?[6] These external issues form the basis of discussion in the next chapter.

Besides these areas of focus, there are other important issues to keep in mind. For example, the Europeanization of policy, as discussed in the previous

---

Box 8.1   The Nobel Peace Prize for the European Union

The EU won the Nobel Peace Prize in December 2012. The Nobel Committee praised the EU for advancing efforts to bring peace, reconciliation, democracy, and human rights to the European continent. The committee highlighted an important transformation of Europe as going from a continent of almost constant war to one of relative peace, and believed much of this success was because of the actions, moral leadership, and soft power of the EU. This prize recognized efforts to transform the countries of CEE into democracies and welcome many of them to EU membership. Whether the EU was worthy of the Nobel Prize, or possesses the capacity to enforce peace in Europe, remains a source of debate across the continent.[a]

Note: Nobel Prize Organisation, "The Nobel Peace Prize 2012," https://www.nobelprize.org/prizes/peace/2012/summary/.

---

chapter, considers the degree to which states have shaped the direction of EU policy or, in turn, the manner in which the EU gets to mold national foreign policies. Can we witness a European identity developing in EFP, or is it simply the result of lowest common denominator negotiations and bargaining? Reuben Wong considers three main facets of the Europeanization of foreign policy. First is the national adaptation model, where member states adapt their foreign policies to EU norms and treaties. Second is the national projection model, where states utilize the EU to promote their own national agendas. The third concerns identity reconstruction, where elite socialization helps to create a culturally integrated and transnational EU.[7]

Another useful method to gauge European foreign policy is through the capability-expectations gap model developed by Christopher Hill.[8] This model considers the expectations we have for European policy compared with the ability to achieve such goals. It is in the area of foreign policy where this gap appears to be at its largest, underlining the shortcomings of EFP in not reaching the potential of treaty language. One further issue to consider is that of the differentiation of goals and action within the EU27. There has long been an understanding that not all members can fully agree to implement all policies within the EU. There are multiple possibilities for members to opt out of certain aspects of treaty law, and this differentiation makes a comprehensive EFP more difficult.[9] With Brexit, there are now not only competing elements of differentiated integration, but also the specter of various models of differentiated disintegration.

The Development and Machinery of EFP

The end of the Cold War prompted a reexamination of European security and foreign policy cooperation in light of concerns about future US disinterest in Europe (and its engagement in the Gulf War of 1993) in addition to the uncertain developments in CEE as Russian influence over the region diminished. This prompted the development of the Common Foreign and Security Policy within the framework of the Treaty on European Union in 1993, alongside the movement toward membership in the North Atlantic Treaty Organization and the EU by many newly emerging states in CEE.[10]

This transition in CEE, with problems especially in the former Yugoslavia, led to further overhaul of EFP in 2003. This included the development of the first European Security Strategy (ESS) in December 2003 (updated in 2009) as an attempt to organize consistent security action in European policy.[11] In addition, there was the creation of a distinctive EU foreign policy bureaucracy, the European External Action Service (EEAS) in 2010. The Lisbon Treaty also created the post of high commissioner for foreign policy, essentially an EU-wide foreign minister. This role strengthened in 2013 when the high commissioner's position straddled both the European Commission and Council. Questions continue, however, about the effectiveness of the EFP machinery. As William Wallace points out, "The EU's national governments pursue their own policies, occasionally in parallel with those negotiated in Brussels, and retain effective vetoes over EU action."[12]

The EU published its Global Strategy (EUGS) in June 2016, just a few days after the Brexit referendum had taken place, as a clear attempt to bolster EU foreign policy.[13] This was an updated and more comprehensive strategy than the ESS, and is the current strategy for EFP. Its bleak opening summed up an ongoing crisis for the EU: "We need a stronger Europe. . . . We live in times of existential crisis, within and beyond the European Union. Our Union is under threat."[14] Elsewhere, the EUGS summed up: "In this fragile world, soft power is not enough: we must enhance our credibility in security and defence."[15] The EUGS emphasizes the need for resiliency to promote the European project and to maintain Europe's position and policies in the world. Resiliency is central to the view that uncertainty in different policy arenas makes it difficult to create rigid policy, but requires states and the EU to maintain considerable flexibility in the promotion of goals.[16]

As part of the EUGS, the EU developed a European Security and Defence Policy in 2017, establishing the Permanent Structured Cooperation (PESCO), the European Defence Industry Program, and the European Defence Fund. These struggled to take off for a variety of reasons, notably that observers perceived

Box 8.2 A European Army?

The contests between rival European armies or alliances of armies have heavily shaped European history, so a call for peace in Europe needs to deal with this issue. The Cold War, though in a way relatively peaceful in avoiding catastrophic war, saw two nuclear-armed forces, NATO and the Warsaw Pact, facing each other menacingly across the iron curtain. The end of the Cold War brought initial optimism that Europe could become a post-conflict society, though smaller conflicts, such as in the Balkans, have occurred. EU members remain divided over whether to pursue a European army to promote peace.

Many states remain supportive of NATO as the ultimate enforcer of peace, and believe that an EU army will lack the (political) willpower to be a credible force. Tellingly, everyone turned to a NATO response to the Russian invasion of Ukraine in February 2022 rather than to the EU. Despite discussions about European defense since the 1950s, there is little forward movement as defense issues are primarily a national (or NATO) decision. France and Germany have flirted with ideas about joint forces, but with little suc-cess, even though President Emmanuel Macron continues to promote the ideas of a European "strategic autonomy."

With significant military forces—Russia, Turkey, the UK, as examples—outside of the EU umbrella, there seems little prospect of any kind of European army developing. There is little enthusiasm anywhere in Europe to spend more money on the military (even for NATO), preferring to send resources to other public goals. As of 2021, only seven European members of NATO spent the requisite 2 percent of GDP on defense spending, with Germany a notable exception.[a] What we do see are EU peacekeeping forces made up by troops from various EU members, but these are primarily observer rather than fighting forces, largely deployed in Eastern Europe and Africa.[b] There is also a divergence across Europe in terms of whether or not to have conscription, with relatively few countries—Austria, Cyprus, Denmark, Estonia, Greece, Norway, Russia, Sweden, Switzerland, Turkey—having some form of compulsory national service.[c]

Notes: a. Those European NATO countries meeting the 2 percent obligation in 2021 are (from highest percentage contribution to lowest) Greece, Poland, the UK, Croatia, Estonia, Latvia, and Lithuania. France and Norway contributed just under 2 percent. *Defence Expenditures of NATO Countries 2014–2021* (Brussels: NATO, 2022), https://www.nato.int/cps/en/natohq/news _193983.htm.

b. Jolyon Howorth, "The European Union's Security and Defence Policy: The Quest for Purpose," in Christopher Hill, Michael Smith, and Sophie Vanhoonacker (eds.), *International Relations and the European Union,* 3rd ed. (Oxford: Oxford University Press, 2017), chap. 15.

c. Xenia Zubova, "Which Countries Still Have Conscription?" *Forces,* December 3, 2021, https://www.forces.net/world/which-countries-still-have-conscription; also *World Population Review,* "Country Rankings" (Walnut, CA), https://worldpopulationreview.com/country-rankings /countries-with-mandatory-military-service.

these as vehicles for French ambition to dominate Europe, the inability of national arms manufacturers to relinquish their interests to a European body, and the vocal opposition of the Donald Trump administration in the United States.[17] The ability to build European capabilities in these areas is key, but difficult. The incoming European Commission in September 2019 doubled-down on these issues by proclaiming themselves the "Geopolitical Commission," highlighting the severe challenges to European influence in the world.[18] The Commission is promoting the idea of strategic autonomy for the EU and a more forceful role in the world, but this is problematic, as discussed further in Chapter 9.[19]

Eastern and Southern Europe: The EU Neighborhood

The European Neighborhood Policy developed after the 2004 enlargement as a way to link countries on the rim of Europe to the EU.[20] At the outset of the ENP, the European commissioner for external relations and European Neighborhood Policy, Benita Ferrero-Waldner, wrote that "it is designed to offer a privileged form of partnership now, irrespective of the exact nature of the future relationship with the EU."[21] Implicit in this was the EU's aim to attempt to maintain the political stability of those on its borders and to claim to lead by moral example.[22] The ENP governs the relationship with sixteen neighboring states, six of which are to the east of the EU: Armenia, Azerbaijan, Belarus, Georgia, Moldova, and Ukraine. This Eastern Partnership (EaP) formalized in Prague in May 2009. These states are possible future EU members, though this seems challenging given Russia's opposition and inclusion into its zone of interest, as all these countries were part of the USSR before 1991 and claimed by Russia as within the post-Soviet space.[23] Russia's invasion of Ukraine in 2022 underlined this opposition. The EU has also struggled to deal with this eastern group of states because of their poor economic performance and diverse interests.[24]

The other ten states are to the south, and are important trade and political partners, but are unlikely to become EU members. This Southern Partnership (essentially large sections of the Middle East and North Africa [MENA]) grew out of the broader 1995 Euro-Mediterranean Partnership, or the Barcelona Process, based on agreements made at a meeting in Barcelona linking together a broader group of states around the Mediterranean. This morphed into the Union for the Mediterranean in 2009, a loose intergovernmental organization comprising the EU members and fifteen partners around the Mediterranean (essentially ENP partners, plus Balkan states and Turkey). The southern members of the ENP are Algeria, Egypt, Israel, Jordan, Lebanon, Libya, Morocco, Palestine,

Syria, and Tunisia. The primary goal of the EU through the ENP and the UfM is political stabilization, rather than democratization, as the EU has struggled with the diversity of issues emanating from the region.[25] These organizations also create the concept of a wider European strategic arena centered on the Mediterranean embracing Europe, the Middle East, and North Africa, bringing us back to ideas regarding the perception of Europe discussed in Chapter 1.[26]

The ENP is a set of EU policies aimed at these two groups of states. It specifically addresses political association, issues, programs of economic integration, and offers for increased mobility for people. However, these are not uniform policies for the complete group of states, and each member has its own priorities in terms of its dealings with the EU. This is unsettling in that dissimilar treatment of ENP members causes different reactions and anxieties. As Karen E. Smith remarks, "The two dimensions inside the ENP, however, make awkward bedfellows, especially given that the east European countries are (reluctantly) seen as potential member states, while the Mediterranean countries have not been considered eligible for EU membership."[27]

When the ENP began, Russia's response was muted and somewhat disinterested. Vladimir Putin began to see EU advances in this geographical arena, however, in zero-sum terms as direct competition to Russia. In 2011, he launched a Eurasian Customs Union with Kazakhstan and Belarus, with the intention of drawing eastern ENP members into the Russian orbit. The role of Russia toward the ENP took a further turn with Russia's incursion into Ukraine and its annexation of Crimea in 2014, displaying Putin's willingness to use a mix of military and soft power.[28] Likewise, Russian intervention earlier in 2008 in Georgia, another member of the ENP, affected the ENP and EU strategy. The EU placed sanctions against Russia for the Ukraine incursions, but was unwilling to raise the stakes of its opposition to Putin. Russia's involvement in the Syrian Civil War after 2011, and its overt backing of the Bashar al-Assad regime, is in contrast to the EU's limited policy role in Syria. These issues have also undermined ENP policies in both its regions.[29] Georgia, Moldova, and Ukraine (the "Trio") remain committed to eventual EU membership and continue to work with the EU on increasing economic access. Ukraine and Moldova made formal membership applications to the EU following the Russian invasion of Ukraine in February 2022. The intransigence of Russia threatens to undermine further movement, and splits EU members as to steps forward, with some not wanting to antagonize Putin.[30] Greater unity of purpose occurred following the 2022 invasion, after EU members initially struggled to agree on the level of sanctions to pursue, but it is uncertain how long this resolve will last.

The hopes of the Arab Spring, ignited by the burst of democratization in Tunisia in 2011, have dissipated following the destabilizing events in Egypt,

Libya, and Syria, as well as crackdowns in many other countries across the region. The EU's policy leans more toward political stability than democratization, somewhat undermining its claims of moral leadership. Its belief that Arab leaders would emulate the democratic path of Europe were severely misplaced. As one scholar concluded, "Overall, the EU has asserted itself as neither a strategic actor nor a normative power, but rather as a bystander, trapped in its internal institutional process and content to passively react to crisis events by proposing long-term solutions that have little impact in the short run."[31]

Prospects for Europe's neighborhood policy appear dim, with four key problems. First, the cluster of right-wing or populist governments in Central Europe opposed to greater EU actions in the ENP include Austria and Hungary, and to a certain extent the Czech Republic and Slovakia. This group of countries makes EU expansion eastward problematic. Second, while the EU maintained sanctions on Russia for its actions in Georgia and Ukraine in 2008 and 2014, it is evident that there was little resolve to intensify actions or maintain high-level sanctions for a long period. Some EU members expelled Russian diplomats for the nerve agent attack in the UK in March 2018, but many states were silent on this issue. More evidence of the business as usual strategy was Germany's approval of further energy pipelines from Russia in March 2018, even as they expelled Russian diplomats.[32] Europe did nothing about Syria, nor did it intervene in Russia's cyber warfare against Ukraine or its cyberattacks on elections, including in France, Germany, and the UK. The outright invasion of Ukraine in 2022 by Russia shattered European peace and challenged the EU directly, leading to increased sancions, but it is uncertain the extent to which this will strengthen the ENP, the CFSP, or the area of common military defense.

Third, there is an ongoing concern about US commitment to Europe's security, especially in terms of NATO defense. The fact that the EU at the best of times has never been able to agree on hard security issues or the expansion of European common forces makes it difficult to see much progress on this even in the current circumstances. This is especially the case given the fear of any potential weakening of US support for NATO as had occurred under the Trump administration (though post-Brexit Britain is likely to remain a prominent member). President Joe Biden's firm support against Russia in 2022 was positive, but many Europeans feared this was temporary, given the increasing costs of that support and with uncertainty about US policy after the 2024 presidential elections.

Finally, the impact of Europe's soft power and its moral influence on its neighboring states appears weak and perhaps waning. If the EU prevaricates on many issues, does not seek to maintain support for democratization with its southern neighbors, and does not consistently stand up to Russia, then perhaps it loses its moral authority.

Foreign Policy, Borders, and Migration

A key part of the EU is the concept of free trade and free movement of people, and the removal of borders inside of Europe is a critical element to that plan. Given early strong opposition from a number of members, the agreement initially occurred outside of the EU framework in Schengen, Luxembourg, in 1985. As more members came on board, it was included in the EU through the Treaty of Amsterdam in 1997. Today, there are twenty-six members in the Schengen zone.[33] Of the EU27, some twenty-two countries participate, and those outside—Bulgaria, Croatia, Cyprus, and Romania—are committed to joining at some point. Ireland also remains outside of Schengen because of its special trade and open borders relationship with the UK—never a member of Schengen—as well as because of its open border with Northern Ireland. The status of Northern Ireland's border is a key issue in the post-Brexit negotiations between the EU, Ireland, and the UK.

Some non-EU members, however, are members of Schengen, notably the members of the European Free Trade Association (EFTA): Iceland, Liechtenstein, Norway, and Switzerland. The Schengen Agreement enables the free flow of people across the twenty-six countries signed up without passport controls. This is important for the 420 million Europeans who are part of Schengen, as they no longer face borders per se. But it is also significant for non-EU citizens, as once they gain access to a Schengen country they have open access without borders to other countries in the grouping for a visit of up to ninety days. Visitors obtain a "Schengen visa" to carry them through the twenty-six countries. This policy also provides an opportunity for refugees to travel freely within Europe, rather than remain in a single country. This has caused some countries to pause their Schengen participation, preferring border controls to limit refugees. Likewise, the Covid-19 pandemic in 2020–2022 forced a halt to Schengen openness, as most countries reinstalled border controls to prevent the movement of people. It is unclear if this imposition of border controls to contain the virus will have longer-term effects on the free movement of people, or when Schengen movement will return fully.

Immigration and Migration Policy

Immigration and migration policy, regular and irregular, for those outside of the EU is a politically sensitive topic. Traditionally, member countries have had full control of these issues, but over the past decade, the EU has increased its role and now has competence to determine the number of migrants entering the EU. This shift in policy came through the Lisbon Treaty, but also was a necessary reaction to the Syrian refugee crisis following 2015. The European Court of Justice now holds jurisdiction over migration and asylum.[34] The EU enables citizens of any member to reside and work in any other member state as part of the single market. Some restrictions emerged following the accession of a large number of Central European states in 2004 and 2007, as some West European countries feared a surge of residents coming from these CEE states. Residents can vote in local and European elections from their place of domicile, though they are restricted from voting in national elections unless they are actually citizens. As of 2019, some 23 million non-EU citizens lived in the EU, about 5 percent of the total EU population.[35]

Migration in general is a source of contention among far-right nationalist parties, especially in countries with stronger economies.[36] There is a string of examples including France, Germany, Italy, and the UK, but CEE states such as Hungary and Poland are also opposed to accepting large numbers of migrants. As discussed in Chapter 6, such issues have helped to fuel populist movements across the continent, especially if the EU can determine who countries should accept.

It is in the realm of migration and refugees where some of the biggest tests have confronted the EU, especially concerning the million or more Syrian refugees fleeing war in their country after 2015. The EU attempted a policy to spread these refugees across members as part of the Dublin Agreement, but many balked.[37] Countries such as Hungary simply refused. In the end, Germany and Sweden took the largest share, with significant internal political consequences. In Germany, following well-publicized attacks by migrants against German women in December 2015, the tide of support for refugees began to shift, and this opposition is now prominent across the continent.[38]

The EU also has to continue to seek support from Turkey to maintain a cordon against the refugees, and this caused unease for many for siding with the unpopular Recep Tayyip Erdoğan regime. Continuing crises of refugees fleeing North Africa, and the humanitarian challenges of many of them drowning in the Mediterranean, keep the spotlight on the EU's policy regarding refugees. These refugee crises highlight the limitations of EU policy and the impact on such areas as health policy, as well as the residual influence of member countries.[39] The crises also embarrass the EU, which has to pursue somewhat draconian measures to keep out migrants, contrary to its ideal of being a humanitarian, benevolent, and moral power. As an example, the EU's European Migration Network received 612,700 applications for asylum in 2019, but accepted only 21,200.[40] These measures were in full view in November 2021, when the EU forced back thousands of Middle Eastern and Afghan refugees who attempted to cross the Polish border from Belarus. This EU hostility and sanctions toward the

Alexander Lukashenko regime in Belarus, which appeared to have a hand in organizing the refugees, complicated the crisis. In contrast, EU members were much more open to the flood of over a half-million Ukrainians fleeing westward in the first week after Russia's 2022 invasion, rising to about four million by May. Most believe that the refugee flow will be temporary, but these numbers could cause political problems if the war drags on indefinitely.

Frontex and Borders

The European Border and Coast Guard Agency, based in Warsaw, holds responsibility for policing the border of the Schengen zone.[41] This role is in coordination with member countries. One of the primary goals is to try to prevent illegal border crossings by migrants, and this put the agency in the spotlight during the Syrian refugee crisis. In the first six months of 2020, for example, Frontex agents stopped 36,400 illegal crossings into the EU, and this was down 20 percent from a similar period in 2019, largely due to the coronavirus halting refugee movements. Frontex often receives criticism for the harsh treatment handed out to prospective migrants. This is likely to continue, as migrants seek access to Europe and border agents aim to keep them out using whatever tools they have. Neither national governments nor the EU desire open borders to the outside of Europe, and policing them firmly is a policy with wide agreement. This is an ongoing debate within the EU, however, in terms of how exactly to control its borders, and one that is too politically contentious to expect a complete resolution in the near future.[42]

Foreign Relations Within Europe

The majority of foreign policy interaction and trade of European countries is with other European countries. There should be no surprise here, given geographical proximity and the history of relationships across the continent. Bilateral relations between European states remain important, but are in tandem with relationships within the EU. Relationships between any random (non-neighboring) groups of EU member states—Sweden with Greece, Poland with Spain, Latvia with Luxembourg—are mostly defined in terms of the parameters of the EU. The foreign policy of prospective members of the EU, such as Albania and North Macedonia, must meet the requirements for EU membership. The EU is also a critical filter for, and shaper of, policy in external relations with non-EU European states, such as Russia, Turkey, the UK, and Ukraine, as well as with countries outside of Europe—and vice versa.

Part of the discussion regarding a common external policy for EU countries relates to the debate over the core mission of the EU itself. For many, the idea of a United States of Europe, or even a close partnership of European states, calls for not only coordination in economic areas and trade, but also in the "high politics" of defense and external relations. How can the EU be a union if countries pursue any type of foreign policy they wish? How can the world take the EU seriously as a political entity if it cannot coordinate policies among its members? How can the EU actually survive if its members are pursuing widely different and potentially aggressive or destabilizing policies toward each other?

In terms of intra-EU trade by the member states, there is clear evidence to show the importance of these intraregional trade patterns. Only two EU members, Cyprus (41 percent) and Ireland (37 percent), have intra-EU trade less than 50 percent of their total export trade. At the other end of the spectrum, four countries (Czech Republic, Hungary, Luxembourg, and Slovakia) have more than 75 percent of their exports go to other countries within the EU. More than 60 percent of this intra-EU trade is in manufactured and industrial products, and chemicals. Only three countries, namely Germany, Ireland, and Italy, have a trade surplus with EU countries and with countries outside of the EU bloc.[43] Significantly, the EU remains the UK's largest trade partner even after the fateful Brexit referendum of 2016. In 2019, UK exports to the EU were 43 percent of total UK exports, and its imports from the EU were 52 percent of the total.[44] Such reliance exacerbates the difficult divorce proceedings between the two parties.

In the next sections, I look briefly at some important and interesting foreign policy relationships within Europe, with examples from EU and non-EU members. Although I am emphasizing their interaction with other European countries, I also allude to their role beyond the continent when relevant.

France and Germany

At the core of Europe and the EU lies the relationship between France and Germany and, for this reason, we look at the two countries together. Antagonistic for centuries, the countries fought each other three times from 1870 to 1945. The success of the EU, and hopes for European peace as a whole, require Franco-German rapprochement in the heart of Europe, as Robert Schuman pointed out in 1950. This cooperation has succeeded in holding the EU together, and remains central to a functioning union and a functioning Europe in general. Charles de Gaulle and Konrad Adenauer cemented this partnership in the Elysée Treaty, signed in January 1963. In a way, this helped to end the era of post-1945 tensions and pointed to a way forward for closer ties between the countries, even though much tension remained. Little policy can take place in the EU, realistically, without the support of the two governments. Both countries, however, maintain this partnership and their role in the EU from quite different starting points and perspectives.

France approaches the relationship as a residual great power, a permanent member of the UN Security Council, a nuclear power, a country (unlike Germany) with territorial possessions still scattered around the world. France also possesses considerable soft power in terms of its culture, its food and wine, its luxury consumer brands, its sense of fashion, and its wealth of history. As an occupying power of Germany immediately after World War II, this also added an element to relations with West Germany in plans for European cooperation. Nevertheless, its occupation by Germany during the war and the trauma of its Vichy government also provided a realism to French policy that an accommodation with Germany was important. French support for building back a prominent Europe clashed with its own failings in the 1950s, with defeat in Vietnam, the collapse of control in Algeria, and the crumbling of its democratic institutions.

France exerted its influence strongly in the early days of the EU, particularly under the leadership of Charles de Gaulle, who never missed an opportunity to pursue French interests. French foreign policy remained aloof from the EU's, notably in maintaining its (military) sphere of influence in Africa. Subsequent leaders were possibly a little less intransigent than de Gaulle and worked harder to blend French and European interests together.

In recent years, President Emmanuel Macron has bolstered French support for the EU, including efforts to promote tighter cooperation in many fields, including strategic autonomy for Europe. He is clearly frustrated with the performance of the EU, and sees an existential threat looming. In a statement in 2019, he argued, "Europe is on the edge of a precipice. If we don't wake up . . . there's a considerable risk that in the long run we will disappear geopolitically, or at least that we will no longer be in control of our destiny."[45] Macron, in turn, receives criticism for speaking on behalf of all of Europe, but he sees EU interests as inextricably linked to the interests of France.[46] He was also proactive on behalf of France and the EU in negotiations with Russia after its invasion of Ukraine in 2022.

Germany's perspective on this partnership is a little different. Although Germany was undoubtedly Europe's most powerful country in the 1930s in terms of population, economy, and military might, by the mid-1940s World War II had made it physically and economically decimated, humiliated, divided, and occupied by four armies. To promote new growth, Germany had to commit to a peaceful partnership in Europe, particularly with France. Germany had no colonies, was not allowed into the United Nations (as two distinct countries, West and East) until 1973, and had to rebuild within borders forced on the country that continued to change until reunification in 1990. In contrast to France, German foreign policy required alignment to that of Europe—modest, unassuming, deferential, even if sotto voce.

After reunification, Germany increasingly flexed its muscles within the EU, especially trying to bring discipline in matters of money, debts, and the euro. Germany played an important role in the expansion of the EU to CEE countries, for political and economic reasons, as Germany expanded its influence there, much to France's unhappiness. Under Angela Merkel, German insistence on policy became more visible, as programs over Greek debt and Syrian migration attest. Germany is also the world's second-largest provider of foreign development assistance (second only to the United States), and this provides important influence across the world.

Chancellor Angela Merkel acted with slightly less enthusiasm in recent years, given the complexities of Germany's internal politics with the rise of the Alternative for Germany and her weakening grip as she prepared for retirement at the end of 2021. There is also an ongoing question regarding the motivations of Germans to remain (constrained) inside of the European embrace and French partnership, or to move to take on a more nationalistic platform.[47] Merkel's leadership during the Syrian refugee crisis and the Covid-19 pandemic, and the resultant criticism of her policies within Germany, also indicated a stance less willing to bow to EU pressures. Ongoing national political differences among members have prevented the EU from finding greater harmony. Some see this as a negative in terms of EU cooperation stalling, but others see the increasing importance of national political opinions as a more realistic way to recalibrate the EU and bring more modesty to its ambitions.[48]

The economic fallout from the Covid-19 pandemic provides a challenge for EU leadership in coming to any regional solution. Unlike with the actions taken in the Greek economic crisis in the early 2010s, the EU struggled to come to any regional consensus to tackle the pandemic. The first signs of action came near the end of May 2020 when France and Germany agreed on the outlines of an EU pandemic fund to alleviate conditions.[49] Merkel's relative weakness in Germany, however, along with the ongoing opposition to Macron inside France make this critical partnership rather soft. It is difficult to envisage scenarios where these two countries could mount a forceful promotion of EFP. The departure of Merkel from political power in 2021, and the relative weakness of Macron despite winning the 2022 presidential election, provide uncertainty for future France-Germany relations, as well as for the EU itself, though both countries coordinated policies following the Russian invasion of Ukraine in 2022.

Norway

Norway is mentioned here as an example of a somewhat independent foreign policy of a wealthy country outside of the EU. Norway's potential membership of the EU was defeated in two national referenda in 1972 and 1994, and Norway remains outside of the EU but inside the European Economic Area and the Schengen zone. This enables Norway to maintain trade and other economic partnerships across the EU, but not be a party to political agreements that it does not favor. Norway has a tradition of independence in foreign relations, choosing neutrality in both world wars. This did not prevent Germany from invading Norway during World War II, primarily to control its strategic coastline. As a response to this, the Norwegian government chose to join NATO as a founding member in 1949, but still attempts to play the honest broker role as a small state in trying to ease international tensions. The Oslo Accords, for example, in 1993 and 1995 were important in pushing forward negotiations between Israel and the Palestinians.

Norway's ability to stay removed from the EU stems from a popular desire to promote a nationalistic perspective, as well as by the economic good fortune to have significant oil supplies and revenue. Its GDP per capita of $75,419 in 2019 is one of the highest in Europe, more than double that of Italy, for example. The government places a lot of emphasis on development and aid policy, and through the Norwegian Agency for Development Cooperation contributes about 1 percent of its gross national income to development assistance, being among the top three providers of foreign aid in the world on this criterion (with Luxembourg and Sweden).[50] Much of its aid is also "untied" allowing recipients to use the aid without political strings attached. Norway is only one of five countries in the world that consistently matches the UN's goal of providing 0.7 percent of GNP to development assistance, a figure Norway has surpassed every year since the mid-1970s.

Poland

Poland has a long and proud history, but located in the center of Europe with no obvious defensible borders, the country has felt the full force of the shifting tides of Europe's power politics. The country disappeared from the map during the nineteenth century, only to reemerge at Versailles in 1919. As discussed in Chapter 2, Poland suffered greatly during World War II, with Germany's invasion sparking the formal outbreak of the war, with massive loss of life especially among its Jewish population, and with a significant (forced) shift in its geographical borders in 1945 by the UK, the United States, and the USSR. These vulnerabilities are key to understanding Polish foreign policy today. Once Soviet control ended after 1989, Poland moved quickly to escape the Russian bear by joining NATO and the EU. As the largest of the emerging CEE countries joining the EU, Poland gained from significant financial assistance from the EU, and opened its economy to international trade, with an especially close relationship with Germany. It is one of the better-performing CEE economies, but its GDP per capita still lags behind Western Europe at only about one-third of the German figure.

In the past decade, however, Poland's policies have shifted somewhat as the populist government strengthened its grip on power. The government has upset the EU with its nationalistic and seeming antidemocratic programs, even though Poland remains closely tied to NATO. Poland has also been supportive of bringing countries on its eastern border into the EU and NATO, as a further buffer against Russia, and has taken in modest numbers of Ukrainian refugees. It is uncertain whether Poland will modify its policies in light of opposition from Brussels.

Russia

As the world's largest country in physical terms spreading across eleven time zones, Russia is not simply a European country. It has many close interests in South and East Asia, as well as a border with the United States, and these are topics to return to in the next chapter. Although Russia has long interacted with other European neighbors, especially the Nordic countries, perhaps a key turning point was the construction of St. Petersburg in the early eighteenth century (on captured Swedish territory), with Peter the Great moving Russia's capital there in 1712. The capital switched to Moscow during the 1917 revolution. The country enjoyed a positive reputation for its cultural strength, with its writers and musicians, but its economic stature lagged in the nineteenth century in contrast to countries of Western Europe because of its lack of industrialization and the continuance of serfdom. Its surprise naval defeat at the hands of Japan in 1905 combined with the jolt caused by the Russian Revolution of 1917 took the country out of a major role in the organization of Europe after World War I. The country's rapid industrial and military growth in the 1930s made it a formidable foe for Germany after its invasion and, as shown in Chapter 2, gave the Soviet Union tremendous sway over much of CEE after 1945.

Russia's underlying economic weakness ultimately undermined the country's influence, but most observers did not foresee its rapid demise between 1989 and 1991, when the USSR disintegrated. This is critical to understanding the stance of contemporary Russian policy today; namely, to build back its rightful respect in Europe and across the world, and to revive its perception of itself as a traditional great power. In the 1990s, Russia struggled to develop a cohesive foreign policy, but attempted to corral the newly emerging former Soviet republics into new political and economic relationships, while at the same time gaining its footing in relations with the rest of Europe and the United States.[51] Europeans hoped for an enhanced and friendly relationship with Russia, but such hopes dissipated.[52] In a prescient summation in the 1990s, relations between Russia and the emerging countries sandwiched between it and the EU were seen as "the most dangerous aspect of the [near future], both for the internal prospects for democracy in Russia and for Russia's relations with the West."[53]

This tension increased with the rise to power of Vladimir Putin. With little prospect of, and no real interest in, EU membership, Russia's resource base of oil, gas, and minerals allow the Putin government strong leverage over energy deficient EU states, in particular Germany. With aspirations of renewed empire and grandeur, Putin pursues policies demanding attention and respect from the EU and other European countries. Cooperation between the two sides was strong, with the EU relatively unwilling to use leverage over Moscow—until the 2022 invasion of Ukraine. The economic partnership blunts many EU countries wanting to hold Russia to account for its day-to-day human rights abuses, cyber-crimes, or antidemocratic policies.

One of the core elements in the construction of the EU going back to the late 1940s was as a bulwark against the Soviet Union. At the end of the Cold War, opportunity emerged in the 1990s with a weakened Russia for the EU (and NATO) to encroach into former Soviet-controlled CEE and add new members. The 1993 Copenhagen Criteria, as discussed in Chapter 2, laid down the road map and conditions for such enlargement, and the Baltic and Central European states joined the EU in 2004 (followed by Bulgaria and Romania in 2007). Putin's rise to power in Russia after 1999 stopped the unchallenged growth of and humiliation by the EU, indicated by Russia's intervention in Ukraine and its annexation of Crimea in 2014. Ukraine became the redline in EU-NATO-Russia relations, and Russia continues to threaten Ukraine's independence and directly opposes any further encroachment of the EU or NATO, as the 2022 invasion of Ukraine displayed.[54] Putin's declared aim was to reintegrate Ukraine into Russia, but he could settle for a smaller goal of controlling Russian-speaking regions of the Donbas along with the agricultural and energy resources of that territory. The shock and severity of this military action, however, radical-ized EU policies to counter Russia at levels unseen since the Cold War.

Putin has increasingly intervened in European politics, aiding right-wing populists, dabbling in the Brexit campaign, undertaking cyber warfare opera-tions, and muddying the waters of European democracy. Russia is especially interested in energy policy, including Arctic policy, as climate change makes

Siberia and the Arctic more open to trade routes and exploitation. How to react to Russia divides the EU, with many, led by Germany, seeking a continual rapprochement or "pragmatic" diplomacy to maintain vital energy supplies despite all the transgressions of the Russian government. According to the World Bank, Germany is Russia's third-highest importer, and Russia's second most important export market, underlying the important economic linkages between the two countries.[55] The UK generally muted its criticism of Russia prior to 2022 for fear of diverting the large amounts of Russian funds invested or held in Britain. In short, Russia normally had little to fear from the rest of Europe.

Trump's repeated questioning of NATO's Article 5 and automatic protection against Russia left many in Europe uncertain about their ability to stand up to Moscow. The EU and NATO could do little about Russia's continuing occupation of parts of Ukraine. The alleged involvement of Russia in assassination attempts in Germany and the UK soured, but did not breach, relations. The EU opposed the outcome of elections in Belarus in 2020 but, with Russia's support and protection for the country, the EU did little to act against Belarus. Russia's expulsion of diplomats from Germany, Poland, and Sweden in February 2021, after their protests against the imprisonment of activist Alexei Navalny, did not completely damage relations, nor did the expulsion of Russians in retaliation.[56] In April 2021, the massing of Russian troops on the border with Ukraine along with tit-for-tat expulsion of diplomats between it and the Czech Republic heightened tensions between Russia and much of the rest of Europe.[57] Relations were further inflamed early in 2022 as 190,000 Russian troops massed on the Ukraine border. The invasion in February helped to solidify NATO and European sanctions against Russia, at least in the short term. With constitutional changes completed in Russia during 2021 that will allow Putin to remain in office until 2036, much of Europe seems likely to remain unsettled and divided over its relations with Russia despite its virtually unified hostility after the 2022 invasion.

Turkey

As the Ottoman Empire, the predecessor empire to Turkey had considerable sway over European affairs. As its powers waned in the nineteenth century, the country's role in Europe weakened to the extent that considerable chunks of its territory were lost to other European countries around the time of World War I. The Turkish War of Independence between 1919 and 1923 staved off further erosion of Turkish land to European "invaders" (Armenia, France, Greece, Italy, and the UK) and brought the independence of modern-day Turkey in 1923. Turkish governments strove to keep the country away from too many entanglements in Europe, so Turkey did not join the League of Nations until 1932, and it stayed neutral in World War II until near its end.

The Dardanelles and the Bosporus, a strategic waterway, again became significant during the Cold War as a potential choke point for the Soviet fleet entering the Mediterranean. Turkey's pivotal position as a geographical gateway to the Middle East also increased its significance, and the country joined NATO in 1952. Successive governments have been negotiating potential entry into the EU for decades. For Turkey, its centrality as the geographical crossroads of Europe, Africa, the Middle East, and Asia has been the center of its foreign policy pursuits and leverage. In recent years, Turkey has come closer to Russia, buying military equipment from the country (to the anguish of NATO allies) and carving out spheres of influence with Moscow over the fluid situation in Syria, where there are Turkish troops on the ground. Of utmost importance to both countries is the Caucuses region, which borders and separates them. The 2020 war between Azerbaijan, backed by Turkey, and a separatist self-proclaimed Republic of Artsakh, supported by Armenia, showed the volatility of the region, and led to a brokered cease-fire by Russia.

President Biden's declaration in April 2021 that Ottoman Turkey (Muslim) undertook genocide against (Christian) Armenia in its attack of 1915 highlighted the continuing tensions in the region and Turkey's vulnerability on human rights issues. Turkey's hostility to Biden's announcement fostered even greater tensions in relations between Turkey, the United States, and the EU. The European Commission and Parliament have consistently called on Turkey to recognize this genocide as a condition for continuing negotiations over EU membership.

One of the biggest challenges from the EU perspective is with the regime of President Erdoğan in Turkey, who has consolidated power since 2003.[58] Following a coup attempt in 2016, the government clamped down on and imprisoned thousands of alleged dissidents and conspirators. This led to much squeamishness in EU policy, as Turkey's support is required to stem the tide of refugees into the EU—particularly from Syria and Afghanistan—but Turkey's disdain of democracy is embarrassing to EU leaders. This also has shaped the ongoing and interminable negotiations over Turkey's membership in the EU, something seemingly as unlikely to happen as at any time since negotiations began in 1995, with all the various EU institutions involved.[59] Turkey, naturally enough, is working hard to leverage its foreign policy position by playing off Russia and the EU, and extracting concessions from the EU to hold firm on migrants. Likewise, it used its bargaining position as a member of NATO to delay applications by Finland and Sweden to join that organization in 2022 as it sought concessions from those states regarding their support for Kurdish opposition groups, as well as from the United States.

Box 8.3   Greece and Turkey

There are many seemingly intractable problems in Europe, and one of them is the relationship between Greece and Turkey. Prominent civilizations in their own right for centuries, Greece fell under the control of the Ottoman Empire in the mid–fifteenth century, only gaining independence through war in the 1820s, supported by France, Russia, and the UK. These three defined the independent state of Greece by treaty in 1832. Greece consolidated itself as primarily a Christian, Greek Orthodox state in contrast to the Islamic Ottoman Empire. Greece invaded the Ottoman Empire in the aftermath of World War I to gain additional (long lost) territory as the empire collapsed, with major losses and atrocities on both sides. The war ended with massive displacements of Greeks and Turks to their own respective homelands. Both countries entered NATO at the same time in 1952, but relations again soured following the Turkish invasion of Cyprus in 1974. In recent years, tensions have grown over disputed islands (and potential oil and gas wealth) in the Aegean Sea, currently under the control of Greece but claimed by Turkey. Greece has an ultimate veto over Turkey's accession to the EU, and tensions seem likely to continue.[a]

Note: a. Jean Marcou, "The Conundrum of the Great Gas Game and the Ensuing Strategic Realignment in the Eastern Mediterranean," Robert Schuman Foundation Policy Paper, no. 571, September 22, 2020, https://www.robert-schuman.eu/en/doc/questions-d-europe/qe-571-en.pdf.

The United Kingdom

The UK has a long history of independent foreign policy action and colonial rule. During the eighteenth and nineteenth centuries, many observers (and everyone in Britain) regarded it as the world's superpower, with the British pound as the world's leading currency. As discussed in Chapter 2, Britain's rapid fall from power in the space of a few decades in the twentieth century undercut its leadership role, even though many in the country refused to recognize this decline. Britain was a skeptic of the EU even when joining in 1973, notably twenty years after core West European countries formed the organization. The country remained outside of the euro and the Schengen zone, for example, and was not enthusiastic over issues such as the Common Agricultural Policy and the EU's Social Policy agenda. Nevertheless, the UK retained EU membership until January 2020.

Following the leave campaign's narrow victory in the June 2016 referendum on Britain's EU membership, the relationship between the EU and the UK remains testy, challenging, and uncertain. Several years of negotiations brought little progress, and the parties formally completed their separation only in January 2020. Unfortunately, this is just the beginning of the agonizing pathway to resolving the future relationship between Britain and the EU. An agreement put in place in December 2020 avoided a hard Brexit (no agreement) and potential trade chaos, but even with this deal, many years of negotiations remain to organize the myriad details of the new arrangement. Disagreements over pandemic policy in 2020–2022 and the supplies of vaccine are examples of likely disagreements going forward, as are hardening battle lines over the status of Northern Ireland and its interaction with Ireland.[60]

For Britain, besides the questions of how to interact with the EU as its leading trade partner, there are issues at home regarding immigration and borders, services, potential calls for Scottish independence, and the difficulties of dealing with the vexing issue of Northern Ireland.[61] Its overseas challenges are perhaps even more formidable, not just in a trade cooperation agreement with the EU, but also in seeking a free-trade deal, or at least a recalibration of its relationship, with the United States.[62] This new path, what Prime Minister Boris Johnson labeled "Global Britain," assumes that Britain remains important in the world, and others perceive it to be so.[63] It depends on Britain's ability to negotiate favorable trade terms with other countries, beginning with the EU itself. These negotiations with the EU did not begin propitiously, and severe differences over fishing rights, especially with France, dogged talks in 2021. Tensions further flared in October 2021 after France lost a lucrative submarine contract with Australia to the UK and the United States, and remained high over disagreements concerning migrants trying to cross the Channel.

The UK did sign a new Transatlantic Charter with the United States in June 2021, symbolic of the original agreement eighty years earlier, along with a trade deal with Australia in the same month. It is difficult to envisage, however, how the UK will expand its influence in the future over potential major trade partners, notably China, Russia, and the United States. As Lawrence D. Freedman points out, Britain needs to plot a more realistic and less ambitious course in a rapidly changing global environment, though perhaps still including a major role in European defense.[64] The EU and the UK will most likely have to continue to deal with the Brexit fallout for the near future, as the issue is not simply going to disappear.

The Foreign Relations of Neutral States

In a continent historically resonant with war, it is not surprising that countries would attempt to maintain neutrality to promote their own national interest, although there is no formal way to guarantee this. At times, invaders ignore such neutrality, as we saw earlier with Norway during World War II. Sweden also has a tradition of neutrality since 1834, which spared it from invasion during World War II, but more because of Germany's inability to launch an active campaign against it rather than Adolf Hitler's respect for neutrality. Sweden remained neutral until Russia's invasion of Ukraine made it seek NATO membership in May 2022, even though it is uncertain whether Sweden will take part in any military-related policymaking in the EU.[65] Spain also strategically promoted neutrality during World War II, as this came right on the heels of the Spanish civil war, but the country's pro-fascist stance left the country outside of Hitler's glare. Spain's neutrality remained until its accession to NATO in May 1992. The Soviet Union's Nonaggression Pact with Germany was akin to a temporary neutrality, but ultimately did not protect the USSR from invasion by Germany in 1941.

Switzerland is perhaps the best example of long-term neutrality, which has kept the country out of wars. Switzerland began its neutrality in 1515 after its military defeat to France, although this did not prevent Napoleon invading Switzerland in 1798. At the end of the Napoleonic wars at the 1815 Congress of Vienna, European countries affirmed the "perpetual" neutrality of Switzerland, as all countries benefited in some way from this neutral zone in the center of Europe. Switzerland built on this platform, hosting the International Committee of the Red Cross after the 1860s, the League of Nations in the interwar period, and the European headquarters of the United Nations after World War II (in the vacated Palais des Nations used by the League). Switzerland is an armed neutral state, so this is not a pacifist stance. Neutrality also kept Switzerland from joining the UN until a referendum marginally supported membership in 2002. Switzerland is not a member of the EU nor of NATO.

Switzerland's neighbor Austria is also a neutral state. Following World War II, allied troops occupied Austria similarly to Germany. As part of the settlement to remove these occupying forces, Austria signed a permanent neutrality agreement in 1955. Through this agreement, Austria remains outside of NATO, but it did not prevent the country joining the EU in 1995. Finland signed a neutrality pact with the USSR in 1948, and this is the basis of its neutrality. The fear of Russian intervention in Finnish affairs during the Cold War led to a form of limited sovereignty and low profile policies for Finland, a status referred to as "Finlandization." Finland did join the EU at the same time as Austria and Sweden in 1995 as Cold War tensions subsided, similar to other neutral countries such as Cyprus and Malta in 2004. Like Sweden, however, Finland decided to change its policy of neutrality in May 2022 by seeking membership in NATO out of security fears following Russia's invasion of Ukraine. Ireland also maintains neutrality—it stayed out of World War II—and remains outside of NATO, but this policy is primarily because it wishes to retain independence from the UK and any military organization (NATO) to which the UK belongs. This relates to Ireland's long-standing goal of unification of the island of Ireland, something opposed by the UK government.

The Foreign Relations of Small States

Europe possesses a number of small states in terms of territory and population, and here I use a benchmark of below 1 million people. Almost by definition, the policies of small states tend to be reactive to larger states around them, often seeking protection or pursuing a neutral stance as often as possible. Such small states have less opportunity for major economic production, so normally specialize today in tourism or banking. Luxembourg is a good example with a population of about 620,000, but with significant banking, finance, and tax haven infrastructure. On a GDP per capita basis, Luxembourg is the highest-ranking country in the EU. Small island states such as Cyprus (875,000) and Malta (500,000) are similar in terms of a specialization in finance, as are the microcountries such as Andorra (77,000), Liechtenstein (39,000), Monaco (39,000), and San Marino (34,000). All of these have high economic performance rates, as shown in the Country Profiles section at the end of the book. Liechtenstein, for example, has embraced casinos since 2010, with five of them, even though rural conservatives there are less enamored. All these small countries or principalities are dependent on the benevolence of their neighbors for their existence, although they all are members of the Council of Europe.

Box 8.4   Denmark and Greenland

Greenland is an island about one-third the size of Australia, but with less than 60,000 people. Its physical location makes it North American, from where its population (largely Inuit) originally migrated. After a thousand years of Norwegian and Danish influence starting with the Vikings, Greenland became a Danish colony in 1814. The Danes fully integrated Greenland as part of Denmark in 1953, even though Greenland is 1,800 miles (2,900 kilometers) from Denmark and ten times the size. Greenland obtained home rule in 1979, and after a referendum in 2008 gained greater autonomy, even though Denmark retains control of defense and foreign policy. Greenland left the EU in 1985, even though its citizens technically remain part of the EU through Danish citizenship. The United States has tried unsuccessfully to purchase Greenland several times, most recently during the Donald Trump administration, but retains a large military base there.[a] Greenland is seeking a free-trade agreement with the United States. In a national election in April 2021, government changed hands and put into power a left-leaning party that opposes a controversial mining operation, and is more assertive of claims to full Greenland independence. With its strategic location in the Arctic Circle and the North Atlantic, the future of Greenland is an important foreign policy issue in Europe and beyond.

Note: a. Martin Breum, "How a US Pivot to the North Changes the European Artic," *Arctic Today,* August 12, 2020, https://www.arctictoday.com/how-a-us-pivot-to-the-north-changes-the-european-arctic/.

One final country of note is the Vatican City or Holy See, with a total population of under 1,000. It is the smallest independent state in the world, and the city of Rome surrounds it. Dating back to the early days of Christianity, the Pope as leader of the Vatican had considerable sway over significant regions of Italy, but Italy received most of those lands on its unification and this transformed the Pope's powers from a traditional head of state to the religious leadership we see today. The protection by Swiss Guards dates back to the recruitment of Swiss mercenaries to fight for papal interests in the fifteenth century, but today forms more of a ceremonial guard to the Pope. Guards today still must be Catholics to serve.

Organizations for European Foreign Policy Cooperation

In this final section, I consider briefly how European countries use a variety of other international organizations based in Europe to pursue or coordinate their foreign policies. Unlike the EU, these are all purely intergovernmental, where the organization has little to no autonomy to go beyond what member states desire. Member governments are free to ignore any programs that they oppose. These organizations, nevertheless, are often useful to promote national, or regional, political agendas.

Council of Europe

As discussed in previous chapters, the Council of Europe (COE) predates the EU, formed by calls for European solidarity after World War II (and should not be confused with EU institutions such as the European Council or the Council of the European Union). Established in 1949 in Strasbourg with an initial membership of ten Western European countries, the COE encompasses forty-seven European states today, essentially the whole of Europe including all EU members, Armenia, Russia, and Turkey, but with Belarus as an observer.[66] As discussed in Chapter 1, the COE excluded Russia following its invasion of Ukraine in 2022. The Council is a loose intergovernmental organization, focusing on the three areas of human rights, democracy, and the rule of law. The unwillingness of the original members to embrace tighter political and economic cooperation led to a small group splintering to develop the EU institutions. The COE has continued to be purely intergovernmental, and operates separate, but parallel, to the EU.

The core institutions of the COE are the Committee of Ministers, comprised of ministerial representation by member states, and a Parliamentary Assembly, made up of 324 parliamentarians elected by national parliaments. A secretary-general leads the COE. The premier element of the COE is the European Convention on Human Rights, signed in 1950, which shapes human rights across the continent, and whose enforcement is monitored by the European Court of Human Rights.[67] The court began operations in 1959 and comprises forty-seven judges elected by the Parliamentary Assembly. Each judge originates from a different member state, even though judges must take a European perspective in their deliberations. The court handles cases brought by individuals or member governments, and is a final arbiter on such matters.

The COE created the twelve-star flag of Europe in 1955 as a symbol of European unity, along with a European anthem. The EU adopted the flag and anthem in 1985, and now both organizations use these. The "Anthem of Europe" is the final movement of Beethoven's "Ninth Symphony," and the COE adopted this originally in 1972. Even though the Council has little to no ability to enforce its policies or keep countries in check, it serves as a useful venue for discussion of topics of relevance to Europe as a whole.

European Free Trade Association

The European Free Trade Association (EFTA) began operations in 1960, largely promoted by the UK as a counterweight organization to the developing EU. EFTA emphasizes free trade and intergovernmental cooperation, and eschews plans for supranational cooperation. The UK's support for EFTA turned out to be short-lived, as it applied for membership in the EU in 1963 (only successfully completing this in 1973 after two French vetoes), but EFTA remains for a handful of countries not willing to fully join the EU. There is speculation that the UK may rejoin EFTA post-Brexit.

The four current members of EFTA are Iceland, Liechtenstein, Norway, and Switzerland. All of them are relatively prosperous states with small populations, with a preference for intergovernmental cooperation only. EFTA's loose intergovernmental structure comprises a Council of Ministers from member states, as well as a small Secretariat based in Geneva. There is a link between EFTA and the EU, nevertheless, through the European Economic Area, which allows EFTA members (excluding Switzerland) many of the benefits of EU membership without the actual necessity of joining. Such benefits include participation in the single market (trade without borders) along with open borders with EU members through the Schengen zone agreements.[68] Possible negatives of this participation in the EEA include the inability to shape EU policy, the lack of representation within the EU organizations, and the fact that these countries are not eligible for any EU payments (though they would most likely be net contributors to the EU).

Nordic Council

The Nordic Council, established in 1952, is an interparliamentary organization of the five Nordic countries, including the associated territories of the Faroe Islands and Greenland (both Denmark), and the Aland Islands (Finland).[69] The eighty-seven representatives are members of the parliaments of their home country, and assigned to represent their country in the Nordic Council. An intergovernmental group, the Nordic Council of Ministers, began in 1971 to provide formal cooperation between governments. A core mandate for the organizations is sustainability.

Organization of the Black Sea Economic Cooperation

Founded in 1992, with its headquarters in Istanbul, the Black Sea Economic Cooperation (BSEC) is a loose political and economic intergovernmental organization comprising twelve states around the Black Sea. Members include Bulgaria, Greece, and Romania from the EU, as well as Turkey and Russia. Many countries in the Caucuses and Balkan regions are present here, countries that form a part of the EU's European Neighborhood Program. This is a region of immense strategic value, especially in terms of the sea route to and from the Black Sea, as well as strong oil and gas reserves. It has a similar administrative structure to the Council of Europe, with a ministerial council and a parliamentary assembly. Membership of Russia and Ukraine did little to ameliorate the tensions between the two following Russia's annexation of Crimea in 2014, or after Russia's full invasion of Ukraine in 2022, but there are some positive signs of economic cooperation between members.[70]

United Nations Economic Commission for Europe

Europe hosts various other influential international organizations that have a predominant focus on European economic affairs (but do include other issue areas). These organizations, however, also contain members from outside of Europe, making them not exclusively European. Not all European countries belong to these organizations, but these organizations are worthy of a quick mention.

The United Nations Economic Commission for Europe (UNECE), based in Geneva at the UN headquarters, is one of the regional bodies of the United Nations established to promote economic stability and policy dialogue between members. The UNECE increased its membership significantly after the collapse of the Soviet Union, and today has a membership of fifty-six countries.[71] The United States and Canada are core members, and today membership includes Kazakhstan, Kyrgyzstan, Tajikistan, Turkmenistan, and Uzbekistan of the former USSR as well as Israel, on top of all countries of Europe including Russia and Turkey. One of the core programs of UNECE over the past several decades has focused on improving the transition economies of CEE.

As with all UN bodies, the UNECE is a loose intergovernmental association and does not really promote any strong political agenda. The organization is modestly successful in promoting economic development and sustainability in the region.

Organisation for Economic Co-operation and Development

The OECD, based in Paris, is the primary organization drawing together the leading industrialized, developed countries in the world. It began life as the Organisation for European Economic Co-operation in 1948, established under US pressure to handle disbursement to European countries of the US European Recovery Act funds, better known as the Marshall Plan named after the secretary of state, George Marshall.[72] In a way, the OEEC was the initial organization to draw together European countries into economic cooperation, and this experience directly led to the establishment of other European institutions, notably the Coal and Steel Community in 1951, and subsequently the EU.

The OEEC became the OECD in 1961, following the relatively successful recovery and rebuilding of Western Europe after the war. The OECD took on a broader mandate to coordinate economic policy and trade among the leading (capitalist) economic players in the world.[73] With thirty-seven member countries, the OECD accounts for about 80 percent of world trade and investment. It includes most EU members, with the notable exceptions of the weaker economies such as Bulgaria, Cyprus, Malta, and Romania. Turkey is a member of the OECD, but not Russia (or China). The EU Commission participates in the OECD, though without voting authority. Core goals of the OECD are to coordinate economic policies in the world's leading capitalist countries, and to promote better business practices. The OECD is a leader in the promotion of anticorruption programs and corporate responsibility.

European Bank for Reconstruction and Development

The European Bank for Reconstruction and Development (EBRD), aptly borrowing its name from the International Bank for Reconstruction and Development (World Bank), began operations in 1991 with headquarters in London. The EBRD is a multilateral development bank focusing on providing finance and investment into transition economies.[74] At the collapse of the Soviet Union and the rapidly changing economic environment in CEE, the EBRD capitalized on the need to provide development assistance to the economies of the region. Such investment helped to develop those economies and prepare them for EU membership after 2000.

Initial projects focused on growing the private sector as a basis for economic transformation. Major funding occurs today in other critical fields, such as infrastructure, telecommunications, and nuclear safety. The EBRD also increased its range of countries to invest in, recently adding projects in the Middle East and around the southern and eastern rim of the Mediterranean Sea.

Arctic Council

The Arctic Council is perhaps a less well-known organization, but arguably will be increasingly central as economic development and climate change occur in the Arctic region. The Arctic Council has only eight members, as geographical presence inside the Arctic Circle is a condition for membership. These members include the five Nordic countries (Denmark [via Greenland], Finland, Iceland, Norway, and Sweden) plus Russia in Europe, along with Canada and the United States. Eight other European countries have observer status, as do China and India. The Arctic Council began in 1996 as an intergovernmental organization, and as issues grew in number, a small Secretariat formed in Tromso in the far north of Norway in 2013 to manage its business.[75]

The council focuses on sustainability and environmental protection, and has a large mandate to protect Indigenous communities in the region. As climate change continually melts the Arctic icepack, there are increasing economic opportunities for mining and transportation routes across the Arctic, objectives that Russia in particular is aggressively pursuing. This is becoming a hotly contested region, and one in which not only Scandinavia but many other European countries will engage, as will China as an observer.

Other Global Organizations Based in Europe

There are many other international organizations based in Europe, but that do not necessarily focus their energies on Europe. Their location in Europe is often a product of history. For example, numerous organizations based in Geneva are tied to the presence of the League of Nations and the UN. Notable for Europe is the World Trade Organization, established in Geneva in January 1995 (absorbing the General Agreement on Tariffs and Trade), which attempts to manage rules regarding international trade. As EU members depend on a rule-based trading system, the WTO has been important, and the EU negotiates there as a single bloc. The WTO's appeals process has engaged the United

States and the EU many times in their trade disputes. The EU, as of 2021, had complained to the WTO in 104 cases, and had responded as defendant in 88 cases. This is second in total only to the United States, and the majority of these cases were disputes between the EU and the United States.[76] A full slate of UN agencies is also important for European states in Geneva, and elsewhere in Europe, such as the United Nations Industrial Development Organization (UNIDO) in Vienna, the United Nations Educational, Scientific and Cultural Organization (UNESCO) in Paris, or the UN Food and Agriculture Organization (FAO) in Rome.

Similarly, in terms of international law, The Hague hosts the UN's International Court of Justice (ICJ) and the International Criminal Court (ICC). The ICJ took over from its predecessor in the League, the Permanent Court of International Justice, after the League ended in 1946. The ICJ handles a few cases a year when states allow it to adjudicate. The ICC is an international court separate from the UN system, and it prosecutes individuals for war crimes and genocide. Established in 2002, the ICC has prosecuted several people over war crimes in the Balkans in the post–Cold War era, notably the Srebrenica ethnic massacre, or genocide, of 8,000 Bosnian Muslim men by Serbs in July 1995.

One final note on international organizations is to make mention of prominent nongovernmental organizations that began in Europe, and which continue to have their headquarters there. There are literally hundreds to mention here, but notable examples include Amnesty International ([AI], founded in London in 1961), Doctors Without Borders ([MSF], Médicins Sans Frontières, founded in 1971 in Paris, now headquartered in Geneva), and the International Committee of the Red Cross and Red Crescent ([ICRC], founded in Geneva in 1863). Many of these nongovernmental organizations in Europe are heavily engaged in dialogue with the EU institutions as well as with other international agencies.

Conclusion

Europe is a complex mosaic of more than forty countries pursuing their interests while maintaining peaceful relations as much as possible. In previous centuries, war was a common occurrence, but since 1945 various international organizations have assisted in trying to navigate relations between countries. The most prominent is the EU, where efforts to harmonize policies among the twenty-seven members are extended to countries around the EU's periphery or "neighborhood." That Europe is living in one of its longest ever periods of peace is a tribute to the EU, but other prominent organizations assist, notably NATO. A prominent theme of this book is the constant flux of Europe and European relations, and there are many areas of interest to keep our focus as we look forward. What is the likelihood of the continuing positive economic and political influence of the EU on its members and the continent as a whole? Will the EU foster closer coordination of national foreign policies, or will the EU erode into blatant national voices? How can Europe contain divergent policies, not just from populist movements but also from major powers such as Russia and Turkey? Will peace in Europe continue, or will there be a new Cold War?

The challenges within Europe are always daunting, as this chapter discusses. Similarly, Europe's relations with the world outside of the continent provide further challenges and opportunities, and it is to these external relations that we turn in the next chapter.

Notes

1. Christopher Hill, Michael Smith, and Sophie Vanhoonacker (eds.), *International Relations and the European Union,* 3rd ed. (Oxford: Oxford University Press, 2017).

2. Simon Duke and Sophie Vanhoonacker, "The European Union as a Subsystem of International Relations," in Christopher Hill, Michael Smith, and Sophie Vanhoonacker (eds.), *International Relations and the European Union,* 3rd ed. (Oxford: Oxford University Press, 2017), chap. 2.

3. Andrew Moravcsik, "Preferences and Power in the European Community: A Liberal Intergovernmentalist Approach," *Journal of Common Market Studies* 31(4), 1993: 473–524.

4. Omar Serrano, *The Domestic Sources of European Foreign Policy: Defence and Enlargement* (Amsterdam: Amsterdam University Press, 2013), p. 123.

5. Ian Manners, "Normative Power Europe: A Contradiction in Terms?" *Journal of Common Market Studies* 40(2), 2002: 235–258.

6. Münevver Cebeci, "European Foreign Policy Research Reconsidered: Constructing an 'Ideal Power Europe' Through Theory," *Millennium: Journal of International Studies* 40(3), 2012: 563–583.

7. Reuben Wong, "The Role of the Member States: The Europeanization of Foreign Policy?" in Christopher Hill, Michael Smith, and Sophie Vanhoonacker (eds.), *International Relations and the European Union*, 3rd ed. (Oxford: Oxford University Press, 2017), chap. 7.

8. Christopher Hill, "The Capability-Expectations Gap, or Conceptualizing Europe's International Role," *Journal of Common Market Studies* 31(3), 1993: 305–328.

9. Benjamin Leruth, Stefan Gänzle, and Jarle Troudal, "Differentiated Integration and Disintegration in the EU After Brexit: Risks Versus Opportunities," *Journal of Common Market Studies* 57(6), 2019: 1383–1394.

10. For a helpful review of the development of these mechanisms, see Steve Wood and Wolfgang Quaisser, *The New European Union: Confronting the Challenges of Integration* (Boulder: Lynne Rienner, 2008), chap. 5. See also Frederiga Bindi (ed.), *The Foreign Policy of the European Union: Assessing Europe's Role in the World* (Washing-

ton, DC: Brookings Institution, 2010); Brian White, *Understanding European Foreign Policy* (Houndmills: Palgrave, 2001).

11. Jolyon Howorth, "The European Union's Security and Defence Policy: The Quest for Purpose," in Christopher Hill, Michael Smith, and Sophie Vanhoonacker (eds.), *International Relations and the European Union*, 3rd ed. (Oxford: Oxford University Press, 2017), chap. 15; see also Council of the European Union, *European Security Strategy: A Secure Europe in a Better World* (Brussels: EU Council, 2009), https://www.consilium.europa.eu/media/30823/qc7809568enc.pdf.

12. William Wallace, "European Foreign Policy Since the Cold War: How Ambitious, How Inhibited?" *British Journal of Politics and International Relations* 19(1), 2017: 80.

13. European Union, *Shared Vision, Common Action: A Stronger Europe: A Global Strategy for the European Union's Foreign and Security Policy* (Brussels: European Union, 2016), https://eeas.europa.eu/topics/eu-global-strategy/17304/global-strategy-european-unions-foreign-and-security-policy_en.

14. European Union, Shared Vision, Common Action, p. 7.

15. European Union, Shared Vision, Common Action, p. 44. See also Jean-Dominique Giuliani, Arnaud Danjean, Françoise Grossetête, and Thierry Tardy, "Defence: Europe's Awakening," Robert Schuman Foundation Policy Paper, no. 474, May 22, 2018, https://www.robert-schuman.eu/en/doc/questions-d-europe/qe-474-en.pdf.

16. Jonathan Joseph and Ana E. Juncos, "Resilience as an Emergent European Project? The EU's Place in the Resilience Turn," *Journal of Common Market Studies* 57(5), 2019: 995–1012; see also Nathalie Tocci, "Towards a European Security and Defence Union: Was 2017 a Watershed?" *Journal of Common Market Studies* 56 (Special Supplement), 2018: 131–141; Karen E. Smith, "A European Union Global Strategy for a Changing World?" *International Politics* 54, 2017: 503–518; Wolfgang Wagner and Rosanne Anholt, "Resilience as the EU Global Strategy's New Leitmotif: Pragmatic, Problematic or Promising," *Contemporary Security Policy* 37(3), 2016: 414–430.

17. Howorth, "The European Union's Security and Defence Policy," chap. 15.

18. Pierre Mirel and Xavier Mirel, "Challenges and Constraints Facing a 'Geopolitical Commission' in the Achievement of European Sovereignty," Robert Schuman Foundation Policy Paper, no. 560, May 26, 2020.

19. Maxime Lefebvre, "Europe as a Power, European Sovereignty and Strategic Autonomy; a Debate that Is Moving Towards an Assertive Europe," Robert Schuman Foundation Policy Paper, no. 582, February 2, 2021, https://www.robert-schuman.eu/en/doc/questions-d-europe/qe-582-en.pdf.

20. For a general official EU overview of the European Neighborhood Policy, see European Union External Action, "EEAS: European Neighbourhood Policy," https://www.eeas.europa.eu/eeas/european-neighbourhood-policy_en . See also European Union Neighbours, "Policy," https://www.euneighbours.eu/en/policy.

21. Benita Ferrero-Waldner, "The European Neighbourhood Policy: The EU's Newest Foreign Policy Instrument," *European Foreign Affairs Review* 11, 2006: 140.

22. Esther Barbé and Elisabeth Johansson-Nogués, "The EU as a Modest 'Force for Good': The European Neighborhood Policy," *International Affairs* 84(1), 2008: 81–96.

23. Michael O. Slobodchikoff, *Building Hegemonic Order Russia's Way: Order, Stability and Predictability in the Post-Soviet Space* (Lanham MD: Lexington Books, 2014).

24. Ganna Kharlamova, "Economic Prospects in the Context of Growing Regional Interdependencies: The European Union and the Eastern Partnership," *Ekonomika* 94(2), 2015: 47–72.

25. Rosa Balfour, "EU Political Dilemmas in North Africa and the Middle East: The Logic of Diversity and the Limits to Foreign Policy," in Gergana Noutcheva, Karolina Pomorska, and Giselle Bosse (eds.), *The EU and Its Neighbours: Values Versus Security in European Foreign Policy* (Manchester: Manchester University Press), chap. 4.

26. Jean Casabianca, "Mediterranean Sea: A Paradigm of Contemporary Conflicts," Robert Schuman Foundation Policy Paper, no. 564, June 23, 2020, https://www.robert-schuman.eu/en/doc/questions-d-europe/qe-564-en.pdf.

27. Karen Smith, "The Outsiders: The European Neighbourhood Policy," *International Affairs* 81(4), 2005: 759.

28. Fyodor Lukyanov, "Putin's Foreign Policy: The Quest to Restore Russia's Rightful Place," *Foreign Affairs* 95(3), 2016: 30–37. See also Ivan Krastev and Mark Leonard, "Europe's Shattered Dream of Order: How Putin Is Disrupting the Atlantic Alliance," *Foreign Affairs* 94(3), 2015: 48–58; see also G. Doug Davis and Michael O. Slobodchikoff, *Cultural Imperialism and the Decline of the Liberal Order: Russian and Western Soft Power in Eastern Europe* (Lanham, MD: Lexington Books 2019).

29. Karolina Pomorska and Gergana Noutcheva, "Europe as a Regional Actor: Waning Influence in an Unstable and Authoritarian Neighbourhood," *Journal of Common Market Studies* 55, 2017: 165–176; see also Karen E. Smith, "Enlargement, the Neighbourhood, and European Order," in Christopher Hill, Michael Smith, and Sophie Vanhoonacker (eds.), *International Relations and the European Union*, 3rd ed. (Oxford: Oxford University Press, 2017), chap. 14.

30. Pierre Mirel, "The Eastern Partnership: Between Resilience and Interference," Robert Schuman Foundation Policy Paper, no. 589, March 30, 2021, https://www.robert-schuman.eu/en/doc/questions-d-europe/qe-589-en.pdf.

31. Gergana Noutcheva, "Institutional Governance of European Neighborhood Policy in the Wake of the Arab Spring," *Journal of European Integration* 37(1), 2015: 34.

32. Andrew Rettman, "Germany Still Backs New Russia Gas," *EU Observer,* March 5, 2018, https://euobserver.com/energy/141204.

33. European Commission, "Migration and Home Affairs: Schengen Area," https://ec.europa.eu/home-affairs/what-we-do/policies/borders-and-visas/schengen_en.

34. European Parliament, "Fact Sheets on the European Union: Immigration Policy," https://www.europarl.europa.eu/factsheets/en/sheet/152/immigration-policy.

35. Eurostat, "Migration and Migrant Population Statistics," https://ec.europa.eu/eurostat/statistics-explained/index.php?title=Migration_and_migrant_population_statistics.

36. Andrew Geddes and Peter Scholten, *The Politics of Migration and Immigration in Europe*, 2nd ed. (London: Sage, 2016).

37. European Commission, "Migration and Home Affairs: Country Responsible for Asylum Application (Dublin Regulation)," https://ec.europa.eu/home-affairs/what-we-do/policies/asylum/examination-of-applicants_en.

38. Markus M. L. Crepaz, *European Democracies*, 9th ed. (New York: Routledge, 2017), chap. 8.

39. Christine Crudo Blackburn and Paul E. Lenze Jr., *Syrian Forced Migration and Public Health in the European Union* (Lanham, MD: Lexington Books, 2019).

40. European Commission, "Migration and Home Affairs: European Migration Network (EMN)," https://ec.europa.eu/home-affairs/what-we-do/networks/european_migration_network_en.

41. Frontex: European Border and Coast Guard Agency, https://frontex.europa.eu/.

42. Stefanie Buzmaniuk, "The Union's External Borders: A European Debate Revisited," Robert Schuman Foundation Policy Paper, no. 585, February 23, 2021, https://www.robert-schuman.eu/en/doc/questions-d-europe/qe-585-en.pdf.

43. Eurostat, "Intra-EU Trade in Goods—Main Features," https://ec.europa.eu/eurostat/statistics-explained/index.php?title=Intra-EU_trade_in_goods_-_main_features&oldid=452727#Evolution_of_intra-EU_trade_in_goods:_2003-2019.

44. UK Parliament, House of Commons Library, "Statistics on UK-EU Trade," https://commonslibrary.parliament.uk/research-briefings/cbp-7851/.

45. "Emmanuel Macron on Europe's Fragile Place in a Hostile World," *The Economist*, November 7, 2019.

46. Ronald Tiersky, "Macron's World: How the New President Is Remaking France," *Foreign Affairs* 97(1), 2018: 87–96.

47. Robert Kagan, "The New German Question: What Happens When Europe Comes Apart?" *Foreign Affairs* 98(3), 2019: 108–120.

48. Matthias Matthijs, "The Right Way to Fix the EU: Put Politics Before Economics," *Foreign Affairs* 99(3), 2020: 160–170.

49. Steven Erlanger, "Germany and France Aim to Lead Continent Out of Crisis. Will It Follow?" *New York Times*, May 20, 2020.

50. Organisation for Economic Co-operation and Development, "Official Development Assistance," https://www.oecd.org/dac/financing-sustainable-development/development-finance-standards/official-development-assistance.htm.

51. For a review of this time period and transition, see Daniel C. Diller, *Russia and the Independent States* (Washington, DC: Congressional Quarterly, 1993).

52. Ivan Krastev and Mark Leonard, "Europe's Shattered Dream of Order." See also a series of articles on Putin's intentions in *Foreign Affairs* 95(3), 2016.

53. Daniel Yergin and Thane Gustafson, *Russia 2010: And What It Means for the World* (New York: Random House, 1993), p. 265.

54. Mirel, "The Eastern Partnership."

55. World Bank, World Integrated Trade Solution (WITS), "Russia Trade," https://wits.worldbank.org/countrysnapshot/en/RUSSIA.

56. Steven Erlanger and Megan Specia, "Russian Envoys Expelled from EU in Retaliation," *New York Times,* February 9, 2021.

57. Michael Schwirtz, "Russia Expels 20 Czech Diplomats as Tensions Escalate," *New York Times*, April 18, 2021.

58. Kaya Genc, "Erdogan's Way: The Rise and Rule of Turkey's Islamist Shapeshifter," *Foreign Affairs* 98(5), 2019: 26–34.

59. Elena Baracani, *EU-Turkey Relations: A New Direction for EU Foreign Policy?* (Cheltenham: Edward Elgar, 2021).

60. Ian Bremmer, "Troubling Times in Northern Ireland," *Time,* April 26–May 3, 2021, p. 25. See also Marie-Claire Considère-Charon, "Brexit and the Irish Question," Robert Schuman Foundation Policy Paper, no. 583, February 9, 2021, https://www.robert-schuman.eu/en/doc/questions-d-europe/qe-583-en.pdf.

61. Philomena Murray and Alex Brianson, "Rethinking Britain's Role in a Differentiated Europe After Brexit: A Comparative Regionalism Perspective," *Journal of Common Market Studies* 57(6), 2019: 1431–1442; see also Simon Hix, "Brexit: Where Is the EU-UK Relationship Heading?" *Journal of Common Market Studies* 56 (Special Supplement), 2018: 11–27. Concerning the potential fracture of the UK itself, see "From United Kingdom to Untied Kingdom," *The Economist*, April 17, 2021.

62. Tim Oliver and Michael John Williams, "Special Relationship in Flux: Brexit and the Future of the US-EU and US-UK Relationship," *International Affairs* 92(3), 2016: 547–567.

63. In a scathing criticism of Brexit by the former French ambassador to the UK, we get a glimpse of the official European disgust of the UK's departure; see Jon Henley, "A Sad Adieu: A Diplomat on Watching the Brexit 'Revolution,'" *The Guardian*, February 26, 2021, https://www.theguardian.com/politics/2021/feb/26/lying-is-no-longer-a-sin-sylvie-bermann-on-brexit-and-boris-johnson. The interview is based on the ambassador's book, Sylvie Bermann, *Goodbye Britannia: Le Royaume-Uni au défi du Brexit* (Paris: Stock, 2021).

64. Lawrence D. Freedman, "Britain Adrift: The United Kingdom's Search for a Post-Brexit Role," *Foreign Affairs* 99(3), 2020: 118–130. The challenges facing the UK increased after Boris Johnson's own Conservative Party forced him to resign as prime minister in July 2022.

65. North Atlantic Treaty Organization, "Neutral European Countries: Austria, Switzerland, Sweden, Finland, Ireland," http://nato.gov.si/eng/topic/national-security/neutral-status/neutral-countries/.

66. Council of Europe, https://www.coe.int/en/web/portal/home.

67. Council of Europe, "European Court of Human Rights," https://www.echr.coe.int/Pages/home.aspx?p=home.

68. European Free Trade Association, https://www.efta.int/.

69. Nordic Council, https://www.norden.org/en/nordic-council.

70. Organization of the Black Sea Economic Cooperation, http://www.bsec-organization.org/.

71. United Nations Economic Commission for Europe, https://www.unece.org/info/ece-homepage.html.

72. Organisation for Economic Co-operation and Development, "Organisation for European Economic Co-operation," https://www.oecd.org/general/organisationforeuropeaneconomicco-operation.htm.

73. Organisation for Economic Co-operation and Development, https://www.oecd.org/.

74. European Bank for Reconstruction and Development, https://www.ebrd.com/.

75. Arctic Council, https://arctic-council.org/en/.

76. World Trade Organization, "Dispute Settlement: The Disputes," https://www.wto.org/english/tratop_e/dispu_e/dispu_by_country_e.htm.

9

The Contest for
Global Influence

IT IS A SIMPLE OBSERVATION TO MAKE THAT EUROPE HAS INTERACTED
with the outside world throughout history. Examples exist from every century,
such as the Roman Empire; the Crusades; the "discovery" and integration of the
Americas into European trade patterns; the colonial expansions into Africa,
Asia, and the Middle East; and the export of the Industrial Revolution from
Europe in the nineteenth century. The igniting of two world wars in the twentieth century also reflects the importance of Europe, although perhaps not posi-
tively and with a weakening of Europe after each. These important historical
trends were the focus of the first two chapters of this book.

Most of these events were not "European" as such, of course, but centered
on the actions of specific European countries. These were individual foreign
policies of countries, such as France, Germany, the Netherlands, Portugal,
Spain, and the United Kingdom, with little or no coordination, and often with
considerable hostility between them. Europe's colonization of Africa during the
latter half of the nineteenth century, for example, surged because of intense
national rivalries between European countries, only partially umpired by the
1884–1885 Berlin Agreements. World War I and World War II were essentially
conflicts between individual European countries, with the major powers of
France, Germany, Russia, and the UK contesting for dominance (not so unlike
the Napoleonic wars of the early nineteenth century), and the United States ultimately playing the decisive role in each.

It is difficult not to imagine individual European states continuing to
attempt to play a strong role in world politics today. France and the UK, for
example, cling to their permanent seats in the UN Security Council, though with

questionable justification. Russia's status in the UN hierarchy is perhaps more complex, as it remains the world's second-largest nuclear power even though its economic prowess is less impressive. Its sheer territorial size, resources, and continuing projection of itself as a global power provide it a strong role in global affairs. Germany remains the dominant economic power of the continent, and ranks among the world's top three exporters. The City of London continues its role as a critical center of global business and finance, far outstripping the nominal strength of the British economy, and notwithstanding Brexit. Countries around the world continue to speak the languages of Europe, with English the world's default language or lingua franca—thanks to the UK's colonization of what would become the United States, rather than anything intrinsic about the UK or the language today. There continues to be considerable respect for European culture and products around the world, and this helps to project soft power.

In this chapter, I look briefly at foreign relations outside of the European continent, emphasizing individual national policies as well as attempts to coordinate policy within the European Union's twenty-seven members. It begins by considering what it is that European countries project in terms of power, and then moves on to discuss some of the more important relationships with different sets of countries around the world.

Europe's Hard, Soft, and Moral Power

In past centuries, Europe's relations with the outside world were virtually always a projection of hard or military power. Even while proselytizing and working to convert others to Christianity, force was always in play. No group of people willingly asked for colonization, but force was the factor that made it happen. During the colonial period, Europeans reorganized local economies to benefit European interests, and tended to exact harsh trade policies on the colonized. A significant portion of Europe's wealth over the past few centuries came off the backs of colonies (or slaves) and the manipulation of trade rules.

In the contemporary world, European countries, and the EU27, still have some residual influence in shaping trade policies, and that is an area where the EU in particular has potential leverage and focuses some energy.[1] The EU is the world's largest economy, accounting for over 20 percent of the world's total GDP at around €14 trillion. The EU has €3,142 billion of exports, and €2,842 billion of imports. As a trade bloc, the EU has a significant positive trade balance with the United States, but an almost equal trade imbalance with China.[2] Where European countries do exert influence is with developing countries, especially in terms of the African, Caribbean, and Pacific group (ACP) of poorer countries (all former colonies). EU countries are the top trade partner for some eighty countries, many of which are developing. European countries have a tougher time in negotiating their economic relationship with the United States and, increasingly, China, as well as with fast-emerging economies such as Brazil and India. European countries put much emphasis on the World Trade Organization in their trade negotiations, as discussed earlier in the book, but the weakening of the WTO in the face of national policymaking also weakens European influence. European countries account for 35 percent of the world's inward foreign direct investment, and 41 percent of the world's outward investment.[3]

European countries are less likely today to project hard power through military force. Military force was certainly a factor in the post–World War II era to try to cling on to recalcitrant colonies, as discussed in Chapter 2. One could make a case that for countries such as France and the UK, it is economics rather than military force that keep overseas territories within their orbit. France uses some military force in Africa, but this is often couched more in terms of helping the international community combat terrorism, or protecting locals, than a direct effort to maintain some residual influence (though in the case of France, this is still a factor). In Russia's case in the Middle East, the use of force is more blatant to exert continuing influence in the region. The EU has a sizable number of peacekeeping missions in developing countries, and these are more humanitarian and economic rather than outright military in nature.

One area to take note of here is the continuing importance of arms sales by many European countries. Although these are not directly influencing states through military means, large arms sales perpetuate economic linkages and provide ties in the military realm. The United States is the world's largest arms exporter, but Russia, France, and Germany round out the top four. The UK, Spain, Italy, and the Netherlands are other European exporters among the top ten. Overall, European manufacturers account for about one-quarter of all the world's arms sales.[4]

Europe as a whole still exerts considerable soft or cultural power around the world, and this is an important ingredient in countries' relationships. Based on the original proposal by Joseph Nye, soft power occurs when one country gets other countries to want what it wants or, in this case, the EU can influence other countries to follow its policies without the threat of force.[5] Besides the power of language, Europe boasts of prestigious luxury products, iconic places to visit, incredible museums and history (often with artifacts plundered during colonialism), music, film, and theater—a significant cultural heritage. All this links to efforts by governments to brand their countries and portray them in the most positive light as stable democracies, helping to promote the service sector and tourism earnings. There is no better place for an autocrat to deposit their ill-gotten gains than a European bank. Is much of Europe on its way to becoming simply a tourist haven with declining significance in the world? That may perhaps be too strong a description of a complex subject, as countries try to utilize the benefits from soft power to leverage improved trade and political relations around the world. Such leverage may well be gradually diminishing, as discussed in this chapter.

A final topic to raise here is one mentioned briefly in the previous chapter; namely, that of Europe, and especially the EU, becoming a moral power, or a moral force for leadership in the world. The concept of Normative Power Europe implies a postconflict, postnationalist, postselfish approach to international affairs, where the EU has the role of moral leadership with mature experience in peacefully resolving tensions. After centuries of relentless plunder of the world—and other European countries—it is ironic that we should now try to overlook the past and see a reformed, pacific, benevolent Europe. It is unclear whether countries outside of the EU perceive the EU in such a light, or that this is simply European hubris. In fact, for some, notably China and Russia, the pursuit of NPE is simply indicative of Europe's declining significance in world politics because of diminishing economic and military power.

Individual countries perhaps flirt with the concept of moral power, such as those in the Nordic bloc, but even those countries in the past had their fair share of conquest, plunder, and empire. As smaller military powers, however, they tend to pursue mediated solutions to problems today. Nordic independence is noted as providing UN Secretaries-General from Europe (Trygve Lie of Norway and Dag Hammarskjöld of Sweden), although we can add Austria (Kurt Waldheim) and Portugal (António Guterres) to that list. Nordic countries are also among the world's leaders in development aid on a per capita basis, arguably another measurement of moral force.

Overall, the apparently diminishing importance of Europe in world politics is a theme that permeates the rest of this chapter, though there will be different reactions from European countries in varying circumstances.[6]

Relations with the United States

Relations between Europe and the United States are arguably among the most important in the world in terms of diplomacy and trade. Together, the EU27 and the United States account for about half of the world's GDP and for almost a third of all of the world's trade. The United States is the EU27's largest market for exports, and the second-largest market for imports (behind China, with the UK in third place).[7] Prior to 1945, there is much of interest in the Europe-US partnership, but I note only a few points briefly here. The transatlantic slave trade, the colonization of North America, the revolutionary wars and stabilization of the United States, the expansion of the United States in terms of territory and trade, and the key intervention of the United States in the two world (yet principally European) wars of the twentieth century—all these were markers in the evolution of the US-European partnership.

The rise of US influence in the global system came at the expense particularly of the UK, but nominally the whole of Europe. This challenge came in terms of military influence, as Rule Britannia gave way to Pax Americana. US isolationism in the interwar period somewhat masked this transfer of hegemony, but became a critical element of transatlantic relations after 1945. The UK's weakness and inability to continue its leadership role in Greece and Turkey (and in 1948, Israel) led directly to what President Harry S. Truman expressed in the Truman Doctrine in 1947, and logically to the Marshall Plan and the European Recovery Program immediately after, and then to NATO.[8] The UK's dramatic decline precipitated the demise of the "special relationship" (if there was such a thing), leading to Britain's reluctant realization—with significant prodding by the John F. Kennedy presidency—in the early 1960s that its best path forward lay in membership in the EU.[9]

The transatlantic partnership came under significant pressure during the 1980s and 1990s with growing US militarism targeted primarily at the USSR under President Ronald Reagan unsettling many European partners.[10] A whole list of trade disputes in the 1990s further undermined relations. These focused on topics such as hormones in beef, genetically modified food, protectionism and subsidies, audiovisual equipment, and intellectual property rights.[11] Differences also surfaced over external issues, such as disagreements over policies toward countries like Cuba and Iran.[12] President Bill Clinton launched negotiations for a New Transatlantic Agenda in 1995 (just as his immediate predecessor, George H.W. Bush, had done in 1990) linking Europe and the United States, but they made little headway in the tensions of the 1990s. In the immediate post–Cold War era, there was little threat from any adversary to push either the United States or Europe into serious negotiations.

The attacks on the United States on September 11, 2001, provided an opportunity for renewed friendship across the Atlantic. Genuine European dismay at the terrorist attacks led to a common stance on tackling the Taliban in an offensive on Afghanistan. Despite widespread European offers of assistance, the United States under President George W. Bush forged ahead on a strategy of attack with minimal European participation. Surrounding the president was a neoconservative leadership who saw little benefit in a partnership with Europe, and much to gain in the promotion of a unilateral preemptive "shock and awe" action by the sole global superpower.[13] Whatever goodwill remaining disappeared with the move to invade Iraq in 2003, this time with the virtual complete opposition of Europe, with the major exception of Britain under Prime Minister Tony Blair. The ill will generated on both sides of the Atlantic, fanned by the Bush administration's scorn of traditional partners as "old Europe," left little hope for better relations between the United States and Europe.[14]

This divergence also undermined the perception of the EU, held by some across the European continent, that it was a superpower in its own right worthy of equal partnership with the United States.[15] The list of tensions in EU-US relations grew longer. These issues included the role of the United Nations; tactical nuclear weapons in Europe; defense spending, and Europe's reluctance to pay its share to NATO; the International Criminal Court; Kyoto and climate change; landmines; privacy of data; agricultural subsidies; and genetically modified foods.[16] This was essentially the status of the relationship until Barack Obama's electoral victory in November 2008 offered hope of a change in direction.

President Obama was able to repair some of the damage done to NATO and political relations, but Europe was not his real focus. Besides the ongoing wars in Iraq and Afghanistan and Obama's efforts to live up to his 2009 Nobel Peace Prize, the continuing challenge of terrorism, rebuilding the economy after the 2008 crash, and the incessant attacks from within a unified and hostile Republican Party, Obama's pivot was more to Asia, and in particular the challenge posed by China. Obama also lost support in Europe by his inaction over Israel and Syria, and by the increasing use of drone attacks in conflict zones, often killing innocent civilians. Near the end of his second term, Obama appeared to turn belatedly to Europe, in particular shoring up the alliance in the face of the struggling euro, the refugee crisis, the Russian incursion into Ukraine, and the threat to Britain and the EU posed by the Brexit vote.[17] Obama was unusually blunt in admonishing the leave camp of Brexit, albeit without success.

Efforts to promote a free-trade area across the Atlantic have been discussed on and off since the Clinton administration in the early 1990s, but came back on to the agenda officially in 2013.[18] The focus of the Trans-Atlantic Trade and Investment Partnership (T-TIP) was to promote trade by removing barriers, but many in Europe feared that T-TIP would erode many social and economic protections that Europeans enjoy. Support also eroded because of opposition to Donald Trump's policies, though many saw T-TIP as a geostrategic partnership rather than a mere trade alliance, "an economic NATO."[19] Continuing negotiations could not guarantee success, as the United States and EU have not really seen eye to eye on trade for many years, exacerbated recently through the Trump tariff wars. Negotiations on T-TIP ended

Box 9.1   EU-US Trade Relations and Competition

One of the popular phrases of the 1990s was that the continent was becoming a "fortress Europe," with the idea that European companies were privileged whereas those from outside of Europe faced discrimination and barriers. This has proved to be an idea without much foundation, as companies from around the world operate openly in the single market. In terms of EU relations with the United States, however, there have been many areas of contention, many of which have played out in the WTO. These include EU actions against US technology companies, as mentioned earlier, as well as the ongoing battle in 2021 between Airbus and Boeing concerning subsidies. Numerous other areas of conflict exist, however, often over food, including Europe's reluctance to allow into the market genetically modified foods, such as corn, or chicken and beef raised with hormones. For example, a two-decade dispute regarding US companies exporting Latin American bananas into the EU market was finally resolved by the WTO in November 2012. The United States also railed against the preferential trade relationships forged between EU countries and their former colonies, leading the WTO to call on Europe to modify these. These antagonistic relations continued for more than two decades, and increased with the tariff wars unleashed by the Donald Trump administration after 2017. Despite EU claims to promote an open market, there are good grounds to conclude that protectionism (albeit often on health grounds) against various US products is present, with the WTO concurring. The EU uses the size of its economy as a lever in trade negotiations with the United States, and hopes to continue this trend with other countries, notably post-Brexit Britain, Canada, China, and Japan, as well as with the African continent. Despite claims to support open markets and globalization, the EU protects itself and could become more of an entrenched economic bloc. Looming in the near future are debates about US technology companies and cybersecurity and ways to agree on mechanisms of management.[a]

Note: a. Christopher Kolmos, "Bridging the Transatlantic Cyber Rift: Recommendations for Cyber Cooperation Between NATO and the EU," The Streit Council, February 24, 2021, https://www .streitcouncil.org/post/bridging-the-transatlantic-cyber-rift-recommendations-for-improving-cyber -cooperation-between-nato?utm_campaign=6479d524-7782-4f89-acc9-eb5135b378b7&utm_source =so&utm_medium=mail&cid=65bb845c-0491-4a62-9f53-3c10a4b07a05.

in 2019 and it is unclear whether they will restart. There are hopes for a better European-US relationship under the Joe Biden administration, but many areas of tension are likely to remain.[20]

Russia's relationship with the United States has been adversarial since the end of World War II (in fact, since the 1917 Russian Revolution). Russians believe that they did not receive sufficient credit for the role they played during the war in defeating fascism. They are opposed to the actions of and perceived threat from NATO, which now sits at its border. Russia faced considerable pressure during the

Cold War, and subsequent humiliation in its defeat and the disintegration of the USSR in 1991. Its contemporary foreign policy goal is to be treated as an equal by the United States and, certainly, by the EU, but these relations have been fraught. Russia's interference in US elections blatantly since 2016, and its continuing cyber warfare with the United States, are likely to be markers in a continuing downturn of Russian-US relations, especially following the inauguration of the Biden administration in January 2021. The Ukraine invasion in February 2022 displayed Russia's weakening of soft power in the region and served to increase tensions considerably, as the United States rejuvenated NATO and provided significant military supplies to Ukraine. A full-blown renewed Cold War is possible, even likely.

On a final note in this section, the UK has tried to maintain a special relationship with the United States, as mentioned above. Based loosely on common cultural heritage, the relationship was pushed to promote favorable trade and political ties, and Winston Churchill bolstered this for political gain during World War II. Following Brexit, the special relationship has served as a possible lever for the UK to access favorable trade relations, and a potential trade partnership, with the United States. This idea gained relatively little traction during the Trump administration, which was favorably disposed to the UK post-Brexit, and receded further from possibility with the Biden administration. This undermined a key component of the Global Britain strategy, to maneuver nimbly around the international system, though did not limit the UK government's rhetoric on the subject.

North Atlantic Treaty Organization

The North Atlantic Treaty Organization formed in 1949 at the beginning of the Cold War to provide protection for the countries of Western Europe (including West Germany, which did not join the organization until 1955) against potential Soviet pressure or threat of invasion. The USSR saw the existence of NATO as a major provocation and a threat to its existence. NATO began with its headquarters in Paris, but following disagreements over policy with France, it left for Brussels in 1967 where it has remained. Twelve countries established this Western Alliance, with the core being those of Western Europe along with Canada and the United States. In 1952, Greece and Turkey joined, but the major growth in the organization came in the 1990s when many countries in CEE joined, again to Russia's dismay. There are thirty NATO members as of June 2022, and these include most of the EU with the notable exceptions of Finland (historical tensions with Russia and a stance of neutrality), and Ireland and Sweden (neutrality) as discussed in the previous chapter.[21] The newest member, North Macedonia, joined in 2020, and Finland and Sweden applied to join in May 2022 as a response to Russia's invasion of Ukraine.

There are two key organs within NATO: the North Atlantic Council, primarily for political consultations, and the Military Committee. At the end of the Cold War, many observers believed that NATO might disappear, but continuing tensions with Vladimir Putin's Russia keep NATO forces in Europe. Others thought that the EU would develop its own military to take over protection of Europe, but this has not really materialized, partly because many EU countries prefer US protection (and spending) within NATO. The organization has also started to operate beyond Europe, such as in Afghanistan and Libya, and there is little likelihood that NATO will become less relevant in the near future, especially as the contest with Russia continues. Indeed, NATO appeared unified and buoyant in its confrontation with Russia over Ukraine in 2022, even as a number of challenges for the organization remain.[22]

Organization for Security and Co-operation in Europe

Another product of the Cold War is the Organization for Security and Co-operation in Europe (OSCE), which brings together fifty-seven countries of Europe, Central Asia, and North America to discuss issues of security in its broadest sense, including human rights, peaceful elections, environmental protection, and arms control.[23] The OSCE grew out of détente during the 1970s and a (temporary) softening of the Cold War, specifically through discussions within the Conference on Security and Cooperation in Europe (CSCE), leading to the Helsinki Accords in 1975. This was an initial agreement to promote dialogue and security across the continent, including the promotion of fair elections and human rights.

Following the collapse of communism and the rapid transformation of CEE, the CSCE morphed into the OSCE in 1994, and increased its membership to fifty-seven states along with its scope of business. Today, it mirrors in some respects the Council of Europe. Most notable is the membership of Russia in the OSCE, as a way to bolster its own position in Europe and to mitigate some of the more provocative actions of NATO toward it. The OSCE has its headquarters and secretariat in Vienna, but has offices in other European cities. It has institutional structures similar to the Council of Europe, with summit meetings of political leaders, a ministerial council, and a parliamentary association. It attempts to pursue policy by consensus, and this tends to water down any policy prescriptions for the organization.

China

Europe's relations with China date back at least 2,000 years to the establishment of the Silk Road that brought Chinese silk and other goods (tea, porcelain) to Europe and European goods to China. The Silk Road also connected the flow of ideas, culture, and religion between the two regions. Aggressive European interventions into a weakened China in the nineteenth century disrupted this relationship, notably through the two opium wars that further weakened China considerably. By the end of the nineteenth century, France, Germany, Portugal, and the UK all held territorial control over a segment of China. The memory of this occupation continues to sour Chinese perspectives toward Europe.

Following the Chinese Revolution of 1949, relations with China were difficult until the death of Chairman Mao Tse-tung in 1976, when China's modernization path allowed closer relations to develop. The end of formal European colonial occupation in China—of Hong Kong in 1997 and Macau in 1999—helped remove a point of contention, and trade relations flourished.

Economic opportunity has been central to Europe's increasing embrace of China in the past decade. The CEE countries have been especially open to investment by China, and the Chinese have viewed this as a cheaper way to access the EU markets. Recent concerns have emerged with the increasingly assertive global policies of China, and with the consolidation of power by President Xi Jinping, with internal crackdowns and human rights abuses particularly against the Uighurs in western China and aggressive political actions toward Hong Kong threatening its democracy. European countries have attempted to stake out opposition to China on human rights grounds, but their views are unconvincing and the Chinese reaction harsh. Lithuania, for example, opposed the use of Chinese phones because of their tracking devices, spoke out against human rights abuses, and favored trade with Taiwan, but suffered significantly after 2021 from Chinese trade reprisals. For China, European government threats are hollow, and its use of force virtually nonexistent. The EU had a trade deficit with China of €164 billion in 2019,[24] and questions arise about Chinese investments in Europe especially in the field of sensitive technology, notably recently with Huawei and strategic communications within the fifth generation of cellular broadband (5G). These issues are dividing the EU in terms of how to face China, with President Emmanuel Macron of France highly vocal in trying, unsuccessfully, to maintain a common European stance vis-à-vis China.[25]

At the EU level, increasing trade and investment partnerships with China have grown significantly over the past decade. A new investment agreement signed in December 2020 allowed for expansion of activities in each other's market, though it remains uncertain whether there is enough political support in the EU institutions to implement this.[26] Germany leads in terms of trade partnerships with China, and is a big supporter of closer EU ties to China (and overlooking human rights abuses), but all states are attempting to improve relations. Support in Europe for China's Belt and Road Initiative (BRI) is growing, and growth of EU relations with China seem inevitable.[27] The UK hopes to improve trade with China as part of its Global Britain initiatives, but its potential military actions in the region in support of China's neighbors might undermine that goal.[28] At a broader level, the rise of China to be a global economic power—potentially improved in the short term by its rebound from Covid-19—and its use of soft power, displayed during the 2022 Beijing Winter Olympics, challenge the status and influence of Europe's trade (in addition to the United States'). This competition between political capitalism (China) and liberal capitalism (Europe and the United States) seems destined to be a key event of the next decade.[29] In November 2021, the EU tentatively opened a trade dialogue with Taiwan to try to counterbalance China's dominant role, but all current signs are that the EU will not be able or willing to challenge China's increasing assertiveness in the global economy and politics, as President Xi is less deferential to the declining influence of Europe.

Box 9.2   Europe and Hong Kong

The UK took possession of Hong Kong during the First Opium War in 1842, and signed a ninety-nine-year treaty in 1898 for its control, including its expansion to the north to include the "new territories." Hong Kong was a backwater at the beginning, but served a useful strategic purpose at the mouth of the Pearl River just to the south of the major trading port of Guangzhou, and its prominence as a manufacturing, trading, and banking center developed during the twentieth century. As the treaty wound up, the British had little option but to negotiate their departure, and did so in July 1997. Within that agreement was a fifty-year commitment by the Chinese government not to change Hong Kong's distinct status with the rest of China, and to protect democratic institutions there. China maintained these agreements more or less until 2014, but has essentially ended

Hong Kong's democracy and independence over the past several years. European governments have opposed China's actions, but can do little for fear of damaging their important economic relationship with China. The UK government began to sketch out an increased military presence in the South China Sea to protect erstwhile allies in the region as part of its Global Britain (with echoes of Rule Britannia) strategy, but it remains unclear what the UK can do against China, and how much support it can engender. The Portuguese enclave of Macau just a few miles to the west of Hong Kong reverted to Chinese control in 1999, after being in Portuguese possession since 1557. Macau is one of the largest casino centers in the world. There is little dispute over Macau, where issues regarding assimilation back into China are nothing in the range of Hong Kong.

China poses a slightly different set of challenges to Russia, partly because they share a common border of about 2,615 miles (4,209 kilometers). The border presents important opportunities for both countries in trade, and encourages a partnership between them. Russian leaders also see China as a strategic partner to counterbalance Europe and the United States (and NATO). China is Russia's top export and import partner, and it will remain important as ongoing sanctions hover over Russia's relations with Europe and the United States. Russia refrains from criticizing China, and China reciprocates. Although there is clearly a rivalry between the two countries, both governments make efforts to minimize tensions and their partnership is growing, including in outer space. In some ways, Russia and China work together to combat EU policies on democratization and human rights, and they share a goal to weaken the EU as an organization.

A final point to note is China's strong interest in the development of the Arctic, which will be another arena where it competes against Russia and other European states. Although China is not within the Arctic Circle, it has claimed permanent observer status in the Arctic Council, and has laid out a forceful "polar silk road" concept where it eyes the significant natural resources of the Arctic as critical to its future as a world power.[30]

Free-Trade Agreements with Canada and Japan

Two countries that share Europe's basic philosophy of free trade, democracy, and human rights are Canada and Japan. Canada developed from its British and French colonial roots, whereas Japan possesses more of an inward culture less affected by European influence. Both countries have a substantial political and economic relationship with Europe.

Canada has close proximity to Greenland, a European territory as part of Denmark. The EU signed a trade agreement with Canada in 1976, but then expanded this into a Comprehensive Economic and Trade Agreement (CETA), essentially a free-trade agreement with the EU. The trade agreement is provisionally in operation removing most tariffs between the parties, though some disputes remain unsettled, notably regarding consumer protection for Europeans. CETA could potentially expand into closer relations for EU countries with Canada, such as a complete free-trade zone, or even potential Canadian membership of the EU (or the EEA). This could benefit Canada in gaining more room for maneuver away from the United States, but also benefit the EU in locking down another major trade partner. Alternatively, it is difficult to get all EU members, the European Parliament, and Council to ratify CETA, and so membership in the EU looks to be an even heavier weight to lift.

The oil crises of the 1970s enabled Japanese car manufacturers to gain strong footholds in many European countries, and with the creation of the Single Market in the 1990s brought many of those manufacturers to set up plants inside of Europe. A significant trade imbalance developed in favor of Japan, and this set off political reactions in Europe leading to calls for export restraints on Japan. Both parties signed tighter trade partnerships in the early 2000s, leading to an EU-Japan Economic Partnership Agreement in July 2018. This is the world's largest bilateral free-trade agreement accounting for about one-third of global GDP. The agreement with Japan faces less political opposition within Europe than the agreement with Canada. It is also useful to counter the protectionist policies of the United States, especially those promoted by the Trump administration.[31]

Non-EU European countries need to maintain relations with Canada and Japan outside of these arrangements. For Russia, there are potential political difficulties. With Canada, Russia faces a significant challenge in its attempt to expand its Arctic policy and resource mining. In terms of Japan, Russia has a simmering hostility because of tensions over the Kurile Islands taken from Japan immediately before the end of World War II. Japan's unwillingness to cede permanently these territories limits cooperation. For the UK, there is a long-standing partnership with Canada as a former colony and member of the Commonwealth, though it is unclear whether the British can gain any kind of favorable trade agreement with Canada as part of its Global Britain strategy. The UK, likewise, has good relations with Japan, though it is difficult to see how the UK government can leverage these relations any further for its benefit.

South, Southeast, and Pacific Asia

Europe has had a long and complex relationship with the continent of Asia. During the Cold War, much of Europe's relationship with Asia fell in line with the policies of the United States. The Chinese Revolution in 1949 and the Korean War starting in 1950 set the ideological tone of those relations, with European states predominantly linked to Japan, Taiwan, and South Korea. By the 1970s, these countries had become significant trading partners, and indeed competitors, with EU countries.

Another important trading bloc for the EU are the countries of the Association of Southeast Asian Nations (ASEAN). With these countries mostly being former European colonies, the relationship between the two blocs has a long and often bitter history. The ASEAN group is one of the more successful trading blocs in the world, building political and economic linkages in that region.

Singapore and Malaysia have recorded strong economic growth in recent years, and have become major trading partners with the EU. Indonesia, the world's largest Muslim state, also has become an important partner of Europe.[32]

ASEAN's relationship with the dominant economic powers of Asia— namely China and India—offer a challenge to Europe. The goal is to maintain these countries as European trading partners, and not have them drawn completely into the orbit of their larger Asian neighbors. At the same time, Europe aims to utilize links to ASEAN members as important partners in their own right, but also as launching pads for expanding trade across Asia. Relations with India also were somewhat subdued because of lingering antipathy toward British colonization, and India's autarkic and protectionist economic policies. Indian liberalization after the 1990s opened avenues to trade and investment, while the prevailing democratic environment of India allowed relations to take place without an overarching political tension.

The EU and India signed a cooperation agreement in 1994, and since 2007 have been attempting to get a free-trade agreement signed, but differences remain. The EU is India's largest trading partner, accounting for just over 10 percent of India's total trade. As tensions between China and India grew after 2020 with continuing military clashes in Kashmir, the Indian government sought to revive and accelerate prospects of a trade deal with the EU. Likewise, European countries favored increased trade opportunities with India to boost economic performance after the Covid-19 pandemic. The UK is also looking to India for increased trade and security partnerships as part of its post-Brexit Global Britain initiative.

Europe's fear of retaliation against them by China limits relations with Taiwan. EU officials tread carefully in their relations, but there is an EU trade office in Taipei. It is improbable that any European country will risk its relations with China by being too supportive of Taiwan or building too strong an economic relationship there, as the Lithuania example shows. There is no chance that European forces will provide any military protection to Taiwan in a dispute with China, unless it was some kind of NATO action.

European relations with Australia and New Zealand reflect a long relationship with the UK, and by Queen Elizabeth technically remaining head of state of both countries. Although historically these countries saw their core trade partners as European, increasingly they turned toward Asia and became major competitors in trade with Europe in those markets. The expansion of the European Single Market also raised barriers to certain aspects of trade from Australia and New Zealand, causing resentment but also prompting greater assertiveness in markets closer to home. Australia remained a vehement opponent to European agricultural subsidies, and through the Cairns Group of states attempted to maintain pressure on the EU (and the United States) to reduce or eliminate such subsidies within the Common Agricultural Policy.

Russia remains committed to Asia, given that it belongs there as an Asian and Pacific power and as a counterweight to relations with Europe. Russia has long sought favorable political and economic relations with India, and attempts to remain disengaged from the tensions between China and India in Kashmir. Russia will increasingly have to balance its desire to secure allies across Asia, thereby challenging somewhat China's policy in the region, while at the same time the Russian government is intent to try to partner with China in its disagreements with the EU and the United States. This is a dynamic and fluid relationship, and one that needs close monitoring

The Middle East

The *Middle East* is a term that gained prominence at the beginning of the twentieth century, primarily in the UK as its government sought to maintain control over large swaths of the region that is technically Southwest Asia. The biblical birthplace of Christianity and the connection to the Roman Empire offer at least 2,000 years of ties. The power of the Ottoman Empire for centuries spread Islam to many parts of Europe. European colonization in the nineteenth and twentieth centuries created the modern map of the region, as the British and French in particular carved up the region for their own benefit. The discovery of oil, and its subsequent development by European companies, provided a core economic rationale for close trade relations to present. The previous chapter touched on some of these relations in terms of the EU's Neighborhood Policy, but here we take a broader perspective.

The legacy of colonial activities by France and the UK in the region is strong. An Anglo-French consortium built the Suez Canal in the 1880s largely to get to the Indian Ocean trade routes—and, for the UK specifically, to its prized colony of India—but also to facilitate trade within the Middle East itself. During World War I, Europeans made many promises for independence and alliances, but broke these after the war as France and the UK tightened their grip on territories, especially those grabbed after the demise of the Ottoman Empire. European formal control over the Middle East quickly shrank after World War II, as their declining capacity to control became evident. The UK's most difficult exit in the region was perhaps in Palestine, where it came under significant military pressure from Israeli nationalist forces. In 1948, the UK handed over the territory to the United Nations, leading to the creation of the State of Israel. European promises to provide a Palestinian state fell by the wayside.

Box 9.3   Europe and the Palestinians

The Palestinians received European promises to create their own state during World War I, but European governments reneged on these, and Palestinians did not approve of the UN decision to create Israel in 1948. The EU maintains strong support for a two-state solution to the ongoing crisis, and is the largest source of funds for the Palestinian government. The EU also attempts to maintain favorable relations with Israel and to promote a negotiated settlement, although the EU stepped up its opposition to Israeli settler expansion in the West Bank. The EU requires labeling of products emanating from the occupied West Bank, but stopped short of supporting a boycott. The EU also maintains support for Jerusalem as the Palestinian capital. Cyprus, Malta, Hungary, Poland, and Slovakia recognized Palestine as a state (though not the Czech Republic) before becoming EU members, and Sweden was the first to recognize the state while as an EU member. In recent years, the EU divided over how to deal with the expansion of Israeli settlements, and how to move forward on the Palestinian issue, though they generally held together in opposition to moves in the region by the Donald Trump administration. In May 2021, Ireland was the first EU member to label Israeli settlements officially as "annexations" of Palestinian land. Outside of the EU, the UK remains supportive of Palestinian statehood, but it has not recognized the state. Russia has given formal recognition to Palestine as a state, but the Russian government tries to play a mediating role, carefully balancing support for Israel and Palestinians. It is unlikely that Europeans will play the decisive external hand in helping to resolve the plight of the Palestinians, as that role likely rests with the United States.

Elsewhere, relations between the newly independent countries and former European colonial rulers remained cordial, as Europe provided welcome technology to develop the oil fields. These relations shifted with the creation of the Organization of the Petroleum Exporting Countries (OPEC) in 1960, and more markedly after 1973, when these countries wrestled more control over their oil industries and oil pricing. The UK acknowledged its economic and military weaknesses and officially marked the end of its active military "protection" of the region with its East of Suez policy declaration to withdraw in June 1967.

European significance in the region slipped with the growing influence of the United States and its expansion of military power to protect oil interests in the region. European viewpoints and actions became secondary to the United States', and often fell in line behind the United States. The evidence of this was most notable in 1956 when the United States refused to condone the British, French, and Israeli intervention in Egypt and the taking over of the Suez Canal to try to block its nationalization by Egypt, forcing a humiliating withdrawal by the Europeans. The US invasion of Iraq in 2003 weakened this compliance somewhat and, in any case, it would be wrong to imply that European countries did not continue to pursue their own trade interests in the region. Sales of weapons and technology in general were important, especially to Saudi Arabia, as was the business of European banks.

The EU took a particular interest in a fellow regional trade organization, the Gulf Cooperation Council, for political and economic reasons. Many European countries were also open to trade with Iran after the 1979 revolution, despite pressure from the United States opposing this. In addition, the EU was more supportive of the Palestinian cause vis-à-vis Israel than any US administration. Europe still supports a two-state solution to the Palestinian crisis, and does not recognize Jerusalem as the Israeli capital. These divisions accentuated during the Trump administration between 2017 and 2021. The harsh reactions of many Gulf states including Saudi Arabia to calls for democratization have brought little if any condemnation from the EU, and business as usual continues. In reality, countries in this region may still tend to look toward the United States to take their lead, rather than to the EU. Europe also maintains a commitment to the treaty with Iran to prevent the growth of their nuclear capability.

Russia has had considerable interest in the region for centuries, as it has a geographical border with many countries in the region. Russia constantly opposed the UK's expansion of interests in the region and in India, with constant clashes. The most notable was in the 1850s with the Crimean War, where combined British, French, Italian/Sardinian, and Ottoman/Turkish forces eventually defeated Russia. The Iranian Revolution in 1979 sparked concerns in Moscow about further Islamic mobilization on its southern borders, and led to the rather disastrous invasion of Afghanistan. The Russian government also intervened to make sure that US-led NATO forces were not successful in their ongoing war against the Taliban after 2001. Russia's intervention since 2015 in the Syrian civil war on the government's side is a continuing manifestation of its desire to maintain influence in the region vis-à-vis other European countries and the United States. In a similar vein, Russia actively has tightened its relationship with Israel and the United Arab Emirates.[33]

Turkey's role in the region is continuous, as it sits inside, and at the crossroads, of both Europe and the Middle East. In an earlier form as the Ottoman Empire, it shaped policy in the region, but its decline weakened its ability to influence. Today, its policy is to capitalize on its strategic location in economic and political arenas. Turkey has important interests in maintaining stability in the region, acting forcefully when necessary against Kurds and to combat the Islamic State in Iraq and Syria (ISIS). In recent years, despite its NATO membership, Turkey has forged a partnership with Russia in the region, partly for each country to pursue their own interests without clashing, as well as for trade.

Turkey diverged from Russia, however, following the latter's invasion of Ukraine in 2022. Turkey also cleverly plays its migration card with the EU, extracting concessions in return for holding back excessive numbers of (Islamic) migrants trying to enter the EU. Turkey's influence in the region appears set to grow in the coming years.

The African, Caribbean, and Pacific Group

The ACP group comprises seventy-nine developing states, all former European colonies in one shape or form. The vast majority of the ACP countries is in sub-Saharan Africa (forty-eight), with the Caribbean and Pacific groups being composed primarily of small island states. The ACP also accounts for the poorest group of states with which the EU trades, and so it is the recipient of considerable aid and assistance.[34]

The initial EU agreements were with a primarily francophone group of African states in the Yaoundé Agreement. Once the UK joined the EU in 1973, there was a need to develop a set of policies to assist former British colonies, as Yaoundé excluded them. An agreement signed in the Togolese capital of Lomé in 1975 set up the first of several arrangements with this wider group. The ACP acted on the principle of solidarity and strength in numbers, though never really had the clout or resources to stand as equals with the EU. The ACP gained preferential access for goods to the EU, particularly for agricultural exports. This Stabex scheme guaranteed prices for those commodities, though some critics believed that this only served to perpetuate the ACP's dependence as primary producers.

The Lomé agreements were renewed in 1980, 1985, and again in 1990, when they were put in place for a decade. Disillusionment with the poor level of success of Lomé, along with pressure from the United States and the WTO to disband the agreement as discriminatory, led to negotiations for Economic Partnership Agreements (EPAs) through the Cotonou Agreement, signed in 2000. Under the Cotonou Agreement, the EU offered less preferential access, and set out to establish more open trade agreements.[35] Whereas the ACP attempted to negotiate these terms as a bloc, the EU preferred bilateral arrangements, or talks with a regional group of countries. These talks were controversial, with many ACP countries reluctant to sign, and the negotiations dragged on for a decade. Nevertheless, the ACP maintained close ties with the EU through various consultative frameworks and hoped that a new era of relationships could be opened.

An important element of the ACP-EU relationship was the Millennium Development Goals (MDGs), signed within a UN framework in 2000. The EU placed significant effort on reaching these targets, with specific strategies agreed on to enable this. The EU-Africa strategy, for example, focused on core aspects of the MDGs, calling on EU donor states to meet their commitments. Despite such rhetoric, European countries bar a few failed to provide the necessary finance for the MDGs. Much development assistance now focuses on the UN's revamped Sustainable Development Goals, from 2015 to 2030, which the EU supports.

Relations with Pacific Islands were similarly difficult. Europeans had many colonial possessions in the Pacific, despite the great distance from Europe. As independence was granted to most islands, European preoccupation remained mostly connected with mineral exploitation and fishing rights, and most Islanders complained that the relationship was not to the benefit of them. A similar sentiment was heard in the Caribbean, where hopes for Caribbean Community (CARICOM) links to the EU were muted.

These agreements have brought together EU policy from divergent interests, with countries such as France and the UK maintaining close ties to their former colonial possessions (for France, this includes military action in regions such as West Africa), whereas the Nordic countries lean toward the promotion of development agendas.[36] The EU-ACP agreement expired in 2020, and countries are currently engaged in negotiations to promote a further extension of these agreements. It is not quite clear what will materialize, as ACP states attempt to "decolonize aid."[37] In Africa in particular, governments remain unhappy with the terms of the EU's previous partnership agreements, and are pursuing increasing possibilities of trade with China. The sixth EU-Africa summit in February 2022 did little to bridge divisions between the two groups of states, as African leaders bristled at European intransigence over loosening migration flows and Covid-19 vaccine patents. Conversely, the Beijing-based Asian Infrastructure Investment Bank (AIIB) opens up the prospect of development financing from China rather than through the EU or the World Bank. The EU has agreed to raise its level of aid to developing countries but, with the exception of Nordic countries, they have been unable to reach these targets. Support for providing aid to the ACP group within the European population, however, remains strong. A Eurobarometer poll published in April 2021 showed more than 80 percent of Europeans polled wanted greater assistance given to the ACP states, not only economic assistance but also aid to promote greater sustainability and climate mitigation strategies.[38]

Latin America

There is a paradox in relations with Latin American countries. In many ways, Latin American countries have had the longest and most significant relations with Europe, with 500 years of colonial and postcolonial relations, primarily through Portugal and Spain, though also including France, the Netherlands, and the UK in Central America and the Caribbean. Despite this history, Latin America as a continent appears to hold minor interest in the minds of Europeans, and in terms of European trade. This can be partly explained by the strength of the United States in those markets in the past century or so, and especially with various trade and diplomatic partnerships within the Americas. These include concepts within the Monroe Doctrine and the Roosevelt Corollary, apparently giving the United States the right to shape affairs in the Americas. In addition, there is the post–World War II creation of the Organization of American States (OAS), and the more recent attempts to sign bilateral free-trade agreements as well as comprehensive continental agreements, notably the Free Trade Area of the Americas (FTAA).

On the European side, the fact that Spain and Portugal possessed nondemocratic governments until the mid-1970s, and remained outside of EU membership until the mid-1980s, left Latin American interests somewhat off the mainstream of the EU policy radar. Neither did Latin America offer the challenges to development that the ACP group offered Europe, nor did it seem to offer the potential of large markets for growth, such as those in Asia. Furthermore, geographical proximity of North Africa and the Middle East, along with large movements of migrants from those regions into European countries, made those arenas more significant than the more distant countries in South America. Finally, the fact that neither Portugal nor Spain are considered policy setters for Europe helped to keep Latin America somewhat in the periphery of European policy.

The signing of the North American Free Trade Agreement (NAFTA) in 1994 by Canada, Mexico, and the United States caused fears in Europe that this agreement would ease out European countries from increased trade with Mexico as well as other Latin American countries to the south. This prompted the signing of an EU-Mexico trade agreement in 2000. This was replaced by a new association agreement signed in 2018 to expand further trade possibilities and again offset the renewed United States–Mexico–Canada Agreement (USMCA).[39]

All this should not keep us from realizing that EU-Latin American relations are, nevertheless, extensive and important to both sets of parties. Trade relations are strong, especially for Portugal and Spain, and the rise to emergent power status for Brazil has intensified relations and trade between Brazil and Europe. Argentina also has a significant trade relationship with Europe, and particularly with the UK, the odd war in the Falkland Islands notwithstanding. It is noteworthy that the UK went to war with Argentina in 1982 to protect control over the Falkland (Malvinas) Islands some 8,000 miles (13,000 kilometers) from the UK with a population of about 2,000 people. Besides helping the unpopular Mar-

Box 9.4   Europe and Cuba

Europe's connection to Cuba goes back to 1492 and the arrival of Christopher Columbus, and what soon turned into 400 years of Spanish colonial rule and exploitation. Much of Cuba's population today are descendants of slaves brought to the island by Spain. The United States defeated Spain in 1898 and took over the Philippines and Guam from the Spanish. Cuba nominally gained its independence in 1901, but remained under the control of the United States. Cubans rose up in 1959 under the leadership of Fidel Castro to claim freedom from US control and intervention, and quickly became embroiled in the Cold War when the Soviet Union sought military advantage by placing ballistic weapons on Cuba in 1962, only 100 miles away from Florida. Although the USSR withdrew these weapons, it maintained close and cordial relations with Cuba, helping the country stay afloat especially with sugar exports under a withering US embargo. Today, Russia retains close diplomatic and trade relations with Cuba, and it is attempting to extend its role across Latin America, notably with Nicaragua and Venezuela, as it builds back its global reach. EU members also maintain solid economic relations with Cuba, but pushed what was known as a "common position" requiring improved human rights in Cuba since 1996. This provided tension in the relationship without too much forward movement, and in 2016 the EU replaced this with a political dialogue and common agreement with Cuba. European companies are active in helping to revive and promote Cuba's tourism industry, with direct flights from nine European countries and one-third of total tourism arrivals coming from the EU27. The EU remains the largest investor in Cuba.

garet Thatcher government win a general election in 1983, the war was arguably about resources and continuing British access and claims to parts of the Antarctic. Rule Britannia still has some life.

Conclusion

It is incorrect to say that European countries are not serious players in global politics and economics, but it is also a mistake to overemphasize their importance today. The EU does not possess sufficient unity of purpose or action to impose its will on the world or its leading players, but does have sufficient influence to remain an important piece of the global jigsaw, especially in countries on the rim of Europe and in the Global South. This acknowledges that Europe is just one of many centers of power in an increasingly multipolar and complex world. Has the EU lived up to its profile of being a moral or civilizing power? Is this moral power more likely to be evident in the next few years? The answer to both of these questions is essentially no. Despite some good intentions and utterances, the EU has not been convincing in such a role, even though its adherence to democracy and the rule of law within Europe remains consistent.

Is the EU more likely to develop its hard power and utilize military forces in promoting its policies? Besides the occasional peacekeeping operation, the answer here should be a rather unambiguous no. Can the EU raise its game to be a major economic power, backed by the euro and led by bustling global companies? The EU is obviously an important economic player on paper, but the United States and China eclipse it in shaping global policy. The mild recession caused by Covid-19 will further limit leadership and could exacerbate divisions within Europe and the eurozone.

Closer integration of foreign policy and strategic autonomy continue to be challenging, unless some major unforeseen crisis hits Europe—such as the end of NATO. Differentiation of policy looks to be increasingly the norm, with the continuing prominence of national interest and intergovernmental bargaining at the fore. For some observers, such as Andrew Moravcsik, the core mission of the EU remains to promote national interest through intergovernmental cooperation rather than supranationalism, and he sees the current performance of the EU as quite productive on that score.[40]

The existing post–World War II international order, of which Europe played a significant role in creating, is under strain, but the EU is unable to shift into the vacuum to prop it up. The EU is also not in a position to challenge China, and Russian influence across Europe continues. As President Macron of France summarized in 2019, "With America turning its back, China rising, and authoritarian leaders on the EU's doorstep, the result is the exceptional fragility of Europe, which, if it can't think of itself as a global power, will disappear."[41] There is little to suggest that the EU can galvanize itself to unite on common policies and try to retain a dominant place in the international system. The invasion of Ukraine in 2022 offered a glimpse of European unity against Russia, but this seemed driven by the United States and NATO more than Europe itself. The EU will continue to lack the political will or capability to deploy military force in any meaningful manner, or to challenge the major powers.[42] There is little evidence that other European countries outside of the EU, such as the UK, can have a marked impact on global affairs. The EU seems set to continue promoting itself economically, perhaps through informal smaller state groupings on certain issues, but not projecting unified policy or convincing authority around the world.[43] In "a world of predictable unpredictability," resiliency will continue to be a key element in monitoring the world beyond Europe, but it will also be increasingly necessary for the EU to maintain its resilience inside of Europe.[44]

Notes

1. For a review of the earlier development of the EU and its global trading relations, see Klaus Heidensohn, *Europe and World Trade* (London: Pinter, 1995). For a general overview of EU trade policy, see European Commission, "Making Trade Policy," https://policy .trade.ec.europa.eu/eu-trade-relationships-country-and-region/making-trade-policy_en.

2. European Commission, "EU Position in World Trade," https://ec.europa.eu /trade/policy/eu-position-in-world-trade/.

3. Eurostat, "World Direct Investment Patterns," https://ec.europa.eu/eurostat /statistics-explained/index.php/World_direct_investment_patterns.

4. Alice Tidey, "Quarter of World's Arms Sales from European Companies," *Euronews,* December 9, 2019, https://www.euronews.com/2019/12/09/quarter-of-world -s-arms-sales-from-european-companies-sipri; see also the Stockholm International Peace Research Institute for a complete breakdown of these sales, https://www.sipri.org /media/press-release/2019/global-arms-industry-rankings-sales-46-cent-worldwide-and -us-companies-dominate-top-5.

5. Joseph S. Nye, "Soft Power," *Foreign Policy* 80, 1990: 153–171.

6. Simon Tisdall, "Global Predators Are Circling a Weak and Unstable Continent," *The Guardian Weekly,* November 26, 2021.

7. European Commission, "Trade: United States," https://ec.europa.eu/trade/policy /countries-and-regions/countries/united-states/; see also World Bank, World Integrated Trade Solution, "European Union Trade," https://wits.worldbank.org/countrysnapshot /en/EUN/textview.

8. Sherrill Brown Wells, *Pioneers of European Integration and Peace 1945–1963: A Brief History with Documents* (Boston: Bedford/St. Martin's, 2007).

9. Although I recognize the distinction between, and time frames of, the terms *European Economic Community, European Community,* and *European Union,* for the sake of convenience I am continuing to use the term *European Union* throughout.

10. H. W. Brands, *What America Owes the World: The Struggle for the Soul of Foreign Policy* (Cambridge: Cambridge University Press, 1998); Kevin Featherstone, "The EC and the US: Managing Interdependence," in Juliet Lodge (ed.), *The European Community and the Challenge of the Future,* 2nd ed. (New York: St. Martin's, 1993), pp. 271–282; Clifford Hackett, *Cautious Revolution: The European Community Arrives* (New York: Praeger, 1990).

11. Miles Kahler, *Regional Futures and Transatlantic Economic Relations* (New York: Council on Foreign Relations, 1995).

12. Richard N. Haass (ed.), *Transatlantic Tensions: The United States, Europe, and Problem Countries* (Washington, DC: Brookings Institution, 1999).

13. Glenn Hastedt, *American Foreign Policy* (Upper Saddle River, NJ: Pearson, 2011); see also Naomi Klein, *The Shock Doctrine: The Rise of Disaster Capitalism* (New York: Picador, 2008).

14. Simon Serfaty (ed.), *Visions of the Atlantic Alliance: The United States, the European Union, and NATO* (Washington, DC: Center for Strategic and International Studies Press, 2005).

15. T. R. Reid, *The United States of Europe: The New Superpower and the End of American Supremacy* (New York: Penguin, 2004); see also Robert J. Guttman, *Europe in the New Century: Visions of an Emerging Superpower* (Boulder: Lynne Rienner, 2001).

16. Michael Smith and Rebecca Steffenson, "The European Union and the USA," in Christopher Hill, Michael Smith, and Sophie Vanhoonacker (eds.), *International Relations and the European Union,* 3rd ed. (Oxford: Oxford University Press, 2017), chap. 17; see also Elizabeth Pond, *Friendly Fire: The Near-Death of the Transatlantic Alliance* (Pittsburgh: European Union Studies Association/Washington, DC: Brookings Institution, 2004).

17. Anne Applebaum, "Obama and Europe: Missed Signals, Renewed Commitment," *Foreign Affairs* 94(5), 2015: 37–44.

18. See the official US government site at Office of the United States Trade Representative, "TTIP," https://ustr.gov/ttip.

19. Tim Oliver and Michael John Williams, "Special Relationship in Flux: Brexit and the Future of the US-EU and US-UK Relationship," *International Affairs* 92(3), 2016: 547–567.

20. Simon Serfaty, "The Biden Transition," Robert Schuman Foundation Policy Paper, no. 580, January 12, 2021, https://www.robert-schuman.eu/en/doc/questions-d-europe/qe-580-en.pdf.

21. North Atlantic Treaty Organization, https://www.nato.int/nato-welcome/index.html.

22. Michael O. Slobodchikoff, G. Doug Davis, and Brandon Stewart (eds.), *The Challenge to NATO: Global Security and the Atlantic Alliance* (Lincoln: University of Nebraska Press, 2021).

23. Organization for Security and Co-operation in Europe, https://www.osce.org/.

24. Pierre Mirel and Xavier Mirel, "Challenges and Constraints Facing a 'Geopolitical Commission' in the Achievement of European Sovereignty," Robert Schuman Foundation Policy Paper, no. 560, May 26, 2020, p. 3.

25. "Emmanuel Macron on Europe's Fragile Place in a Hostile World," *The Economist*, November 7, 2019.

26. Jack Ewing and Steven Lee Myers, "EU and China Reach Investment Deal, but Political Hurdles Await," *New York Times,* December 31, 2020.

27. Giovanna De Maio, *Playing with Fire: Italy, China, and Europe* (Washington, DC: Brookings Institution, May 2020).

28. Patrick Wintour, "A Great Trade Off: Why Britain Is Tilting Towards the Indo-Pacific," *The Guardian Weekly,* March 26, 2021.

29. Branko Milanovic, "The Clash of Capitalisms: The Real Fight for the Global Economy's Future," *Foreign Affairs* 99(1), 2020: 10–21. See also Sylvain Kahn and Estelle Prin, "In the Time of Covid-19 China's Mask Has Fallen with Regard to Europe," Robert Schuman Foundation Policy Paper, no. 569, September 8, 2020, https://www.robert-schuman.eu/en/doc/questions-d-europe/qe-569-en.pdf. China has gradually eaten into Europe's traditional sphere of influence in Africa; see Deborah Brautigam, *The Dragon's Gift: The Real Story of China in Africa* (Oxford: Oxford University Press, 2009).

30. *The New Arctic: Navigating the Realities, Possibilities, and Problems* (Washington, DC: Walsh School of Foreign Service, 2018).

31. Hiroko Tabuchi and Jack Ewing, "Europe and Japan Near Trade Deal as US Takes Protectionist Path," *New York Times,* June 23, 2017.

32. Stephen Keukeleire and Tom De Bruyn, "The European Union, the BRICS, and Other Emerging Powers: A New World Order?" in Christopher Hill, Michael Smith, and Sophie Vanhoonacker (eds.), *International Relations and the European Union,* 3rd ed. (Oxford: Oxford University Press, 2017), chap. 18.

33. Eugene Rumer and Andrew S. Weiss, "A Brief Guide to Russia's Return to the Middle East," Carnegie Endowment for International Peace, October 24, 2019, https://carnegieendowment.org/2019/10/24/brief-guide-to-russia-s-return-to-middle-east-pub-80134.

34. Organisation of African, Caribbean and Pacific States, http://www.acp.int.

35. Olufemi Babarinde and Gerrit Faber (eds.), *The European Union and the Developing Countries* (Leiden: Martinus Nijhoff, 2005).

36. Maurizio Carbone, "The European Union and International Development," in Christopher Hill, Michael Smith, and Sophie Vanhoonacker (eds.), *International Relations and the European Union,* 3rd ed. (Oxford: Oxford University Press, 2017), chap. 13. See also Jack Mangala (ed.), *Africa and the European Union: A Strategic Partnership* (New York: Palgrave Macmillan, 2013).

37. Maurizio Carbone, "The Calm After the Storm: Plurilateral Challenges to the Post-2020 EU-ACP Partnership," *Journal of Common Market Studies* 57 (Special Supplement), 2019: 141–151; see also Albert Mashika and Maria Nyman, "Does New EU-ACP Deal Really 'Decolonise' Aid?" *EU Observer,* April 8, 2021, https://euobserver.com/opinion/151472?utm_source=euobs&utm_medium=email.

38. European Commission, "Eurobarometer: EU Citizens Strongly Support Cooperation with Partner Countries and Youth to Reduce Poverty," April 29, 2021, https://ec.europa.eu/commission/presscorner/detail/en/ip_21_1550.

39. European Commission, "EU—Mexico Agreement," https://policy.trade.ec.europa.eu/eu-trade-relationships-country-and-region/countries-and-regions/mexico/eu-mexico-agreement_en. See also European Parliament, "United States-Mexico-Canada Agreement (USMCA): Potential Impact on EU Companies," https://www.europarl.europa.eu/RegData/etudes/ATAG/2018/630341/EPRS_ATA(2018)630341_EN.pdf.

40. Andrew Moravcsik, "Ever-Further Union," *Foreign Affairs* 99(1), 2020: 159–165.

41. "Emmanuel Macron on Europe's Fragile Place in a Hostile World."

42. Andrew Cotley, "Astrategic Europe," *Journal of Common Market Studies* 58(2) 2020: 276–291.

43. Lisbeth Aggestam and Federica Bicchi, "New Directions in EU Foreign Policy Governance: Cross-Loading, Leadership and Informal Groupings," *Journal of Common Market Studies* 57(3), 2019: 515–532.

44. European Union, *Shared Vision, Common Action: A Stronger Europe: A Global Strategy for the European Union's Foreign and Security Policy* (Brussels: European Union, 2016), p. 46, https://eeas.europa.eu/topics/eu-global-strategy/17304/global-strategy-european-unions-foreign-and-security-policy_en.

10

Ongoing Transitions and the Future of Europe

PREVIOUS CHAPTERS OF THIS BOOK EXPLAIN IN DEPTH THE DEVELOP-
ment and current nature of European politics and society. Chapters 1 and 2 considered the many historical legacies that shape today's Europe. One core idea is
the centrality of the European experience to the rest of the world, even though
its influence is diminishing as the twenty-first century unfolds. The following
five chapters analyzed the issues, policies, and machinery of European national
politics, highlighting common trends where possible and pointing out differences. For a Europe comprised of the forty-seven member countries of the
Council of Europe, the commonalities are evident when the study is at a general (30,000 feet) level, but once we focus in on individual countries the differences become obvious. Support for social democracy and democratic goals is a
shared element of most European countries, but at a closer level, this is less evident in certain countries, especially those around the eastern rim of Europe. In
that sense, we can contest the extent to which countries such as Russia and
Turkey are typically European, or even European at all.

Chapters 8 and 9 considered the international cooperation evident inside
Europe, notably regarding the European Union, as well as Europe's relationship
with countries around the world. The EU is arguably the most developed example of a contemporary regional organization, with well-established institutions
and policies. It works alongside nation-states, but also with other international
organizations in the continent. The presence of these organizations gives cre-
dence to the viewpoint of Europe as a mature continent comfortable with relationships transcending national borders. These chapters discussed the extent to

which we can see an EU foreign policy emerging, as well as examples of non-EU actors and their external relations.

In this final chapter, I pull together our thoughts about contemporary European politics and try to consider some potential directions for the continent and its countries. It is a truism to state that Europe is in transition, as to some extent all countries and regions in the world are always in transition. At first glance, many assume that Europe's long history has brought it to a position of stable political and social development, with confidence in the status quo. In reality, this is quite far from the truth, as this book highlights. Whether it is the expansion of the EU, the disintegration of the Soviet Union and the rise of Russia, the specter of war in Eastern Europe and the prospect of a new Cold War, or the growth of nationalism and populism, as evidenced from Belgium to the Balkans, much is in transition and flux in the continent.

The purpose of this final chapter is not so much to make firm predictions as to what the continent will transition to in the near future—say, 2030 as a benchmark—though there is an element of such crystal ball gazing. The goal, rather, is to highlight important trends in Europe and discuss scenarios in their evolution over the next few years. There are many issues to consider, but here we isolate critical topics and trends to gauge the most important pathways the continent appears to be following. There are undoubtedly going to be completely new developments appearing that are impossible to foresee at this time, or that are foggy in the crystal ball. Likewise, trends that appear so obvious and locked in now could turn out to be fleeting and unimportant in a year or two. How many people accurately predicted the Europe of 2010 back in 2000 or, even more problematic, the Europe of 1991 back in 1988? How different will the Europe of 2030 be to the Europe of 2022? So with sufficient hedging and insurance in place, what are the most important trends?

I highlight seven broad sets of issues, or clusters of questions, that appear likely to engage Europeans in the near future. They are: (1) the continuing commitment to social democracy and social justice across Europe, and places where such a commitment may waver; (2) the evolution of the EU enterprise, where enhanced cooperation appears uncertain; (3) the continuing forces of nationalism, populism, and identity politics across Europe, and their impact on national politics, as well as policies of the EU; (4) the continuing strength of Germany within Europe, and a possible movement to greater German independent policy outside of the confining parameters of the EU; (5) the continuing resurgence of the role of Russia in the world in general, and in European affairs in particular; (6) the evolution of transatlantic and trans-Asian relations in a broadening global environment, where the role of Europe is likely to diminish, especially vis-à-vis the United States and China. The seventh and final topic relates to the increased efforts to promote climate change and human development policies, including the pressures on countries from such factors as more (climate) refugees, or the challenges to many European countries of the changing Arctic (political) environment.

The Commitment to Social Democracy

I argued in earlier chapters that most European countries embed the notion of social democracy in terms of political openness and electoral competition, as well as in terms of the government providing and guaranteeing core elements of social welfare. This may differ in the degree of commitment and implementation across the continent, but most hold to the core beliefs. The support for political openness is under threat in parts of CEE, notably Hungary and Poland, and has never really been embraced in Belarus, Russia, or Turkey, except in terms of lip service. In recent years, however, such unmitigated support for social democracy has waned somewhat even across Western Europe, and it appears likely that these trends will continue to challenge and weaken the status quo during the 2020s.

Part of the challenge comes from a changing political landscape. The radical reformist (some might say "revolutionary") policies of the Margaret Thatcher government in the UK in the 1980s promoted a neoliberal agenda of privatization and markets, and these types of policies have become mainstream across Europe. Though perhaps less strident in content and ideology than the Thatcher government, European countries increasingly have begun to chip away at the alleged excesses of social welfare programs, loosening safety nets for health and unemployment, and in turn trimming state expenditure. Countries with strong welfare policies, such as France, Germany, and Sweden, have felt the need to trim social expenditures, though not completely undermining the prevalent support for social assistance. Sweden is a model for open markets and capitalist economic competition, with many Swedish companies being global leaders in their fields.

If the political and economic drift has been toward drawing back from perceived excessive social expenditure, then what has accelerated the trend has been the ongoing global economic and financial problems since the 2008 global recession, compounded by the pressures of the Covid-19 pandemic in 2020–2022. The lack of confidence in the euro a decade ago contributed to the excessive austerity programs forced on Greece by the EU as the price to pay for financial support, with the consequence that the social safety net in Greece was badly damaged. An emergency budget in the UK in June 2010 slashed public spending by all-time record levels, and austerity programs continued for a decade, to some observers threatening the very fabric of British society. The concept of "belt-tightening" in Europe meets little resistance today, and the trend is clearly to spend less on social programs rather than more in the coming years, a direction supported by the EU. The 2020–2022 pandemic rattled Europe and led to some short-term, high-spending economic recovery plans to prop up European economies. The economic dislocation of the pandemic, however, is likely to be longer term, at least into the mid-2020s, and increased austerity programs are probable once the initial impact of the pandemic has passed. Rapid inflation and supply chain problems across Europe in 2022 as a result of the pandemic and the Ukraine war added to the economic challenges.

A core trend to consider with this neoliberal social transformation in recent years is the resistance by those most affected by these changes. In particular, how trade unions and government employees react to sweeping changes in their way of life will determine to some extent what evolves by 2030. Some countries will force through change: others, such as France, may struggle to implement such change because of societal opposition. Note the opposition to the neoliberal policies of Emmanuel Macron over several years. The result of these policy choices will have significant impact on the social arena of Europe and on the vitality and economic competitiveness of states. It is possible that Europe in 2030 will partially resemble the social and economic philosophy of the United States, much to the disgust of many socially minded Europeans. The mantra of global competitiveness could push the reform (neoliberal) agenda in Europe, with increasing economic weakness vis-à-vis China and the United States likely to maintain pressures to trim budgets and reform European economies. The Global Britain platform of the UK Conservative government can work only with a tight neoliberal framework, despite protestations of leveling up by increased spending in the poorer regions of the North of England. This is more a search for election votes rather than a change of economic philosophy.

We can also see an allied trend in the political arena. Shifts from left to right, and vice versa, are common features of European politics, and difficult to predict. Just when pundits declare Europe to be on a permanent move to the right, several countries will swing to the left. In 2022, certainly in some of Europe's larger economies—France, Italy, and the UK, as well as larger populations such as Poland, Russia, and Turkey—the forces of the political right appear to be ascendant, and could hold sway at least into the mid-2020s, and perhaps beyond. The victory of the Social Democratic Party and their alliance partners in Germany in December 2021, however, exemplifies the fluidity of the situation, even though this government is unlikely to change government spending radically, especially as it has committed more funds to defense spending. It

Box 10.1   The Future of the City of London

London, or more precisely the City of London, has developed over decades to serve as a global financial center and the premier financial hub of Europe. With the UK's messy divorce from the EU, there is considerable speculation whether London can maintain its preeminence in finance, and how the UK's departure from the EU could hamper this status. The financial services sector contributes about 7 percent to the UK's GDP, so is vital to the UK economy.[a] Other smaller financial centers, such as Amsterdam, Frankfurt, and Paris, have vied to take the mantle from London, but it is not clear how this will materialize. The City of London has major connections with markets outside of the EU, and it hopes to build on these as part of its renewed global outreach. London will remain an attractive and safe home for finance, economically and politically, but it may be difficult to create more partnerships in the post-Brexit environment, and the City may lose ground. The exposé of the Pandora Papers in 2021 and the role of the City in shielding wealthy patrons from taxation could potentially bring tighter controls to lessen London's attractiveness to investors, even though it does not look likely to lose innovators.[b] Likewise, efforts by the UK government to sanction questionable Russian funds in London in response to Russia's invasion of Ukraine in 2022 may also have a longer term impact.

Notes: a. Eshe Nelson, "How Will Britain Defend Its Financial Fief After Brexit?" *New York Times,* April 16, 2021, https://www.nytimes.com/2021/04/16/business/london-financial-hub-worries.html; Harry Wilson and Neil Callanan, "The City of London Is Now at the Mercy of Brexit's Tug of War," *Bloomberg Businessweek,* February 2, 2021, https://www.bloomberg.com/news/articles/2021-02-03/brexit-agreement-london-s-future-as-global-financial-hub-is-unclear.
b. Gina Clarke, "London Calling: How the City Became a Global Hub for Fintech," *Time,* October 11–18, 2021; "From Big Bang to a Whimper: How to Revive Britain's Stockmarket," *The Economist,* October 2, 2021.

is likely that neoliberal economic decisions and debt reduction programs will bring anger and anxiety in many countries. Even if there is a swing to the left, it is extremely unlikely that those political forces will be in a position to implement major social spending.

With the rise of far-right political forces in many parts of Europe, invigorated by their opposition to vaccination policies during the Covid-19 pandemic and essentially shifting the mainstream political spectrum to the right, it is unlikely that they will promote greater social spending or the politics of social inclusion. These forces would undermine political freedoms enshrined for decades under the umbrella of social democracy, focus more on a nationalistic rather than a European perspective, and limit funds spent on certain social groups. Overall, the trends toward a lessening of the social democratic framework, both economic and political, appear likely to continue during the decade, and could be quite transformative for the continent by 2030. Whether the 2030s will take Europe back to the stark days of the 1930s is difficult to say, but should not be completely excluded as a possibility. There is little to suggest that outlier states, such as Russia or Turkey, or recalcitrant EU members such as Hungary or Poland, will deviate from their current economic and social pathways and embrace social democracy unless there is some transformative event or force to make this happen.

The Evolution of the European Union Enterprise

That the EU has survived and thrived over the seventy years since its beginnings would probably come as a huge surprise to its founders if they were living today. Nobody of sane mind could have predicted such success coming out of the ashes of yet another European slaughter during World War II, just some twenty years after the carnage of the Great War (World War I), and with the intensity of the Cold War and nuclear-armed camps dividing Europe at the time. Back in 1996, George Soros asked, "Can Europe Work?" and was not certain about his answer.[1] With the advantage of hindsight, we should take care not to underestimate the EU's resilience or staying power, nor to overestimate the problems facing the EU in the coming decade. The EU's ability over time to wriggle its way out of seemingly insurmountable problems is quite impressive, and such scenarios are often the foundation for further integration. Conversely, we should be equally vigilant not to overestimate what the EU might be capable of achieving, nor underestimate the real problems facing the organization.[2] It is most likely that the EU will remain in existence in 2030, but its actual scope and status are difficult to predict. We are unlikely to return to the Euro-optimism days from over a decade or more ago, even though the EU had a burst of unity in opposition to Russia's invasion of Ukraine in 2022. What are the trends likely to shape the EU by 2030? Will the EU continue to edge toward an ever closer union, or potential federalism as the founders expressed, or will the EU be weaker, divided by nationalism of its members, and more circumscribed than it is today as it operates on differentiated and multispeed agendas?

Various trends are present to shape the EU in the coming decade. Despite the fundamental shock to European stability of Russia's invasion of Ukraine in 2022, there is still a high expectation that there will be relative peace in the continent, at least to the west of Ukraine. This is significant given our knowledge of European history, and provides grounds by itself to try to maintain the EU. While there certainly will be tensions and disagreements, the prospect of outright war in Europe is slim, certainly within the twenty-seven members of the bloc, as well as with EFTA members and the UK. The EU will also continue to try to maintain peace on the geographical rim of the organization, though certainly in concert with NATO. As Balkan states join the EU (e.g., Albania or North Macedonia, or at least be on their best behavior as candidate countries to try to join the EU), this region should be more stable with the EU's presence than without it. Bigger problems lie elsewhere. Any major crisis in the Middle East that prompted a mass exodus of refugees—like in the mid-2010s with the Syrian civil war—could exacerbate tensions in the southeast of the continent, and aggravate relations between Turkey and its neighbors. Ongoing political instability in countries such as Belarus and Ukraine can destabilize the Eastern flank of Europe and relations with Russia, as we witnessed in 2022, as can stronger efforts by the EU (and NATO) to include these countries in membership negotiations.

Perhaps actions by Russia and Turkey could provide the biggest problems for European peace and stability. If NATO does not remain united, Russia could feel emboldened to probe further Europe's Eastern flank, perhaps in the Baltics as well as Ukraine, or will likely invest more in the destabilization of national political and cyber arenas and NATO. Turkey also is likely to remain an unpredictable neighbor and partner, especially as prospects of EU membership become more remote when its democratic credentials further tarnish. Turkey's closer ties to Russia, along with increased belligerence toward its centuries-old foe (and NATO "ally") Greece, could lead to some level of military confrontation in the region. The EU, in contrast to NATO, has never shown much willingness or political capacity to use military muscle in its disputes, and this trend may well continue, the actions over Ukraine in 2022 notwithstanding.

Another issue concerns the operations of the EU itself. Although the EU's ambitions to move toward closer integration have failed in the past only to have the EU leap forward suddenly, it seems unlikely that any new major initiatives are possible. Indeed, it would be quite remarkable if the EU could maintain the status quo by 2030. The euro's usage seems unlikely to expand much beyond the existing nineteen states (plus Croatia after 2023), a constitution is beyond reach, and the scope and vigor of the EU's foreign policy agenda look unlikely to grow. Similarly, new policy initiatives do not appear obvious, nor does it look like EU membership can continue its inexorable growth. Potential new members, such as Albania or North Macedonia, have little to offer the EU's cause by way of political or economic strength. For example, Albania's GDP is approximately 250 times smaller than Germany's, and North Macedonia's is even smaller. Any developments in membership in the East, such as with Ukraine or other former Soviet republics, are currently in hiatus because of Russia's vehement opposition and military threats, as exemplified in 2022.

At this stage, closer integration within the EU membership seems unlikely, and so we can only realistically expect at best piecemeal changes, minor modifications, and tweaks to the existing EU framework. We must keep in mind the distinction between what the formal rules of the EU are in contrast to what the actions of the members are. There is always a gap between these, and the chances are that this gap will grow as member governments pursue their own agendas.[3] Many citizens enjoy the EU for easy travel, a quick and painless way to get to a warm beach, and they think less if at all about the intrinsic benefits of deeper European cooperation. One key breakthrough would be for the EU to embrace fully the concept of differentiated integration, allowing multiple tracks and speeds for participation in the organization. This could provide the flexibility to develop, and allow some members to integrate more closely than others. What would push the EU to make such a move is difficult to foresee at present, and raises questions about the future efficacy of the EU. Perhaps such flexibility would strengthen the EU's resiliency over time, or perhaps the fracturing of the membership into subgroups would weaken the overall integrity of the EU.

Could we potentially witness the unraveling of the EU, with the realization that the EU has already peaked in terms of its level of cooperation? Divisions have always existed between EU member states, notably between those favoring supranationalism against those wanting intergovernmental cooperation, between the fiscally conservative and those looser with their budgets, between the inner original core of members and those joining later. Several trends, however, threaten to challenge the EU further. The UK's decision to leave the EU following the Brexit referendum of 2016 is the first example of an EU departure (with a note of Greenland's departure in 1985). Is it possible that other disaffected states could follow, or will Britain's transition problems deter others from leaving? Tensions are likely to continue between the EU and the increasingly deviant members Hungary and Poland, for instance. It is possible that muted hostilities will continue, but that the organization will muddle through. Increased recriminations and pressure exerted by the EU against these recalcitrant members could lead to further EU departures. It is also going to become increasingly difficult, if not impossible, to get agreement within the EU on such major issues as refugees and migration, on a budget, or on how to deal with Russia, so that tensions will flare. If the EU simply serves the interests of the members, as supporters of the intergovernmental approach argue, then increasing nationalism in Europe could serve to heighten competition, rather than cooperation, within the EU.

The lessons of the Covid-19 pandemic are instructive here. The Schengen agreement failed, open borders failed, and cooperative health policy failed.

What did shine through the crisis was individual national interest and policy trumping coordinated EU interests. The EU struggled significantly to put together a fiscal package to manage the economic chaos caused by the coronavirus, and only slowly managed to improve cooperation on the virus. It is not too difficult to imagine similar issues challenging the EU's ability to cooperate. A permanent cut in energy supplies from Russia, a full-scale trade war with China, a major influx of long-term Ukrainian refugees, a rise in populist (anti-EU) governments across Europe—all these would provide major challenges to EU cohesion that the organization could fail to handle. EU solidarity in the early days after Russia's invasion of Ukraine in 2022 was heartening, but also surprising given the EU's inability normally to agree on policy. Can such solidarity last? Is it likely also that the EU's global influence overall will continue to diminish as other centers of power arise? Is it possible that we will see the EU settle for middle-range status as a moral influence in the world, and give up its quest to be a major actor? In light of these challenges, simply maintaining the status quo of the EU to 2030 could actually turn out to be a major success.

Nationalism, Populism, Migration, and Identity Politics

Among the biggest trends in European society, as I previously discussed, is the rise of populism and identity politics. It is difficult to come up with any meaningful examples of countries that have not faced these issues, and it is evident that such pressures will grow over the next few years. Although populists exist on the left and right of the spectrum, the groups on the right appear to be more influential and provocative, especially those promoting ethnonationalism.[4] As we witnessed in the UK with the Brexit and UKIP parties, such populism normally vents against the EU, and so it is possible to imagine other countries leaving the EU. More likely, however, is heightened pressure to dilute policies of the EU and to push back on any attempts by the EU to increase its activities. Such populism, for example, makes it difficult for the EU to envisage European-wide refugee and migrant policies, unless it is to close off Europe's borders, a trend that is likely to strengthen in the coming years.

Are populations going to perceive of themselves as European, and continue to support the EU venture, or is nationalism and anti-EU sentiment going to change fundamentally the trajectory of Europe? There is a sense that Europeans are forgetting the lessons of recent history, the wars that tore Europe apart, and see a peaceful Europe in terms of nation-states rather than an overarching European institution. There appears to be little to slow populism in terms of its support for national identity and interests, national pride, and national destiny—to the detriment of a desire to maintain European identity. One foreseeable trend is these groups' increasing participation in coalition governments.

If the challenges are significant at the EU level, then we should also focus in on the pressures of populism at a national level. Populist groups, by definition, challenge the status quo in terms of government structures and party affiliations. Italy provides a pertinent example of the changes that can appear when populists enter government and upend the existing political structures. We see similar examples in Hungary and Poland. Even outside of government, however, populists shape existing political dialogue, and have a tendency to shift political discussions to the right of the political spectrum. With the ongoing dynamic of European politics, and with continuing intervention and support from Russia, one can envisage a rise of populism and populist governments, in the coming years. This will likely fracture national politics further, and lead to harsher and more exclusionary political discourse, beating the drum against migration and minority groups in particular. Will the harsh reaction to Putin's invasion of Ukraine stem the tide of populism, or merely promote it?

The politics of identity is also likely to increase in other areas, potentially in the weakening of existing states with disaffected populations. Belgium always springs to mind as a country that can barely hold itself together in terms of the Flemish and Walloon divisions. Is this the time when Belgium rationalizes itself as two countries? Perhaps, but other examples seem more pressing. The UK has teetered for a while on the edge of division, but conditions now seem ripe for the country to split. Scotland wants to maintain its EU connectivity in a post-Brexit world, and seeks another referendum on independence, a situation exacerbated by its general distaste for the London-based UK government. Northern Ireland is adrift following the Brexit agreement with the EU, and may be drifting toward unification with Ireland, much to the disdain of unionists. Tensions within Northern Ireland seem likely to continue to rise, along with the potential for a return to low-grade civil war. The loss of either Scotland or Northern Ireland would severely dent the UK government's grandiose strategy of the new Rule Britannia—namely, Global Britain—and would undermine the status quo of British politics.

Other cases of identity politics could be equally impactful. The ongoing Catalan separatist movement in Spain, or the (Northern) League's calls for separation in Italy, are going to remain loud and vocal in the coming decade. We still need to iron out (ethnic) differences in the Balkans, especially in terms of the future of Bosnia and Herzegovina and Kosovo, which seem likely to drag on (with increased Russian involvement on the side of Serbia). No central government is willing to give up territory and population, and yet one hopes that the decade precedes more along the lines of the Velvet Divorce of Czechoslovakia rather than the ethnic bloodshed of Yugoslavia. The success of the EU to date provides impetus for some of these secessionist movements to be able to operate within a broad, open, democratic space of Europe. Spain (and Italy), however, would likely veto any claim to EU membership by a breakaway Scotland for fear of encouraging its own secessionists. Perhaps the declining influence of the EU could make these encounters more stark and dangerous. The increasingly bellicose nationalism in the contest between Greece and Turkey is another case in point.

One other important aspect of identity involves the group rights of migrants and minorities, and in particular the growing presence of Muslim cultural and religious identity, where racism plays a key role. In many countries, we have witnessed a backlash against Muslims, whether from the Middle East or Africa, who face ostracism for their differences. These pressures have been in the form of increased support for Christian identity, or national (racial) identity, or in a country such as France, as a way supposedly to support a secular identity. Whether these are policies limiting the use of the hijab in France, or the building of minarets in Switzerland, or the opposition to Turkish (resurgent Islamic) membership in the EU, religious identity is an issue building in strength. Those who

---

Box 10.2   Microstates: Plus ça change . . .

Although I have stressed the fluidity of the European political environment, one of the ongoing constants appears to be that of microstates. The map of Europe has changed quite dramatically over the past 100 years, but not for the microstates that do appear to be anachronistic relics from a bygone age. They have flourished through economic specialization, through astute government policies, and by remaining below the radar of major European issues. There is little to suggest that the next decade will see any significant change to these small states, even though there could be major changes across the continent.

Indeed, the survival of these small principalities could possibly become a model for Europe, as large multinational states face pressures to fissure. The Balkans provides an example of this trend. This also ties in to ideas about globalization and the pressures that weaken national regulation of economies and perhaps the state itself. These pressures bring about overlapping authorities and multiple loyalties, a concept known as new medievalism.[a] It is unlikely that such a major shift will take place within Europe in the next decade, but this is something to monitor.

Note: a. Jörg Friedrichs, "The Meaning of New Medievalism," *European Journal of International Relations* 7(4), 2001: 475–501.

promoted the Christian character of the continent in the past had appeared to be fighting a losing battle, but had wanted to fight it anyway. Today, this is not true, and the ideals of multiculturalism in the continent could diminish in influence as the 2020s continue. The issue of Islamic inclusion is a major challenge, and it likely will destabilize many countries, in addition to the EU itself. These are difficult problems to resolve, but easy ones to draw onto the political stage. Without strong, enlightened leadership on these issues—seemingly lacking in the 2020s—then this can turn explosive. This also creates an environment of hate and fear, and likely social disorder, a trend in process for some time.[5]

As a final note, language is a core element of identity. Greater multilingualism within the continent offers the prospect of greater cultural understanding and harmony. This is especially the case with the continuation of the ERASMUS program, helping students learn firsthand about other European cultures. Unfortunately, only a small (privileged) proportion of Europe's youth gets to have such an opportunity, and the vast majority of people remain within their national confines, consuming country-based (and at times xenophobic) rather than European political discourse. Greater awareness of other cultures does not automatically mean greater respect, of course. The ability of many Europeans to communicate with each other is positive, either through multilingualism or through the lingua franca of English, but this may be insufficient to stunt the residual and staying power of national language and identity.

Germany at the Heart of Europe

Germany has played a pivotal role in Europe since its initial unification in 1871, in positive and negative terms. Its burgeoning power and large population upset the frail balance of power at the beginning of the twentieth century, contributing to World War I. Similarly, in the 1930s there was little to stop its expansion under Adolf Hitler, except perhaps for the country's overreach in invading the Soviet Union. After 1945, a divided Germany remained pivotal in Europe as the front line of the Cold War, and West Germany as a critical founding member of the EU. This tying of Germany to the European project is essential to the success of the EU and the maintenance of peace in Europe. Will it last?

Countries change their policy positions constantly based on perceived needs—note the UK departing the EU after forty-seven years of membership (1973–2020)—and so there is the possibility that Germany's quiet leadership role in Europe, remaining deferential to the overall project, could change, even though the country would likely remain in the EU. Several factors are worthy of consideration. First, Germany has the largest population in the EU and the largest economy in Europe, quite capable of surviving in the global economic system by itself.[6] In fact, in terms of trade with China and Russia, it has embarked on autarkic policies to benefit itself rather than the European project, a normal aspect of national foreign policy. Second, Germany has earned its reputation as the policer of EU policy, particularly regarding budgets and the role of the euro. It could be possible that German leaders will see this as not worthwhile, hampering the German economy. Why be constrained in continually bailing out fragile economies to the South or East, and is the EU as a whole worth this?

The third factor could be a game-changer. The rise of the Alternative for Germany points to evidence that a significant number of Germans agree with the first two points, and may not agree to the maintenance of the policing role of the EU if it constrains German freedom to act independently. The AfD may not be openly calling for Germany's exit from the EU, but it clearly wants German interests to be first above those of the EU. If Germany continues to lead the EU, it should be to benefit German interests according to the AfD. Although the AfD's performance in the 2021 elections was flat, its role will continue to keep these ideas in play.

With the erosion in support for Germany's Christian Democrats following their stumbles during the pandemic, along with the retirement of long-term chancellor Angela Merkel in December 2021, a resurgent Green party may try to grab the political center, altering the scope of Germany's economic and social landscape by promoting policies to mitigate against climate change.[7] A polarization of German politics is possible, however, with the continuing presence of the AfD, emboldened in 2022 by protests against German vaccination policies.[8] There is no guarantee that German leaders post-Merkel will have the same legitimacy or capability to manage a diverse set of pressures. Such a change of parties and policies at the heart of the federal government would be significant in terms of altering Germany's relationship with the EU, but this potential realignment inside German politics makes this an important trend to watch post-Merkel.[9] The strength of the far-right in neighboring France, even after its defeat in the 2022 presidential election, could also unsettle the Franco-German alliance on which much of Europe's stability lies.

Russia Resurgent

As shown in Chapters 1 and 2, the role of Russia in Europe ebbs and flows depending on its status at the time. When Czar Peter the Great built St. Petersburg in the country's far western corner and declared it Russia's capital in 1713, this was the start of a period of Russia's major involvement as a European power. Since then, Russia has had an uneven impact, such as with its weakness following the 1917 revolution, and again following the demise of the Soviet Union and communism in the 1990s and its loss of influence over large swaths of Central and Eastern Europe.

Since 2000, however, Russia's role in Europe—and the world—has revitalized, in no short measure linked to the rise of Putin. What are the trends to watch here? Across Europe, Russia continues to play an important trade role in energy supplies, and this is likely to continue until the time when alternative and sustainable energy is abundant, even though the Ukraine war in 2022 brought some EU energy sanctions and broader economic sanctions. Such dependence on Russian energy at least in the short-term makes Europe somewhat under Russian influence, or potential interference. Russia's ability to cut off supplies when tensions rise and temperatures drop is always present. Russia is also likely to continue to meddle in the politics of Europe in real and in cyber terms, continuing to fund and support populist movements to the detriment of broader social democracy, and exploit differences within countries.

Russia's invasion of Ukraine in February 2022 altered the dynamic of Russia's role in Europe by galvanizing opposition to Putin. The speed and severity of sanctions against Russia within the first three months were unprecedented, with even neutral countries such as Finland and Sweden offering military assistance to Ukraine (and applying for NATO membership), and Switzerland freezing Russian banking transactions. Energy companies, such as BP and Shell, withdrew from the Russian market, while widespread sanctions curtailed Russia's ties to the global financial system and transportation. Also unprecedented was the level of agreement and coordination within the EU and NATO, something barely imaginable before Putin's reckless adventure. It is difficult to foresee how all this plays out, whether the political and economic damage to Russia will be long-lasting, and whether the EU's and NATO's singularity of purpose and resilience will hold. Putin was probably surprised by this unified reaction, and his own fate appears to be in the balance, as does his desire to extend the conflict beyond Ukraine. Similarly, Europe's boldness of action may only survive behind a strong and resurgent NATO, and any wavering by NATO (such as after the 2024 US elections) could strengthen Russia's hand.

Countries geographically close to Russia, such as Belarus and Ukraine, as well as those around the Caspian Sea, will likely continue to feel Russia's hand more heavily than other states. The promotion of the EU's Neighborhood Policy will continue to face Moscow's opprobrium. Relations between Russia and the EU will remain tense and complex. It is difficult to see a different scenario unless there is a tumultuous change in Russian politics. Likewise, we must expect to see an increasing role for Russia inside the Arctic Circle in terms of raw materials and transportation routes, putting the country at odds with other European Arctic members. A new Cold War seems imminent, stretching to an even Colder War in the Arctic.

Within Russian politics and Putinology, the game appears to be Putin's to play, assuming he withstands domestic pressures over Ukraine. He has engineered constitutional amendments to allow him to retain power through the ballot box potentially until 2036. If Russia continues with Putin, then it will be a path of increasing repression and minimal democracy. Whether the forces of Russian civil society or the business elite have the capacity to change this dynamic is to be tested. Observers said similar things about CEE in early 1989, so we should keep an open mind. The least likely option is a blossoming of Russian social democracy, with a full embrace of, and by, Europe. That would be a radical transformation, and would take time.

What appears likely, certainly under Putin's leadership, is a continuation of the rather subversive role in world politics, undermining the stability of Western democracies and partnering with China when possible in upsetting the established world order. Russia will persist in its demand for respect as a world's leading power.[10] Its economic influence will continue only with the West's dependence on traditional energy commodities, as it has failed to diversify its economy. A rapid shift to sustainable energy strategies would undercut its influence to a considerable extent, though not necessarily its meddling, especially in the realm of cybersecurity. With a focus on 2030, it is difficult to see how Russia would change track in any significant way, although some believe that Putin's grasp on power is more precarious than it seems, even before the invasion of Ukraine.[11] At this point, however, a continuation of an underperforming domestic political and economic system is most likely.

Transatlantic and Trans-Asian Relations: European Relevancy?

The likelihood that the twenty-first century is to be the century of Asian economic power driven primarily by China and India raises important questions for Europe (and, of course, the United States). Although the EU remains somewhat influential in global terms as the world's largest trade bloc, it is already facing challenges from the growing influence of the Asian powerhouses, especially China, as well as the traditional competition with the United States. Although EU policies along with the euro provide some capacity for regional cooperation to face outward, the European continent still comprises small national component states that are involved in promoting their own individual agendas.

Can Europe maintain unity during the 2020s to face growing external economic competition? From a rational perspective, one might say yes, as European countries combined within the EU27 have much more chance of negotiating policy and leveraging strength collectively than as separate units. There are signs, however, that European unity over trade may not hold, as countries seek to make their own opportunistic deals. International organizations relied on by the EU to police trade policies and agreements, such as the World Trade Organization and the Group of 20 (G-20), will likely continue to decline in significance and struggle to manage the norms of the system. As the United States and China line up as rival global economic leaders, with no real leadership within the international system, the EU's voice may continue to recede, its "moral" power notwithstanding. This raises the prospect of increasing calls for protectionism and subsidy within Europe, or a declining multilateral perspective.

The last two US presidents, Barack Obama and Donald Trump, placed little emphasis on a closer relationship with Europe. Obama perhaps pivoted to Europe as an afterthought near the end of his second term, but Trump was outspoken in his hostility toward the EU and NATO (and just about everyone else in the global system, except Russia). President Joe Biden talks of close relations with traditional partners and allies (in Europe), but challenges for the United States on every horizon will likely make difficult an implementation of substantial policy. The United States will continue to want European partners to carry more of the burden of European defense. The logic of a US-EU partnership to counter the rising power of China seems unimportant and unlikely from a US perspective, though is one that some in Europe continue to think is a possibility, even though many in Europe remain opposed. These are trends to follow, which could easily be upset in the volatile arena of US politics. Although talks of a transatlantic free-trade area have been around for decades, but have stalled in recent years, this is a topic to keep an eye on. The UK, post-Brexit, certainly hopes to make a trade agreement with the United States, but this is unlikely to be large enough to change either country's trajectory. A EU-US deal could be important, though there are still many detractors on both sides of the Atlantic who would not favor such a partnership. Spats over trade discrimination and subsidy—Boeings, bananas, and beef—that were previously accentuated may not fully subside, but one would expect calls for cooperation would outweigh nationalistic and regional tendencies in the 2020s. Whether such a free-trade area across the Atlantic will emerge by 2030 depends on a whole host of factors, but it remains an outside possibility.

To some extent, the transatlantic relationship may rely on the relations with Asia (both European and US). Asia, of course, is not monolithic, and tensions between China and India, such as over Kashmir, are just as likely to burst out as are desires for cooperation. Most Asian countries remain cautious and concerned by the increasingly forceful Chinese economic and strategic agenda. Europe can continue to build partnerships along the rim of China, notably with India and Japan, who themselves fear China. The EU is likely to strengthen its partnership with ASEAN and other trading groups. The Global Britain agenda appears to pin much of its hopes on a strengthening of UK ties in this region. Europe, including Russia, will continue, however, to seek the best possible trade relationship with China, so all this requires significant balancing. Europe's relationship with Asia will grow, perhaps to the extent that trans-Asia becomes as significant as transatlantic, and that is something to watch.

Both these sets of relationships are dependent on what happens within the internal European market. Can Europe maintain its competitive economic edge with the demands of the social agenda within the continent? Can Europe maintain its unity and economic relevance in the world in 2030, especially within the markets of Asia? European economies are generally strong and competitive, so they are not going to shrivel in the next few years. This question, though, addresses the economic and political strength of Europe to maintain its relevance in shaping global policy up to 2030.

Climate Change and Human Development

The final trend to watch is a topic in which Europe genuinely appears to be a global leader, and that is on issues of climate change and the promotion of human development, including human rights. The EU along with the UK and members of EFTA maintain a strong commitment to common environmental policies, and to support of the Paris Agreement to counter climate change. This is also an area with widespread public support across the continent. This puts Europe in a different position from those countries with lukewarm or less active strategies to combat climate change, notably China, Russia, and the United States. Europe hoped to hold center stage in June 2022 when Stockholm hosted the fiftieth anniversary of the original Stockholm conference on climate and development, but this meeting did not get the world's attention. European leaders can continue to exert soft power in the promotion of these agendas during the 2020s, promoting higher levels of foreign assistance and efforts to meet the 2030 Sustainable Development Goals laid out by the UN. Although Europe's relations with the developing world, notably the African, Caribbean, and Pacific group of states, are not without critics, European countries are likely to maintain their levels of developmental support. Despite difficult negotiations, it is also likely that the EU will find a way to conclude another round of economic partnership agreements with the ACP.

Europe does not have the capacity, however, to bring recalcitrant environmental countries into the fold, but it does have the ability to continue to champion climate policies. It is unlikely that Europe has the capacity to extend climate into bargaining chips with rival trade powers—though it could with weaker countries in the developing world—and it is uncertain whether the EU would act against its own members who were dragging their heels. The EU, for example, faced huge difficulties in negotiating a minimal energy sanctions package against Russia in 2022. In terms of climate change as an existential threat to the planet, Europe's generally strong support for climate policies puts the continent on the right side of history, Russia excepted. Volvo's announcement in March 2021 that all its cars would be electric powered by 2030 is a trend that vehicle manufacturers across the continent will likely take up.[12] This is an area where we expect continuing European policy proposals and leadership, rippling into areas such as energy usage and transportation. We can expect to see rising tensions over the Arctic, with increasingly forceful actions by Russia in the region facing opposition from Western European Arctic members. Policies by Russia will promote more exploitation and less conservation.

Such support for climate, human development, and human rights continues to provide the EU with some semblance of moral leadership in the world, and this may increasingly become the main type of leadership that Europe can portray. This is certainly a critical decade for Europe and the world on climate and human development, and arguably an important decade for Europe on many different fronts.

Conclusion

This book attempts to explain key factors and trends in European politics and society. Rather than showing a stable and slow-moving continent, I have shown a continent in flux, with significant and often unpredictable changes in the continent since 1945 and, arguably, more changes coming in the near future. The EU serves as something of an anchor for the continent, an organization that shapes Europe for members and nonmembers alike. Its constant efforts to remake itself will likely continue, but it is difficult not to conclude that its efforts and energies are limited, especially as many European countries remain outside of the organization. What is interesting is whether this serves as an indicator of a larger issue, that after centuries dominating and shaping the world, Europe's influence and reputation are waning. This may not be a dramatic or sudden collapse, but rather a steady, yet inevitable, one. Unity and cooperation tied to economic strength could maintain Europe's prestige and influence, but the Europe of the 2020s still appears nationalistic and a place where countries push their own agendas albeit under the military protection of NATO. The stability of its largely social democratic framework is also possibly wavering. The outcome of Russia's war with Ukraine will also likely shape the future of Europe in the next decade. No outcome is definite or preordained, and so watching Europe in the coming years makes for an interesting pastime.

Notes

1. George Soros, "Can Europe Work? A Plan to Rescue the Union," *Foreign Affairs* 75(5), 1996: 8–14.

2. Douglas Webber, *European Disintegration? The Politics of Crisis in the European Union* (London: Red Globe, 2019); Simon Duke, *Europe as a Stronger Global Actor: Challenges and Strategic Responses* (London: Palgrave Macmillan, 2017); William Drozdiak, *Fractured Continent: Europe's Crises and the Fate of the West* (New York: Norton, 2017).

3. Herman Lelieveldt and Sebastiaan Princen, *The Politics of the European Union,* 2nd ed. (Cambridge: Cambridge University Press, 2015), chap. 12.

4. Milada Anna Vachudova, "Populism, Democracy, and Party System Change in Europe," *Annual Review of Political Science* 24, 2021: 1–28.

5. Walter Laquer, *The Last Days of Europe: Epitaph for an Old Continent* (New York: St. Martin's, 2007).

6. Germany has Europe's fourth-largest military, behind France, Russia, and Turkey, though there is little to suggest that anyone is thinking seriously about the use of the German military.

7. Kate Connolly and Philip Oltermann, "Post Merkel: Is the CDU Facing Disaster?" *The Guardian Weekly*, March 19, 2021; Frank Baasner and Stefan Seidendorf, "A Year of Electoral Uncertainty: Germany Turns the Page on Merkel," Robert Schuman Foundation Policy Paper, no. 593, April 27, 2021, https://www.robert-schuman.eu/en/doc/questions-d-europe/qe-593-en.pdf.

8. Katrin Bennhold, "Line Blurs in Germany Between Pandemic Protesters and Far Right," *New York Times,* March 1, 2022.

9. Constanze Stelzenmüller, "The Singular Chancellor: The Merkel Model and Its Limits," *Foreign Affairs* 100(3), 2021: 161–172.

10. Michael Kofman and Andrea Kendall-Taylor, "The Myth of Russian Decline: Why Moscow Will Be a Persistent Power," *Foreign Affairs* 100(6), 2021: 142–152.

11. Timothy Frye, "Russia's Weak Strongman: The Perilous Bargains that Keep Putin in Power," *Foreign Affairs* 100(3), 2021: 116–127.

12. Jack Ewing, "Volvo Sets 2030 as Year All New Cars Are Electric," *New York Times*, March 3, 2021. The all-time record heatwave across Europe in July 2022, along with efforts by many European countries to wean themselves off Russian oil and natural gas, could further propel the movement toward electric cars and sustainable energy initiatives.

Acronyms

ACP	African, Caribbean, and Pacific group
AfD	Alternative for Germany (Alternativ für Deutschland) party
AI	Amnesty International
AID	United States Agency for International Development
AIIB	Asian Infrastructure Investment Bank
ALDE	Alliance of Liberals and Democrats for Europe
ASEAN	Association of Southeast Asian Nations
BDA	Confederation of German Employers' Association
BDI	Federal Association of German Industry
BRI	Belt and Road Initiative
BSEC	Black Sea Economic Cooperation
CAP	Common Agricultural Policy
CARICOM	Caribbean Community
CDU	Christian Democratic Union
CEE	Central and Eastern European
CETA	Comprehensive Economic and Trade Agreement
CFP	Common Fisheries Policy
CJEU	Court of Justice of the European Union
CMEA	Council for Mutual Economic Assistance
CND	Campaign for Nuclear Disarmament
COE	Council of Europe
CoR	Committee of the Regions, EU
COREPER	Committee of Permanent Representatives
CSCE	Conference on Security and Cooperation in Europe

CSU	Christian Social Union
DAF	Van Doorne's Automobiel Fabriek (the Netherlands)
DRC	Democratic Republic of Congo
EAFRD	European Agricultural Fund for Rural Development
EAGF	European Agricultural Guarantee Fund
EAP	Environmental Action Program
EaP	Eastern Partnership
EBRD	European Bank for Reconstruction and Development
ECB	European Central Bank
ECJ	European Court of Justice
ECSC	European Coal and Steel Community
EEA	European Economic Area
EEAS	European External Action Service
EEC	European Economic Community
EESC	European Economic and Social Committee, EU
EFP	European Foreign Policy
EFTA	European Free Trade Association
EHEA	European Higher Education Area
EMA	European Medicines Agency
EMFF	European Maritime and Fisheries Fund
EMU	European Monetary Union
ENA	École Nationale d'Administration
ENP	European Neighborhood Policy
EP	European Parliament
EPA	Economic Partnership Agreements
EPI	Environmental Performance Index
EPP	European People's Party
EU	European Union
ERASMUS	European Region Action Scheme for the Mobility of University Students
ERDF	EU Regional Development Fund
ESS	European Security Strategy
EU-OSHA	European Agency for Safety and Health at Work
EUGS	European Union Global Strategy
EUIPO	European Union Intellectual Property Office
Euratom	European Atomic Energy Community
Europol	European Police Office
EU27	EU twenty-seven member countries
FAO	UN Food and Agriculture Organization
FDP	Free Democratic Party

FIFA	International Federation of Association Football (Fédération Internationale de Football Association)
FPTP	first-past-the-post
Frontex	European Border and Coast Guard Agency
FTAA	Free Trade Area of the Americas
GDP	gross domestic product
GDPR	the General Data Protection Regulation
GDR	German Democratic Republic
GSC	General Secretariat
G-20	Group of 20
ICC	International Criminal Court
ICJ	International Court of Justice
ICRC	International Committee of the Red Cross and Red Crescent
IOC	International Olympic Committee
LGBTQ	lesbian, gay, bisexual, transgender, and queer/questioning (one's sexual or gender identity)
LNG	liquefied natural gas
MAN	Maschinenfabrik Augsburg Nürnberg (Germany)
M&A	merger and acquisition
MDGs	Millennium Development Goals
MENA	Middle East and North Africa
MSF	Doctors Without Borders (Médicins Sans Frontières)
NAFTA	North American Free Trade Agreement
NATO	North Atlantic Treaty Organization
NPE	Normative Power Europe
OAS	Organization of American States
OECD	Organisation for Economic Co-operation and Development
OEEC	Organisation for European Economic Co-operation
OPEC	Organization of the Petroleum Exporting Countries
OSCE	Organization for Security and Co-operation in Europe
PCF	French Communist Party
PDS	Party of Democratic Socialism
PESCO	Permanent Structured Cooperation
PHARE	Poland and Hungary: Assistance for Restructuring Their Economy
PIIGS	Portugal, Ireland, Italy, Greece, and Spain
PR	proportional representation
QMV	qualified majority vote
SPD	Social Democrats (in Germany)
STV	single transferable vote

TGV	high-speed train links (Train à Grande Vitesse)
T-TIP	Trans-Atlantic Trade and Investment Partnership
UEFA	Union of European Football Associations
UfM	Union for the Mediterranean
UKIP	UK Independence Party
UNECE	United Nations Economic Commission for Europe
UNESCO	United Nations Educational, Scientific and Cultural Organization
UNIDO	United Nations Industrial Development Organization
USMCA	United States-Mexico-Canada Agreement
USSR	Union of Soviet Socialist Republics
VAT	value-added tax
VVD	People's Party for Freedom and Democracy
WEF	World Economic Forum
WTO	World Trade Organization

Country Profiles

THESE PROFILES PROVIDE BASIC DETAILS ABOUT THE FORTY-SEVEN member countries of the Council of Europe. Data have been drawn from multiple public sources, including the European Union, the Council of Europe, the Organisation for Economic Co-operation and Development, the World Bank, the United Nations, and Transparency International's Corruption Perceptions Index 2020 (the smaller the number, the less corrupt).

Albania
Population: 2,854,190
Official Name: Republic of Albania
Capital: Tirana
Land Area (sq. km): 27,400
Life Expectancy: 78
Population Density (per sq. km): 105
Type of Political System: Parliamentary, Unitary, Unicameral
Head of State: President
Head of Government: Prime Minister
Current Gross Domestic Product (GDP) ($) millions
  (World Bank [WB] 2019): 15,279.18
GDP per Capita ($) (WB 2019): 5,353.2
Public Social Spending as a Percentage of GDP (2019): 11.75 (est.)
Corruption World Rank: 104

Andorra

Population: 77,140
Official Name: Principality of Andorra
Capital: Andorra la Vella
Land Area (sq. km): 470
Life Expectancy: 81
Population Density (per sq. km): 164
Type of Political System: Parliamentary, Unitary, Unicameral
Head of State: President of France and Bishop of Urgell
Head of Government: Sindic, or President of the General Council
Current GDP ($) millions (WB 2019): 3,154.06
GDP per Capita ($) (WB 2019): 40,886.40
Public Social Spending as a Percentage of GDP (2019): not available (N/A)
Corruption World Rank: N/A

Armenia

Population: 2,057,730
Official Name: Republic of Armenia
Capital: Yerevan
Land Area (sq. km): 28,470
Life Expectancy: 75
Population Density (per sq. km): 104
Type of Political System: Parliamentary, Unitary, Unicameral
Head of State: President
Head of Government: Prime Minister
Current GDP ($) millions (WB 2019): 13,672.80
GDP per Capita ($) (WB 2019): 4,622.70
Public Social Spending as a Percentage of GDP (2019): N/A
Corruption World Rank: 60

Austria

Population: 8,877,070
Official Name: Republic of Austria
Capital: Vienna
Land Area (sq. km): 82,520
Life Expectancy: 82
Population Density (per sq. km): 107
Type of Political System: Parliamentary, Federal, Bicameral
Head of State: Federal President
Head of Government: Federal Chancellor
Current GDP ($) millions (WB 2019): 445,075.39

GDP per Capita ($) (WB 2019): 50,137.70
Public Social Spending as a Percentage of GDP (2019): 26.9
Corruption World Rank: 15

Azerbaijan
Population: 10,023,320
Official Name: Republic of Azerbaijan
Capital: Baku
Land Area (sq. km): 82,654
Life Expectancy: 73
Population Density (per sq. km): 120
Type of Political System: Semipresidential, Unitary, Unicameral
Head of State: President
Head of Government: Prime Minister
Current GDP ($) millions (WB 2019): 48,047.65
GDP per Capita ($) (WB 2019): 4,793.6
Public Social Spending as a Percentage of GDP (2019): N/A
Corruption World Rank: 129

Belgium
Population: 11,484,060
Official Name: Kingdom of Belgium
Capital: Brussels
Land Area (sq. km): 30,280
Life Expectancy: 82
Population Density (per sq. km): 377
Type of Political System: Parliamentary, Federal, Bicameral
Head of State: Monarch
Head of Government: Prime or First Minister
Current GDP ($) millions (WB 2019): 533,097.46
GDP per Capita ($) (WB 2019): 46,420.7
Public Social Spending as a Percentage of GDP (2019): 28.9
Corruption World Rank: 15

Bosnia and Herzegovina
Population: 3,301,000
Official Name: Bosnia and Herzegovina
Capital: Sarajevo
Land Area (sq. km): 51,200
Life Expectancy: 77
Population Density (per sq. km): 65

Type of Political System: Parliamentary, Federal, Bicameral
Head of State: President of the Federation
Head of Government: Prime Minister
Current GDP ($) millions (WB 2019): 20,164.19
GDP per Capita ($) (WB 2019): 6,108.5
Public Social Spending as a Percentage of GDP (2019): 18.5
Corruption World Rank: 111

Bulgaria

Population: 6,975,760
Official Name: Republic of Bulgaria
Capital: Sofia
Land Area (sq. km): 108,560
Life Expectancy: 75
Population Density (per sq. km): 65
Type of Political System: Parliamentary, Unitary, Unicameral
Head of State: President
Head of Government: Minister-Chairman
Current GDP ($) millions (WB 2019): 68,558.82
GDP per Capita ($) (WB 2019): 9,828.1
Public Social Spending as a Percentage of GDP (2019): 16.4
Corruption World Rank: 69

Croatia

Population: 4,067,500
Official Name: Republic of Croatia
Capital: Zagreb
Land Area (sq. km): 56,590
Life Expectancy: 78
Population Density (per sq. km): 72
Type of Political System: Parliamentary, Unitary, Unicameral
Head of State: President of the Republic
Head of Government: President of the Government
Current GDP ($) millions (WB 2019): 60,752.59
GDP per Capita ($) (WB 2019): 14,936.1
Public Social Spending as a Percentage of GDP (2019): 21.2
Corruption World Rank: 63

Cyprus

Population: 1,198,580
Official Name: Republic of Cyprus

Capital: Nicosia
Land Area (sq. km): 9,240
Life Expectancy: 81
Population Density (per sq. km): 129
Type of Political System: Presidential, Unitary, Unicameral
Head of State and Government: President
Current GDP ($) millions (WB 2019): 24,948.94
GDP per Capita ($) (WB 2019): 27,858.4
Public Social Spending as a Percentage of GDP (2019): 17.7
Corruption World Rank: 42

Czech Republic

Population: 10,669,710
Official Name: Czech Republic
Capital: Prague
Land Area (sq. km): 77,200
Life Expectancy: 79
Population Density (per sq. km): 138
Type of Political System: Parliamentary, Unitary, Bicameral
Head of State: President
Head of Government: Chairman of the Government
Current GDP ($) millions (WB 2019): 250,680.50
GDP per Capita ($) (WB 2019): 23,494.6
Public Social Spending as a Percentage of GDP (2019): 19.2
Corruption World Rank: 49

Denmark

Population: 5,818,550
Official Name: Kingdom of Denmark
Capital: Copenhagen
Land Area (sq. km): 40,000
Life Expectancy: 81
Population Density (per sq. km): 145
Type of Political System: Parliamentary, Unitary (with some devolution of
    powers), Unicameral
Head of State: Monarch
Head of Government: Minister of State
Current GDP ($) millions (WB 2019): 350,104.33
GDP per Capita ($) (WB 2019): 60,170.13
Public Social Spending as a Percentage of GDP (2019): 28.3
Corruption World Rank: 1

Estonia
Population: 1,326,590
Official Name: Republic of Estonia
Capital: Tallinn
Land Area (sq. km): 43,470
Life Expectancy: 78
Population Density (per sq. km): 30
Type of Political System: Parliamentary, Unitary, Unicameral
Head of State: President
Head of Government: Head Minister
Current GDP ($) millions (WB 2019): 31,4711,10
GDP per Capita ($) (WB 2019): 23,723.3
Public Social Spending as a Percentage of GDP (2019): 17.7
Corruption World Rank: 17

Finland
Population: 5,520,310
Official Name: Republic of Finland
Capital: Helsinki
Land Area (sq. km): 303,920
Life Expectancy: 82
Population Density (per sq. km): 18
Type of Political System: Parliamentary, Unitary (with some devolution of
    powers), Unicameral
Head of State: President
Head of Government: Head Minister
Current GDP ($) millions (WB 2019): 269,296.31
GDP per Capita ($) (WB 2019): 48,782.8
Public Social Spending as a Percentage of GDP (2019): 29.1
Corruption World Rank: 3

France
Population: 67,059,890
Official Name: Republic of France
Capital: Paris
Land Area (sq. km): 547,557
Life Expectancy: 83
Population Density (per sq. km): 122
Type of Political System: Semipresidential, Unitary, Bicameral
Head of State: President
Head of Government: Prime Minister

Current GDP ($) millions (WB 2019): 2,715,518.27
GDP per Capita ($) (WB 2019): 40,493.9
Public Social Spending as a Percentage of GDP (2019): 31
Corruption World Rank: 23

Georgia
Population: 3,720,380
Official Name: Georgia
Capital: Tbilisi
Land Area (sq. km): 69,490
Life Expectancy: 74
Population Density (per sq. km): 65
Type of Political System: Parliamentary, Unitary, Unicameral
Head of State: President
Head of Government: Prime Minister
Current GDP ($) millions (WB 2019): 17,477.26
GDP per Capita ($) (WB 2019): 4,697.7
Public Social Spending as a Percentage of GDP (2019): N/A
Corruption World Rank: 45

Germany
Population: 83,132,800
Official Name: Federal Republic of Germany
Capital: Berlin
Land Area (sq. km): 349,380
Life Expectancy: 81
Population Density (per sq. km): 237
Type of Political System: Parliamentary, Federal, Bicameral
Head of State: Federal President
Head of Government: Federal Chancellor
Current GDP ($) millions (WB 2019): 3,861,123.56
GDP per Capita ($) (WB 2019): 46,445.2
Public Social Spending as a Percentage of GDP (2019): 25.9
Corruption World Rank: 9

Greece
Population: 10,716,320
Official Name: Hellenic Republic
Capital: Athens
Land Area (sq. km): 128,900
Life Expectancy: 82

Population Density (per sq. km): 83
Type of Political System: Parliamentary, Unitary, Unicameral
Head of State: President
Head of Government: Prime Minister
Current GDP ($) millions (WB 2019): 209,852.76
GDP per Capita ($) (WB 2019): 19,582.5
Public Social Spending as a Percentage of GDP (2019): 24
Corruption World Rank: 59

Hungary
Population: 9,769,950
Official Name: Hungary
Capital: Budapest
Land Area (sq. km): 91,260
Life Expectancy: 76
Population Density (per sq. km): 107
Type of Political System: Parliamentary, Unitary, Unicameral
Head of State: President of the Republic
Head of Government: Minister-President
Current GDP ($) millions (WB 2019): 163,469.04
GDP per Capita ($) (WB 2019): 16,731.8
Public Social Spending as a Percentage of GDP (2019): 18.1
Corruption World Rank: 69

Iceland
Population: 361,310
Official Name: Republic of Iceland
Capital: Reykjavik
Land Area (sq. km): 100,830
Life Expectancy: 83
Population Density (per sq. km): 3
Type of Political System: Parliamentary, Unitary, Unicameral
Head of State: President
Head of Government: Prime Minister
Current GDP ($) millions (WB 2019): 24,188.04
GDP per Capita ($) (WB 2019): 66,944.8
Public Social Spending as a Percentage of GDP (2019): 17.4
Corruption World Rank: 17

Ireland
Population: 4,941,440

Official Name: Ireland
Capital: Dublin
Land Area (sq. km): 68,890
Life Expectancy: 82
Population Density (per sq. km): 71
Type of Political System: Parliamentary, Unitary, Bicameral
Head of State: President
Head of Government: Taoiseach
Current GDP ($) millions (WB 2019): 388,698.71
GDP per Capita ($) (WB 2019): 78,661.0
Public Social Spending as a Percentage of GDP (2019): 13.4
Corruption World Rank: 20

Italy
Population: 60,297,400
Official Name: Republic of Italy
Capital: Rome
Land Area (sq. km): 297,730
Life Expectancy: 83
Population Density (per sq. km): 203
Type of Political System: Parliamentary, Unitary (with devolution of powers),
   Bicameral
Head of State: President
Head of Government: President of the Council of Ministers
Current GDP ($) millions (WB 2019): 2,003,576.15
GDP per Capita ($) (WB 2019): 33,228.2
Public Social Spending as a Percentage of GDP (2019): 28.2
Corruption World Rank: 52

Latvia
Population: 1,912,790
Official Name: Republic of Latvia
Capital: Riga
Land Area (sq. km): 62,090
Life Expectancy: 75
Population Density (per sq. km): 31
Type of Political System: Parliamentary, Unitary, Unicameral
Head of State: President
Head of Government: Minister-President
Current GDP ($) millions (WB 2019): 34,102.91
GDP per Capita ($) (WB 2019): 17,828.9

Public Social Spending as a Percentage of GDP (2019): 16.4
Corruption World Rank: 42

Liechtenstein

Population: 38,020
Official Name: Principality of Liechtenstein
Capital: Vaduz
Land Area (sq. km): 160
Life Expectancy: 83
Population Density (per sq. km): 237
Type of Political System: Parliamentary, Unitary, Unicameral
Head of State: Monarch
Head of Government: Prime Minister
Current GDP ($) millions (WB 2019): 6,876.98
GDP per Capita ($) (WB 2019): 181,402.8
Public Social Spending as a Percentage of GDP (2019): N/A
Corruption World Rank: N/A

Lithuania

Population: 2,786,840
Official Name: Republic of Lithuania
Capital: Vilnius
Land Area (sq. km): 62,630
Life Expectancy: 76
Population Density (per sq. km): 45
Type of Political System: Semipresidential, Unitary, Unicameral
Head of State: President
Head of Government: Minister-President
Current GDP ($) millions (WB 2019): 54,627.41
GDP per Capita ($) (WB 2019): 19,601.9
Public Social Spending as a Percentage of GDP (2019): 16.7
Corruption World Rank: 35

Luxembourg

Population: 619,900
Official Name: Grand Duchy of Luxembourg
Capital: Luxembourg
Land Area (sq. km): 2,430
Life Expectancy: 82
Population Density (per sq. km): 250
Type of Political System: Parliamentary, Unitary, Unicameral

Head of State: Monarch
Head of Government: Prime Minister
Current GDP ($) millions (WB 2019): 71,104.92
GDP per Capita ($) (WB 2019): 114,704.6
Public Social Spending as a Percentage of GDP (2019): 21.6
Corruption World Rank: 9

Malta

Population: 502,650
Official Name: Republic of Malta
Capital: Valletta
Land Area (sq. km): 320
Life Expectancy: 82
Population Density (per sq. km): 1,514
Type of Political System: Parliamentary, Unitary, Unicameral
Head of State: President
Head of Government: Prime Minister
Current GDP ($) millions (WB 2019): 14,989.42
GDP per Capita ($) (WB 2019): 29,820.6
Public Social Spending as a Percentage of GDP (2019): 15.1
Corruption World Rank: 52

Moldova

Population: 2,657,640
Official Name: Republic of Moldova
Capital: Chisinau
Land Area (sq. km): 32,885.3
Life Expectancy: 72
Population Density (per sq. km): 94
Type of Political System: Parliamentary, Unitary, Unicameral
Head of State: President
Head of Government: Prime Minister
Current GPD ($) millions (WB 2019): 11,968.71
GDP per Capita ($) (WB 2019): 4,503.5
Public Social Spending as a Percentage of GDP (2019): N/A
Corruption World Rank: 115

Monaco

Population: 38,960
Official Name: Principality of Monaco
Capital: Monaco

Land Area (sq. km): 2
Life Expectancy: 89
Population Density (per sq. km): 19,083
Type of Political System: Quasi-Parliamentary, Unitary, Unicameral
Head of State: Monarch
Head of Government: President
Current GDP ($) millions (WB 2019): 7,188.24
GDP per Capita ($) (WB 2019): 185,829.0
Public Social Spending as a Percentage of GDP (2019): N/A
Corruption World Rank: N/A

Montenegro
Population: 622,140
Official Name: Montenegro
Capital: Podgorica
Land Area (sq. km): 13,450
Life Expectancy: 77
Population Density (per sq. km): 46
Type of Political System: Parliamentary, Unitary, Unicameral
Head of State: President
Head of Government: Prime Minister
Current GDP ($) millions (WB 2019): 5,542.58
GDP per Capita ($) (WB 2019): 8,908.9
Public Social Spending as a Percentage of GDP (2019): N/A
Corruption World Rank: 67

Netherlands
Population: 17,332,850
Official Name: Kingdom of the Netherlands
Capital: Amsterdam
Land Area (sq. km): 33,670
Life Expectancy: 82
Population Density (per sq. km): 512
Type of Political System: Parliamentary, Unitary (with devolution of powers), Bicameral
Head of State: Monarch
Head of Government: Minister-President
Current GDP ($) millions (WB 2019): 907,050.86
GDP per Capita ($) (WB 2019): 52,331.3
Public Social Spending as a Percentage of GDP (2019): 16.1
Corruption World Rank: 8

North Macedonia
Population: 2,083,460
Official Name: Republic of North Macedonia
Capital: Skopje
Land Area (sq. km): 25,220
Life Expectancy: 76
Population Density (per sq. km): 83
Type of Political System: Parliamentary, Unitary, Unicameral
Head of State: President
Head of Government: Prime Minister
Current GDP ($) millions (WB 2019): 12,547.04
GDP per Capita ($) (WB 2019): 6,022.2
Public Social Spending as a Percentage of GDP (2019): N/A
Corruption World Rank: 111

Norway
Population: 5,347,900
Official Name: Kingdom of Norway
Capital: Oslo
Land Area (sq. km): 365,107.8
Life Expectancy: 83
Population Density (per sq. km): 15
Type of Political System: Parliamentary, Unitary, Unicameral
Head of State: Monarch
Head of Government: Prime Minister
Current GDP ($) millions (WB 2019): 403,336.36
GDP per Capita ($) (WB 2019): 75,419.6
Public Social Spending as a Percentage of GDP (2019): 25.3
Corruption World Rank: 7

Poland
Population: 37,970,870
Official Name: Republic of Poland
Capital: Warsaw
Land Area (sq. km): 306,170
Life Expectancy: 78
Population Density (per sq. km): 124
Type of Political System: Semipresidential, Unitary, Bicameral
Head of State: President
Head of Government: President of the Council of Ministers
Current GDP ($) millions (WB 2019): 595,858.21

GDP per Capita ($) (WB 2019): 15,692.5
Public Social Spending as a Percentage of GDP (2019): 21.3
Corruption World Rank: 45

Portugal
Population: 10,269,420
Official Name: Republic of Portugal
Capital: Lisbon
Land Area (sq. km): 91,605.6
Life Expectancy: 81
Population Density (per sq. km): 112
Type of Political System: Semipresidential, Unitary, Unicameral
Head of State: President
Head of Government: Prime Minister
Current GDP ($) millions (WB 2019): 238,785.09
GDP per Capita ($) (WB 2019): 23,252.1
Public Social Spending as a Percentage of GDP (2019): 22.6
Corruption World Rank: 33

Romania
Population: 19,356,540
Official Name: Romania
Capital: Bucharest
Land Area (sq. km): 230,080
Life Expectancy: 75
Population Density (per sq. km): 85
Type of Political System: Semipresidential, Unitary, Bicameral
Head of State: President
Head of Government: Prime Minister
Current GDP ($) millions (WB 2019): 250,077.44
GDP per Capita ($) (WB 2019): 12,919.5
Public Social Spending as a Percentage of GDP (2019): 14.7
Corruption World Rank: 69

Russia
Population: 144,373,540
Official Name: Russian Federation
Capital: Moscow
Land Area (sq. km): 16,376,870
Life Expectancy: 73
Population Density (per sq. km): 9

Type of Political System: Semipresidential, Federal, Bicameral
Head of State: President
Head of Government: Prime Minister
Current GDP ($) millions (WB 2019): 1,699,876.58
GDP per Capita ($) (WB 2019): 11,585.0
Public Social Spending as a Percentage of GDP (2019): N/A
Corruption World Rank: 129

San Marino

Population: 33,860
Official Name: Republic of San Marino
Capital: San Marino
Land Area (sq. km): 60
Life Expectancy: 85
Population Density (per sq. km): 563
Type of Political System: Parliamentary, Unitary, Unicameral
Head of State: Captains Regent (Two, Elected)
Head of Government: Senior Secretary of State
Current GDP ($) millions (WB 2019): 1,655.30
GDP per Capita ($) (WB 2019): 48,995.1
Public Social Spending as a Percentage of GDP (2019): N/A
Corruption World Rank: N/A

Serbia

Population: 6,944,980
Official Name: Republic of Serbia
Capital: Belgrade
Land Area (sq. km): 87,460
Life Expectancy: 76
Population Density (per sq. km): 80
Type of Political System: Parliamentary, Unitary, Unicameral
Head of State: President
Head of Government: Prime Minister
Current GDP ($) millions (WB 2019): 51,475.02
GDP per Capita ($) (WB 2019): 7,411.8
Public Social Spending as a Percentage of GDP (2019): 19
Corruption World Rank: 94

Slovak Republic

Population: 5,454,070
Official Name: Slovak Republic

Capital: Bratislava
Land Area (sq. km): 48,080
Life Expectancy: 77
Population Density (per sq. km): 113
Type of Political System: Parliamentary, Unitary, Unicameral
Head of State: President
Head of Government: Chairman of the Government
Current GDP ($) millions (WB 2019): 105,079.67
GDP per Capita ($) (WB 2019): 19,266.3
Public Social Spending as a Percentage of GDP (2019): 17.7
Corruption World Rank: 60

Slovenia

Population: 2,087,950
Official Name: Republic of Slovenia
Capital: Ljubljana
Land Area (sq. km): 20,136.4
Life Expectancy: 81
Population Density (per sq. km): 103
Type of Political System: Parliamentary, Unitary, Bicameral
Head of State: President
Head of Government: President of the Government
Current GDP ($) millions (WB 2019): 54,174.23
GDP per Capita ($) (WB 2019): 25,946.2
Public Social Spending as a Percentage of GDP (2019): 21.1
Corruption World Rank: 35

Spain

Population: 47,076,780
Official Name: Kingdom of Spain
Capital: Madrid
Land Area (sq. km): 499,603.5
Life Expectancy: 83
Population Density (per sq. km): 94
Type of Political System: Parliamentary, Unitary (with devolution of power),
    Bicameral
Head of State: Monarch
Head of Government: President of the Government
Current GDP ($) millions (WB 2019): 1,393,490.52
GDP per Capita ($) (WB 2019): 29,600.4

Public Social Spending as a Percentage of GDP (2019): 24.7
Corruption World Rank: 32

Sweden
Population: 10,285,450
Official Name: Kingdom of Sweden
Capital: Stockholm
Land Area (sq. km): 407,310
Life Expectancy: 83
Population Density (per sq. km): 25
Type of Political System: Parliamentary, Unitary, Unicameral
Head of State: Monarch
Head of Government: Minister of the State
Current GDP ($) millions (WB 2019): 530,883.87
GDP per Capita ($) (WB 2019): 51,615.0
Public Social Spending as a Percentage of GDP (2019): 25.5
Corruption World Rank: 3

Switzerland
Population: 8,574,830
Official Name: Swiss Confederation
Capital: Bern
Land Area (sq. km): 39,516
Life Expectancy: 84
Population Density (per sq. km): 215
Type of Political System: Parliamentary (with direct democracy), Federal,
   Bicameral
Head of State: President of the Federal Council
Head of Government: President of the Federal Council
Current GDP ($) millions (WB 2019): 703,082.44
GDP per Capita ($) (WB 2019): 81,993.7
Public Social Spending as a Percentage of GDP (2019): 24.6
Corruption World Rank: 3

Turkey
Population: 83,429,620
Official Name: Republic of Turkey
Capital: Ankara
Land Area (sq. km): 769,630
Life Expectancy: 77

Population Density (per sq. km): 107
Type of Political System: Parliamentary, Unitary, Unicameral
Head of State: President
Head of Government: President
Current GDP ($) millions (WB 2019): 761,425.50
GDP per Capita ($) (WB 2019): 9,126.6
Public Social Spending as a Percentage of GDP (2019): 12
Corruption World Rank: 86

Ukraine

Population: 44,385,150
Official Name: Ukraine
Capital: Kyiv
Land Area (sq. km): 579,400
Life Expectancy: 72
Population Density (per sq. km): 77
Type of Political System: Semipresidential, Unitary, Unicameral
Head of State: President
Head of Government: Prime Minister
Current GDP ($) millions (WB 2019): 153,781.07
GDP per Capita ($) (WB 2019): 3,659.0
Public Social Spending as a Percentage of GDP (2019): N/A
Corruption World Rank: 117

United Kingdom

Population: 66,834,400
Official Name: United Kingdom of Great Britain and Northern Ireland
Capital: London
Land Area (sq. km): 241,930
Life Expectancy: 81
Population Density (per sq. km): 275
Type of Political System: Parliamentary, Unitary, Bicameral
Head of State: Monarch
Head of Government: Prime Minister
Current GDP ($) millions (WB 2019): 2,829,108.22
GDP per Capita ($) (WB 2019): 42,330.1
Public Social Spending as a Percentage of GDP (2019): 20.6
Corruption World Rank: 11

Bibliography

Abdelal, Rawi, and Kimberly A. Haddad. *A Wider Europe: The Challenge of EU Enlargement*. 9-703-021. Cambridge, MA: Harvard Business School, 2003.

Acemoglu, Daron, and James A. Robinson. "Why Did the West Extend the Franchise? Democracy, Inequality, and Growth in Historical Perspective." *Quarterly Journal of Economics* 115(4), 2000: 1167–1199.

Aggestam, Lisbeth, and Federica Bicchi. "New Directions in EU Foreign Policy Governance: Cross-loading, Leadership and Informal Groupings." *Journal of Common Market Studies* 57(3), 2019: 515–532.

Alderman, Liz. "France Announces a Vast Expansion of Nuclear Power." *New York Times*, February 11, 2022.

Almond, Gabriel A., and G. Bingham Powell. *Comparative Politics: A Developmental Approach*. Boston: Little, Brown, 1966.

Almond, Gabriel A., Russell J. Dalton, and G. Bingham Powell Jr. (eds.). *European Politics Today*. New York: Longman, 1999.

Almond, Gabriel A., and Sidney Verba. *The Civic Culture: Political Attitudes and Democracy in Five Nations*. Princeton: Princeton University Press, 1963.

Ambrose, Jillian. "Watts Up: Sea Change for British Wind Power." *The Guardian Weekly,* January 15, 2021.

Anderson, Robert. "Social Democracy: What's Left in Central Europe?" *Balkan Insight*, March 26, 2020, https://balkaninsight.com/2020/03/26/social-democracy-whats-left-in-central-europe.

Applebaum, Anne. "Obama and Europe: Missed Signals, Renewed Commitment." *Foreign Affairs* 94(5), 2015: 37–44.

Asen, Elke. "Top Individual Income Tax Rates in Europe." *Tax Foundation*, February 22, 2019, https://taxfoundation.org/top-individual-income-tax-rates-europe-2019.

Baasner, Frank, and Stefan Seidendorf. "A Year of Electoral Uncertainty: Germany Turns the Page on Merkel." Robert Schuman Foundation Policy Paper, no. 593, April 27, 2021. https://www.robert-schuman.eu/en/doc/questions-d-europe/qe-593-en.pdf.

Babarinde, Olufemi, and Gerrit Faber (eds.). *The European Union and the Developing Countries.* Leiden: Martinus Nijhoff, 2005.

Bale, Tim. *European Politics: A Comparative Introduction,* 4th ed. London: Palgrave Macmillan/Red Globe, 2017.

Balfour, Rosa. "EU Political Dilemmas in North Africa and the Middle East: The Logic of Diversity and the Limits to Foreign Policy." In Gergana Noutcheva, Karolina Pomorska, and Giselle Bosse (eds.). *The EU and Its Neighbours: Values Versus Security in European Foreign Policy.* Manchester: Manchester University Press, 2013, chap. 4.

Ballinger, Pamela. "Colonial Twilight: Italian Settlers and the Long Decolonization of Libya." *Journal of Contemporary History* 51(4), 2016: 813–838.

Baracani, Elena. *EU-Turkey Relations: A New Direction for EU Foreign Policy?* Cheltenham: Edward Elgar, 2021.

Barbé, Esther, and Elisabeth Johansson-Nogués. "The EU as a Modest 'Force for Good': The European Neighborhood Policy." *International Affairs* 84(1), 2008: 81–96.

Bennhold, Katrin. "Line Blurs in Germany Between Pandemic Protesters and Far Right." *New York Times,* March 1, 2022.

Bierbach, Mara. "Who Makes Up the New Bundestag?" *Deutsche Welle (DW)*, October 24, 2017, https://beta.dw.com/en/germanys-new-bundestag-who-is-who-in-parliament/a-41082379.

Bindi, Frederiga (ed.). *The Foreign Policy of the European Union: Assessing Europe's Role in the World.* Washington, DC: Brookings Institution, 2010.

Birkland, Thomas. *An Introduction to the Policy Process: Theories, Concepts, and Models of Public Policy Making,* 5th ed. New York: Routledge, 2020.

Birnbaum, Michael. "'Would This Have Happened If I Had Worn a Suit and a Tie?': EU President Ursula von der Leyen Denounces Sexism in 'Sofagate' Incident." *Washington Post*, April 26, 2021.

Bloj, Ramona. "Women's Europe." Robert Schuman Foundation Policy Paper, no. 587, March 9, 2021. https://www.robert-schuman.eu/en/doc/questions-d-europe/qe-587-en.pdf.

Bradford, Anu. *The Brussels Effect: How the European Union Rules the World.* New York: Oxford University Press, 2020.

Bremmer, Ian. "Troubling Times in Northern Ireland." *Time,* April 26–May 3, 2021.

Breum, Martin. "How a US Pivot to the North Changes the European Artic." *Arctic Today*, August 12, 2020.

Brzezinski, Zbigniew. "A Plan for Europe: How to Expand NATO." *Foreign Affairs* 74(1), 1995: 26–42.

Burnham, James. *The Machiavellians.* Chicago: Gateway, 1943.

Buzmaniuk, Stefanie. "The Union's External Borders: A European Debate Revisited." Robert Schuman Foundation Policy Paper, no. 585, February 23, 2021. https://www.robert-schuman.eu/en/doc/questions-d-europe/qe-585-en.pdf.

Caiani, Manuela, and Ondřej Cisař (eds.). *Radical Right Movement Parties in Europe.* Abingdon: Routledge, 2019.

Calance, Madalina. "The Resurgence of Nationalism in the European Union." Centre for European Studies Working Paper 4(1), 2012, pp. 24–34. https://www.econstor.eu/bitstream/10419/198153/1/ceswp-v04-i1-p024-034.pdf.

Caparros, Martin. "Vox and the Rise of the Extreme Right in Spain." *New York Times*, November 13, 2019.

Carbone, Maurizio. "The European Union and International Development." In Christopher Hill, Michael Smith, and Sophie Vanhoonacker (eds.), *International Relations and the European Union,* 3rd ed. Oxford: Oxford University Press, 2017, chap. 13.

Carbone, Maurizio. "The Calm After the Storm: Plurilateral Challenges to the Post-2020 EU-ACP Partnership." *Journal of Common Market Studies* 57 (Special Supplement), 2019: 141–151.

Carroll, Rory. "Peace Under Fire." *The Guardian Weekly*, April 16, 2021.

Cartier, Emmanuel, Basile Ridard, and Gilles Toulemonde (eds.). "The Impact of the Health Crisis on the Functioning of Parliaments in Europe." Robert Schuman Foundation Policy Paper, December 15, 2020. https://www.robert-schuman.eu/en/doc/ouvrages/FRS_Parliament.pdf.

Casabianca, Jean. "Mediterranean Sea: A Paradigm of Contemporary Conflicts." Robert Schuman Foundation Policy Paper, no. 564, June 23, 2020. https://www.robert-schuman.eu/en/doc/questions-d-europe/qe-564-en.pdf.

Cebeci, Münevver. "European Foreign Policy Research Reconsidered: Constructing an 'Ideal Power Europe' Through Theory." *Millennium: Journal of International Studies* 40(3), 2012: 563–583.

The Charter of Fundamental Rights of the European Union. Official Journal of the European Union, C326. Brussels, 2012. https://eur-lex.europa.eu/legal-content/EN/TXT/PDF/?uri=CELEX:12012P/TXT&from=EN.

Chin, Rita. *The Crisis of Multiculturalism in Europe: A History*. Princeton: Princeton University Press, 2017.

Christensen, Thomas, Knud Erik Jørgensen, and Antje Wiener. "The Social Construction of Europe." *Journal of European Public Policy* 6(4), 1999: 528–544.

Christensen, Thomas, Knud Erik Jørgensen, and Antje Wiener (eds.). *The Social Construction of Europe*. London: Sage, 2001.

Clarke, Gina. "London Calling: How the City Became a Global Hub for Fintech." *Time,* October 11–18, 2021.

Clayton, Anthony. *The Wars of French Decolonization*. Abingdon: Routledge, 2013.

Close, Caroline, and Emilie Van Haute (eds.). *Liberal Parties in Europe*. Abingdon: Routledge, 2019.

Connolly, Kate. "Stark Divides Persist, 30 Years After Reunification." *The Guardian Weekly,* September 25, 2020.

Connolly, Kate, and Philip Oltermann. "Post Merkel: Is the CDU Facing Disaster?" *The Guardian Weekly,* March 19, 2021.

Considère-Charon, Marie-Claire. "Brexit and the Irish Question." Robert Schuman Foundation Policy Paper, no. 583, February 9, 2021. https://www.robert-schuman.eu/en/doc/questions-d-europe/qe-583-en.pdf.

Cotley, Andrew. "Astrategic Europe." *Journal of Common Market Studies* 58(2), 2020: 276–291.

Council of the European Union. *European Security Strategy: A Secure Europe in a Better World*. Brussels: EU Council, 2009. https://www.consilium.europa.eu/media/30823/qc7809568enc.pdf.

"Covid-19: How Europe Has Mishandled the Pandemic." *The Economist,* March 31, 2021.

Crepaz, Markus M. L. *European Democracies,* 9th ed. New York: Routledge, 2017.

Croci, Osvaldo. "Taking the Field: The European Union and Sport Governance." In Ingeborg Tömmel and Amy Verdun (eds.), *Innovative Governance in the European Union: The Politics of Multilevel Policymaking*. Boulder: Lynne Rienner, 2009, chap. 10.

Crosby, Alfred W., Jr. *The Columbian Exchange: Biological and Cultural Consequences of 1492*. Westport, CT: Greenwood Press, 1972.

Crudo Blackburn, Christine, and Paul E. Lenze Jr. *Syrian Forced Migration and Public Health in the European Union*. Lanham, MD: Lexington Books, 2019.

Cumming-Bruce, Nick. "Swiss Narrowly Approve Ban on Face Coverings." *New York Times,* March 8, 2021.

Cvijic, Srdjan, and Lorenzo Zucca. "Does the European Constitution Need Christian Values?" *Oxford Journal of Legal Studies* 24(4), 2004: 739–748.

Davis, G. Doug, and Michael O. Slobodchikoff. *Cultural Imperialism and the Decline of the Liberal Order: Russian and Western Soft Power in Eastern Europe.* Lanham, MD: Lexington Books 2019.

Defence Expenditures of NATO Countries 2014–2021. Brussels: NATO, 2022. https://www.nato.int/cps/en/natohq/news_193983.htm.

De Groot, David. "EU Legislation and Policies to Address Racial and Ethnic Discrimination." European Parliamentary Research Service, PE 690.525. May 2022. https://www.europarl.europa.eu/RegData/etudes/BRIE/2021/690525/EPRS_BRI(2021)69025_EN.pdf.

Delanty, Gerard. *Inventing Europe: Idea, Identity, Reality.* Houndmills: Palgrave Macmillan, 1995.

De Maio, Giovanna. *Playing with Fire: Italy, China, and Europe.* Washington, DC: Brookings Institution, May 2020.

Denk, Thomas, Henrik Serup Christensen, and Daniel Bergh. "The Composition of Political Culture—A Study of 25 European Democracies." *Studies in Comparative International Development* 50(3), 2015: 358–377.

De Schutter, Olivier. *The European Social Charter in the Context of Implementation of the EU Charter of Fundamental Rights.* Brussels: European Parliament, 2016. https://www.europarl.europa.eu/RegData/etudes/STUD/2016/536488/IPOL_STU(2016)536488_EN.pdf.

De Vries, Catherine E., Sara B. Hobolt, Sven-Oliver Proksch, and Jonathan B. Slapin. *Foundations of European Politics: A Comparative Approach.* Oxford: Oxford University Press, 2021.

Diller, Daniel C. *Russia and the Independent States.* Washington, DC: Congressional Quarterly, 1993.

Dinan, Desmond. *Ever Closer Union: An Introduction to European Integration,* 4th ed. London: Red Globe, 2010.

Dinan, Desmond. *Origins and Evolution of the European Union*, 2nd ed. Oxford: Oxford University Press, 2014.

Donadio, Rachel. "France's Obsession with Decline Is a Booming Industry." *New York Times,* February 3, 2017.

Drozdiak, William. *Fractured Continent: Europe's Crises and the Fate of the West.* New York: Norton, 2017.

Duke, Simon. *Europe as a Stronger Global Actor: Challenges and Strategic Responses.* London: Palgrave Macmillan, 2017.

Duke, Simon, and Sophie Vanhoonacker. "The European Union as a Subsystem of International Relations." In Christopher Hill, Michael Smith, and Sophie Vanhoonacker (eds.), *International Relations and the European Union,* 3rd ed. Oxford: Oxford University Press, 2017, chap. 2.

Duverger, Maurice. *Political Parties: Their Organization and Activity in the Modern State.* London: Methuen, 1954.

Duverger, Maurice. "A New Political System Model: Semi-Presidential Government." *European Journal of Political Research* 8, 1980: 165–187.

Elections in Central and Eastern Europe: A Compendium of Reports on the Elections Held from March Through June 1990. Washington, DC: Commission on Security and Cooperation in Europe, 1990.

"Emmanuel Macron on Europe's Fragile Place in a Hostile World." *The Economist,* November 7, 2019.

Erlanger, Steven. "Germany and France Aim to Lead Continent Out of Crisis: Will It Follow?" *New York Times,* May 20, 2020.

Erlanger, Steven, and Megan Specia. "Russian Envoys Expelled from EU in Retaliation." *New York Times,* February 9, 2021.

European Commission. *Corporate Social Responsibility, Responsible Business Conduct, and Business and Human Rights: Overview of Progress.* Staff Working Document, 143. Brussels: European Commission, 2019. https://ec.europa.eu/docsroom/documents/34482.

European Union. *Shared Vision, Common Action: A Stronger Europe: A Global Strategy for the European Union's Foreign and Security Policy.* Brussels: European Union, 2016. https://eeas.europa.eu/topics/eu-global-strategy/17304/global-strategy-european-unions-foreign-and-security-policy_en.

Ewing, Jack "Volvo Sets 2030 as Year All New Cars Are Electric." *New York Times,* March 3, 2021.

Ewing, Jack, and Steven Lee Myers. "EU and China Reach Investment Deal, but Political Hurdles Await." *New York Times,* December 31, 2020.

Eyerman, Ron, and Giuseppe Sciortino (eds.). *The Cultural Trauma of Decolonization: Colonial Returnees in the National Imagination.* Cham: Springer/Palgrave, 2020.

Farrell, David. *Electoral Systems: A Comparative Introduction,* 2nd ed. London: Red Globe/Macmillan, 2011.

Featherstone, Kevin, "The EC and the US: Managing Interdependence." In Juliet Lodge (ed.), *The European Community and the Challenge of the Future,* 2nd ed. New York: St. Martin's, 1993, pp. 271–282.

Ferrero-Waldner, Benita. "The European Neighbourhood Policy: The EU's Newest Foreign Policy Instrument." *European Foreign Affairs Review* 11, 2006: 139–142.

Fleega, Jonas, "Football's 'Super League'—An Own-Goal for EU Soft Power." *EU Observer,* April 23, 2021. https://euobserver.com/opinion/151638?utm_source=euobs&utm_medium=email.

Fontaine, Pascale. *Jean Monnet, a Grand Design for Europe.* Luxembourg: European Communities, 1988.

Ford, Robert, and Will Jennings. "The Changing Cleavage Politics of Western Europe." *Annual Review of Political Science* 23, 2020: 295–314.

Franz, Romeo. "After 50 Years, Where Do Roma Rights Stand Now?" *EU Observer,* April 8, 2021. https://euobserver.com/opinion/151466?utm_source=euobs&utm_medium=email.

Freedman, Lawrence D. "Britain Adrift: The United Kingdom's Search for a Post-Brexit Role." *Foreign Affairs* 99(3), 2020: 118–130.

Friedrichs, Jörg. "The Meaning of New Medievalism." *European Journal of International Relations* 7(4), 2001: 475–501.

"From Big Bang to a Whimper: How to Revive Britain's Stockmarket." *The Economist,* October 2, 2021.

"From United Kingdom to Untied Kingdom." *The Economist,* April 17, 2021.

Frye, Timothy. "Russia's Weak Strongman: The Perilous Bargains that Keep Putin in Power." *Foreign Affairs* 100(3), 2021: 116–127.

Gallagher, Michael, and Paul Mitchell (eds.). *The Politics of Electoral Systems.* Oxford: Oxford University Press, 2008.

Geddes, Andrew, and Peter Scholten. *The Politics of Migration and Immigration in Europe,* 2nd ed. London: Sage, 2016.

Gellner, Ernest. *Nations and Nationalism.* Ithaca: Cornell University Press, 1983.

Genc, Kaya. "Erdogan's Way: The Rise and Rule of Turkey's Islamist Shapeshifter." *Foreign Affairs* 98(5), 2019: 26–34.

Gibbon, Edward. *The Decline and Fall of the Roman Empire*. Abridged by D. M. Low. London: Book Club Associates, 1960.

Giraud, Jean-Guy. "The European Council: A Self-Proclaimed 'Sovereign' Off the Rails." Robert Schuman Foundation Policy Paper, no. 574, October 13, 2020. https://www.robert-schuman.eu/en/doc/questions-d-europe/qe-574-en.pdf.

Giuliani, Jean-Dominique, Arnaud Danjean, Françoise Grossetête, and Thierry Tardy. "Defence: Europe's Awakening." Robert Schuman Foundation Policy Paper, no 474, May 22, 2018. https://www.robert-schuman.eu/en/doc/questions-d-europe/qe-474-en.pdf.

Graziano, Paolo, and Maarten P. Vink (eds.). *Europeanization: New Research Agendas*. Houndmills: Palgrave Macmillan, 2007.

Greer, Germaine. *The Female Eunuch*. New York: McGraw Hill, 1971.

Guarascio, Francesco. "EU Demands Immediate Access to UK-Made Vaccines in AstraZeneca Legal Battle." Reuters, April 28, 2021. https://www.reuters.com/world/europe/eu-legal-case-against-astrazeneca-begins-brussels-court-2021-04-28/.

Guttman, Robert J. *Europe in the New Century: Visions of an Emerging Superpower*. Boulder: Lynne Rienner, 2001.

Haass, Richard N. (ed.). *Transatlantic Tensions: The United States, Europe, and Problem Countries*. Washington, DC: Brookings Institution, 1999.

Hackett, Clifford. *Cautious Revolution: The European Community Arrives*. New York: Praeger, 1990.

Hancock, M. Donald. "Sweden: Where Is the Power?" In M. Donald Hancock, Christopher J. Carman, Marjorie Castle, David P. Conradt, Raffaella Y. Nanetti, B. Guy Peters, William Safran, and Stephen White (eds.). *Politics in Europe,* 5th ed. Washington, DC: CQ Press, 2012, pp. 455–456.

Hancock, M. Donald, Christopher J. Carman, Marjorie Castle, David P. Conradt, Raffaella Y. Nanetti, B. Guy Peters, William Safran, and Stephen White (eds.). *Politics in Europe,* 5th ed. Washington, DC: CQ Press, 2012.

Hardy, Paula. "Sinking City: How Venice Is Managing Europe's Worst Tourism Crisis." *The Guardian,* April 30, 2019.

"Health Measures and Travel Conditions." Robert Schuman Foundation Policy Paper, November 6, 2020. https://www.robert-schuman.eu/en/doc/actualites/FRS_Health_measures.pdf.

Heidensohn, Klaus. *Europe and World Trade*. London: Pinter, 1995.

Henley, Jon. "A Sad Adieu: A Diplomat on Watching the Brexit 'Revolution.'" *The Guardian,* February 26, 2021.

Henley, Jon. "Netherlands Election: Mark Rutte Claims Fourth Term with 'Overwhelming' Victory." *The Guardian,* March 18, 2021.

Hill, Christopher. "The Capability-Expectations Gap, or Conceptualizing Europe's International Role." *Journal of Common Market Studies* 31(3), 1993: 305–328.

Hill, Christopher. "The Geo-Political Implications of Enlargement." Working Paper RSC no. 2000/30. Florence: European University Institute, 2000.

Hill, Christopher. "Powers of a Kind: The Anomalous Position of France and the United Kingdom in World Politics." *International Affairs* 92(2), 2016: 393–414.

Hill, Christopher, Michael Smith, and Sophie Vanhoonacker (eds.). *International Relations and the European Union,* 3rd ed. Oxford: Oxford University Press, 2017.

Hitler, Adolf. *My Struggle*. London: Paternoster Library, 1938.

Hix, Simon. "Brexit: Where Is the EU-UK Relationship Heading?" *Journal of Common Market Studies* 56 (Special Supplement), 2018: 11–27.

Hofstede, Geert. *Culture's Consequences: International Differences in Work-Related Values*. London: Sage, 1984.

Holder, Josh, Karl Russell, and Stanley Reed. "How Russia's Natural Gas Powers the Market in Europe." *New York Times,* February 17, 2022.

Hooghe, Liesbet, and Gary Marks. *Multi-Level Governance and European Integration*. Lanham, MD: Rowman and Littlefield, 2001.

Horowitz, Jason. "Italy's New Leader Outlines Recovery, Appealing for Unity and Sacrifice." *New York Times,* February 18, 2021.

Houeix, Romain, and Françoise Marmouyet. "Diversity Gains Ground in France's New-Look National Assembly After Vote." *France 24*, June 21, 2017. https://www.france24.com/en/20170621-france-diversity-gains-ground-new-look-national-assembly-after-legislative-election.

Howorth, Jolyon. "The European Union's Security and Defence Policy: The Quest for Purpose." In Christopher Hill, Michael Smith, and Sophie Vanhoonacker (eds.), *International Relations and the European Union,* 3rd ed. Oxford: Oxford University Press, 2017, chap. 15.

Human Development Report 2020: The Next Frontier: Human Development and the Anthropocene. New York: UN Development Programme, 2020.

Hutton, Will. *The State We're In*. London: Vintage, 1996.

Illien, Noele. "Swiss Voters Approve Law Mandating Paternity Leave." *New York Times,* September 28, 2020.

Inglehart, Ronald. *The Silent Revolution: Changing Values and Political Styles Among Western Publics*. Princeton: Princeton University Press, 1977.

Joseph, Jonathan, and Ana E. Juncos. "Resilience as an Emergent European Project? The EU's Place in the Resilience Turn." *Journal of Common Market Studies* 57(5), 2019: 995–1012.

Kagan, Robert. "The New German Question: What Happens When Europe Comes Apart?" *Foreign Affairs* 98(3), 2019: 108–120.

Kahler, Miles. *Decolonization in Britain and France: The Domestic Consequences of International Relations*. Princeton: Princeton University Press, 1984.

Kahler, Miles. *Regional Futures and Transatlantic Economic Relations*. New York: Council on Foreign Relations, 1995.

Kahn, Sylvain, and Estelle Prin. "In the Time of Covid-19 China's Mask Has Fallen with Regard to Europe." Robert Schuman Foundation Policy Paper, no. 569, September 8, 2020. https://www.robert-schuman.eu/en/doc/questions-d-europe/qe-569-en.pdf.

Kennedy, Robert, and Amy Sandler. *Shock Therapy in Eastern Europe: The Polish and Czechoslovak Economic Reforms*. 9-797-068. Cambridge MA: Harvard Business School, 1999.

Kershaw, Ian. *The Global Age: Europe 1950–2017*. New York: Viking, 2019.

Keukeleire, Stephen, and Tom De Bruyn. "The European Union, the BRICS, and Other Emerging Powers: A New World Order?" In Christopher Hill, Michael Smith, and Sophie Vanhoonacker (eds.), *International Relations and the European Union,* 3rd ed. Oxford: Oxford University Press, 2017, chap. 18.

Kharlamova, Ganna. "Economic Prospects in the Context of Growing Regional Interdependencies: The European Union and the Eastern Partnership." *Ekonomika* 94(2), 2015: 47–72.

Kofman, Michael, and Andrea Kendall-Taylor. "The Myth of Russian Decline: Why Moscow Will Be a Persistent Power." *Foreign Affairs* 100(6), 2021: 142–152.

Kolmos, Christopher. "Bridging the Transatlantic Cyber Rift: Recommendations for Cyber Cooperation Between NATO and the EU." The Streit Council, February 24, 2021. https://www.streitcouncil.org/post/bridging-the-transatlantic-cyber-rift -recommendations-for-improving-cyber-cooperation-between-nato?utm_campaign =6479d524-7782-4f89-acc9-eb5135b378b7&utm_source=so&utm_medium=mail &cid=65bb845c-0491-4a62-9f53-3c10a4b07a05.

Krastev, Ivan, and Mark Leonard. "Europe's Shattered Dream of Order: How Putin Is Disrupting the Atlantic Alliance." *Foreign Affairs* 94(3), 2015: 48–58.

Krause-Jackson, Flavia. "Socialism Declining in Europe as Populism Support Grows." *Independent*, December 29, 2019, https://www.independent.co.uk/news/world/europe /socialism-europe-parties-populism-corbyn-left-wing-francois-holland-snp-a9262656 .html.

Kubicek, Paul. *European Politics,* 3rd ed. Abingdon: Routledge, 2021.

Landler, Mark. "Two Prominent British Firms Say They'll Pay Reparations for Slavery." *New York Times,* June 19, 2020.

Landler, Mark, and Stephen Castle. "UK and France Call in the Navy, Sort of, in Channel Islands Fishing Dispute." *New York Times,* May 7, 2021.

Laquer, Walter. *The Last Days of Europe: Epitaph for an Old Continent.* New York: St. Martin's, 2007.

Lefebvre, Maxime. "Europe as a Power, European Sovereignty and Strategic Autonomy: A Debate That Is Moving Towards an Assertive Europe." Robert Schuman Foundation Policy Paper, no. 582, February 2, 2021. https://www.robert-schuman.eu/en/doc /questions-d-europe/qe-582-en.pdf.

Lelieveldt, Herman, and Sebastiaan Princen. *The Politics of the European Union,* 2nd ed. Cambridge: Cambridge University Press, 2015.

Lendvai, Paul. *Orbán: Hungary's Strongman.* New York: Oxford University Press, 2016. (Subsequently titled *Orbán: Europe's New Strongman.*)

Leonard, Mark. *Making Europe Popular: The Search for European Identity.* London: Demos/Interbrand, 1998.

Leruth, Benjamin, Stefan Gänzle, and Jarle Troudal. "Differentiated Integration and Disintegration in the EU After Brexit: Risks Versus Opportunities." *Journal of Common Market Studies* 57(6), 2019: 1383–1394.

Lessem, Ronnie, and Franz-Friedrich Neubauer. *European Management Systems: Towards Unity Out of Cultural Diversity.* New York: McGraw Hill, 1994.

Lichfield, Gideon. "Having It Both Ways: A Survey of Russia." *The Economist* (Special Survey), May 22, 2004.

Lijphart, Arend. *Democracy in Plural Societies: A Comparative Exploration.* New Haven: Yale University Press, 1977.

Lijphart, Arend. *Patterns of Democracy: Government Forms and Performance in Thirty-six Countries.* New Haven: Yale University Press, 1999.

Lindell, Martin, and Jouko Arvonen. "The Nordic Management Style in a European Context." *International Studies of Management and Organization* 26(3), 1997: 73–91.

Lisi, Marco (ed.). *Party System Change, the European Crisis and the State of Democracy.* Abingdon: Routledge, 2019.

Livingstone, Katie, and Colm Quinn. "Was Portugal's Election a Breakthrough for the Far-Right?" *Foreign Policy,* January 26, 2021. https://foreignpolicy.com/2021/01/26 /portugal-presidential-election-far-right-breakthrough-ventura-rebelo-sousa/.

Lukyanov, Fyodor. "Putin's Foreign Policy: The Quest to Restore Russia's Rightful Place." *Foreign Affairs* 95(3), 2016: 30–37.

Machiavelli, Niccolò. *The Prince.* New York: Norton, 2020.

Magone, José M. *Contemporary European Politics: A Comparative Introduction,* 2nd ed. Abingdon: Routledge, 2019.

Mangala, Jack (ed.). *Africa and the European Union: A Strategic Partnership.* New York: Palgrave Macmillan, 2013.

Manners, Ian. "Normative Power Europe: A Contradiction in Terms?" *Journal of Common Market Studies* 40(2), 2002: 235–258.

Marcou, Jean. "The Conundrum of the Great Gas Game and the Ensuing Strategic Realignment in the Eastern Mediterranean." Robert Schuman Foundation Policy Paper, no. 571, September 22, 2020. https://www.robert-schuman.eu/en/doc/questions-d-europe/qe-571-en.pdf.

Marty, Olivier, and Damien Ientile. "Reforming European Economic Policies." Robert Schuman Foundation Policy Paper, no 588, March 23, 2021. https://www.robert-schuman.eu/en/doc/questions-d-europe/qe-588-en.pdf.

Mashika, Albert, and Maria Nyman. "Does New EU-ACP Deal Really 'Decolonise' Aid?" *EU Observer,* April 8, 2021. https://euobserver.com/opinion/151472?utm_source=euobs&utm_medium=email.

Matthijs, Matthias. "The Right Way to Fix the EU: Put Politics Before Economics." *Foreign Affairs* 99(3), 2020: 160–170.

Maurice, Eric. "European Democracy, a Fundamental System to Be Protected." Robert Schuman Foundation Policy Paper, no. 578, December 1, 2020. https://www.robert-schuman.eu/en/doc/questions-d-europe/qe-578-en.pdf.

Maurice, Eric. "Protecting Checks and Balances to Save the Rule of Law." Robert Schuman Foundation Policy Paper, no. 590, April 6, 2021. https://www.robert-schuman.eu/en/doc/questions-d-europe/qe-590-en.pdf.

Méheut, Constant. "France Eases Access, a Little, to Its Secrets." *New York Times*, March 10, 2021.

Milanovic, Branko. "The Clash of Capitalisms: The Real Fight for the Global Economy's Future." *Foreign Affairs* 99(1), 2020: 10–21.

Minder, Raphael. "Gibraltar Gets a Deal of Its Own on Borders." *New York Times,* January 1, 2021.

Mirel, Pierre. "The Eastern Partnership: Between Resilience and Interference." Robert Schuman Foundation Policy Paper, no 589, March 30, 2021. https://www.robert-schuman.eu/en/doc/questions-d-europe/qe-589-en.pdf.

Mirel, Pierre, and Xavier Mirel. "Challenges and Constraints Facing a 'Geopolitical Commission' in the Achievement of European Sovereignty." Robert Schuman Foundation Policy Paper, no. 560, May 26, 2020.

Moravcsik, Andrew. "Preferences and Power in the European Community: A Liberal Intergovernmentalist Approach." *Journal of Common Market Studies* 31(4), 1993: 473–524.

Moravcsik, Andrew. *The Choice for Europe: Social Purpose and State Power from Messina to Maastricht.* Ithaca: Cornell University Press, 1998.

Moravcsik, Andrew. "Ever-Further Union." *Foreign Affairs* 99(1), 2020: 159–165.

Mueller, Benjamin. "Royal Rift Reveals Britain's Underbelly: A Very Big Silence Around Race." *New York Times,* March 12, 2021.

Mueller, Benjamin, and Matina Stevis-Gridneff. "Italy Stops 250,000 Doses from Leaving Europe." *New York Times,* March 5, 2021.

Muis, Jasper, and Tim Immerzeel. "Causes and Consequences of the Rise of Populist Radical Right Parties and Movements in Europe." *Current Sociology* 65(6), 2017: 909–930.

Murray, Philomena, and Alex Brianson. "Rethinking Britain's Role in a Differentiated Europe After Brexit: A Comparative Regionalism Perspective." *Journal of Common Market Studies* 57(6), 2019: 1431–1442.

Neal, Larry, and Daniel Barbezat. *The Economics of the European Union and the Economies of Europe.* Oxford: Oxford University Press, 1998.

Nelson, Brent F., and Alexander Stubbs (eds.). *The European Union: Readings on the Theory and Practice of European Integration,* 4th ed. Boulder: Lynne Rienner, 2014.

Nelson, Eshe. "How Will Britain Defend Its Financial Fief After Brexit?" *New York Times,* April 16, 2021.

The New Arctic: Navigating the Realities, Possibilities, and Problems. Washington, DC: Walsh School of Foreign Service, 2018.

Newell, Michael. "Top 5 Largest Fines Levied on Tech Companies by the European Commission." *The New Economy*, February 18, 2019. https://www.theneweconomy.com /business/top-5-largest-fines-levied-on-tech-companies-by-the-european-commission.

Norris, Pippa, and Ronald Inglehart. *Cultural Backlash: Trump, Brexit, and Authoritarian Populism.* Cambridge: Cambridge University Press, 2019.

Noutcheva, Gergana. "Institutional Governance of European Neighborhood Policy in the Wake of the Arab Spring." *Journal of European Integration* 37(1), 2015: 19–36.

Noutcheva, Gergana, Karolina Pomorska, and Giselle Bosse (eds.). *The EU and Its Neighbours: Values Versus Security in European Foreign Policy.* Manchester: Manchester University Press, 2013.

Novak, Benjamin. "Hungary Further Expands Executive Power and Curtails Gay Rights." *New York Times,* December 16, 2020.

Nye, Joseph S. "Soft Power." *Foreign Policy* 80, 1990: 153–171.

OECD (Organisation for Economic Co-operation and Development), "Constitutions of Central and Eastern European Countries and the Baltic States." SIGMA Paper no. 2. Paris: OECD, 1995. https://doi.org/10.1787/5kml6gf26mvk-en.

OECD Tourism Trends and Policies 2020. Paris: OECD, 2020.

Official Journal of the European Union. *Treaty Establishing a Constitution for Europe.* C310, Vol. 47. Brussels, December 2004. http://publications.europa.eu/resource /cellar/7ae3fd7e-8820-413e-8350-b85f9daaab0c.0005.02/DOC_1.

Oliver, Tim, and Michael John Williams. "Special Relationship in Flux: Brexit and the Future of the US-EU and US-UK Relationship." *International Affairs* 92(3), 2016: 547–567.

Olsen, Jonathan, and John McCormick. *The European Union: Politics and Policies,* 6th ed. Boulder: Westview, 2017.

Onishi, Norimitsu. "In Simmering Race and Gender Struggle, France Blames US Ideas." *New York Times,* February 10, 2021.

Onishi, Norimitsu, and Constant Méheut. "Pushing Change, Student Union Touches a Nerve in France." *New York Times,* April 5, 2021.

Opello, Walter C., Jr., and Katherine A.R. Opello. *European Politics: The Making of Democratic States.* Boulder: Lynne Rienner, 2009.

Outhwaite, William. *Contemporary Europe.* Abingdon: Routledge, 2017.

Pagden, Anthony (ed.). *The Idea of Europe: From Antiquity to the European Union.* Cambridge: Cambridge University Press/Woodrow Wilson Center Press, 2002.

Palese, Michela. "Which European Countries Use Proportional Representation?" *Electoral Reform Society*, December 26, 2018. https://www.electoral-reform.org.uk /which-european-countries-use-proportional-representation/.

Pèlegrin, Clémence. "Economic Recovery and Climate: For Europe and the World, Two Battles to Fight at Once." Robert Schuman Foundation Policy Paper, no. 579, December 8, 2020. https://www.robert-schuman.eu/en/doc/questions-d-europe/qe-579-en.pdf.

Pinder, David (ed.). *The New Europe: Economy, Society and Environment.* Chichester: Wiley, 1998.

Pomorska, Karolina, and Gergana Noutcheva. "Europe as a Regional Actor: Waning Influence in an Unstable and Authoritarian Neighbourhood." *Journal of Common Market Studies* 55, 2017: 165–176.

Pond, Elizabeth. *Friendly Fire: The Near-Death of the Transatlantic Alliance.* Pittsburgh: European Union Studies Association/Washington, DC: Brookings Institution, 2004.

Popov, Vladimir. *A Russian Puzzle: What Makes the Russian Economic Transformation a Special Case.* Research for Action Paper 29 (Helsinki: United Nations University/World Institute for Development Economics Research, 1996).

Postelnicescu, Claudia. "Europe's New Identity: The Refugee Crisis and the Rise of Nationalism." *Europe's Journal of Psychology* 12(2), 2016: 203–209.

Pronczuk, Monika. "EU Proposal Seeks to Close Gender Pay Gap by Requiring Companies to Reveal It." *New York Times,* March 5, 2021.

Reid, T. R. *The United States of Europe: The New Superpower and the End of American Supremacy.* New York: Penguin, 2004.

Rettman, Andrew. "Germany Still Backs New Russia Gas Pipeline." *EU Observer,* March 5, 2018. https://euobserver.com/energy/141204.

Rimkus, Ron. "Parmalat." *CFA Institute,* November 29, 2016. https://www.econcrises.org/2016/11/29/parmalat/.

Risse, Thomas. *A Community of Europeans? Transnational Identities and Public Spheres.* Ithaca: Cornell University Press, 2010.

Roberts, Ivor, and Beverly Springer. *Social Policy in the European Union: Between Harmonization and National Autonomy.* Boulder: Lynne Rienner, 2001.

Roman, Michal, Monika Roman, and Arkadiusz Niedziolka. "Spatial Diversity of Tourism in the Countries of the European Union." *Sustainability* 12, 2020: 1–16. https://www.mdpi.com/2071-1050/12/7/2713.

Roskin, Michael G. *The Rebirth of East Europe,* 3rd ed. Upper Saddle River, NJ: Prentice Hall, 1997.

Ross, George. *Jacques Delors and European Integration.* New York: Oxford University Press, 1995.

Rumer, Eugene, and Andrew S. Weiss. "A Brief Guide to Russia's Return to the Middle East." Carnegie Endowment for International Peace, October 24, 2019. https://carnegieendowment.org/2019/10/24/brief-guide-to-russia-s-return-to-middle-east-pub-80134.

Sachs, Jeffrey D. "Russia's Struggle with Stabilization: Conceptual Issues and Evidence." *Proceedings of the World Bank Annual Conference 1994.* Washington, DC: World Bank, 1995.

Safran, William. "The Context of French Politics." In M. Donald Hancock, Christopher J. Carman, Marjorie Castle, David P. Conradt, Raffaella Y. Nanetti, B. Guy Peters, William Safran, and Stephen White (eds.). *Politics in Europe,* 5th ed. Washington, DC: CQ Press, 2012, chap. 2.1.

Sampson, Anthony. *The Changing Anatomy of Britain.* London: Hodder and Stoughton, 1986.

Sapolsky, Robert. "This Is Your Brain on Nationalism: The Biology of Us and Them." *Foreign Affairs* 98(2), 2019: 42–47.

Satariano, Adam. "Ireland Fines Facebook's WhatsApp over Data Transparency." *New York Times,* September 3, 2021.

Schuman, Robert. "The Schuman Declaration." May 9, 1950. Robert Schuman Foundation, https://www.robert-schuman.eu/en/declaration-of-9-may-1950.

Schwab, Klaus (ed.). *The Global Competitiveness Report 2019.* Cologny: World Economic Forum, 2019. http://www3.weforum.org/docs/WEF_TheGlobalCompetitivenessReport 2019.pdf.

Schwirtz, Michael. "Russia Expels 20 Czech Diplomats as Tensions Escalate." *New York Times,* April 18, 2021.

Serfaty, Simon (ed.). *Visions of the Atlantic Alliance: The United States, the European Union, and NATO.* Washington, DC: Center for Strategic and International Studies Press, 2005.

Serfaty, Simon. "The Biden Transition." Robert Schuman Foundation Policy Paper, no. 580, January 12, 2021. https://www.robert-schuman.eu/en/doc/questions-d-europe/qe -580-en.pdf.

Serrano, Omar. *The Domestic Sources of European Foreign Policy: Defence and Enlargement.* Amsterdam: Amsterdam University Press, 2013.

Shepard, Todd. *The Invention of Decolonization: The Algerian War and the Remaking of France.* Ithaca: Cornell University Press, 2006.

Sherwood, Harriet. "Europe's Jewish Population Has Dropped 60% in Last 50 Years." *The Guardian,* October 25, 2020. https://www.theguardian.com/world/2020/oct/25 /europes-jewish-population-has-dropped-60-in-last-50-years.

Shreeves, Rosamund, and Nessa Boland. "Women in Politics in the EU: State of Play." European Parliamentary Research Service, PE 689.345, March 2021. https://www.europarl .europa.eu/RegData/etudes/BRIE/2021/689345/EPRS_BRI(2021)689345_EN.pdf.

Slobodchikoff, Michael O. *Building Hegemonic Order Russia's Way: Order, Stability and Predictability in the Post-Soviet Space.* Lanham MD: Lexington Books, 2014.

Slobodchikoff, Michael O., G. Doug Davis, and Brandon Stewart (eds.). *The Challenge to NATO: Global Security and the Atlantic Alliance.* Lincoln: University of Nebraska Press, 2021.

Smith, Karen E. "The Outsiders: The European Neighbourhood Policy." *International Affairs* 81(4), 2005: 757–773.

Smith, Karen E. "Enlargement, the Neighbourhood, and European Order." In Christopher Hill, Michael Smith, and Sophie Vanhoonacker (eds.), *International Relations and the European Union,* 3rd ed. Oxford: Oxford University Press, 2017, chap. 14.

Smith, Karen E. "A European Union Global Strategy for a Changing World?" *International Politics* 54, 2017: 503–518.

Smith, Michael, and Rebecca Steffenson. "The European Union and the USA." In Christopher Hill, Michael Smith, and Sophie Vanhoonacker (eds.), *International Relations and the European Union,* 3rd ed. Oxford: Oxford University Press, 2017, chap. 17.

Soros, George. "Can Europe Work? A Plan to Rescue the Union." *Foreign Affairs* 75(5), 1996: 8–14.

Standard Eurobarometer 94, Winter 2020–2021. "Public Opinion in the European Union." Brussels: European Commission, 2021.

Stelzenmüller, Constanze. "The Singular Chancellor: The Merkel Model and Its Limits." *Foreign Affairs* 100(3), 2021: 161–172.

Stevis-Gridneff, Matina, and Benjamin Novak. "Hungary's Ruling Party Breaks with Conservative EU Allies that Shielded It." *New York Times,* March 4, 2021.

Stewart, Conor. "Number of New Coronavirus (Covid-19) Deaths in Europe Since February 2020." *Statista*, May 8, 2022. https://www.statista.com/statistics/1102288/coronavirus-deaths-development-europe/.

Stockemer, Daniel, and Andre Blais. "Voters and Abstainers in National and European Elections." *European Review* 27(2), 2019: 300–315.

Stockwell, Sarah. *The British End of the British Empire.* Cambridge: Cambridge University Press, 2018.

Tabuchi, Hiroko, and Jack Ewing. "Europe and Japan Near Trade Deal as US Takes Protectionist Path." *New York Times,* June 23, 2017.

Thomas, Martin, Bob Moore, and L. J. Butler. *Crises of Empire: Decolonization and Europe's Imperial States,* 2nd ed. London: Bloomsbury, 2015.

Thucydides. *The Peloponnesian War.* Harmondsworth: Penguin, 1972.

Tiersky, Ronald. "Macron's World: How the New President Is Remaking France." *Foreign Affairs* 97(1), 2018: 87–96.

Tisdall, Simon. "Global Predators Are Circling a Weak and Unstable Continent." *The Guardian Weekly,* November 26, 2021.

Tocci, Nathalie. "Towards a European Security and Defence Union: Was 2017 a Watershed?" *Journal of Common Market Studies* 56 (Special Supplement), 2018: 131–141.

Tömmel, Ingeborg, and Amy Verdun (eds.). *Innovative Governance in the European Union: The Politics of Multilevel Policymaking.* Boulder: Lynne Rienner, 2009.

Vachudova, Milada Anna. "Populism, Democracy, and Party System Change in Europe." *Annual Review of Political Science* 24, 2021: 1–28.

Van Malderen, Gauthier. "Europe Is Increasingly Innovative." Robert Schuman Foundation Policy Paper, no. 105, January 26, 2021. https://www.robert-schuman.eu/en/doc/entretiens-d-europe/ee-105-en.pdf.

Vásquez, Ian, and Fred McMahon. *The Human Freedom Index 2020: A Global Measurement of Personal, Civil, and Economic Freedom.* Washington, DC: Cato Institute/Vancouver: Fraser Institute, 2020. https://www.cato.org/sites/cato.org/files/2020-12/human-freedom-index-2020.pdf.

Vitrey, Anne, and Sébastien Lumet. "Multi-Annual Financial Framework and Next Generation EU: Review of an Unprecedented, Tumultuous European Budgetary Chapter." Robert Schuman Foundation Policy Paper, no. 575, October 27, 2020. https://www.robert-schuman.eu/en/doc/questions-d-europe/qe-575-en.pdf.

Wagner, Wolfgang, and Rosanne Anholt. "Resilience as the EU Global Strategy's New Leitmotif: Pragmatic, Problematic or Promising." *Contemporary Security Policy* 37(3), 2016: 414–430.

Wallace, Paul. *The Euro Experiment.* Cambridge: Cambridge University Press, 2016.

Wallace, William. "European Foreign Policy Since the Cold War: How Ambitious, How Inhibited?" *British Journal of Politics and International Relations* 19(1), 2017: 77–90.

Webber, Douglas. *European Disintegration? The Politics of Crisis in the European Union.* London: Red Globe, 2019.

Wells, Sherrill Brown. *Pioneers of European Integration and Peace 1945–1963: A Brief History with Documents.* Boston: Bedford/St. Martin's, 2007.

Wendt, Alexander. *Social Theory of International Politics.* Cambridge: Cambridge University Press, 1999.

Wettengel, Julian. "Germany and the EU Remain Heavily Dependent on Imported Fossil Fuels." *Clean Energy Wire*, March 14, 2022. https://www.cleanenergywire.org/factsheets/germanys-dependence-imported-fossil-fuels.

White, Brian. *Understanding European Foreign Policy.* Houndmills: Palgrave, 2001.

White, Stephen. "The Context of Russian Politics." In M. Donald Hancock, Christopher J. Carman, Marjorie Castle, David P. Conradt, Raffaella Y. Nanetti, B. Guy Peters, William Safran, and Stephen White (eds.). *Politics in Europe,* 5th ed. Washington, DC: CQ Press, 2012, chap. 6.1.

"Why Emmanuel Macron Wants to Abolish ENA, France's Most Elite College." *The Economist,* May 4, 2019.

Wight, Martin, *Power Politics.* London: Pelican, 1979.

Wilke, Richard, Jacob Poushter, Laura Silver, Kat Devlin, Janell Fetterolf, Alexandra Castillo, and Christine Huang. "Political Parties." *Pew Research Center,* October 14, 2019. https://www.pewresearch.org/global/2019/10/14/political-parties.

Williams, Zoe. "The Family Arsenal." *The Guardian Weekly,* March 12, 2021.

Willsher, Kim. "Former French President Nicolas Sarkozy Sentenced to Jail for Corruption." *The Guardian,* March 1, 2021. https://www.theguardian.com/world/2021/mar/01/former-french-president-nicolas-sarkozy-sentenced-to-three-years-for-corruption.

Wilson, Harry, and Neil Callanan. "The City of London Is Now at the Mercy of Brexit's Tug of War." *Bloomberg Businessweek,* February 2, 2021. https://www.bloomberg.com/news/articles/2021-02-03/brexit-agreement-london-s-future-as-global-financial-hub-is-unclear.

Wimmer, Andreas. "Why Nationalism Works: And Why It Isn't Going Away." *Foreign Affairs* 98(2), 2019: 27–34.

Wintour, Patrick. "A Great Trade Off: Why Britain Is Tilting Towards the Indo-Pacific." *The Guardian Weekly,* March 26, 2021.

Wong, Reuben. "The Role of the Member States: The Europeanization of Foreign Policy?" In Christopher Hill, Michael Smith, and Sophie Vanhoonacker (eds.). *International Relations and the European Union,* 3rd ed. Oxford: Oxford University Press, 2017, chap.7.

Wong, Reuben, and Christopher Hill (eds.). *National and European Foreign Policies: Towards Europeanization.* Abingdon: Routledge, 2011.

Wood, Steve, and Wolfgang Quaisser. *The New European Union: Confronting the Challenges of Integration.* Boulder: Lynne Rienner, 2008.

Worland, Justin, "The Art of the Green Deal." *Time,* November 2–9, 2020.

Wright, Stephen. "Are the Olympics Games?: The Relationship of Politics and Sport." *Millennium: Journal of International Studies* 6(1), 1977: 30–44.

Yergin, Daniel, and Thane Gustafson. *Russia 2010: And What It Means for the World.* New York: Random House, 1993.

Young, Crawford. *Politics in Congo: Decolonization and Independence.* Princeton: Princeton University Press, 1965.

Youngs, Richard, and Camino Mortera-Martinez. "A Liberal-Centrist Vision for Europe?" Carnegie Europe, March 14, 2019. https://carnegieeurope.eu/2019/03/14/liberal-centrist-vision-for-europe-pub-78533.

Zeff, Eleanor E., and Ellen B. Pirro (eds.). *The European Union and the Member States,* 2nd ed. Boulder: Lynne Rienner, 2006.

Zubova, Xenia. "Which Countries Still Have Conscription?" *Forces,* December 3, 2021. https://www.forces.net/world/which-countries-still-have-conscription.

Index

337

About the Book

WHAT CONSTITUTES EUROPE TODAY? IS THERE AN IDENTIFIABLE EURO-pean culture that transcends state boundaries? How do the various national political, economic, and social structures and institutions work? To what extent does the European Union influence policy in the region for members and nonmembers alike? Stephen Wright's comprehensive discussion of contemporary European politics addresses these fundamental questions in a book that notably encompasses all of Europe, from the UK to the Russian Federation.

Both thematic and comparative, with numerous examples used to illustrate key points, *Politics and Society in Contemporary Europe* integrates political, economic, and social factors to provide a thorough—and accessible—text.

Stephen Wright is professor emeritus of politics and international affairs at Northern Arizona University.